THIS BOOK IS DEDICATED TO the one person who has bothered herself enough to read everything I have written over some thirty years, *Kathleen Louise dePass*, my source of inspiration and the one person who has always believed I should continue my work in public discourse, even when I spoke only of quitting.

The Hydra of Carnage:
Bush's Imperial War-making and The Rule of Law

An Analysis of the Objectives and Delusions of Empire

By Craig B Hulet?

Former Special Assistant to Congressman Jack Metcalf

Craig B Hulet was *Special Assistant* to Congressman Jack Metcalf (R, WA) for *Special Projects* and periodically a consultant (Domestic Militia Movement) to The United States Treasury Department's Bureau of Alcohol Tobacco and Fire-arms (ATF). He served in Vietnam with the 101st Airborne as a weapons expert (MOS 45J20). Mr. Hulet has appeared on the Arsenio Hall Show, CNN, and has over 10,000 hours of media interviews over the past twenty years. He presently is Government Policy Analyst, KC & Associates (business/political consultants) in Washington State. His website is www.craigbhulet.com (360) 288-2652, KC&A, P.O. Box 710, Amanda Park WA 98526-0710

Published by The Artful Nuance
P.O. Box 37, Quinault, WA
98575-0037. (360) 288-2652

KC & Associates Investigations Research Associates
P.O. Box 710, Amanda Park, WA 98526-0710

Printed by Gorham Printing
334 Harris Rd., Rochester, WA 98579

Printed and bound in the United States of America

ISBN 0-9677886-2-5
www.kcandassociates.org

BOOKS, ART AND SCREEN PLAY BY THE SAME AUTHOR

Books:

Human All-Too-Human
A Nietzschean Retrospective
Copyright © *1999 The Artful Nuance*
ISBN 0-9677886-0-9

Global Triage
a Nietzschean history of a future
Imperium in Imperio
Copyright © *1999 The Artful Nuance*
ISBN 0-9677886-1-7

Foreign Affairs Affects Domestic Policies
A *Foreign Affairs* Special Anthology
Copyright 1988, 1990, 1992, 1993
The Council on Foreign Relations, Inc. and Craig B Hulet

Blue Bear's Rain Forest Adventures
A Children's Book to Color
Copyright © *1999 The Artful Nuance*

Screenplay and Treatments:

Temple Heart
Registered SP: Writer's Guild of America, west, Inc.
09/26/96 by Craig B Hulet

The Militia
Registered TRT: Writer's Guild of America, west, Inc.
10/31/95 by Craig B Hulet

Manchurian Candidate
Registered TRT: Writer's Guild of America, west, Inc.
05/06/97 by Craig B Hulet

Fine Art Pen & Inks:

Rain Forest Memories
Copyright © *1993 The Artful Nuance*

Rain Forest Awakened
Copyright © *1999 The Artful Nuance*

Heaven & Earth
Copyright © *1995 The Artful Nuance*

TABLE OF CONTENTS

Forward / 9

Part One

Part Two

If one reflects on the ruses, stratagems, schemes, and artifices with which evil princes are equipped to despoil the people—fiscal laws, amendments, false pretexts, pretended wars, denunciations, family alliances, it seems that the eagle is not worthy to bear the name of king.

—Erasmus

FORWARD

> *It has been fairly well established that*
> *there is a strong human inhibition*
> *against killing other people.*
> *...this would be overcome—overwhelmed*
> *is a better word—by what psychologist Eric Erikson*
> *calls "pseudspeciation," the notion that one's enemies are*
> *not really human and therefore are appropriate*
> *objects of lethal violence.*
>
> —ROBERT L. O'CONNELL
> *The Ride of the Second Horseman*

"A FORWARD IS MUCH LIKE A THRESHOLD wherein reader and author have a brief encounter, the former making his entrance, and the latter his exit. During this meeting the writer can make a few remarks about his work." (M. Maisels, *Thought and Truth*, Vision Books, p. 3, 1956). So the reader may make his entrance and I shall make my few remarks about this work.

This book is not just about the *jolly little war* in Afghanistan and the alleged war on terrorism globally that Mr. George Bush Jr. and Mr. Tony Blair claim they shall pursue, allegedly against al Qaida. We shall all find, soon enough, that this is a falsehood of immense proportions, but one with enough believability to fly in the face of truth for most. It is about the American-led corporate Empire which is well on its way to becoming a reality. According to very recent (January 2002) Pentagon disclosures this *jolly little war* will last no less than six years and probably more like a decade. The Department of Defense of course wants a great deal more money to fight the war and Mr. Bush and an utterly obedient Congress shall most certainly concede. I shall argue this war shall last the rest of my lifetime and yours too; that this war is just the beginning of both Empire's closure on the world but the growing global dimensions of the resistance against Empire. I will argue this war is not just what it seems and terrorism is no longer what we have all come to understand. Not any longer.

This book is really not about the war itself and so there shall be little of the glitz, CNN style; little of the jazz, network news provides; little of the repeating, word for word, on White House press releases, New York Times style. Nowhere else but here in this introduction, will I quote from one of those exalted ecstatic moth-balled Air Force generals brought out of retirement by the networks and CNN, to smugly state how exiting it all is, or was in their heyday, "to feel the ground quake under your feet like a slow earthquake..." regarding the carpet bombing of the poorest country on earth by the richest. The sole untamed superpower. These retired generals, and *retired for good reason*, should stay home and be still.

No, this book is a collection of works that began for the most part immediately on the day of September 11, 2001; five pieces were written prior to the close of 2001 and they have been rewritten and updated: chapter two, *On War*; chapter four, *A New Theory of International Urban Guerrilla Warfare*; chapter five, *The Hydra of Carnage*; chapter eight, by far the longest and most important piece included here, *Oil and Sovereignty*; and chapter nine, *Strategic Analysis*. Several earlier essays are herein included which few outside of my private client base and Congressman Jack Metcalf and a few of his staffers ever saw: chapters three, six, seven, eleven and twelve were essays written originally as speeches or briefings and are here rewritten for this volume; these were written during 2000 at the time for Congressman Jack Metcalf (Retired) while I was his *Special Assistant for Special Projects*. The remainder of the text is all new material as is much of the former five pieces written in response to 9/11/01. The appendices are made up of four sections which includes an essay, *The Folklore of Corporatism: The Coronation of George*, written during early 1999 for my client base; it was intended to give the reader a feel for what kind of prince our new leader Mr. Bush Jr. might become. It is included with no changes except where spelling and grammar were improved some.

I do not fancy myself a writer by any stretch. My two other books were collections of aphorisms and each held a collection of poetry written during the summers, respectively, 1997, 1998. It was in the one volume, *Human All-Too-Human*, that I wrote a poem, *Emperor's Own*, declaring Mr. Bush Jr. would be the next president of the United States, an argument I had been making since around 1993 during radio and television interviews, well before Mr. Bush Jr. was elected governor of Texas. The fact of the prognostication, not prediction (a term which reeks of a false metaphysics), is well-known to those who have followed my public work for the past twenty-odd years; I only state this here as an attempt to induce the unwary reader to buy yet another book of mine.

I wish I had a list of famous university names to thank for their efforts at proofing my pathetic prose, sloppy syntax, or a fine woman's name (like every Oxford Don has on tap) which I could then compliment for her unending editorial pursuit to make my manuscript readable. Just one professor of philosophy which could have suggested I quiet my expletives, shun my exaggerations and reduce the incredible number of redundancies throughout the text, would have been most welcome. Alas, the reader is stuck with what it is. Just a book written by a technical political analyst with some military and security background, who alone decided he had something to say. I will likely, and quite understandably, regret having made the attempt. On the one hand, it is not a work of fiction; it is on the other a work of general truths, factoids, empirical evidence and a lot of it, and of course my interpretation of those facts. It is in the interpretation where everyone gets into trouble and I will certainly be no different. Thus my whiney response is very much akin to our own Bill Clinton's, "I did the best I could." Those who really take issue with my arguments, I can only whine, Clintonian-like, "I didn't do anything wrong."

.

*   *   *

The question remains whether Mr. Bush Jr. has been entirely honest with the American people? Was Osama bin Laden really the mastermind behind the air attacks on the American and global infrastructure. Mr. Bush has refused to supply any significant evidence of it arguing it would give up intelligence gathering techniques and therefore create some risk to our national security. The reader will find I have left the first section of chapter two almost as I first wrote it during September; I raised the doubt then that bin Laden and his al Qaida network were the masterminds behind the event. I argued that it had all the earmarks of one or more nation-state's intelligence involvement. Those who are already convinced of bin Laden's guilt, and had never heard these arguments before, reading them here may find it disturbing; it is now passe to even question this. Mr. Bush and Mr. Blair have done the job well by the constant repetition that it was this organization alone who is guilty; my argument flies in the face of these assertions, but I no longer press the issue in interviews nor throughout the remainder of this book. The reason is, it is not important any longer and the argument is now quite moot. I leave it in the chapter only for the reason that the present reader should understand how I approached the subject from the beginning. I could have left it out and avoided those who will get fixated, bogged down, in the supposed bin Laden details, and that Mr. Blair and Mr. Bush have purportedly provided solid evidence. The reader then claiming I erred from the start. I hope the more reasonable reader finds the argument of historical interest at the least, and understands that every working hypothesis must work through much to discover, often very little, by way of conclusive anything. As a Nietzschean I am faced with *becoming* rather than *being*; that is to say, I am still, myself, very much a work in progress; I have few convictions left and these will be thrown out soon enough.

I also originally argued that there is a "perception" by many that there is an American-led Empire; I used the word *perception* during interviews so as to avoid getting bogged-down with the host or callers that I was of the belief that there is "in fact" such an empire, and not just some "other's" perception. This use of the term *perception* now seems to me to be a term used to allow, specifically American, media personalities the opportunity to avoid making any commitment to the issue, as it does not reflect well on America's elite (whom the host may often want [desperately] to interview after my own). Here, in this volume, even though I return to the term "perception" where some of the "others" may be concerned, which seems appropriate in the abstract, I do not use it where my own is concerned. After thirty years of work in the field, military, corporate, security and political, I am fully cognizant of this Empire "as fact," and American-led; its ideology of *Corporatism* and the *process* and *support* it finds, no, needs, in the double-edged sword of technology and globalization is abundantly clear to me.

This all to say only this, in the past I said there were those with the perception that there is an American-led empire; here I am asserting with full knowledge and forethought that, from my point of view, research and some past personal participation of my own, there is "in fact" an American-led Empire being put into place globally. Not *American*, American, but an economic regime led by multinational corporations and international governing organizations (IGO); a regime defended by the United States Central Intelligence Agency (CIA) and the Pentagon; offered as the *one best way* through the World Trade Organization (WTO) and its bureaucratic institutions like the World Trade Center (WTC). Those who already disagree with me on this point must agree to disagree, if they choose to go on.

September 11, 2001: To be fair, it is standard fare to always begin any discussion about the Afghan issues and Usamah bin Laden, spelled here properly as the Arabic translation would be, (Osama bin Laden throughout the text), whether critical or affirming, with some syrupy line about the victims. I too will follow this pattern so all readers can feel I am just as sympathetic towards the victims of the air attacks on American soil as the next. And admittedly I was at the time. That having been said, I will add that most Americans, and I mean a very large majority, really felt little, or nothing whatsoever; in our sappy *Oprah- moment* culture the outpouring of emotional posturing, especially when there is a camera near, then comes the weepy teary-eyed displays, always quite visible, of sentimentality begins in real earnest; it hides more than it reveals. It is a sad truth, only the strictest of philosophers would openly concede, Americans, by and large, care not one whit for anyone in the world with the sole exception, themselves.

The flags a-waving all over this nation, in my Nietzschean opinion, is an effort to *demonstrate* that they do care, an effort to *show* they still care; a raw and faux-caring display of thoughtless self-interest is the reality. That is why the need to make "a show of it." As Leonard Cohen's lyrics note in his recent album, "Look through a paper...make sure to cry...no one cares if the people,... live or die." (Secret Life) The reader may wish to not continue with a book that is going to pursue, with Nietzschean-like rigor, a critique of my country's underbelly. A look at a country turning its face to empire, a look at a nation of mostly *politically* ignorant subjects; some forty percent of adults functionally illiterate. A people that are prepared to bomb and kill at will. As long as someone else does the killing, someone else the bombing. There have been small mobs on street corners waving flags with huge signs saying "Honk if you support Bush!" I am the only guest which has appeared on the talk-show circuit to say this, in regard to those citizens which blindly endorse our Mr. Bush, "Honk if you've enlisted."

I am not a classical pacifist. I am not opposed to all war by nature. I have stated publicly that should America be actually invaded, foreign troops on our soil, I would immediately join ranks and help train *Wayne's World* to return fire. A hapless act without much hope of success (see my redundancy) given that the American youth today are not required to attend any kind of physical education; indeed, competition is seen as a gross injustice in the American government school system. One can but ponder, does this have any correspondence to the recent surveys indicating the per capita weight gain of Americans which has crossed over into the forty pounds mark? The youth are those with the highest gains, not in grades but in caloric intake.

If all this seems unseemly to point out at the very apex of patriotic passion I blame only myself. My first two books (here I go again, hint, hint) were both Nietzschean in their flavor: the first, *Human-All-Too-Human: A Nietzschean Retrospective*, the second, *Global Triage: a Nietzschean history of a future, Imperium in Imperio*. This volume takes my government to task for a war that never needed to be fought on Afghanistan's soil; fought for an additional political/economic objective which Mr. Bush and Mr. Blair will never come to publicly admit: it is my effort alone. My effort is, then, an act of patriotic fortitude, of patriotic duty on my part. In the frame of mind, if not in the good taste, of Thomas Paine (a Nietzschean himself in spirit, although there is of course no way he could have read Frederich Nietzsche's works). I offer this dissent from my country's war-making.

My one great asset in life, since early puberty, was to never care what anybody thinks of me. I still do not give a damn what anyone thinks of me; what they think of the book itself? I don't know: I hope it is but a good read for some, additional data to fill up the enquiring mind for others (you know the ones I mean, the scribblers that show up at a public lecture wide-eyed with pen and legal pad in hand); and a pain in the ass for those blind partymen of both parties; a thorn in club opinion.

I like waves on the ocean, a lot. I hate *waves* at a football game, therefore I do not attend nor view games on television; in fact I have not had a working television for over twenty years. I live in a rain forest on the upper edge of the Olympic Peninsula, of Washington State. I probably read too much and brood, over much of what I do read. Often I am not a *happy camper* in the American penchant for silly colloquialisms. But I do love life; it seems to matter to me that so many Americans care so little for the deaths of so many for so many decades caused by so few partymen in our own corporate government. Regarding these men, who send others to die and kill, it was said best in a quip only the English still retain: these are men "who wouldn't say boo to a Taliban goose." (John Pilger)

In America, Mr. Bush & Company, Bush, Inc., have resurrected the phrase, "America, Love it or Leave it." Well, I do not much like what we are evolving into, I do not care much for the many American's brazen arrogance and self-superiority; and it is my patriotic duty as a citizen of the world to stay put and point this out. Leave it? No, I think I shall stay and see if I can't take some of the "jolly" out of Mr. Bush's *jolly little war*. So with these few remarks, I shall make my exit.

CHAPTER ONE
Bush's War on the Rule of Law

The civilized world is engaged in a guerilla war it did not seek.
It is a war with small groups of alienated individuals
too weak to mount open assault.
No country can ever have an army
large enough to protect its
people against such attacks.
But the United States government does have the
ability and resources to organize a world-wide hunt
for the perpetrators and their sponsors.
Self-defense is the oldest law of nature.
[But], Vengeance is not cured by blind vengeance,
nor wrong by another wrong.
—HANS F. SENNHOLZ

The rule of law....unless it has become deformed
by the tactics of Machiavellian manipulation,
is for the most part beneficial to the interests
of the weaker groups in society.
—EDGAR BODENHEIMER

Wherever and whenever the government or
political parties are able to instigate
paroxysms of fear of danger,
imagined or real, the people are
prepared to give up much of their own
liberties and guarantees of due process, but they are
even more eager to sacrifice such guarantees
for their neighbors, especially those who
belong to the lower classes.
—MIECZYSLAW MANELI

THE RULE OF LAW

BEFORE I BEGIN TO ARGUE THE CASE FOR yet another unspoken political/commercial objective of yet another Bush administration once again, in Afghanistan, I feel compelled to begin with the closing aspect of the so-called war. Mr. Bush and Mr. Blair both declare we won, its all over in Afghanistan. We'll see. But the treatment of the captured *evil doers* as Mr. Bush likes to call them, and the prosecution of the war itself has received almost no serious coverage at all in America with regard to the latter and is being dismissed out of hand regarding the former.

I shall begin with the captured al Qaida members, so-called, and the Taliban soldiers. It was reported that "The first arrivals are being held in temporary maximum security facilities which were built in the last few days," a US spokesman said. "Those facilities are essentially outdoor cages or outdoor cells." The cages, constructed from chain-link fences topped with canvas roofs, are encircled by several yards of razor wire. Each of the compounds are lit by blazing halogen floodlights 24 hours a day to ensure that the prisoners are constantly monitored. Each prisoner will be given a mattress and two towels, one to be used as a prayer mat. They will be given three meals a day and have access to "a few toiletries" - a washcloth, toothpaste, soap and shampoo. The same spokesman said "They will not be given blankets and will not be given repellant to ward off the swarms of mosquitoes," that thrive in the tropical swamp which forms the bay at Guantanamo Bay Naval Base, Cuba.

Mr. Bush and his Secretary of Defense Donald Rumsfeld have no problem with the treatment of these troops because according to the newest of our regular fare of newspeak, these individuals are not prisoners of war but "detainees."

Lt. Gen. Hamid Gul Haq, the former head of the ISI security service in Pakistan, said at the time this was reported: "I think it is very strange behavior that one didn't expect from the Americans . . . They are setting new trends in state behavior by coining new terms like battlefield detainees." He added "One can safely say they are violating all norms of behavior and violating the Geneva Convention." Even in Great Britain there were a few raised eyebrows and Donald Anderson, the Labor MP and chairman of the Commons foreign affairs select committee, added this "Whatever the formal category, these prisoners still have legal rights and what we have heard already suggests that human rights are indeed being put in jeopardy." (UnitedStates.com)

Mr. Bush Goes His Own Way

Most have read something about this president's persistence in going his own way; as if the world no longer exists; Mr. George Bush Jr. shall rewrite the rules of game. It is this autocratic tendency which shall certainly get this president into trouble sooner or later. Most of the discussion of the Bush administration's anti-terrorism reconfiguration of the justice system has focused on whether or not these changes violate the U.S. Constitution and specifically the Bill of Rights. But there is another legal standard that Mr. Bush's administration appears to be tossing out as so much gobbledegoop: The Geneva Convention. For instance the plan to hold secret military tribunals on US aircraft carriers or in remote islands in US possession. Mr. Bush argues that we did something similar during World War Two; not quite Mr. Bush, but even had this been true, the Geneva Conventions were drawn up after World War Two during 1949 with Protocol II adopted as international law during 1977. For Bush to make such a false statement can only be attributed to his utter contempt for Americans given their lack of knowledge over such issues. Given Nuremberg and all that went with it, his argument is not going to hold up under scrutiny. Consider the plan to try some accused terrorists in secret military tribunals and wiretap their meetings with lawyers. The Fourth Convention (which can be viewed at <http://www.unhchr.ch/html/menu3/b/92.htm>), was issued in 1949 and titled "Relative to the Protection of Civilian Persons in Time of War," and safeguards "as a minimum" the rights of all "persons *taking no active part in the hostilities*, including members of armed forces who have laid down their arms" and those removed from combat "by sickness, wounds, *detention*, or any other cause ..." [emphases added]. As one journalist pointed out "Clearly this stricture of international law is intended to protect throughout the course of a war all civilians and all fighters who are put out of action. And it goes on to say that none of these people can be sentenced without trial in a 'regularly constituted court' that affords all guarantees, 'which are recognized as indispensable by civilized peoples.' Surely the rights to an open trial, a ban on secret evidence, and freedom from warrantless government wiretaps are among those guarantees." (Unconventional Un-wisdom, How the Bush administration is breaking the rules of war. By Scott Shuger, December 6, 2001) The author makes this lucid argument at some length and it bears quoting in length:

> The Fourth Convention also requires countries to apply to war detainees the law as it existed at the time of their offenses. Since U.S. courts have generally extended to defendants the protections mentioned in the previous paragraph, it's therefore at least a violation of the spirit of the convention to drop them now. And what of the 548 civilians who are still being detained unnamed and uncharged in the United States as part of the government's post-9/11 investigation? Attorney General John Ashcroft's steadfast refusal to release any information about

them certainly seems to violate the GC's requirement that countries shall "immediately" give out information about detainees so that their next of kin can be notified "quickly." And the GC explicitly states that this information should "make it possible to identify the protected person exactly." Certainly the United States would demand such basic information if any of our troops in Afghanistan were taken prisoner. Therefore it should likewise provide it to Taliban officials now. And once the United States has done this, maintaining its current refusal to inform American lawyers and reporters would be reduced to the nonsense that Mullah Omar is entitled to know things about the U.S. justice system the American people are not.

Mr. Shugar is probably right when he adds "Perhaps the administration would respond that the Geneva Convention is irrelevant here because it covers wars between nations while the United States' anti-terror campaign is being waged against a rump band that hijacked a country and the criminal gang they hosted." That completely misinterprets the Geneva Convention and Mr. Bush presumably understands this. It seems clear where it states that its key provisions also apply "[i]n the case of armed conflict not of an international character occurring in the territory of one of the High Contracting Parties." In other words, and Mr. Shugar is correct in pointing this out, "it doesn't matter if the Taliban isn't a ["recognized" (by whom?)] nation—the Geneva Convention applies to any land belonging to a country that has signed it. And since both the United States and Afghanistan are signatories, anyone taken prisoner in the course of this war should enjoy its protection."

Both President Bush and Ashcroft have consistently defended their changes to our legal system by citing the demands of war. But they seem to have forgotten that war doesn't just entail special demands that must be met. It also entails special laws that must be obeyed. (Ibid.)

A more thorough look at these enforceable laws, is in order, to add to what Mr. Shugar has touched upon regarding the Geneva Convention and other legal documents which are to guide the rules of war. Only one group, the four Geneva Conventions are specific enough not to be ignored. Of the approximately twenty sources presently existing in this area of international law, sources containing a total of more than 600 articles, only this one agreement, containing twenty-eight articles, is directly related to the problem of internal armed conflicts. It is here we find the intent of the law. This document is the Additional Protocol, adopted in 1977, to the Geneva Conventions of August 12, 1949. This Protocol is where we find the concerns addressed regarding the treatment of and protecting the victims of, armed conflicts of a "non-international nature," (Protocol II) further supplementing Article 3, which is common to all four 1949 Geneva Conventions of 1949. The war Bush started in Afghanistan is and remains a war of a non-international character, unless Mr. Bush and Mr. Blair decide to make it a global war against other sovereign nation-states; then the entire Geneva Accords and the United Nations Charter and Security Council itself would be faced with denouncing the US actions. Take a careful look at how Mr. Bush and Mr. Blair are violating the law:

> Article 3 of the Geneva Conventions of 1949, the first international law provision designed to be applied "[i]n the case of an armed conflict not of an international character," remained for almost three decades, right up to the time when Protocol II entered into force, the sole requirement under international law of humane treatment, by each of the parties to a conflict, under all circumstances and without discrimination, of "[p]ersons taking no active part in the hostilities, including members of armed forces who have laid down their arms, and those placed *hor de combat* by sickness, wounds, detention or any other cause." Article 3 introduces into current international law a legislative prohibition against carrying out the following actions against the persons listed above:
>
> (a) violence to life and person, in particular, murder of all kinds, mutilation, cruel treatment and torture;
> (b) taking of hostages;
> (c) outrages upon personal dignity, in particular humiliating and degrading treatment;
> (d) the passing of sentences and the carrying out of executions without previous judgment pronounced by a regularly constituted court, affording all the judicial guarantees which are recognized as indispensable by civilized peoples. (S.A. Yegorov, *International Law and International Security: Military and Political Dimensions*, 1991, M.E. Sharpe, Inc.)

There can be no question that the reason why Mr. Bush has decided independently of all the rules of war, all the rules of civilized peoples, all the legal aspects of international law, and has once again chosen to go his own way, is that he knows he has already violated international law and specifically Protocol II adopted 1977; signed by virtually all nations including Afghanistan and the United States. This, though not alone, created the legal obligations Mr. Bush cannot simply ignore. The Military Tribunals violate international law; trials held in secret outside regularly constituted courts, violate international law; wire-tapping of prisoners and their lawyers violate international law; the treatment of the twenty (so far) prisoners of war, shaving their heads, outdoor cages, no protection from the environment (mosquitoes, rain and heat), the secret base confinement, violates the laws of decency and international law; the sick (several prisoners wearing masks because they have tuberculosis) treated inhumanely is, as well, a violation of human rights and international law. But the worst violation of all is the effort to deny the applicability of the Four Geneva Conventions and Protocol II outright, by claiming these are not prisoners of war, but "battlefield detainees," a term, not of legal significance, that has no basis in law, anywhere in law, and is pure deception and an outrage for the United States, *of all nations,* to act upon. As one US citizen, who has served his country, on and off, for more than thirty years in several different capacities, I am obligated to cry out against this President and all those who stand with him. These are the actions of a man who believes he is above the law. A man who believes he and his circle of friends have a right to rule *imperially,* the world, and all the world must therefore obey. As a citizen of both the world and the United States of America (call it dual citizenship if you must) I am as obligated as Thomas Paine was, to see that my country, above all, acts civilized and within the rule of law. Mr. Bush, with Mr. Blair's (sometimes silent) endorsement, have taken the world backwards, backwards to more primitive and feudal times when *might meant right.*

A Preliminary Glance at the Brotherhood

As I point out below in chapters nine and thirteen Mr. Bush had indeed already recognized the Taliban as the legitimate governing body in Afghanistan from February through August of 2001 immediately after taking office. He considered them a "stabilizing force in the region." But as you will see further below, that was only to apply in secret and only if the Taliban took the economic deal (euphemistically called a 'carpet of gold' at the time) offered to them in exchange for recognition. The deal was of course the 1996 proposed pipeline running through Afghanistan from Kazakhstan and Turkmenistan. Moreover, since 1996 the entire Caspian region, had been negotiating with Dick Cheney, Richard Armitage, Paul Wolfowitz, Condoleeza Rice, James A. Baker III, Henry Kissinger and Zbignew Brzezinski, former Senator Lloyd Bentson and a host of others all at the time representing major oil firms as consultants or directors of the firms themselves. This, since early 1996 until 2000, when the first four entered the White House along with Mr. Bush Jr. and the others remain consultants to the US Defense and State Departments, and oil companies of course.

Mr. Bush does not seem to want to follow the rules of International Relations (IR) let alone international law; he has, in many legal scholar's view, not been following the United States Constitution exactly to the letter either. If we can make the argument that Mr. Bush and his administration did in fact recognize the Taliban during the negotiations noted above (and the evidence is now becoming overwhelming that they did) even if later Mr. Bush, once the Taliban did not take the economic deal, suddenly decided they were then *persona non grata* and therefore not any longer recognized, is a moot point. They were recognized by the administration, were negotiated with in good faith, and the Afghan regime did not change, the United States administration changed *their mind.* Moreover, it cannot be argued that the people of

Afghanistan did not, in anything like a majority, recognize the ruling Taliban and in fact obeyed them. The argument to the contrary can not be supported any more than the argument that Saddam Hussein does not have the support of most of his people. Dissidents aside and anti-Hussein elements (and I agree with their position entirely) is none of our concern. The majority of people in Afghanistan did support the Taliban regime and were glad they stopped the carnage perpetrated against the Afghan people by the Northern Alliance up until 1996. In fact, the so-called oppressed women of these supposedly Taliban tyrants were seen in the hills fighting along side their husbands against both the Northern Alliance and US Special Forces. Not that oppressed one might suppose. Mr. Bush Jr. rewrites history in denying all this.

Therefore we are talking about a sovereign nation-state and its sovereign leaders. Mr. Bush never had any legal standing to declare the Taliban leader Mullah Mohammad Omar, "wanted dead or alive." Nor can anyone suggest Donald Rumsfeld wringing his hands over a *missed opportunity* to "kill Omar" outright was anything but diabolical. If we are at war, then we must obey the rules of war; if we are not at war we must obey the rules of civilized human nature. The Taliban had nothing to do with the September 11, 2001 air attacks and this bears repeating often; even if it were proven Osama bin Laden had something to do with it (and nothing anyone publicly has seen, to date January 18th, 2002, proves otherwise) this has no bearing on bombing the country itself, killing civilians and removing the Taliban from power.

This volume has as one of its objectives to prove that there are in fact other objectives being sought and these objectives have been sought for over five years. And it can only be these objectives which has motivated Mr. Bush to dissemble reality to the world in declaring his right to defend America (which was clearly attacked) against the wrong enemy. Yes, the president has a right to defend America; every nation has a right to defend itself. But the laws regarding this defense have been worked out in great detail since World War Two and Mr. Bush violates these as well.

The United Nations

Has Mr. Bush Jr. and Britain's Tony Blair seriously followed the intent of the United Nations Charter? Most Americans *think they might* believe so. The Charter is designed to govern the various nation-states in their respective international relations. It was, and is, to be the beginnings of a rule of law globally. Mr. Bush cited Article 51 of the UN Charter, and Mr. Blair blindly conceded, that Bush was lawfully following the U.N. Charter and *his* (that would be the United States Mr. Bush, of which you are but a term-limited representative) right to "self-defense."

Is this an accurate depiction of the intent of the law? Article 51 authorizes to a state self-defense "if an armed attack occurs." The majority of governments and scholars consider that this means "only if an armed attack occurs." Others have argued that the "inherent right" referred to in Article 51 safeguards this right. But this interpretation would render the phrase "if an

armed attack occurs" redundant, which is not likely to have been intended. It would have made no sense to include it if it were not a limitation.
According to legal scholar, Oscar Schachter,

> [N]ot all uses of force against a state constitute armed attacks. In *Nicaragua v. United States*, the International Court distinguished between an armed attack and a "mere frontier incident," noting that an armed attack must have greater "scale and effects." The Court recognized that an armed attack included the sending of armed bands and "irregulars" into the territory of another state to carry out hostile acts. Assaults of this kind must be of "sufficient gravity," to constitute hostile acts. The court held that assistance to rebels in the form of provision of weapons or logistical or other support does not amount to an armed attack. (*International law and International Security*, pp, 35-38)

The Taliban governing body of Afghanistan had nothing to do with the air attacks on the three American facilities, the one of which, the World Trade Center, an international facility, nor had they sent insurgents to "illegally attack" America; this is not too fine a point to make as the war on terrorism must be fought within the boundaries outlined in the rule of law, not a summary judgment by Mr. Bush and Mr. Blair as to which country's rulers are next to be overthrown and replaced with imperial puppets. In fact Mr. Schachter makes a further point which one finds rather disturbing: "A contrary view expressed in a dissenting opinion is that "substantial involvement" in support of an insurgency can amount to armed attack and justifies individual and collective self-defense in response. (Schwebel, dissenting opinion, paragraph 176; Jennings, dissenting opinion, Page 534. Nicaragua v. United States, Ibid., Schachter)."

Which means that not only was Afghanistan not guilty of an armed attack on the United States, nor were Afghanistan insurgents used against the United States, therefore Bush's "inherent right to self-defense" by attacking Afghanistan and removing the Taliban from power amounts to a violation on the United State's part, not Afghanistan. Furthermore, in the dissenting opinions above, it is the United States, and Mr. Bush proper, which has attacked another sovereign state without provocation, and supplied "substantial involvement" in "support of an insurgency" (The Northern Alliance) which amounted to an "armed attack" justifying the individual self-defense on the part of the Taliban of Afghanistan, not the other way around.

This scenario gains further legal status (ground) when one discovers what has only just begun to come to light in the foreign press, certainly not in the American press; that being, that Mr. Bush and his present administration (and to only some lesser degree the Clinton administration) have been planning this war on Afghanistan and executing a "substantial involvement" with the Northern Alliance "insurgents" through "logistical and other support" well before September 11, 2001. (See chapter fourteen below for the most recent update to these findings [that chapter written while the book was already at the publishers] and added at the last moment before printing.) The meaning becomes clear. Mr. Bush has used an attack by terrorists, which have turned into international guerrilla warfare, to illegally attack another state and supply "illegal support" for an illegal attack by internal insurgents on that state. It is the Taliban ruling Afghanistan which therefore had the "inherent right to self-defense" guaranteed in Article 51 of the United Nations Charter, not Mr. Bush and the United States. In International Relations (IR) language it is Mr. Bush that has provided the *delict* in international law. (See chapter five below for further details of what a *delict* means) When Mr. Bush cited Article 51, he simply hoped no one of importance would note he cited wrongly the intent of the Article in his defense.

> The basic international law principle prohibiting armed intervention by foreign states in internal conflicts is Article 2(4) of the UN Charter. It reads:

> > All Members shall refrain in their international relations from the threat or use of force against the territorial integrity or political independence of any state, or in any other manner inconsistent with the Purposes of the United Nations.

> The principle is also accepted as a rule of customary international law and as a peremptory norm (*jus cogens*) from which no derogation is permitted. Customary international law also includes a general principle of non-interference in internal affairs, formulated by the UN General Assembly as follows:

> > No state or group of States has the right to intervene, directly or indirectly, for any reason whatever, in the internal affairs of any other State. Consequently, armed intervention and all other forms of interference or attempted threats against the personality of the State or against its political, economic and cultural elements, are in violation of international law.

> UN General Assembly Resolution 25/2625 (1970); see also UN General Assembly Resolution 20/2131 (1965). It is obvious from these principles that a foreign state may not use force to support insurgents or opposition elements against the government of a state. (Ibid., Schachter, pp. 37-38)

It is clear from this text that Mr. Bush intends, and likely always intended, to interfere with the personality of Afghanistan; even Mr. Jay Leno's wife must be thrilled that we now have an "el Presidente" (unlike Clinton) who is prepared to illegally intervene in the "cultural elements" of a foreign state and instruct the religious elements on how to dress. All sarcasm aside, Mr. Bush has violated every tenet of international relations: ideas developed over almost 400 years of history to secure for the world, through international law, international peace; international peace being the primary fundamental intent, the Purposes of the United Nations, that is to say.

> The essence of the international legal regime regarding the use of force in the post-World War II world is contained in Article 2(4) of the UN Charter which provides:

>> All members shall refrain in their international relations from the threat or use of force against the territorial integrity and political independence of any state, or in any other manner inconsistent with the Purposes of the United Nations. (William D. Jackson, *Renunciation of Aggression* in *International Law and International Security*, 1991, pg. 2)

Following this prohibition against the use of force or the threat of the use of force, the Charter in Article 2(3) imposes on all members of the United Nations an obligation to settle international disputes "by peaceful means in such a manner that international peace and security, and justice, are not endangered." These words have been seen as a profound change in international law and possess a character of overriding importance "widely acknowledged by jurists and governments alike." (Ibid., pg.3)

Important for our discussion here is what Mr. Jackson had to say regarding Article 51 and the inherent right to self-defense.

> Though the Charter affirmed in Article 51 that all members continued to have "the inherent right of individual or collective self-defense if an armed attack occurs," and "until the Security Council has taken measures to maintain international peace and security," nothing in the language of Article 51 was intended to diminish the comprehensive restriction of Article 2 of the Charter. Rather, the intention of the drafters of the Article, as reflected in Secretary of State Stettinius's report to the President on the work of the San Francisco Conference, was to affirm that as sweeping as the restraints on the use of force were under the Charter, they did not deny members the right to use force defensively if an armed attack occurred and until, as Stettinius stressed, the Security Council acted. The qualifying language of Article 51 itself reflected a view on the part of the government assembled at San Francisco that the nature of modern war required the establishment of restraints on the right to the use of force of a new and highly restrictive character....The same determination to condemn the aggressive use of military force in the

Charter was reflected in the Charter of the International Military Tribunal, which declared the planning or participating in wars of aggression a crime under international law. (Jackson, Ibid., pg. 3)

Mr. Bush has done as much to affect international peace and violate the "Purposes of the Charter," as had the hijackers who commandeered the four aircraft. As heinous as the latter acts were, and they were clearly carried out with great deliberation, nothing in those acts can cry out for blood revenge, a vendetta, or anything so primitive as striking out against the wrong people. Mr. Bush cannot justify his acts of international war by one state against another, using a "criminal element," the al Qaida, which he referred to in his September 20th, 2001 terrorism speech, "as akin to our Mafia," as the reason. The law is clear and Mr. Bush (sometimes much to my own regret here, I have to write this out of a greater sense of justice) has violated the most important ones. But what of the states that make-up his "loose" (a term here used very loosely indeed) coalition; which amounts to Britain and the states which have allowed Mr. Bush to launch his war from their territories?

Adoption by the General Assembly in 1974 of the definition of aggression by a consensus vote led to further specification of the principle of refraining from the threat or use of force. In conformity with this definition, acts of employment by a state of military force which are prohibited by the UN Charter include the following:

(a) The invasion or attack by the armed forces of a State of the territory of another State, or any military occupation, however temporary, resulting from such invasion or attack, or any annexation by the use of force of the territory of another State or any part thereof;
(b) Bombardment by the armed forces of a State against the territory of another State or the use of any weapons by a State against the territory of another State;
(c) the blockade of the ports or coasts of a State by the armed forces of another State;
(d) An attack by the armed forces of a State on the land, sea, or air forces, or marine or air fleets of another State;
...(f) The action of a State in allowing its territory, which it has placed at the disposal of another State, to be used by that other State for perpetrating an act of aggression against a third State; (V.N. Fedorov, *Renunciation of Aggression in International Law and International Security*, pp 12-13)

If the law means anything at all, then by these definitions adopted by all the signatories of the UN Charter and the Four Geneva Conventions inclusive of Protocol II, then Pakistan. Turkmenistan, and Uzbekistan have all violated international law by allowing US and British forces to launch an act of aggression, an act of war, against Afghanistan. Even though the air attacks against the United States must be considered under the same rules of war and international law, as an illegal attack, although and "unarmed" attack by definition, it was an act of war; an act of war which has no relationship to the government of Afghanistan proper even if the alleged, and he remains the alleged, "master mind" was Osama bin Laden. Now that he is hidden somewhere else, say Iran or Syria, or God forbid a country we have better relationships with but no extradition treaty with (like Afghanistan), do we bomb them as well? Bush seems to be contemplating Iran, Iraq, Syria, Sudan, Somalia, and Yemen. Where will Mr. Bush, backed by Mr. Blair, end his war? We must ask not only when will it end, but why America was attacked by these (who were by and large never known before as terrorists) international (many nationalities involved) guerrillas? Why the World Trade Center as opposed to Disneyland? Why has Mr. Bush, representing the world's most devastating war apparatus ever created, been allowed to go his own way in the face of international law 300 years in the making? How has he cowed the UN? How has he cowed a nation of free speech, free press, and free citizens into utter silence, relegating dissent to the vast outreaches of the Internet alone?

Mr. Bush has declared that everything has changed. These are all new circumstances because now America had finally been struck by elements the entire rest of the world has lived with for decades if not centuries. The world has not changed; warfare has not changed. Not really. And the motives for war have not changed at all. This is what this book is really about. That there are always more than one political objective pursued by every government when it decides to act with unbounded aggression, would seem to be a truism anyone could see, relate to, understand. Yet the world stands in stark contradistinction from the one I would have thought would witness these events. Events that I fear may not be duly debated for decades to come. But I am certain of one thing. History will judge and *there are no secrets* for long.

> Just as in domestic societies the kind of conflict which occurs depends on the kinds of wants which society itself instills, among international societies too the different kinds of war that have been fought reflect the different kinds of wants which each society has established. They reflect in other words the ideology of each age, as established by the elites which wield power at each time. (Evan Luard, *War in International Society*, Yale, 1986, pg 392)

CHAPTER TWO
On War: September 11, 2001

*Our most abject failing stems from our poor
capacity to understand other cultures. Officers trained
in anthropology and several of the other
social sciences would be useful.*
—CARL F. BERNARD

*Globalization has diffused economic and technological power
around the world....And globalization also has
the potential of giving rise to a gnawing sense of
impotence as decisions affecting the lives of millions slip
out of local political control.*
—DR. HENRY KISSINGER
America at the Apex: Empire or Leader

*Dulce bellum inexpertis
(Sweet is war to those who know it not.)*
—ERASMUS

ON WAR

SEPTEMBER 11, 2001 WAS A DAY THAT OUR COUNTRY will long remember. Whether the country's citizenry will ever know the truth about what happened is another story. Regardless of what the President and an obedient media states with such forthright assurances, we will not be told the entire truth. The one area we seemingly cannot bear to address is the *why*? Has another nation-state, with possibly participation of its military and intelligence apparatus with or without only al Qaida members, perpetrated an act of war, *not just terrorism*, on American soil? Bush must make all believe, as our latest PR President, that they know all the perpetrators by name. We know who did it and they are going to be brought to justice.

I am a patriot; it was once said of me, "Hulet is in love with what America could be and as one of its harshest critics he is also one of America's best friends." (Professor Dean Picard PhD, reviewing the book, *Human All-Too-Human*, 2000). A patriot must, as well, see his government for what it is and to preserve what it ought to be; according to the Founders, be its greatest critic when it goes astray. Especially when the decision to go to war has been taken, then the true patriots speak out. Thus the reasons for this analysis; hopefully you will begin to understand below.

The Evidence: The *Penttbomb* Investigation

Nobody serious about what happened believes that the FBI had already caught any of the bad-guys. Nor that they know with any certainty who the pilots and others were by name. No reasonable thinking person believes this. No adult law enforcement personnel believe this. No one in the intelligence community, active or retired. This is the pap the President must feed the average unthinking herd. The enemy can only be crazed fanatical Islamic Jihad types. Only religious fanatics would commit suicide for a cause. Nobody sane would want to kill Americans. And that is precisely what has not happened. Soldiers and military pilots and revolutionaries will do precisely the same thing if ordered and they believe their nation(s) are at risk. If some, any, terrorist group planned and executed this act of war alone, they would have taken full credit. (At the time of this rewrite for the book edition, Mr. Bush had displayed a flawed and incredulous tape that did not, I repeat did not, demonstrate Osama bin Laden (spelled throughout the remainder of this text improperly for the reader used to western insults) planned the attack. It is only in taking the credit that their cause becomes understood; even if only understood to exist as their cause. That no group has claimed credit is a tell. They have not claimed it because they did not do it alone. Just like Oklahoma City, the government/media nexus immediately said it was Arab terrorists; I was a lone voice for three days (KABC News Radio) saying it was an act by an American. I knew this for many reasons and one of them was that nobody claimed credit, Why? because no Arab group did it. Here is the main point to this part of the analysis: Even if they were from an Arab State this does not *ipso facto* say they were terrorists. The participation of former military, intelligence, covert operations simply cannot be ruled out; the true originating source is unknown still.

Regarding the FBI's rather bold and sudden claim within a week or so, that they know, absolutely know, who the 19 hijackers were, by name, with addresses, photographs; we will never know if the face on the passport or driver's licenses match the toast in the rubble. But the White House and FBI do not care that this evidence is more wishful thinking than conclusive evidence. We must be seen by Americans to be on top of all this. We cannot even be sure the names are the names of the pilots. The media obediently repeats the names by rote, never questioning it: Satam al-Suqami (who allegedly sat in 10B) and Waleed al-Shehri and Wail al-Shrhri (who allegedly sat in 2B and 2A): while they may have set up the same Hollywood post-office box as their address, are they the persons who they said they were? If I had been one of the pilots I would have had all the same I. D. 's, mail drops and I would have left the same idiotic paper trail for the FBI to diligently "discover" but the name would have been Warren Beatty!

I am not, obviously saying that these men did not stay where the FBI says they stayed, or bought a burger on the 10th of September and a latte at Squirrelly Bob's Dinner; I am saying, does anyone believe these individuals used their real names? That their own, or some other's nation's military and intelligence agencies could not have given them full credentials and identification? In other words "they were washed clean." That some were intelligent enough to carry a Master's Degree in civil engineering and fly the world's most sophisticated airplanes but are so stupid as to leave their *real names* behind? When the FBI "discovered" that several of the alleged suspects (dead now, so we shall never know) spoke German, as witnesses confirmed they spoke German, but the FBI said they were from the Middle East,...why? Because the witness was told they were from the Middle East (Saudi Arabia) by the German speaking gentlemen; and like the diligent FBI they believed this. They spoke German because maybe, just maybe, some were German. later it was admitted that there were two Anglo-Saxons from Britain involved with the Al Qaida network, Chinese were fighting with the Taliban and bin Laden. Some on one flight spoke perfect English; why would they speak perfect English on a suicide mission? Of course much later an American (Walker) was captured in the raids in Afghanistan so we know this is not just a Jihad made up of Islamic fanatics. There is more going on than that. I shall argue throughout this revised volume in book form that we are in fact dealing with a global reaction from many nation-state's peoples against what they believe to be a new form of global empire. An American-led empire.

It was conceded early on that the FBI did not know the nationalities of the

19 men that allegedly were the perpetrators. And nationalities are very important. Not because the FBI and media have assumed all were Arab State's citizens; again several spoke perfect English and others German, others did not speak at all. And this is important. English could mean South African, British, Australian, American, as we now know, or whatever. Nobody will dare suggest that they spoke these languages because that was their country of origin, not the Arab States; that their allegiance might be to a completely different nation-state or to a global cause is not even a consideration, that is just too scary. Indeed, those people that look like Arabs amounts to approximately two thirds of the world's peoples. I have a client which closely resembles a Palestinian who is of Jewish and Nicaraguan parents: he is now a New Yorker, born in San Francisco. With an Arabic name he would easily be identified as Arab. He looks very much like a young bin Laden.

Who is Williams? What Nationality?

In New Jersey, the FBI on a September 2001, Wednesday, searched the Marriott Hotel at Newark Airport, where some or all of the four hijackers of United Airlines flight 93 were believed to have stayed on Monday night. The plane is the one that crashed in western Pennsylvania. It was that flight where either passengers and/or crew members downed the plane rather than become a cruise missile. But here was an interesting aside, reported once then never looked at again.

> Curiously, given that all the suspected hijackers had Arab names, one guest at the hotel, who asked not to be named, said in an interview that during the search, the FBI agents asked each man they encountered, "Are you Williams?"
> (By Christopher Drew: nytimes.com/2001/09/16/nyregion/16ARRE.html)

It does not seem significant to anyone that the Vero Beach, Florida Flight School and others interviewed as well, have no record of almost all of these individuals attending the schools; those which had attended the school and were Saudi citizens, have been absolved of involvement because their names were similar and/or they were alive and in Saudi Arabia. Even if it could be concluded that some (as in maybe two or five) of the hijackers had attended a U.S. Flight School (and this has still not been proven conclusively) it could have likely been to polish-up skills they already possessed (which proved to be the case as late as December 2001). Why do U.S. authorities refuse to seek out the obvious: these pilots may have been already trained, some well-trained. By whom? Since we cannot prove conclusively that the men identified were *not* German, or not English, but only looked this way or that, said they were this or that, any other nation-state could as easily be part of this. And this is not just my suspicion. It was reported once, only once and never repeated again:

It was uncertain whether the 19 names of the hijackers put out by officials today were the true names of the hijackers. The names were apparently those used by the men when they purchased airline tickets, but it was unclear whether they might have used aliases, stolen identities or forged documents.
(By Neil A. Lewis: nytimes.com/2001/09/15/national/15IN-QU.html)

Which of course becomes the only explanation as to why the perpetrators would have openly (and stupidly) purchased tickets on the Internet using their accrued mileage or with credit cards. It was not "their" credit cards, nor their mileage, as it was not really them in whose names they were purchased. This level of tactical skill and planning falls comfortably into nation-state military intelligence levels but hardly *bin Laden's* alone. According to INS these individuals' passports were, with but one exception, not out-of-status with immigration authorities and only one was even said to have been. In other words, these individuals were "clean" and could travel freely. Precisely the case if they were military personnel or individual citizens with (then) no known ties to terrorists or traveling under false identities (washed) and under "orders" in behalf of their nation-state authorities. Under orders; by whom then becomes the real question. It is the blind assumption that these were all followers of *bin Laden*, with laser-like focus and determination, that the FBI and White House refuse to tell the American people to prepare for a protracted war, not with just simple terrorists, but with trained professional military and intelligence personnel from one or more nation's military and likely Air Force being involved at some level. It is becoming better known just how much Iraqi, and Iranian intelligence officers have met with various factions of different terrorist groups. These terrorist groups have evolved into something far more dangerous in my opinion. And there must be, therefore, different reasons why.

Another fact surfaced that was reported twice then never broached again. A senior White House aide told New York Times reporter and later reported in William Safire's column, that Secret Service was contacted and told that Air Force One had been targeted next after the airliners had already begun striking the World Trade Center towers.

According to the high official, American code words were used showing a knowledge of procedures that made the threat credible....(I have a second, on-the-record source about that: Karl Rove, the president's senior advisor, tells me: "When the president said 'I don't want some tinhorn terrorists keeping me out of Washington,' the Secret Service informed him that the threat contained language that was evidence that the terrorists had knowledge of his procedures and whereabouts. In light of the specific and credible threat, it was decided to get airborne with a fighter escort.").
(www.nytimes.com/2001/09/13/opinion/13SAFI.html)

No responsible thinking person believes *bin Laden,* nor any other terror-ists, could have come by such tightly held security data on their own. The military intelligence (spy agencies) of many nation-states, on the other hand, performs precisely such operations. Here is a report from CNN.com that ex-plained why this war was going to be fought with such secrecy: "This new war (is) to be fought with unprecedented secrecy...the Bush administration has decided to clamp down on even routine information because it could prove of some use to potential terrorists." The report spells this out in the Pentagon's own words and one doubts the sincerity of Bush's claims that these are simply al Qaida members. But if he were worried about nation state intelligence capabilities, which we believe is the case, then the clamp down makes sense.

> The actual plans are under close guard and have not been shared with news agencies. The rationale, according to Penta-gon officials: Terrorist organizations lack the intelligence-gath-ering capacity that nations possess, relying instead on news organizations to find out what their enemies are doing. (cnn.com/2001US/09/17/ret.us.secret.war/)

The point of course is not lost and the Pentagon and White House can-not have it both ways. If intelligence capabilities are nation-state's alone and terrorists "lack the intelligence-gathering capacity," then the intelligence re-ported above on Air Force One's codes and procedures could not have been Osama bin Laden generated. Therefore some nation's intelligence capabilities are, by the rules of logic, at work.

It is such facts, reported once or maybe twice, then disappear from the media altogether that suggests the Pentagon is clearly in control, not the FBI. That we are dealing with a different threat than what Bush claims. And there are, I shall argue below, sufficient evidence that this is the case. But not some-thing Mr. Bush will want to readily explain to the unwitting herd of Ameri-cans.

Another fact not reported, why were ATF, Alcohol Tobacco and Firearms *Rapid Response Teams* turned away from the disaster scenes by the FBI when they were ordered by the Secretary of Treasury? Why have so many in other branches of federal law enforcement been kept completely out of the loop, including the ATF already mentioned. The ATF in particular has great ca-pabilities in explosives and arson investigations, neither of which are skills which could have been ruled out, no matter what the FBI says. (I was in-formed later on September 21st, by my sources at ATF, that the ATF had been brought back into the loop.) In any case, if it were criminal terrorists like we have been told, the federal law enforcement authorities would need every hand and brain available. If it were only terrorism that is; but if it is what I am suggesting here, then there would be every reason to tighten the hold on both evidence and information. The first casualty of war is truth; always free speech and a free press. Recall it was an ATF Special Agent Mark Micholic, that actually nailed Timothy McVeigh. (See this authors interviews with Jim Bohannon [Westwood One] and Frank Sontag [KLOS/KABC] where I went on the air with Micholic and Special Agent Luke Franey, 1999.) There can be another reason other than the that which the FBI claims, as to why they had locked down the disaster sites; the Pentagon's Joint Chiefs of Staff are really in charge and the FBI are their spokesmen and cover. They do not want some bright-eyed ATF agent catching another Tim McVeigh and identifying any source not in the Operational Plan. This is going to be seen as terrorism, period...end of story.

Analyzing the Facts Differently

U.S. culture, low-brow or high, radiates outward with an intensity last seen in the days of the Roman Empire— but with a novel twist...cultural sway stopped exactly at their borders. America's soft power, though, rules over an empire on which the sun never sets.

—JOSEF JOFFE
Who's Afraid of Mr. Big?

Here we have the beginnings of what I believe are the facts, properly interpreted. While I may stand to be corrected later on some fact or interpretation, the crux of the argument will hold over time. That is the real intent of this book, to raise questions during a period in my country's history when we are all told "to shut-up and sit-down," by the government. Not only were these not just Islamic terrorists, it is clear this was a secular attack on the very governmental infrastructure of the American-led empire. The empire, which has been efficiently and quietly built for decades under American's turned-up noses. That it is empire is no longer in dispute. That it is a purely western world empire is becoming clearer; that it is an American-led empire is now inarguable.

It is the empire that was attacked; what are seen as its Roman Legions were specifically targeted. This is the second key to any understanding. Hitting the Pentagon, and the intended target of the fourth aircraft was most certainly not Camp David (the President was on Air Force One and the perpetrators knew this), but the United States Capital Building, is striking at the infrastructure of the empire, not just America as America. How do we know this? The second target was the belly of the empire, its *raison d'etre*, its very essence, *Corporatism*.

The World Trade Center (WTC) is not an American institution but a global institution; its child, the *World Trade Organization* (WTO), is what the empire is, as reality and just cause. *Corporatism* is its ideology and means nothing less than this: the largest U.S. based multinational corporations are inextricably tied to the United State's governing apparatus; it is the state, the men within the corporate power structure *are* the cabinet of the White House. When George Shultz speaks to the press, "...*bin laden* did not do this, this is much larger than that..." he speaks as former Secretary of State, Secretary of Labor, Secretary of the Treasury and Undersecretary of the Treasury for Monetary Affairs. But he speaks as the voice of *Corporatism* as well as former CEO of Bechtel, director of Boeing and head of the former USUSSR Trade and Economic Council, among the other hundred plus positions on boards of directors, advisory boards and appointments galore. Now, repeat this scenario several hundred times with different names; George Bush Sr., Casper Weinberger, Philip Habib, Lawrence Eagleberger, Brent Scowcroft, Averill Harriman, McGeorge Bundy, and on and on, ad nauseum, both Republicans and Democrats equally represented and often the one in the other's White House appointments. And for over fifty years this has been the norm. This is not in dispute any longer; not even the haggard American progressive-left will (which always had in the past) dispute this argument any longer.

This has never been a conspiracy theory. This is just what it is, the way it has been, arguably since the dawn of time, but specific to this newest attempt at empire, certainly since the beginning of World War Two, with traces as far back as the turn of the last century.

In Josef Joffe's article quoted briefly above in italics, the editor and publisher of *Die Ziet*, raises the question *why* like this, "No armed coalitions, formal or informal, are being organized by former friends or foes." In this he seems puzzled. Every great empire has found a coalition built against it by former allies or enemies or some ad hoc formation of nations which oppose the one great nation of empire. Joffe's only mistake in this thoughtful piece was to focus entirely on fully developed western nation-states. When looked at through only that lens one finds plenty of complaints about this empire of America's.

> The two [American party] conventions [in 2000] displayed all that is most repugnant and alien in a political system corrupted beyond recognition....God's chosen people, uniquely blessed, nurture a self-image almost as deranged in its profound self-delusion as the old Soviet Union. (*Polly Toyndee*, in the British *Guardian*, quoted in *Newsweek*, December 2000—February, 2, 2001)

Joffe points out that such criticism like that above which he quoted also is directed not at what America does, but what America is. He notes this as a European style, or *un-America* attitude predominately of the industrialized EU (European Union) nations. His only error, in my opinion, is he focused on the wrong continents, the wrong mixed bag of potential coalition makers formed against the newest empire, America (-led, I would note, again and not a purely American Empire at all). But his collection of what he sees as European perspectives towards America gives one pause. If our allies and trading partners view us with such disgust, what of the Arab states, what of under-developed third-world states; it is the *rogue states*, the *pariah* states, this paper considers a greater threat than ever. Let us look at, in brief, what Joffe outlines as attitudes towards America as empire in any case, and extrapolate from there. He notes this elsewhere as "HHMMS" or the *Harvard, Hollywood, McDonald's Microsoft Syndrome.*

HHMMS

America is morally retrograde. It executes its own people, which Europe does not, and likes to bomb others, which Europe does only when dragged along by the United States. It is a land of intolerant, fundamentalist religion, while Europe is charting a path toward enlightened secularism... Internationally, it is "Dirty Harry" and "Globocop" rolled into one—an irresponsible and arrogant citizen of the global community.

America is socially retrograde. It is the land of "predatory capitalism" that denies critical social services, like health insurance, to those who need it most. Instead of bettering the lot of the poor and unskilled, it shunts millions of them, mainly dark-skinned minorities, off to prison. Europe on the other hand metes out rehabilitation, not retribution. America accepts, nay, admires gross income inequalities, whereas Europe cherishes redistribution in the name of social justice. The United States lets its state school system rot, not to speak of the public infrastructure.

America is culturally retrograde. It gorges itself on fatty fast food, wallows in tawdry mass entertainment, starves the arts and prays to one God, which is Mammon. Instead of subsidizing the good and high-minded, as do the Europeans, the United States ruthlessly sacrifices the best of culture to pap and pop. Its great universities (for the rich and well-connected only) conceal vast illiteracy and ignorance of the world. In matters sexual, America is both prurient and prudish, a far cry from the wiser ways of Europe.

The above lengthy quote is from Joffe's article in *The National Interest*, — Summer 2001. This may not be what Joffe himself senses about America (though it's a good bet some of it he does) but what he senses Europeans sense about America. It will seem harsh to some Americans to read this, especially at this time right after the air attacks when all the citizenry of America are swept-up in the hysteria of *America First*, love-it-or-leave-it. It is an argument meant to understand, that while America is so disliked by the European powers, there is no indication of a willingness to form a military coalition to stand against this empire. His Euro-argument may hold. But elsewhere he encounters the question of America's efforts to install the NMD or national missile defense (the newest version of Star Wars) and European, Russian and Chinese opposition to it. America throws out arms control regimes and their treaties America itself foisted on the world during the Cold War: *to wit,* the ABM (Anti-Ballistic Missile) convention; yet proposes to build its own. We are not arguing the merits or demerits of U.S. actions, just pointing out what the rest of the world sees as hypocrisy and raw power politics. Joffe here raises the important question for this juncture of American history after September 11, 2001. He put it this way during February 2001:

> Assume though, by a flight of fancy, that NMD really works. In that case, it will not only devalue the strategic arsenals of lesser players; worse, it will add to America's "proactive" power by enhancing its "escalation dominance." Concretely, if America could shield itself against missiles, it could inhibit Chinese sallies against Taiwan or intervene against any "rogue state" with little risk to itself. That would grant a nice margin of usable power to the United States, a prospect that does not reassure the rest of the world. (Page 48)

Many Americans will agree with Joffe but most will like the idea of such American risk-free hegemony. That is not the point. The point is how the rest of the world perceives the United States as the newest Empire. It is strategic balancing, the balance of power in the world that Joffe is reflecting upon. Without the real balance, he sees a kind of existential sting arising and affecting the world. In the case of America, "...Suffice it to say: he who does not conquer does not provoke literal counter-alliances and war. America's 'hard power' inspires discomfort, not existential angst..." But that is because it is so hard to identify.

> Since America's existential sting is well concealed or well contained, strategic balancing against this hegemon falls short of the classic pattern; it is internal, illicit or implicit. Internal balancing is what the Russians and Chinese do when they try to preserve (Moscow) or expand (Beijing) their military panoplies. Illicit balancing goes by the name of international terror. It is deployed against the United States more or less privately, as by Saudi freelance bombardier bin laden, or more or less officially, as by those Arab countries suspected of being sources of "state-sponsored terrorism." (Page 49.)

It is the *more*, in the more or less above, we are concerned with here. It is not the European powers that Joffe pondered as to "why they have not formed a coalition" against the American empire, "in the classic tradition," but the lesser powers he ignored. The *rogue states* he barely noted in the above as victims of the hegemonic power of America. It is European opinions of America, culturally, morally and socially, that he takes note of. Taking note of what the *rogue states* and their people, the people that have felt more than the "existential sting," of American raw power, is where he should have been looking; and this is precisely why this writer is looking there now.

I had included in Appendix One of my first paper, On War, a September 21, 2001 article that appeared in (www.worldtribune.com/wta/Archive-2001/me_egypt_09_21.html) *Egypt rejects U.S. coalition, upgrades ties with Iraq.* This is just the beginning. Egypt almost immediately established diplomatic ties, opened an embassy and began forming a NAFTA type free-trade agreement with Iraq. I have not included further evidence of Iraqi military intelligence, Iraqi funding and their activities because most will have read about it at some point. One very reliable source, Jane's Security ran a piece stating "Israel's military intelligence service, Aman, suspects that Iraq is the state that sponsored...(the attacks)." (www.janes.com/security/international_security/news/fr/fr010919_1_n.shtml).

> In another development, Mohamed Atta, one of the suspected hijackers on board the first plane to slam into the World Trade Center last week, met with an Iraqi intelligence official somewhere in Europe earlier this year, U.S. officials said Tuesday.

Remarkably in the next paragraph the U.S. officials cautioned..."that the meeting does not mean that Iraq had a role in last week's terrorist attacks." I fear they will eat those words soon enough. (www.cnn.com/2001/US/09/18/inv.investigation.terrorism/)

After making my arguments for nation-state military involvement one half hour after Bush gave his rousing speech, September 20th, on The Jim Bohannon Show (live in Washington D.C.), the very next day the Washington Times (and the others above) began releasing stories with headlines reading "Iraq suspected of sponsoring terrorist attacks."

(Bill Gertz, www.washtimes.com/national/20010921-94732490.htm)

My point remaining is the same as I began with on the morning of September 11th, this is not just terrorism sponsored by some *rogue state*, but **guerrilla warfare** tied directly or loosely to nation-state military and/or military intelligence. Egypt was the first nation to reject the Bush U.S. coalition and was certainly not to be the last. Should more than a few nation-states be behind these horrific events Bush will find himself at war with secular (not religious) leaders of nation-states (not terrorists) and their full military compliment (not individual terrorists brought to justice) of trained (often by the U.S.) military forces. To win a war against nation-states which declare war or perpetrate an act of war on American soil, Bush will have to defeat the governments themselves, defeat their military and occupy their territory. This is a beast of a different color than what Bush outlined in his frenzied speech of September 20th, 2001. Mr. Bush may wish to proceed on these very assumptions though and enter a new era of protracted wars. By December 20th 2001, it was widely reported that Mr. Bush had targeted Iraq, Sudan, Yemen and Somalia and had deployed Special Operations personnel in those countries to make contact with dissident elements which might oppose their existing regimes. Secretary of Defense Donald Rumsfeld referred to this repeatedly as "we have been successful in Afghanistan and we feel it can be repeated elsewhere." Saying these kinds of naive statements when Afghanistan is hardly *settled* does not put this writer at ease.

End of Geography?

To better understand the meaning of this empire one might do well to read chapter three below titled *The World Trade Organization: The End of Geography?* Here I must make a brief return to the issue at hand. In our opinion, this is why the WTC was targeted along with the American political infrastructure. This was *not* a strike at the American people; this was *not* a strike at our religions, traditions or norms; this was not Islamic holy war, no Jihad. This was a secular strike at the empire itself. The attack upon this larger empire, unfortunately for the innocent (known to us when our nation does the same to other nation's people, as *collateral damage*) is as well, an attack on America. But nobody is trying to defeat or destroy America *per se*. They want the empire to go away. They want the empire to recede from their shores, their political and cultural lives. And so this level of attack will happen again. One believes Mr. Bush, and the Arab hating media at one's peril. This was an act of war, a declaration of war on the empire we have all allowed our government to create, not in our (as in the citizenry of the United States) interests, but the monopoly interests of the largest corporations which double as our defense contractors; whose directors and CEO's revolve in and out of our government. The empire is no less shadowy than the shadowy perpetrators in Bush's rhetoric.

> The post-Cold War generation is concerned very little...Nor does it feel guilty about professing a doctrine of self-interest which it pursues strenuously in its own economic activities....This generation is subject to being seduced by the idea of riskless global relations as compensation for the intense competitiveness of its private lives....Such attitudes are possible only because the danger of general war has largely disappeared.
> (Dr. Henry Kissinger, Summer 2001, *The National Interest*)

Until now. After the end of the Cold War and the Berlin Wall fell, the world breathed easier. But others saw raw opportunity at hand. Then President George Bush Sr., began a series of high-level meetings at the White House. I have transcripts and the published reports of these meetings (see chapter eight below), where it was decided that America, as the sole superpower, must move rapidly and seize the future for western hegemony. It was then decided American hegemony was not something to be left to chance, not history, nor our allies. It was decided America would begin a new day, a new order, a New World Order...Bush's words not mine. But virtually nobody had a clue then, nor now, what he meant. You would have to have been reading for years the transcripts and volumes published and only read in IR circles (International Relations) and primarily what the British and French were saying. Out of this US based conceptual brainstorm came a new Directorate (V) within the Central Intelligence Agency's charter (CIA), an economic counter-espionage arm; its sole purpose is the protection of U.S. multinational corporations: trade secrets, corporate espionage, information technology, trade routes, air space over critical facilities, etc.— which raises the obvious question always asked regarding every governmental body — "In whose interests does it serve?" In chapter eight below I name the individuals and their attendant corporate connections in the region in question and globally more generally. This is why, I shall be labeled a *conspiracy theorist.* Which no longer bothers me much because the facts are too well known now. But I do take up these charges in chapter thirteen and sort out why the charges are being made about anyone who dissents from Mr. Bush's iron viewpoint. I also look at Mr. Tony Blairs recent attack on anyone that disagrees with Britain's role or Mr. Bush; set out as charges in a dossier hailing all the victories America and Britain have achieved to date.

The Analysis in Brief

What do we now know about indigenous
cultures in areas where we may commit forces?
—CARL F. BERNARD

Understanding the empire is the beginning. Assuming the reader has accepted my argument so far (if not one may wish to go to chapter three first before going on), let me continue regarding the air attacks. After the rubble has cleared and the body count confirmed (which will never be certain) the picture painting begins. My picture, painted with my own brushes, is different from my government's. These planes were not, and I cannot stress this enough, hi-jacked, they were *commandeered.* They were used as cruise missiles since everyone knows the impossible tactic of trying to enter American airspace without approval. They were not taken by scarf wearing, AK-47 toting, chest strapped with dynamite fanatics. The planes were taken by individuals fighting a new kind of guerrilla war. (The argument as to how well-trained these pilots may have been will never be known as they are all quite dead, assuming once again we really have their correct names.) Were they just a bunch of irregular students that took a course in flying really big planes in Florida? This was a tactical assault of the first rank. Logistics and planning superb. Years in planning and likely many, very many test runs well before the deed.

One high-level intelligence special agent warned me, "...if I were them, they already have more pilots and soldiers on our soil, and they will hit us again," and this was in place for several years. Our intelligence community completely missed it, even as it was being carried out. Why? Because our intelligence groups were looking only for the fanatical Muslim Jihad, the known terrorists, not a *secular* and individual military's involvement of one or more *secular* regimes. They could not have thought to be looking out for newly enlisted guerrilla warriors joining a global revolution. As pointed out recently in *Soldier of Fortune* magazine's Carl Bernard's article, *Pursuit of Intelligence,* (many) "Battles And Wars (are) Lost From Bad Intel." (subtitle to the piece, Oct., 2001). He writes, "Our world has undergone enormous changes with entirely new kinds of terrorist threats. Civil and holy wars require new approaches by intelligence services." The key words are *civil* and holy. While our paranoid world police focus entirely on the holy, the *civil* may have slipped in under the radar. Another reason I will be hard to convince that Osama bin Laden was primarily responsible or had anything substantially to do with this (nor any other Arab terrorist group alone) is this: this was, in my humble opinion, an act set in motion by the civil secular authorities of one or more nation-states, the empire has chosen to not recognize as a legitimate states. Using known terrorists is a given option, but recruiting civilians to fight a guerrilla war globally cannot be traced, tracked like other criminal activities. And there are many of these nation-states.

Rogue States and Pariahs

We call these numerous states *Rogue States*, we vilify them as *Pariahs*, we blame these small developing countries for almost everything that is wrong in the world's trading regimes and they are not allowed to be part of the empire's economic world. None are members in good standing in the WTO. They are not part of world trade; they are sanctioned, embargoed and treated as the stupid little red-haired stepchild of the empire. Many were once our allies, many had their pilots and soldiers trained by our CIA and Special Forces, our Air Force, and Navy. North Korea, Cuba, Iraq and Libya to name a few; now add the sovereign nation-states' (countries) we have intervened in with military force since Vietnam: Panama, Grenada, the Sudan, Somalia, Bosnia; supported the insurrections within the same or others: El Salvador, Nicaragua, Guatemala, Panama, the Philippines, Puerto Rico, South Africa; then add our, *Mr. Bush-Senior's,* Drug Wars throughout all of Latin America: Columbia, Peru, Bolivia; our support of too many a *coup d'etat.* The United States of America, serving the interests of the *global regime of economic interdependence* (this being the explanatory name given this empire by our own elite) has stationed troops in 130 nation's states on every continent. When NATO barks it is in the American vernacular.

I am not arguing against some of this intervention. I am not arguing it is wrong or right. I am simply stating what is. It is what it is. What are the perceptions of others regarding the empire's activities? Perceptions are reality, in the mind's and heart's of the rest of the world's nation-state regimes. Not just their people. This is not just about people, citizens nor subjects; this is about the *recognized authorities* of *not-recognized* states.

Carl Bernard's important article points out our greatest failing as a great power. To paraphrase: we do not even bother to learn their language, we ignore their customs, beliefs and traditions, and we do not even know who our enemies are. How they think? we do not care. How they feel about us, our regime that is? we don't care. When we have bombed them into the stone age, and not to protect sovereign American citizens, but sovereign American corporate interests, we sanction them, embargo their goods and refuse to allow them to participate in the Global Regime. These governments we choose to not recognize, and clearly many are repressive regimes, remain isolated. When Saddam Hussein began taking diplomatic visitors during 2000/2001, in Iraq, both Clinton and Bush Jr. became "alarmed"...they were violating the United Nations orders. Libya's Muammar Qadhafi is supposed to recognize the empire's orders when his nation is one of the *Rogue States* as well? Iraq, Iran, North Korea, Cuba?

Here is the point then, and I made this point over and over in lectures and interviews over ten years ago. You do not have to like the regimes in question. You can be appalled, as I am, at the cruelty of Saddam Hussein, the repressive North Korean and Cuban leaders; one can hand-wring all day over Afghanistan and Libya. But you cannot, then, in good conscience see the American-led empire recognize worse regimes with worse *Human Rights Records,* according to *Amnesty International;* regimes in good standing with the empire: Kuwait, Saudi Arabia, The People's Republic of China. (Which by the way few know this, China had already been granted inclusion into the World Trade Organization by both the United States House and Senate before their "official" inclusion December 2001; see chapter six below and the section granting *Permanent Normal Trade Relations [PNTR] to China,* during 2000.)

Another important point lost on Americans because our own government simply ignores it, these regimes of Muammar Qadhafi and Saddam Hussein are secular regimes *not religious.* Nobody knows this better than the anti-Iraqi and anti-Libyan Arabs living here in America. The same with Cuba, North Korea, the Serbs and the former Russian Republics which make-up the Commonwealth of Independent States (CIS); not to mention China and all of the rest above noted. There are few religious regimes even in power; few religious monarchies remain with the exception of our own allies like Great Britain, Saudi Arabia and Kuwait.

Now here, further, is my point to the above. Saddam Hussein will likely be blamed, once again, for orchestrating this with his military and intelligence apparatus. He will be charged with trying to develop nuclear, biological and chemical weapons of *mass destruction.* Bomb Baghdad, kill Hussein, and nobody really believed America as empire wanted Hussein dead (he remained a bulwark against Iran taking Saudi Arabia and Kuwait) and we will be hit again. Saddam never was a Hitler, nor a madman; indeed, he has outlasted four U.S. Presidents as both ally and threat. He knows if he hit America as a civil state, a *secular state regime* in a declaration of war, he would be nuked. If, and here is where analysis gets tricky for those of us that work such issues,... if Iraq, as a secular military force did help organize this tactical strike at the American empire's *secular institutions* of war and economic might, he did not act alone. President Bush may have his scapegoats in the Taliban and bin Laden for awhile to get Americans back to work, shopping, kids back to school and the busses running on time, but if we hit Iraq over this, or the other reasons above, we may discover he has already built a coalition of allies himself. We may be shocked with whom and just how many. I hope I am wrong about this but then I hope Mr. Bush does not pursue his global war with anything like the present rhetoric.

We may be truly at war for the first time since World War Two. A real bona fide world war with secular military powers, many of which we trained and then turned into *Pariah* states. We may find this enemy not the least bit shadowy. But scattered across the globe. Look at a map, a made-in-America map, and America has always been the center of the universe. Look at it closely now; America has global reach, *overreach* it is called in IR language. Stretched across the globe, the first truly global regime. But upon closer examination, one finds it is simultaneously surrounded by enemies of its own creation. Like Rome, look to the west, the south and east. The enemies are not religious fanatics but secular nation-state regimes that recognize each other even if we do not.

When any enemy of an empire strikes at the heart of the empire other enemies are awaiting to see if the empire stumbles. Should the empire appear weak other states step in, hoping to at least, and if nothing else, knock it down a notch; weakened enough, every terrorist group from east and west will join the fight; domestically, if the enemy is perceived as particularly Arab and Muslim we may find we have enemies within the ranks of our own citizenry — anti-Semitics within radical militia cells, Aryan Nations and the silly KKK. These groups believe Zionists control the American regime, Israel somehow controls just about everything. Wrong-headed, true, but perceptions rule everyone's thought processes. If Mr. Bush makes this an Arab Muslim issue alone he will be dividing more of his own people and the people of the world more than he could possibly imagine. Should Mr. Bush decide, along with government employees like Sarah Brady, it is time to register guns in America, all citizen's guns, he will create another opposition front to this already multinational coalition.

But I do not believe President Bush says what he knows; I believe the government of the United States is looking at this as I am; they just do not want to tell the people. They think we are too ignorant, weak, naive...we will panic. This is a wrong decision. The people must be told every possible direction this war could take.

And it is my understanding that the American government is treating this as precisely what I am describing and not as an act of classical terrorism. Former, retired that is, covert operations personnel have been called and told they may be reactivated with specifications as to where throughout the world they may be stationed. Conscription has already been discussed for our laggardly youth; healthy retired military with specific skill sets and MOS (Military Occupational Standard) are being contacted for re-enlistment. Clearly the government knows this is larger than this president is telling us. Everyone I have spoken with and those I had briefed over the first few days after 9/11/01 concurred, the American people must be told and told now, what we may be facing. Even Kennedy, during the Cuban Missile Crisis, spoke to America about what was really going on, preparing them for war should it come. We are a free republic, the people remain the sovereigns (at least that is way it ought to be) and have a right to be fully informed. We are not Iraq.

Tactical Forces Strategy

An interesting aside to this was the choice of flight routes. Michael Moore, the iconoclast humorist thinks the routes were just wrong because they originated in states (Boston and Washington D.C.) and were flying to states (California) that voted for Gore? But there *is* something here in the choices. Fully fueled (all airline flights are tanked-up before every takeoff in case something mechanical fails; they can then stay aloft for a good length of time) domestic routes were chosen with few passengers. Thus the force deployed had little chance of killing too many foreign citizens, only Americans. Not a perfect plan, there likely were a few foreigners, but very few indeed. Thus world opinion is easier to swallow the reality when all is finally in the open. If this was nation-state inspired, government to government(s), world opinion gets the lesson as well. Stay out of it. You see, this tactic, if so chosen, was ingenious, and certainly not hatched in a Boston coffee shop over lattes by four PLO professors that just happen to be able to fly jumbo jets. Which means this as well: lock-down the airports, declare marshal-law, restrict air travel and strip-search all passengers. Do away with Habeas Corpus, throw out the entire Bill of Rights as Mr. Bush seems intent on doing. National ID cards are all the rave in the media now. Once we have all our security in place and Americans, less some important civil liberties, have traded liberty for security, they can, and will, hit us again.

They can simply take any private business jumbo jet like Armand Hammer's or David Rockefeller's and repeat the performance; a small private Lear Jet will do nicely. This is how a foreign military intelligence would think when trying to breech American airspace. They are only lacking in more pilots and soldiers to continue the air strikes. Air freight and tanker trucks carrying volatile chemicals would do nicely, indeed America is one big geographical target. Here is where I shall begin to look at guerrilla warfare as opposed to simple terrorism. Chapter four covers it in greater detail but a cursory look is here presented.

Guerrilla Warfare

Guerrilla warfare has different objectives than that of terrorism. Terrorism strikes at the heart of the culture, the people themselves are punished for the sins of their government. Guerrilla warfare has as one of its primary objectives to destabilize the regime itself. Make the people no longer believe the governing body can protect them. Make the citizen begin to question the legitimacy of its government by asking why this is happening. A war of attrition. One of guerrilla warfare's goals is if the guerrilla attacks accomplish their objectives the state's citizens will lose most of their fundamental civil liberties. The guerrilla wins, you lose. Now is not a good time to lie or conceal from the American people anything, except tactical intelligence and strategy. Classical guerrilla warfare has always been fought by soldiers, ground troops, tactics well known to most from the Vietnam and Latin American experiences. But guerrilla warfare is a concept first, flexible and modified to fit the enemy's fortifications and intelligence (both kinds). What has happened here for the first time in American history, in my humble opinion, is guerrilla warfare taken to a higher level and it has been brought to our own soil, by an enemy that understands the new world only too well. They are left out of it.

Nobody can breech, still, American airspace. But the borderless world of Walter Wriston and Alan Greenspan, which they are so proud to proclaim as the wonder of the new day, has as its corollary which way the traffic flows. NAFTA (North American Free Trade Agreement) and GATT (General Agreement on Tariffs and Trade) have knocked down borders in behalf of what is called *National Treatment* for U.S. multinational corporations. It grants them nothing short of full legal status as citizens of every country that is part of the WTO wherever the corporations find themselves. *National Treatment* was originally language used within the CIA's lexicon; moved now to appeal to trade regimes, it allows any monopoly giant corporation the right to buy, own and control any business operation in any country if it has enough money to buy in. The domestic citizen's government must treat the foreign *paper company* equally or better, than the domestic citizenry (including business owners). (See chapter six titled, *National Treatment and the World Trade Organization: Ralph Nader's Endorsement.*) This economic invasion of sovereign nation-states' industries and cultures are the basis for much of the world-wide protest of late at WTO meetings: Seattle, Paris and Canada; The OSAC, *Overseas Security Advisory Council* and our State Department's *Consular Information Sheet* the *Worldwide Caution* Reports had warned that the November meeting in Genoa, Italy, of the WTO would see unprecedented protests. One doubts it will take place at all now. (After I originally wrote these lines the WTO, IMF and World Bank all cancelled their upcoming meetings.)

This may mean little to most Americans who base their lives and values primarily on the making of money, forgetting that in many cases, especially at the global level of monopoly corporate power, this is a zero-sum game. Only when the pie is enlarged do the little people see a gain. Our corporate sector is bloated beyond recognition, overpriced stock market valuations and speculation, mergers and acquisitions have created a disparity between the rich and poor that nobody thought possible. The consolidation of every significant industry goes on unabated. Today, of the 100 largest economies in the world, America being the largest, followed by the western industrialized states, 51 are now multinational corporations like Boeing and GM, GE and ATT. (See Appendix Three below for a list of those 51 corporations.)

If this situation is never corrected, or as Leonard Cohen would say (CD, *The Future*) along with the economist Paul R. Krugman, (*The Age of Diminishing Expectations*, 1994, MIT Press) "The rich get richer, the poor stay poor," then only envy shall grow where the standard of living recedes. Revolutions are born of such squalor and despair.

When the citizens of the third-world and these *Rogue States* look to their government for relief, for action, these governments will protect themselves; governments always protect their own first. One way to get the minds of their people off their government is to blame *others*. We in America are their *other*. It does not have to make sense; it is about perceptions not necessarily reality. The reality is raw enough.

Along with this scenario is this troubling thought. If Saddam Hussein does align its military and intelligence capability with one or several other *Pariah* states, America is spread quite thin globally. They would not be fighting to defeat America as a nation-state. Like I pointed out above, Saddam is not crazy, he cannot win a war against America, nor can any terrorists which may have already joined ranks; even if he started it, several nation-states together cannot defeat America. It is not always about winning, the fighting of a war. Often it is the last resort to internal defeat for those in power. This is about power and money and Machiavellianism runs deep in the hearts of the Arab people and their leaders. Each nation will fight to survive, even if they have to fight the giant global hegemon.

As I stated in this office's September, 2001 press releases, and above, I too had hoped it was just some really clever lone nuts and Mr. Bush has them all in custody real soon. Should that be the case we can all sigh a great sigh of relief and snuggled in our little beds, sleep the sleep only Americans know so well. Too many American adults take naps. Should the scenario I have laid out not be true for today, look to tomorrow if the global regime does not change what it does throughout the world. If even some of what I have conceptualized is true today, Mr. Bush will be sending Corporatism's diplomats far and wide, visiting the *Rogue States* individually, promising all enormous sums of money, taxpayer's money, in the hopes that he can bribe them to not align themselves with the one or more *Pariahs*. Corporatism sees bribery as just one more means to an end. "You will be welcomed now into the community of nations if you just go along with us on this. Bridges, water desalinization projects, dams and wonderful technology long denied you are yours for the asking. Pipelines and a carpet of gold." Bush Sr. did precisely this during the Persian Gulf War. President Bush Jr. repeated the same message to Afghanistan from February 2001 right up until five weeks before 9/11/01.

The nations all get the promised goods and services. But recall what else was promised by Mr. Bush Sr.,...democracy and free elections in both Kuwait and Saudi Arabia. To prove their well-meaning intentions in the CIS Caspian region today, the diplomats will be the real ones, the ones that matter. They will be the directors and CEOs of our largest multinational corporations, like George Shultz and former president George Bush Sr.; Dick Cheney was there before he became vice president as a lobbyist for Brown & Root and Halliburton Energy, he is there now seeking vengeance; they call them Corporate Diplomats. I kid you not. In chapters five and eight we will see who these men are and where they came from.

CHAPTER THREE

The World Trade Organization
The End of Geography?

*...in Western democracies, the social source of
intolerance is the political bureaucracy
and the increasing economic power of the
monopolies and giant corporations with their
gradually growing bureaucracy and the
bureaucratization of an increasing number of
social and political fields of activity;
Side by side with these phenomena are the rising sense
of popular injustice, inequality, and needless deprivation.*
—MIECZYSLAW MANELI

*In politics the philosopher is spared many a pitfall
that he might walk into in physics and biology;
his field is limited to human affairs
....He has to consider real events and real forces,
which are all physical, even when they have a mental or
moral accompaniment.In this sense
he is a man of science, with the responsibilities of an
enquirer after the truth, and not, in intention,
a composer of historical romances.*
—GEORGE SANTAYANA

*...what about the modern value of war for
purposes of empire building?
Acidly, Erasmus indicts the classic types of the
empire builder as insane world robbers—
men whose interests were
criminally opposed to those of the vast majority
of humanity.*
—ROBERT P. ADAMS ON ERASUMS

END OF GEOGRAPHY

DURING 1969 C.P. KINDLEBERGER WROTE that "the nation-state is just about through as an economic unit." He added that the U.S. Congress and right-wing know-nothings in all countries were unaware of this. He added: "The world is too small...Two-hundred- thousand ton tank and ore carries... and airbuses, and the like will not permit sovereign independence of the nation-state in economic affairs."

Before that Emile Durkheim stated: "The corporations are to become the elementary division of the state, the fundamental political unit. They will efface the distinction between public and private, dissect the democratic citizenry into discrete functional groupings which are no longer capable of joint political action." Durkheim went so far as to proclaim that through corporations' scientific rationality it "will achieve its rightful standing as the creator of collective reality." (Quoted in *The Unconscious Civilization*)

There is little question that part of these two statements are accurate; America has seen its national sovereignty slowly diffused over a growing number of International Governing Organizations. The WTO is just the latest in a long line of such developments that began right after World War Two. But as the protests in Seattle, Genoa and Paris against the WTO Ministerial Meetings made clear, the democratic citizenry seemed well-prepared for joint political action. Though it has been pointed out that many, if not the majority, of protestors did not know what the WTO was, and much of the protest itself entirely missed the mark regarding WTO culpability in many areas proclaimed, this remains but a question of education. And it is the responsibility of the citizens' representatives to begin that process.

We may not entirely agree with the former head of the Anti-Trust Division of the U.S. Justice Department, Thurman Arnold (1938-1943), when he stated that the United States had

> ...developed two coordinate governing classes: the one, called 'business,' building cities, manufacturing and distributing goods, and holding complete and autocratic power over the livelihood of millions; the other, called 'government,' concerned with preaching and exemplification of spiritual ideals, so caught in a mass of theory, that when it wished to move in a practical world it had to do so by means of a sub rosa political machine. (*The Folklore of Capitalism*, pg. 110)

...but surely the advocate of corporate governance today, housed quietly and efficiently within the corridors of power at the WTO, OECD, IMF and the World Bank...clearly believe.

Corporatism as ideology, and it is an ideology; as John Ralston Saul recently referred to it as, "a hijacking of first, our terms such as individualism and then a hijacking of western civilization," the result being

> (the portrait of) a society addicted to ideologies - a civilization tightly held at this moment in the embrace of a dominant ideology: corporatism. (The Unconscious Civilization)

As we find our citizenry affected by this ideology and its consequences (consumerism) "the overall effects on the individual are passivity and conformity in those areas that matter and non-conformity in those which don't." (Saul) We do know more than ever before just how we got here. The WTO is a creature of the General Agreement on Tariffs and Trade (GATT) which began in 1948 its quest for a global regime of economic interdependence. But by 1972 some members of Congress saw the handwriting on the wall, and it was a forgery. Senator Long, while Chairman of the Senate Finance Committee made these comments to Dr. Henry Kissinger regarding the completion and prepared signing of the Kennedy Round of the GATT accords.

> If we trade away American jobs and farmers' incomes for some vague concept of a new international order, the American people will demand from their elected representatives a new order of their own, which puts their jobs, their security and their incomes above the priorities of those who dealt them a bad deal. (*Foreign Affairs*, Eckes, Vol. 71, No.4)

But we know that few listened and twenty years later the former Chairman of the International Trade Commission, Alfred Eckes, argued that it was the Kennedy Round that began the slow decline in American's living standards. Citing statistics in his point regarding the loss of manufacturing jobs and the like he concluded with what must be seen as a warning.

> The...Uruguay Round and the promise of the North American Trade Agreement all may mesmerize and motivate Washington policy makers. But in the American heartland those initiatives translate as further efforts to promote international order at the expense of existing American jobs. (Ibid., *Foreign Affairs*)

We are still not listening. Certainly the ideologists of Corporatism can not hear us; they in fact are pressing the same ideological stratagem in the journals that matter like *Foreign Affairs* and the books coming out of the elite think-tanks and non-governmental organizations. One such author, Anne-Marie Slaughter proclaimed her rather self-important opinion that state sovereignty was little more than a status symbol and something to be attained now through 'transgovernmental' participation. That would be presumably achieved through the WTO for instance?

Stephan Krasner in the volume *International Rules* goes into more detail by explaining global regimes as functional attributes of world order: environmental regimes, financial regimes and of course trade regimes.

In a world of sovereign states the basic function of regimes is to coordinate state behavior to achieve desired outcomes in particular issue-areas....If, as many have argued, there is a general movement toward a world of complex interdependence then the number of areas in which regimes can matter is growing. (Krasner, *International Rules*, Oxford, pg.,172)

But we are not here speaking of changes within an existing regime whereby elected representatives of free people make adjustments to new technologies, new ideas and further the betterment of their people; the first duty of elected representatives is to look out for their constituency. The WTO does not represent changes within the existing regime but an entirely new regime. It has assimilated an unprecedented degree of American sovereignty over the economic regime of the nation and the world. In the WTO's most important ruling to date (January 15, 2002) America and American business just found out what the loss of nation-state sovereignty means.

Geneva, Jan. 13 (Bloomberg) — The World Trade Organization is likely to rule Monday that a U.S. tax break violates global export-subsidy rules, exposing U.S. companies to threatened European Union sanctions of more than $4 billion.

The EU wants permission to impose the trade tariffs if the WTO rejects a U.S. appeal of an earlier ruling, in a case that affects exporters from Boeing Co. and Microsoft Corp. to Eastman Kodak Co., Archer Daniels Midland Co. and General Electric Co. The potential damages are the highest in the seven-year history of the world trade arbiter. A WTO dispute panel found last August that even after an overhaul, a U.S. law that allows companies to shield income from taxes on a range of sales is an illegal export subsidy to hundreds of companies. (01/13 05:56, WTO Seen Ruling U.S. Tax Law Illegal; $4 Billion EU Duties Loom, By Warren Giles and Blair Pethel)

This may be one more straw for the Bush administration, which clearly like to "go their own way," towards more public understanding. "The issue is of such magnitude that sanctions couldn't possibly be imposed without also affecting a lot of European companies" with U.S. interests, according to William Reinsch, president of the National Foreign Trade Council in Washington, which represents some 550 U.S. manufacturers. Should this appeal go against the United States "as many corporate lobbyists and U.S. legislators expect, the WTO would decide around the end of March the size of sanctions the EU could apply," according to Giles and Pethel. These kinds of sanctions if they are approved by the WTO are usually imposed in the form of increased import tariffs on a range of products. The 15-member EU asked for sanctions of $4.04 billion, U.S. officials have said they would oppose an award of that size.

They argue that $4 billion is the size of the tax law's application to U.S. companies' global exports, not just to Europe, which are much smaller.

Under the revised law, all U.S. taxpayers — including foreign and domestic companies — are eligible for tax breaks that allow them to protect much of their income earned outside the country from U.S. tax, as long as they have paid tax overseas on their earnings. (Ibid.)

The new law was passed in November 2000 after the U.S. missed an earlier deadline. Known as the Extraterritorial Income Act, it replaces the original Foreign Sales Corporation law. This law has become a serious issue with a number of my private corporate clients as well. The outcome matters a great deal for all businesses and not just the monopoly transnationals which clearly stood to gain more than everyone else. It should be clear once again the influence Corporatism has in every administration, Clinton signed the law and it was lobbied for during his tenure. Now the same chief executives which lobbied the Clinton administration return to lobby the Bush regime, only for their defense this time.

Chief executives of major U.S. companies including Archer-Daniels-Midland and General Motors Corp. last year urged President George W. Bush to appeal the ruling to buy more time to negotiate a resolution with the EU. "This isn't a good time," said Paul Brenton, a senior researcher at the Center for European Policy Studies, a Brussels- based research group. "At the start of a new WTO trade round, and with the world economy in a precarious position, the U.S. and EU should be taking the lead in trying to settle disputes amicably." (Ibid.)

Kenneth Dam, U.S. Deputy Treasury Secretary, said in November, 2001, that the ruling sets a standard for taxing corporate income earned abroad that calls into question the tax systems of many countries, including those in the EU. Mr. Dam said if the U.S. can't get a clear reversal of the WTO decision, then the appeal ruling might be specific enough to allow the U.S. to bring the law into WTO compliance by changing the existing legislation. If the EU were to proceed and be granted $4 billion in retaliation — something U.S. Trade Representative Robert Zoellick has said would be like dropping a "nuclear bomb"' on the trade relationship — it may prompt U.S. lawmakers to change the structure of the U.S. business tax system. "I don't see the EU rushing to retaliate," said Reinsch. "The original panel report is so sweeping that there are potential implications for European tax systems."

Currently, the U.S. employs a so-called "global" tax system, under which companies' earnings all over the world are in theory subject to tax. U.S. law then excludes some categories of earnings, a policy the WTO said was illegal.

Several lawmakers, including California Republican Bill Thomas, who chairs the tax-writing House Ways and Means Committee, have said they would prefer to revamp the system entirely
and move to a "territorial" system such as Europe's.

Under that system, only domestic earnings are subject to tax,
although certain foreign profits are taxed. (Ibid.)

When one sees these kinds of developments, developments the public is,
by and large, totally unaware of, one must ask the question, "then who are the
sovereigns"? Is it the people, the "nation" in nation-state? I do not believe so.
I would argue that who governs rules; who rules is sovereign. And the people of America and their elected representatives do not rule nor govern at the
WTO but corporate diplomats (a word decidedly oxymoronic) clearly rules;
even if the ruling goes against the United States as representative of these
corporations, it is clear the private diplomats, i.e., the corporate executives
are as much in control and as sovereign as the public diplomats negotiating in
their behalf. I would suggest this will all be settled behind closed doors, and
Mr. Bush, who is well-known for his allegiance to his corporate partners will
make an all-out concerted effort in the months to come.

Who are these new Sovereigns? Maybe we can get a clearer picture by
looking at what the WTO is in place to accomplish. I took interest in an article
in *Foreign Affairs, - A New Trade Order*), by Cowhey and Aronson.

Foreign investment flows are only about 10 percent of the size
of the world trade flows each year, but intra-firm trade (for example, sales by Ford Europe to Ford USA) now accounts for
up to an astonishing 40 percent of all U.S. trade.(Vol. 72, No. 1)

This complex interdependence we hear of every day inside the beltway, is
nothing short of miraculous according to the policy makers who are mesmerized by all this. But clearly the interdependence is less between the people of
the *nation*-states than between the *corporations* of the *Corporate*-states.

Richard O'Brien in his book titled *Global Financial Integration: The End Of
Geography* states the case this way.

The firm is far less wedded to the idea of geography. Ownership is more and more international and global, divorced from
national definitions...If one marketplace can no longer provide
a service or an attractive location to carry out transactions, then
the firm will actively seek another home. At the level of the
firm, therefore, there are plenty of choices of geography. (O'Bri-
an, The Royal Institute of International Affairs, pg. 100)

O'Brien seems unduly excited when he adds, the "glorious end-of-ge-
ography prospect for the close of this century is the emergence of a seam-
less global financial market...Barriers will be gone, service will be global,
the world economy will benefit and so too, presumably, the consumer..."

Presumably? Counter to this ideological slant, and it is ideological, O'Brien notes the

> ...fact that governments are the very embodiment of geography, representing the nation-state. The end of geography is, in many respects, all about the end or diminution of sovereignty. (Ibid.)

In a rare find a French author published a book titled *The End of Democracy*. Jean-Marie Guehenno, has served in a number of posts for the French government including their Ambassador to the European Union. He suggests this period we live in is an Imperial Age. I would go the one necessary step further and suggest Mr. Bush Jr. may just be the first true Imperial President. And the below quote from 1999 sends chills down the spine of all who understand the implications of Bush Jr.'s war on global dissidence.

> The imperial age is an age of the diffuse and continuous violence. There will no longer be any territory to defend, but only order - operating methods - to protect. And this abstract security is infinitely more difficult to ensure than that of a world in which geography commanded history. Neither rivers nor oceans protect the delicate mechanisms of the imperial age from a menace as multiform as the empire itself.

The Empire itself? Whose Empire? In whose interests? In my second book titled *Global Triage: Imperium in Imperio* I referred to this new global regime as Imperium in Imperio, or power within a power: a *State* within a state. The basis of the theory means that the new sovereigns are the corporations themselves. The theory proposes that these new sovereigns are nothing short of this: "they represent the power not of the natural persons which make up the nations' peoples, nor of their elected representatives, but the power of the legal paper-person recognized in law — the corporations themselves are, then, the new sovereigns. And in their efforts to be treated in law as equals to the citizens of each separate state, they call this *National Treatment*, they would travel the sea and wherever they land ashore they would be citizens here and there!" Not even the Privateers of old would have dared impose this will upon nation-states. (See chapter six below for a further elaboration of what this means.)

Can we claim to know today what this rapid progress of global transformation will portend for democracy here at home? We understand the great benefits of past progress; we are not Luddites here, we know what refrigeration can do for the child in a poor country; what clean water means everywhere to everyone; what free communications has already achieved. But do not be taken-in by Bill Gatesian mythos about the Internet setting us all free making the world more democratic: "The web is not a virtual community; it is a collection of isolated individuals," according to Richard Davis of Oxford University.

> ...the existence of communication technology does not trans-
> form people into political animals. Similarly, the Internet does
> not cause people to suddenly become politically active or even
> interested. Rather, American political behavior will remain es-
> sentially the same regardless of technological innovations de-
> signed to disseminate more political information. (Davis, *The
> Web of Politics*, Oxford University Press, pg. 172)

And this is being proven out today in the face of the American people's
response to Mr. Bush's rhetoric, war-making and apologia for emptying the
Bill of Rights of any meaning. There is almost no dissent in America; what
there is, is on the Internet; what is on the Internet is not being read nor dis-
tributed if read by one of Davis's "isolated individuals." In fact, Davis suggested just this scenario in his book: "This is especially true of the Internet,
it will not revolutionize public interest and knowledge. In fact, in some respects the Internet may well reduce the level of political knowledge held
by Americans." (Ibid., pg 172) I believe the Internet has led to a reaction in
people which has made them use the Internet to avoid information they do
not wish to encounter. Where subscribing to a daily paper forces one to "see"
headlines (at least) to stories one does not wish to know about, the Internet
makes it that much more easy to completely avoid the noxious news of the
day. The reason we were all virtually brainwashed to believe in the Internet as savior of the democratic process was the religious faith we have been
brought to believe in, of "progress." Any progress. The progress being made
in the loss of state sovereignty is one area most care so little about, they flee
a lecturer on the topic, rarely listen to the subject on radio or television and
certainly not going to go to the Internet sites, like my own, to brush up on
such a boring subject.

So, right then, are we as a people, American, British, and French for instance, going to unwittingly sacrifice our national sovereignty on the alter of
this new god, *Progress*. **Is it progress if a cannibal uses a knife and fork?**

Can we claim to know today what this rapid progress of global transformation will portend for national sovereignty here at home? We protect our
way of life; our children's future; our workers' jobs; our security at home, by
measures often not unlike our airports are protected from pistols on planes:
But self-interested ideologies, private greed and private power? *Bad ideas escape our mental detectors.*

We seem to be radically short of leadership where this active participation
in the process of diffusing America's power, all state's power, over to, and
into, the private global monopoly-capitalist regime; today pursued without
questioning its basis at all.

An Empire represented by not just the WTO, but clearly this entirely new
international regime is the core ideological success for Corporatism.

The only step remaining, according the Harvard Professor Paul Krugman, is the finalization of a completed Multilateral Agreement on Investment,
which failed at OECD. According to OECD's staff I worked with during my

tenure with Congressman Metcalf (2000) the agreement's actual success may come through (not a treaty this time) but arrangements within corporate governance itself, using the Memorandum of Understanding process, circumventing legal routes or legislation, and was, at the time, quietly being hashed out at the IMF and World Bank as well as OECD. We are not yet the United Corporations of America. But we are getting ever closer to it.

The WTO needs to be scrutinized carefully, debated, hearings and public participation where possible. We can of course, as author Christopher Lasch notes, peer inward at ourselves as well, when he argued

> The history of the twentieth century suggests that totalitarian regimes are highly unstable, evolving toward some type of bureaucracy that fits neither the classic fascist nor the socialist model. None of this means that the future will be safe for democracy, only that the threat to democracy comes less from totalitarian or collective movements abroad than from the erosion its psychological, cultural, and spiritual foundations from within.

Are we not witness to, though, the growth of a global bureaucracy being created, not out of totalitarian or collectivist movements, but from autocratic corporations which hold so many lives in their balance? And where shall we redress our grievances when the regime completes its global transformation? When the people of each Nation and their State find they can no longer identify their rulers, their true rulers? When it is no longer their State which rules?

The most recent U.N. Development Report documents how globalization has increased inequality between and within nations while bringing them together as never before.

Some are referring to this as *Globalization's Dark Side*, like Jay Mazur recently in *Foreign Affairs*.

> A world in which the assets of the 200 richest people are greater than the combined income of the more than 2 billion people at the other end of the economic ladder should give everyone pause. Such islands of concentrated wealth in the sea of misery have historically been a prelude to upheaval... The vast majority of trade and investment takes place between industrial nations, dominated by global corporations that control a third of world exports. Of the 100 largest economies in the world, 51 are corporations. (Vol. 79, No. 1 January/February 2000)

With further mergers and acquisitions the future, with no end in sight, those of us that are awake must speak up now. (See Appendix three for a list of the 51 largest corporations.)

Or is it that we just can not see at all; believing in our past speculative bubble making a return, which nobody credible believed at the time could be sustained and nobody believes a new bubble can fix what's wrong for 2002. And were we ever wrong!

> US COMPANIES could be forced to write off a total of $1 trillion (£690 billion) in the first three months of this year to cover the cost of acquisitions made at the peak of the Internet boom, analysts said yesterday. Under new accounting rules that have already forced AOL Time Warner to write off up to $60 billion, US companies will have to give details of the amount they overpaid for acquisitions during the boom of the late 1990s and early 2000. The write-offs will be unprecedented in stock market history and will result in US businesses reporting losses of a magnitude never seen before. Although the write-offs are book-keeping exercises that do not involve any cash, they will prove to be embarrassing for many chief executives. (January 10, 2002 *US set for $1 trillion of Internet write-offs*, Chris Ayers, New York Times.)

The article goes on to point out the how, or why this has surfaced and might be of interest. "The new accounting rules, introduced by the Financial Accounting Standards Board (FASB) on January 1, force US companies to declare any fall in the value of "goodwill" they paid for acquisitions. Goodwill is the premium paid for an acquisition over and above what accountants call the "fair value" of its assets."

The fall in the stock market value of high-tech companies since early 2000 has resulted in hundreds of billions of dollars of this goodwill being wiped out. But before the new accounting rules were introduced US companies could spread goodwill charges over a period of up to 40 years, effectively making it irrelevant. Now companies have to report changes to goodwill annually. "According to Alfred King, he and other analysts believe the total could reach $1 trillion. Bob Willens, an accounting analyst with Lehman Brothers, said: "If you add it all up it's pretty easy to get to $1 trillion. I think there will be a certain amount of embarrassment about it. When you write off goodwill you acknowledge that the acquisition is not going to be as successful as you thought," Ayers reported. (Ibid.) All these developments and a soured economic outlook, millions of job losses adds up to greater frustration worldwide not just in America. The middle-class will surely overreact as is their custom to.

The imperial leader missed the growing anger of the last years, fear and frustration of our own people here in America (militia groups, violent environmentalists); we missed the growing anger in less-developed countries (not only Muslim people) where a new level of guerrilla warfare has now surfaced (September 11) against this very empire. Unfortunately the empire is perceived to be primarily American because it is unquestionably American-led. Believing in the myths our policy priests pass on, we missed the dissatisfaction of all workers and the poor throughout the world; and not only the poor, but, as in every revolutionary scenario of the last 300 years, the youth of the better-off join the reaction against autocracy. Believing in the god "progress" our imperial leaders, and too many of the common folk, have lost their vision.

Another warning, this time from Ethan Kapstein in his article *Workers and the World Economy*.

> While the world stands at a critical time in post war history, it has a group of leaders who appear unwilling, like their predecessors in the 1930's, to provide the international leadership to meet economic dislocations. Worse, many of them and their economic advisors do not seem to recognize the profound troubles affecting their societies. Like the German elite in Weimar, they dismiss mounting worker dissatisfaction, fringe political movements, and the plight of the unemployed and working poor as marginal concerns compared with the unquestioned importance of a sound currency and balanced budget. Leaders need to recognize their policy failures of the last twenty years and respond accordingly. If they do not, there are others waiting in the wings who will, perhaps on less pleasant terms. (*Foreign Affairs*: Vol. 75, No. 3)

We ought to be looking very closely at where the new sovereigns intend to take us. We need to discuss the end they have in sight. It is our responsibility and duty.

Most everyone today agrees that socialism is not a threat. Many feel communism, even in China, is not a threat, indeed, there are few real security threats to America that could compare to even our recent past, even after September 11, 2001. Indeed, there will be arguments made that Mr. Bush is working very hard to keep the perception of danger alive so as to assume ever more centralized control over a country whose leaders have long been after just such an opportunity. Be that as it may, when we speak of the global market economy, free enterprise, massage the terms to merge with managed competition and planning authorities, all the while suggesting we have met the hidden hand and it is good, we need to also recall what Adam Smith said but is rarely quoted upon:

> Masters are always and everywhere in a sort of tacit, but constant and uniform, combination, not to raise the wages of labor above their actual rate. To violate this combination is everywhere a most unpopular action, and a sort of reproach to a master among his neighbors and equals. We seldom, indeed, hear of this combination, because it is usual, and one may say, the natural state of things.... Masters, too sometimes enter into particular combinations to sink wages of labor even below this

rate. These are always conducted with the utmost silence and secrecy, till the moment of execution.

And now precisely, whose responsibility is it to keep an eye on the Masters?

(This was, in an edited version, a speech given at the US House of Representatives - May 04, 2000 by Congressman Jack Metcalf [Ret.]; written by Craig B Hulet)

CHAPTER FOUR

A study in the Theory of
International Urban Guerrilla Warfare
The War of the Flea

NEW YORK, Sept. 23 /PRNewswire/
— At a two-day meeting last week of the
Pentagon's Defense Policy Board, which is
Chaired by hard-liner Richard Perle,
eminent conservatives including Henry Kissinger,
James Schlesinger, Dan Quayle and Newt Gingrich
reached a consensus that U.S. military forces
should strike Iraq shortly after an initial blow against
Afghanistan in response to the terror attack on
New York and Washington, Newsweek reports in the current issue.
"When the U.S. loses what may be more than 6,000 people,
there has to be reaction so that the world clearly
knows that things have changed."
—GINGRICH TELLS NEWSWEEK.

Saudi Interior Minister Prince Nayef said
at the weekend that seven Saudis named by the FBI as
suspects in the skyjack attacks were innocent
and still living in the kingdom. It is thought the
real attackers used false or stolen documents.
The Mirror September 26, 2001
—ANDY LINES, U.S. EDITOR

None evil captain was he in the war,
as to which his disposition was more meetly
than for peace...Friend and foe was muchwhat
indifferent: where his advantage grew,
he spared no man's death whose life
withstood his purpose.
—SIR THOMAS MORE

DEFINITIONS OF WARFARE

BEFORE WE CAN BEGIN TO LOOK AT what I believe to be a new level of low intensity conflict or guerrilla warfare and in particular of an urban (even suburban) nature, we need to define our terms. All warfare is force. Civil war is war between two groups of the same nation. Rebellion is open, organized resistance against previously established authority. Revolution is successful rebellion. Revolt and insurrection are armed uprisings in which the outcome is quickly decided. Bandit warfare is armed fighting to support life by plunder. Partisan or orthodox guerrilla warfare is armed fighting by light troops, detached or separately established from the regular army, whose operations they support principally by harassing the common enemy, usually without seizing and defending substantial land areas. Communist revolutionary guerrilla warfare was considered new and was defined thusly: It is a different military effort inspired by international communism, using local adherents to weaken the military, economic, and political unity of an area so that it would fall under communist control. This has also been called revolutionary terrorism at times.

It is the view of this author that we are facing something once again entirely new. Clearly guerrilla warfare is not in itself new; the first true guerrilla warriors have been identified by scholars as having been the Spanish resistance opposing Napoleon. While there is something similar in the revolutionary guerrilla warfare as was practiced by international communism, there is as well, a fundamental difference. Rather than international communism's ideology, this newest form of warfare has no such clear focus nor does it have as its goal the ultimate overthrow of any particular nation-state. That is in part because the *have-nots* are spread across the globe with many nation's peoples clearly categorized as such. It would be a mistake to focus exclusively on the Middle Eastern states and North and West Africa; Latin America and Asia have enormous populations of dissatisfied and repressed people. Therefore it does have as its roots the similar dissatisfaction of the masses of people that communism preyed upon. It should not be surprising that the Middle Eastern terrorist groups have become "seemingly" the first wave in this newest guerilla war internationally as many were significantly funded and sponsored by the Soviet Union and Red China; since the end of the Cold War, this too has changed but not the disparity of wealth and the utter imbalance of power between their nations and America perceived as empire.

It is my belief that the great failing of the U. S. intelligence community where the September 11, 2001 air attacks occurred, was in part due to the utter contempt we hold the developing nation's military capabilities; primarily those states we identify as *rogue states* and *pariah* states, we hold in even greater contempt. It was this contempt for our foes, a complete lack of understanding their perspective, their cultures and their institutions that has brought this home; our contempt has been rewarded with war.

American policy makers, in the recent past, simply could not imagine any one of these numerous nations daring an attack on American soil. I still hear it said, "If Iraq was responsible for orchestrating the attacks (not just sponsoring them as in sponsoring terrorism, which is far more than semantics) then America will go in and wipe them off the map." I feel this is not only unwise in thinking strategically, but the tactic will likely fail in the real world of today. This is not 1990. President George Bush Sr. could then, with all confidence, attack Iraq and intervene in the Middle East with nary a whimper from friend or foe; this could be done *only* because the Soviet Union had *just fallen* and the fall of the Berlin Wall demonstrated to all the world that only America remained the sole superpower. The nations that the Soviet's funded, trained and would have (in the past) stood with in war, was suddenly gone; along with the funding these countries lost all arrogance and confidence in defying American hegemony. Intoxicated with the prospect of global hegemony and riskless global prosperity, America believes this to be still true today.

I should have to argue that this is ten years hence and coalitions will be harder to form in support of intervention and war, and that if Iraq significantly orchestrated this attack (military intelligence, funds and logistical support) Saddam Hussein believes he already has a coalition of his own. He would not have acted alone. The only question remains which state or states he has already quietly made his pact with? Something else has changed as well: Iraq does not believe, nor do any states he may have in tow, that they can defeat America. The Arab terrorist argument of President Bush Jr., the hordes that hate America speech, do not wish to overthrow anything (with the exception of Israel); they do not want to eradicate American Christians nor the American democracy. They do not hate our freedoms nor our way of life. Terrorists in the Middle East want Israel eliminated, that is true enough. But this is not only, or primarily, about Israel nor America as backer of the Israeli state, but something else and something far more important.

Rather than the target being, necessarily, a particular nation-state, and rather than the efforts directed at overthrow of that state, we are, I believe, seeing another model. The perception of much of the western world (inclusive of our allies in Europe) is that the United States has evolved into a significant new form of genuine empire; Dr. Kissinger's *America at the Apex: Empire or Leader?* An empire different than the Roman model in many respects but the most significant is that the Roman empire's cultural sway ended at its borders. In Joseph Joffe's words "America's soft power...rules over an empire on which the sun never sets." This has given rise to an escalation of warfare but with tactics adapted to the new world and the empire's weaknesses. Non-traditional colonialism inspires non-traditional tactics, now called *asymmetric warfare* by the policy analysts in the think tank world of "new terms"; this newest resistance will be in resisting the effects of the perceived empire.

However, this remains a war between the *haves* and *have-nots*; and the most significant haves is of course America; the most significant have-nots (significant because of coming off the fall of Soviet sponsorship), the actively organized Arab groups. The greatest American intelligence failure to come along in some time was September 11, 2001. While America's vast intelligence operations have targeted terrorism as the newest threat to stability and American interests, the experts all concluded that without the support of the past Soviet Union, and China begging at the door of the World Trade Organization (WTO), the United States had no greater enemies than the simple terrorist. (Not that they viewed these terrorists as not worthy of note, they in fact have focused too much on their threat at the expense of nation-state sponsored warfare threats.) One clear reason for this lack of broader focus is that the allure of international communism as an ideology has waned. Without that ambitious ideology American threat assessments lacked their own focus regarding other cultures and other perspectives. Other nations regard their nationalism and their own states as worthy of note equal to that of America's. With the American-led view in international relations (IR), that borders no longer matter in our borderless world, we have violently discovered that that is but our perspective alone. Other peoples, the have-nots, see their nation's governing apparatus as just as worthy of mere existence as the United State's. And the Empire is just that...empire, for the haves.

One must look at the world differently; the borderless world of Alan Greenspan and George Bush Senior. Take a nice flat map and spread it out. America has always portrayed itself as the center of the universe. The first thing that no longer matters are the two major oceans. Neatly trim them away from their respective continents and cut and paste your map together again. In guerrilla wars of the past the enemy would strike anywhere and then run to the hillsides; the mountains and hinterlands is where the guerrilla fighter found refuge (still in countries where this applies).

But in the new world, taking the war to the industrialized nations, the terrorist turned guerrilla must find refuge among the people of each country they are fighting in. They must be able to strike at the heart, the symbols and the true targets of war, the infrastructure of the regime. They then flee to the centers of populations, to disappear, merge within, melt-into the very background of everything familiar. They must be able to "swim with the fish," exist for great lengths of time living among the citizenry of each nation unsuspected of anything improper. They must, as well, and indeed will, move from one nation to another as easily as those in the past could slip off into the hills and jungles of neighboring lands. It is this mobility that is relished by the west that the guerrilla has taken up as tactic and achievement. This is key to understanding the guerrilla from the terrorist. Terrorists have other objectives, other targets and therefore other tactics which I shall look at below. The guerrilla warrior does not come from the ranks of the known terrorists, although he may; as in guerrilla recruitment tactics of past wars, Mexico, Cuba, China and even those of World War Two, the guerrilla soldier comes to the war free of criminal background; free of terrorist connections; free of the security checks; that is to say, the guerrilla becomes what he is without the radical religious or fanatical beliefs of classical terrorists. He is therefore free, clean if you will. He can then operate freely within any society with little detection; even if he chooses to strike, he can simply return to his job the way the agrarian guerrilla of the past returned to his farm. He has an ideology. But not the one President George Bush Jr. proclaimed in his speech of September 20, 2001. One will see emerge from this text a picture of a new world and an order of things quite different from the past. Revolutionary guerrilla tactics will, though, still apply with greater significance and understanding than ever.

Mao Tse-tung is the author of the signal work on guerrilla warfare, others followed. When Mao wrote and fought he paid little attention to urban warfare as the wars of liberation were meant to unseat colonial powers on lesser developed country's soil. Thus the Chinese, Mexican and Cuban experiences became the norm for agrarian guerrilla warfare. Ernesto Che Guevera, on the other hand, saw the urban center populations as a major help. We will begin below by examining Che Guevara's concepts in detail but with a twist; I shall use Che Guevara's text on *Guerrilla War* as my model, adapting it to the new urban (suburban) global guerrilla war I believe we are today facing. I have utilized the work of Che Guevara's based on the U.S. Army Intelligence translation and, as well, the condensed version of Major Harries-Clichy Peterson, U.S. Marine Corps Reserve, July, 1961.

What appears in italics is from the text itself, leaving what Guevara wrote, but the remainder I have left out applying my new interpretation placed in context of the present global regime. This might be akin to writing Guevara's work the way he would write it today for the newest tactics and strategy. We need to understand the terrorists that exist and their metamorphosis into global guerrillas.

Ernesto Che Guevara on Guerrilla Warfare

*The important lessons to be learned from Guevara are
his motives, his method of inciting his followers,
and how he uses the hills as a sanctuary,
thrusting out and attacking regular forces,
then withdrawing and luring them in to be devoured,
all in a vicious pulsating rhythm.*

(HARRIES-CLICHY PETERSON, FROM HIS INTRODUCTION, 1961)

*Withdraw when the enemy advances;
harass him when he stops;
strike him when he is weary;
pursue him when he withdraws.*

—MAO TSE-TUNG

*...a sudden, surprise, furious relentless attack;
then, abruptly, total passivity.
The survivors think things have returned to normal,
when suddenly a fresh blow lands
from a new direction.
An unexpected lightning blow is what counts.*

—CHE GUEVARA

Che Guervara's argument (in italics throughout) begins with what would seem to be obvious: *The people must be shown that social wrongs are not going to be redressed by civil means alone. And it is desirable to have the oppressor, wittingly or not, break the peace first.* In the case of the air attacks on American soil those who committed the atrocity already think the vast majority of people, if not in America, understand their perception that America has broken the peace, first and often, in every corner of the globe. Given that this is the perception of many, and surely the poorer classes, *...Understanding these conditions, popular discontent assumes increasingly positive forms, creating a state of resistance that, provoked by the attitude of the authorities, can easily lead to an outbreak of fighting.* If our theory holds up here, Guevara's argument goes deeper....*if a government has come to power through some form of popular vote, whether fraudulent or not, and if that government maintains at least the appearance of constitutional law, a guerrilla uprising cannot be brought about until all possible avenues of legal procedure have been exhausted.* It is clear to those whom have bothered themselves enough to study the seemingly foreign perceptions of other people throughout the world, they have little or no say in what is happening globally. In the rogue states and those sanctioned and embargoed like Cuba and Iraq, Libya and Lebanon, the people have no say and nor do their governments; nations who are not outside the mainstream of global economic activities have virtually no say globally in this case as well. The International Monetary Fund (IMF), the World Bank, the World Trade Organization (WTO), the General Agreement on Tariffs and Trade (GATT) and the enormous number of distinct international governing organizations (IGO), in many ways dictate a purely western way of doing everything from trade to military alliances; from agriculture to meat patties; milk, soy beans and cotton thread, all come under the macroscopic microscope of thousands of faceless bureaucrats in organizations seen as dominated and pressed forward by the United States and a few other western powers. Our culture, so-called, descends from above via satellite in the form of movies and too much tasteless television (not to mention pornography). That this economic, cultural and global political machine is seen as an American empire is no longer questioned; Joseph Joffe states "It rules over an empire where the sun never sets."

So it should not surprise anyone that the global citizens might wish to rebel at the global regime's indifference to their suffering; all the while the regimes true beneficiaries, the U.S. and western multinational corporations, literally swell in riches and power. The people of the global shrinking planet understand only too well, that the regime is now global.

Thus,...*Guerrilla warfare, the basis of the people's fight for liberation, has many different characteristics and facets. It is obvious—and all who have written about it concur—that war is subject to certain strategic laws, and those who violate these laws will be defeated. Guerrilla warfare, a phase of general warfare, must be governed by all these laws; but in addition it has its own laws, and this unique set of rules must be followed if it is to succeed. Of course, different geographic and social factors in individual countries may call for different methods and forms of guerrilla warfare, but the basic laws apply to all guerrilla campaigns.*

One fundamental change is the sheer power, militarily, the United States has wielded, sometimes with restraint, sometimes with raw abandon. The world understood for decades, nobody could enter American airspace, not the Soviets, not the Chinese. But guerrilla warfare is specifically designed for just such can-do missions. And our "geographic and social factors" gave rise to another means of striking at the enemy so perceived. *One resorts to guerrilla warfare when oppressed by superior numbers and arms. For the individual guerrilla warrior, then, wholehearted help from the local population is the basis on which to start. Popular support is indispensable.* This is, in my opinion, a war against empire and the world's nation-states' people are the popular support needed for the new guerrilla warrior. If nation-state boundaries no longer exist, or are no longer of importance, one must view the world as we are so instructed. Then the people of the world are indeed one whole; within that whole resides the have-nots and there the guerrilla finds popular support amongst the have-nots that are not waging this war. The principle holds. Terrorists in the past have recognized the need to bring all the different dissident and revolutionary groups, terrorists and guerrilla alike, under one enormous cover. We find this from a once secret communique from the terrorist organization Hizballah, or "Party of God," a Shiite terrorist group operating primarily out of Lebanon.

> We strongly urge on all the oppressed of the world the need to *form an international front* that encompasses all their liberation movements so that they may establish full and comprehensive coordination among these movements in order to achieve effectiveness in their activity and to focus on their enemies' weak points....as for Israel, we consider it the American spearhead in our Islamic world... (Source: Joint Publications Research Service, Near East/South Asia Report, 19 April 1985.)

Why does the guerrilla fight? He is a social reformer. He takes up arms in response to widespread popular protest against an oppressor, impetuously hurling himself with all his might against anything that symbolizes the established order. Few past written works, could compare to Guevara's words in describing the attacks on the global empire's symbols: the World Trade Center, the United States Pentagon and either the Capital Building or the White House (CIA Headquarters too comes to mind); and the threat against the President on Air Force One was credible because the warning contained code words and knowledge of Secret Service procedures no terrorist (according to the Pentagon itself) could have known. Interesting to note was a story whose headlines claimed the White House backed off on this threat with CBS News saying the call never took place; but the actual text of the article read the opposite, that the threat was real; the article closed with Vice President Dick Cheney saying "I think it was a credible threat....enough that the Secret Service brought it to me." The urgency of some in the White House to claim no call took place is simply because that call makes the case, not for bin Laden, but for others with military intelligence capabilities which is not the spin the White House wants today.)

When we analyze the tactics of guerrilla warfare, we see that the guerrilla must possess a highly developed knowledge of the terrain on which he operates, avenues of access and escape, possibilities for rapid maneuver, popular support, and hiding places. Che Guevara's text, then, explains the newest form of warfare as an agrarian warrior, living off the land. This newest modification, or better put, metamorphosis, carries with it the same distinctive thought process and tactics. Clearly the pilots and soldiers who commandeered the four flights were never going to be caught (Knowing this, why would one of these alleged terrorists, according the FBI, try to take his last will and testament on board with him?) It would not be too much to assume that the many others, and maybe very many indeed, melted back into society the way Guevara's soldiers melted into the jungle's hills. Their "avenues of access and escape" and "hiding places," keeping the larger contingent completely invisible from the pursuit of the arresting authorities. Watching the FBI pick up each and every Arab-speaking individual whose passport is out of status, ones who "might" have some knowledge of the events, or might have been in contact with Osama bin Laden, in many ways, is making my argument better than I could. The

FBI is in pursuit of an evil individual, and one hopes he is one day caught. But it is not bin Laden's terrorists that got away. Many of those that got away have no relationship to bin Laden. If this theory holds at all, it is on this point. The guerrilla is not a terrorist, he is a soldier. There is a fundamental difference.

There is a saying: "The guerrilla is the maverick of war." He practices deception, treachery, surprise, and night operations. Thus, circumstances and the will to win often oblige him to forget romantic and sportsmanlike concepts. Military strategy and tactics represent the way the group conceives its objectives of taking full advantage of the enemy's weak points. Individual combat is much the same in guerrilla warfare as at the squad level in conventional warfare. When trickery does not work, it's only because the enemy is alert and cannot be caught off guard.

Clearly we are dealing with now, for the first time on American soil, an opponent that will seek out weak points because our strength and strong points are un-breechable; no foreign aircraft can enter American airspace (they will be targeted by an enormous array of technological superiority), there they have no chance. The enemy does not have the technical skill nor weaponry to launch a cruise missile into the tactical targets. The guerrilla finds the targets and deploys the opposition's technology as cruise missile *within* the American airspace. And clearly trickery and surprise was deployed against an enemy who wasn't alert and could be caught of guard. *However, because the guerrilla band commands itself and because the enemy cannot forever guard all areas, surprise is always possible. It is the guerrilla's duty to exploit it!*

The guerrilla is willing to give his life to realize an ideal, not merely to defend it. Here is where President George Bush in his September 20 speech, in my humble view, erred greatly. It was not only untrue what he stated about Arab terrorists generally but he rallied the American people to virtually a holy war against an enemy whose religion may play as little a part, in general, as our own Navy Seals' personal religious choices. President Bush stated,

> They hate what they see right here in this chamber, a democratically elected government. Their leaders are self-appointed. They hate our freedoms, our freedom of religion, our freedom of speech, our freedom to vote and assemble and disagree with each other. They want to overthrow existing governments in many Muslim countries, such as Egypt, Saudi Arabia, and Jordan. They want to drive Christians and Jews out of vast regions of Asia and Africa. These terrorists kill not merely to end lives but to disrupt and end a way of life.

It does not escape every thinking, reasonable person, how attacking the *World Trade Center* will affect the removal of "Christians and Jews from vast regions of Asia and Africa," how striking at the center of the American military infrastructure carries the message that the perpetrators want to overthrow the Egyptian government? Indeed, it was none other than Egypt, the very next morning of September 21st, in all the world's press, announced it would not stand with any American coalition and reopened full diplomatic relations with Iraq in standing violation of U.N. sanctions. Hosni Mubarak went even further: he announced a NAFTA-like free trade agreement between Iraq and Egypt and reappointed a new Ambassador to Iraq.

Muslims, Jews and Christians had lived in peace with one another for over a thousand years, until the United States and Great Britain, after the two world wars, drew the lines in the sand and told the tribal elders this was Iraq, that is Saudi Arabia, this is Syria. And for the past fifty years we have put into power dictator after dictator, kept autocrats and princes, monarchs and despots in power—today our friend, tomorrow our enemy. America trained the Taliban of Afghanistan and Osama bin Laden so as to resist the Soviet Union's efforts in the region. In 1991, the United States put a permanent United States military presence on Saudi soil; nobody believes for any other reason than to protect two of the worst despots in the contemporary world, i.e., Al Sabah family of Kuwait and the Saudi Princedom. In Pakistan, President Bush Jr. forgets to call its leader, so-called, *President* Pervaiz Musharraf, "General" and admit that he came to power no differently than Saddam Hussein, a military coup d'etat. These are simple facts of history. And history never ignores facts.

But it may be argued that they do want to disrupt our way of life. Understanding what our way of life, as global economic empire and world policeman, means to the vast majority of have-nots throughout the world, an ever smaller borderless world, and one begins to see why a global guerrilla movement, nation-state orchestrated and aided by states "unrecognized" in the community of nations, might mean. To many throughout this new world of ours, the United States represents the old world of vast social injustices; injustices made ever more unbearable by the vast expanse of this American-led empire. *Thus the essence of guerrilla warfare is the miracle by which a small nucleus of men—looking beyond their immediate tactical objective—becomes the vanguard of a mass movement, achieving its ideals, establishing a new society, ending the ways of the old, and winning social justice.*

One does not have to agree with Guevara on this point. But one must listen to the enemy and understand him. This empire is quite real; it is primarily led by the United States; its beneficiaries are the multinational corporations. General Electric alone is an economy larger than 49 other nation-states in a count of the largest 100 economies of the world. And GE is one of America's largest defense contractors year after year. One deludes oneself if one thinks the people of the rest of the empire are unaware of this.

Strategy and Tactics

In the case of weapons, consider how they are to be used, the realistic value of such items as tanks and airplanes in guerrilla warfare...his customs, etc. Keep in mind that the guerrilla's most important source of supply is the enemy himself. It was without doubt a brilliant choice in picking the passenger airliners inside American protected airspace, to convert to cruise missiles. That this tactic can be redeployed using many such "vehicles of delivery" becomes clearer upon little reflection. business jets, private and commercial freight carriers, trains and subway and Amtrack, all fall into similar profiles. Any substantial stock-pile of highly flammable or toxic substances would fill the need for a guerrilla warrior's weapon of choice. Small arms like the terrorists utilize and truck bombs rarely escape detection; as I have said elsewhere and above, terrorists would have hit Disneyland, guerrilla warfare strikes at fundamentally different targets; i.e. the empire's infrastructure. You see this is war, not terrorism. The targets are the tell.

The guerrilla's numerical inferiority makes it necessary always to attack by surprise, permitting him to inflict disproportionate losses upon the enemy....The way a guerrilla army attacks also is different: a sudden, surprise, furious, relentless attack; then, abruptly, total passivity. The survivors think things have returned to normal, when suddenly a fresh blow lands from a new direction. An unexpected lightning blow is what counts!

Sabotage is an important revolutionary means, but should be differentiated from terrorism. Indiscriminate terrorism against groups of ordinary people is inefficient and can provoke massive retaliation. ...it should never be used to eliminate unimportant individuals whose death would accomplish nothing but invite retaliation. Guevara does not rule out selective use of terror, but only, *when the oppressor's grip is so tight that nothing can be done anyway, except by force of arms. It comes down to a calculated risk.* It was, the morning of September 11, 2001, and remains, my contention, that the flights were chosen well ahead of time to have as few passengers on board each airplane; as well, the flights were chosen specifically because they were domestic, not international, flights: this was to keep as few random foreigners from the destined fate as possible. Those who died in the WTC were not innocent in the view of the guerrilla, but part of the empire's infrastructure. And this has been going on for some time; it just is not always front page and then only reported in the regions where it takes place. This may be why few Americans understand and continue to ask the lame question..."Why do they hate us so?"

Here is a short list of targets in the Washington D.C. and New York areas for just 1983 and 1984; attention must be paid to the targets (if this were a campaign slogan it would be "It's the Targets Stupid.") as terrorists select random acts against civilians; buses with children, night clubs and theatres, etc.; these targets speak to another issue.

Date	Target	Claimant
16 Dec 82	South Africa Corporation (Elmont, NY)	UFF
16 Dec 82	IBM Corporation (Harrison, NY)	UFF
28 Jan 83	Federal Building/FBI (Staten Island, NY)	RFG
26 Apr 83	National War College (Ft. McNair Wash. DC)	ARU
12 May 83	Army Reserve Center (Uniondale, NY)	UFF
13 May 83	Navy Reserve Center (Queens, NY)	UFF
17 Aug 83	Navy Computer Center (Navy Yard, Wash. DC)	ARU
21 Aug 83	National Guard Armory (Bronx, NY)	UFF
7 Nov 83	U.S. Capital Building (Wash. DC)	ARU
13 Dec 83	Navy Recruiting Center (East Meadows, NY)	UFF
14 Dec 83	Honeywell Corp. (Queens, NY)	UFF
29 Jan 84	Motorola Corp. (Queens, NY)	UFF
19 Mar 84	IBM Corporation (Harrison, NY)	UFF
5 Apr 84	Israeli Aircraft Industries (Manhattan, NY)	RGR
20 Apr 84	Navy Officers Club	RGR
22 Aug 84	General Electric Corp. (Queens, NY)	UFF
26 Sep 84	Union Carbide Corp. (Mount Pleasant, NY)	UFF

The groups that claimed credit for the bombings were: The United Freedom Front (UFF); Red Guerrilla Resistance (RGR); Armed Resistance Unit (ARU). Those who continue to call groups like these "terrorists" in today's climate risks keeping Americans dumbed down as to what our country is really faced with. Even if one chooses to keep calling them terrorists, because it seems less threatening than a guerrilla war directed in large part against America, one must concede, these are certainly unlike anything in the past and this war is not going to end any time soon.

For major attacks, guerrillas can be massed, but immediately thereafter they must withdraw in small, widely dispersed groups. Virtual armies can be organized under a single command without actually merging the various groups. The secret is to be sure to elect the right chief for each band, one who, ideologically and personally, will work well with the maximum leader of the zone.

The Minuet

The minuet is the classic tactic of guerrilla warfare; I include it here as this generation has had no experience in war or even having, in any larger numbers, been in the military. Not even our best active duty personnel over the last twenty-five years have had any real combat experience. This may not be the worst handicap I can think of, as even Mao said one learns guerrilla warfare by doing guerrilla warfare, which only means our troops will learn to fight guerrillas by fighting guerrillas; but they can never learn to become guerrillas themselves. Che Guevara on the minuet: *The guerrilla relies on mobility. This permits him quickly to flee the area of action whenever necessary, constantly to shift his front, to evade encirclement...and even to counterencircle the enemy. (Another) maneuver, frequently used to wear down a larger sized enemy force, is called the "minuet." The guerrillas surround the enemy, an advancing column for example, on all four sides. Five or six guerrillas are stationed on each side, sufficiently spread out to avoid their own encirclement. The dance begins as one side fires on the enemy, who naturally moves towards that side. The guerrillas on that side move back, without breaking visual contact, and succeed in drawing the enemy out. Then another guerrilla side begins firing and draws the enemy to a different side. Thus the partners on all sides participate in the dance, the enemy column is rendered immobile, expends vast quantities of ammunition, and loses morale, while the guerillas remain unharmed.*

Because classical terrorism often mimics the guerrilla in tactics one can be misled into thinking we are dealing with terrorists rather than the greater and more serious threat of guerrilla warfare; this cannot, I believe be stressed enough.

Fighting in built-up areas

Che Guevara was the first of his time to see the value of urban guerrilla warfare. His offerings today seem less valuable but I shall include them here for reasons of history and what the future may hold. Guevara wrote, *(But) first let it be stated that a guerrilla band never arises in a suburban area. Such a band will form only when a favorable environment has been created by others, and the band will always be under direct orders of superiors situated outside. Accordingly, the mission of this band will not be to act independently, but to follow preconceived strategic plans. In other words, the suburban band will not be able to choose between knocking down telephone poles or ambushing patrolling soldiers; it will do exactly as told.... Such a band should not number more than four or five men. This is important because the suburban guerrilla is working in exceptionally unfavorable terrain, where the risks and consequences of exposure are tremendous. There is little distance between the guerrilla's point of action and his refuge, so night action must predominate.*

The apt description of what it takes to be a suburban guerrilla by Guevara seems prescient today in light of what the pilots and soldiers that commandeered the airliners must have been like individually. *Essential qualities of the suburban guerrilla are discipline, probably to a degree unexcelled by any other, and discretion....the importance of suburban fighting has not been fully appreciated . When done effectively and extended over a wide area, it completely paralyzes the everyday life of the sector. The population becomes restless, anguished, almost anxious for the development of violence, in order to bring the violence to an end. If, at the very start of the war, specialists are organized for suburban guerrilla work, quicker action can be obtained, more lives spared, and the nation's valuable time saved.*

The Individual Guerrilla Fighter

We said the guerrilla is a crusader for the people's freedom who, after exhausting peaceful means, resorts to armed rebellion. He aims directly at destroying an unjust social order and indirectly at replacing it with something new. It is here that the guerrilla tactics, taken to the larger global context of international suburban guerrilla warfare has morphed into something quite new, in this analyst's opinion. It is my theory that what we are seeing is the global citizenry, outside the purely western industrialized nations and America in particular, who feel they have exhausted all means of redress of grievances and the empire simply continues to grow ever more powerful; ever more cruel; ever more disinterested in seeing the standard of living of the billions of poor raised by even a smidgen. Rather than agrarian reform, as in the past and still in many underdeveloped countries, this new level of guerrilla activity is directed at the heart of the empire's power. The new tactics address this new enemy and his symbols. The guerrilla, on the other hand, bears the same stamp, branded with the same iron will, as that of guerrillas in the past.

To attain the stature of a true crusader, the guerrilla must display impeccable moral conduct and strict self-control. He must be an ascetic. At first, he will not stress social reform... There is little question that what we are dealing with are extremely disciplined individuals who after the deed flowed back into the "ocean of people, like fish in water," to use Mao's apt phrase. Their silence in not claiming credit for the acts themselves tell us we are dealing with no bragging strutting terrorists waving guns around in front of video cameras. They disappear to await the time when America once again feels their world is secure (after the loss of many civil liberties to guarantee this security). *Little by little the issues sharpen, people are forced to take sides, and conflict breaks out.... The guerrilla provides ideology for social reform by personal example—by his ideas, his plans, and lessons from experience.* Here the ideology is the anti-empire rhetoric that the western powers dismiss as sour grapes; "If they don't like their lot they need to reform and become part of the community of nations." Which is nothing less than to alter your world view, your economic and cultural life, to conform to the international economic policy formulations of the IMF and WTO and the rest of the western world's alphabet soup of IGOs. Become more western, that is to say. But this too, while not as coercive as the economic dictate, is not less intrusive. America produces some of the best films in the world, and as purveyor of pornography, inclusive of the now average PG13 Hollywood output, we are unmatched; the rest of the world reels in front of America's number one export: trashy films. Our grasping for mammon is appalling by many American's and European's own standards but positively heretical to Hindus, Sikhs, Jains, Buddhists and Muslims. Our American Christianity cannot, by and large, be compared to the Christianity of those in the Middle Eastern nations or Latin American Catholicism. Our culture has been described often as non-culture; i.e. no culture at all.

Guevara goes on: *He stresses force of arms and spiritual dedication.* We are not here reading the words of any fundamentalist believer; Guevara and Castro and Mao were atheists. The issues and ideology today are not meant to change American's minds. *The people are united, not by religion, race, custom, or hunger, but common economic and social goals and a common desire to improve their lot. Asia and Africa joined Bandung. Now Cuba is uniting Asia and Africa with colonial America.* Americans represent the enclosed wealthy elite that support this global empire; we are the citizens of empire that benefit, gain greater wealth and security at the expense of our neighbors in the bordering states and counties of the borderless world. The rural countryside of the guerrilla is his backyard, but the targets of guerrilla war must be the metropolitan citadels of gross economic power. The new guerrilla must fight in the international urban centers as the rural centers are decimated nation-states where nobody cares there are people in residence. We are talking about nothing short of a new *international liberation movement* (as opposed to older national liberation movements) not led by communist ideologues nor any other specific faith. American policy makers need to think about what we are doing in the world as empire, and understand, the people of the world may have lost something when communism fell, but they have gained nothing by its demise either.

International Liberation Movement

The guerrilla is physically tough and capable of enduring extremes, not only in deprivation of food, water, clothing, and shelter, but also in bearing sickness and wounds without medical care, for leaving the battle zone brings with it the risk of capture and death. It is my firm belief that of the remaining guerrilla fighters that were part of the alleged 19 the FBI has presumably identified, there remains considerable doubt that the names on passports and mail boxes are the real names of those on the planes. (See elsewhere above the brief story which came out of Saudi Arabia and never picked up by our own emasculated press.) Many may then, still be in the United States; they melted back into the mass of suburbia, back to work, school, and regained the quiet life...waiting further orders to "surprise, ...strike lightning-swift blows." *Men so dedicated must have an ideal.* President Bush's portrayal left little room to understand those that perpetrated the air attacks and the portrayal of some hate-filled Holy Warriors served only to unify the American racial hatred of all Arabs regardless of what many considered Bush's raw sophistry regarding those Muslims living amongst us.

In this type of war, the work of those not directly engaged in fighting is of major importance. Communications have already been cited. Relays to headquarters or to remote guerrilla forces must be set up, utilizing the most modern means in the area. This applies to favorable as well as to unfavorable terrain. Looking at the global regime differently, as I noted above, reveals a porous and real open society; the Internet and the multitude array of communications available to the international urban guerrilla is staggering. And there is really no genuine guaranteed way of stopping it. *Sabotage is one of the invaluable weapons of guerrilla warfare. It is to be conducted outside rebel-held territory and directed by the guerrilla general staff.* In that this newest transformation of guerrilla tactics will not include the rebels ever holding any territory, the goal being that the empire recedes from the rebel's nation-state territory in physical reality or in symbolic retreat, as in withdrawing the IMF, WTO influence throughout the world, this guerrilla war is the easier to fight. *Sabotage is not terrorism. On a national scale, its aim is the interruption of enemy communications—telephone and telegraph installations, bridges, railroads. Vital industries and businesses owned by enemy leaders also may have to be destroyed, but indiscriminate destruction resulting in mass starvation is impermissible.*

This is where the tactical mission and the overall strategy that guides and directs it has completely been overlooked by the administrations of both parties for thirty years and completely lost on the American and western intelligence apparatuses. The new guerrilla understands the enemy, the United States and the western industrialized nations, better than we understand them. They understand the multinational corporate nexus well; its presence is everywhere felt; its corporate tentacles are no different in the guerrilla's perception than Bush's tentacled beast of terrorism. This multi-headed Empire is seen as a hydra, in this author's words a *Hydra of Carnage* as well. The idea of these recent attacks was to provoke an enormous reaction; an all-out war; mass retaliation. That is the purpose of guerrilla warfare, not the purpose of terrorism.

President George Bush seems to be falling into a well-laid trap every guerrilla warrior sets. To get the enemy to attack the guerrillas with impressive force. *Make the enemy reveal himself as the true, hated criminal....Guerrillas seldom can spare any forces to constitute a reserve. Yet, a reserve will be needed in desperate, unforeseen situations. One way to prepare for this need is to compose an elite platoon given special privileges. Call it "the Joker" or "Suicide platoon." Forge its reputation for heroism by committing it to the most difficult combat situations.* Does America face the radical Jihad of American-hating Arab terrorists, as President Bush spins the yarn? Or did we get hit with a guerrilla "Suicide Platoon"? Well, then, that is the real important question is it not?

The War of the Flea

I am going to begin here to look at how and what outcome this newest form of guerrilla warfare is trying to achieve. The typical (for America that is) military intervention has been with mobile United States Marine Expeditionary Forces in swift takeovers and in retaliation of a perceived wrong against American citizens. The act of intervention itself was justified as follows:

> The use of force against a foreign and friendly state, or against anyone within the territories thereof, is illegal. The right of self-preservation, however, is a right which belongs to states as well as to individuals. And in the case of states it includes the protection of the state, its honor and its possessions, and lives and property of its citizens against arbitrary violence, actual or impending, whereby the state or its citizens may suffer irreparable injury. (Harrie-Clichy Peterson, Major, U.S. Marine Corp Reserve)

In President George Bush's September 20th speech he announced what seemed logical and realistic to most Americans. He stated,

> Now, this war will not be like the war against Iraq a decade ago, with the decisive liberation of territory and a swift conclusion. It will not look like the air war above Kosovo two years ago, where no ground troops were used and not a single American was lost in combat....Our response involves far more than instant retaliation and isolated strikes....Americans should not expect one battle, but a lengthy campaign unlike any other we have ever seen, It may include dramatic strikes visible on TV and covert operations, secret even in success.

As I go deeper into my analysis, remember the words above, particularly "a lengthy campaign unlike any other we have ever seen..."

Revolutionary guerrilla wars are wars, of necessity, long in duration. It is customary to speak of guerrilla wars as wars of attrition. A guerrilla war is more subversive than abrasive. Its intended effect on this empire is to wear out the empire's base, economically, politically and culturally. The goal is not to win over wealthy or middle-class Americans; the goal is to win over more and more of the world's impoverished peoples that remain worse off than ever, worse off in many cases due to the fall of communism and its overt operational assistance. Each time the guerrilla strikes at the heart of the United States, cheers go up in every corner of the world and recruits are enlisted to the ranks. True there are tears aplenty that flow as well, prayers from every corner of the world. But these Oprah Moments so cherished by the media and politicians (to prove we were wronged for the latter; the former, to prove we as a people today care when for three decades we have shown no mercy for the poor and disenfranchised the world over), will do nothing to sustain us when Bush is even one year into a global guerrilla war. While I feel as terrible as everyone (not acting superficially that is), these feelings do nothing towards understanding what we are dealing with, what is to come.

Attrition plays a significant role in guerrilla warfare. In the political sphere the government, and in this case, its offspring, the economic global empire's IGOs, are subjected to sustained strain and angst, a constant wearing pressure that comes from the enormous expenditure of tax dollars and loss of life; *blood and coin* it was called in the past. The war of attrition is meant to bring the call from the business community and the banks: "When will it all end? What are you going to do about it?" And from our feminist dominated, left-leaning campuses, should Bush have to reinstate the draft, the roar will be deafening. You will not see the feminists trade-in their shopping bags for duffle-bags. Economic attrition has been discussed above where sabotage is involved. The loss of credit and investment suffered by a country engaged in a guerrilla war cannot be stressed enough. Not even a great nation, rich in productivity and capital reserves can withstand assault after assault over a long period of time. President Bush speaks of a protracted war as though this will, once again, be a one-sided campaign and America proper will never be hit again. The painful fact is unsavory at best; the guerrillas can carry on indefinitely.

The guerrilla has everything invested in his war. He owns nothing and has already decided to die for his cause. His enemies (even if it is just his perception; perception is reality), the multinational corporations included, are housed and vulnerable in 130 countries on three continents. He can strike anywhere at any time. America must chase the guerrillas down wherever we "think" they "might" be. The guerrilla has nothing to lose and everything to gain by not giving up.

> They fight, then, in order to survive. Given their inferiority of resources, they can survive only by avoiding direct confrontation with a superior enemy; that is, battle on the enemy's terms. Guerrilla strategy is dictated from the start by this consideration. The result—if the guerrillas are to be successful and to avoid extermination—is a protracted war. (Page 46)

The above quote is from *The War of the Flea*, (1965) by Robert Taber. I must here point out that every book on guerrilla warfare has been concerned with why they fight, how they fight, and how they have in fact gone about defeating regular armies through attrition and tactics outlined above. I shall not go into the latter in any way as I do not believe these newest formations of guerrillas expect to defeat any nation state and certainly not the United States. I am convinced that their war of attrition, sabotage and hit and run, is directed at the global empire itself. Thus the reason for the targets not being random civilian targets that terrorism strikes at. Given that assumption, and that is what it is, my assumption alone, these international urban guerrillas do not intend to defeat anything more than the loosely knit international bodies that support what they perceive as their repression. It would be hard to argue their perceptions are simply illusions. Therefore, the only way they can win their objectives, not needing to hold or occupy territory, is through a protracted war.

They want a protracted war; they want President George Bush Jr. to bomb and burn the planet in hot pursuit! This is their only chance to achieve their objectives. And their only chance to win converts and world opinion to their side. "Make the enemy reveal himself as the true and hated criminal."

Has President George Bush Jr. inherited his father's will to power? Mr. Bush announces that America must set out to win a "protracted war," the *only* kind of war the guerrillas can win. To quote Taber on this very point:

> A principle can be observed throughout this entire process: the more the enemy holds, the more he has to defend and the broader the insurgent target area. Yet on the other hand, the more the insurgent fights and wins, the more he has with which to fight and win in arms, in manpower, in material resources. Thus the objectives of the government and of the insurgent must be diametrically opposed. The army seeks to end the war as quickly as possible, in order to minimize its losses; the insurgent seeks to prolong it, since he has everything to gain by it. (Page 57)

It is my belief that we are in a guerrilla war with insurgents only at a higher global level; the targets will be American facilities, governmental and private, corporate and international, and these targets are presented in every country on each continent. Of course airplanes, private and commercial, company planes and freight, can be commandeered once again and used as cruise missiles; but heavy trucks carrying highly toxic, poison gasses and chemical containers all present weapons for targets for metropolitan areas; the vast complex of rail systems in each country carry similar payloads. If these new guerrillas are insurgents against the perceived empire they already occupy every nation and there are American, French, British, Japanese and German industries which all meet the criteria of enemy and empire. And we are not even beginning to look at the number of international governing organizations (IGOs) that are spread across the globe. The NATO in Brussels, the United Nations in New York, the WTO, the IMF, The World Bank and the various headquarters of many other trade and economic councils. There are thousands, I am reluctant to warn.

It is not a coincidence that all the above named IGOs shut down and have called off their annual and plenary meetings scheduled for this entire year. I firmly believe Mr. Colin Powell understands this although it is far from certain Mr. Bush will take his advice and move slowly and with less abandon than his other advisors would like.

Communism is Gone,
But not the Ideology against Empire

When trying to understand the ideology of guerrillas in the less-developed countries over the last fifty years, communism and its rhetoric, its stock in trade one might say, was anti-imperialism. The great imperialist was of course seen as the United States. Communism is dead as both ideology and spiritual foundation for active measures against the imperialists. But the argument has, in my opinion, more force than ever now that America is in fact the sole superpower. Therefore the sole perpetrator of the imperialism that rightfully belongs to the great global hegemon. Corporatism as ideology is without doubt understood by this newest crop of global insurgents. The corporation will continue to be and grow ever more, as the target of choice to strike against the regime. See how easily the old argument fits the new regime, quoting Taber once again during and immediately after the last great transformation of guerrilla warfare, the 1970s: Guerrilla warfare,

> [In] the world at large, (it) is destroying the last vestiges of feudalism and of traditional colonialism where these remain. Its full vigor is turned now against neo-colonialism and what, in Marxist terminology, is called imperialism—the economic and political (and often military) domination of the weak, industrially poor nations by the rich, powerful, and technologically superior ones. (page 11)

Taber, writing during 1965, is prescient when he noted, "In its total effect, it is creating new alignments and a new confrontation of powers that vitally relates to and yet transcends the Cold War." Exactly transcends the Cold War. "It is a confrontation, in its essence, of the world's haves and the world's have-nots, of the rich nations and the poor nations." (Ibid.)

> Viewed from one standpoint, it is a potent weapon, a sword of *national* liberation and social justice; viewed from another, it is a subversive and sinister process, a sort of plague of dragon's teeth, sown in confusion, nourished in the soil of social dissension, economic disruption, and political chaos, causing armed fanatics to spring up where peaceful *peasants* toiled. (my emphasis, Ibid.)

Simply alter two significant words in the above quote and I believe we have an appropriate picture of the new guerrilla: *International* for national (liberation) and *workers* (peasants). Mao Tse-tung wrote on *Guerrilla War* and his work was widely read during these past fifty years. One area he notes I think is important, is on guerrilla warfare's political dimensions.

> On politics: Without a political goal, guerrilla warfare must fail, as it must if its political objectives do no coincide with the

aspirations of the people, and their sympathy, cooperation and assistance cannot be gained. The essence of guerrilla warfare is thus political in character. (Mao on Guerrilla Warfare)

It is my contention that these newest international guerrillas have as their political goal, forcing the American-led economic (and military) empire to recede from their individual countries' shores, if you will, restoring the world of nation-state's balance of power; in this they shall certainly find enormous numbers of "people" sympathetic to their cause; many new recruits for every one guerrilla captured or killed; people the world over will rise up against Americans personally in many countries and American corporations attacked as symbols of empire: cooperation and assistance will likely be forthcoming in many countries one might have overlooked initially. Indonesia, Egypt, Korea and Cuba, not to mention India and Turkey. It goes without saying we shall find no cooperation from most of the Arab and Persian states, Iran, Syria, Libya, Algeria, etc.

Time works in the guerrilla's favor; that is all he has is time. The guerrilla's strength comes from the fact that he has nothing to defend and plenty to attack. It takes a war chest to fight the guerrilla war from the perspective of the defenders of empire which costs both money and political capital, neither of which the guerrilla has much of, nor much need of.

This is guerrilla war: the *guerra de guerrillas* fought by Spanish partisans against Napoleon's invading army, refined in our time to a politico-military quasi-science—part Marxist-Leninist social theory, part tactical innovation—that is changing the power relationships of the post-World War II era, and in the process is destroying the verities of the Western general staffs whose professional concern it is, and increasingly will be, to understand and combat it. (Taber, page 10)

And now the western and particularly the American general staffs must seek to understand a new form, a metamorphosis if you will, of the recent past's guerrilla, and look upon the whole world as one enormous nation-state. One world is what the American progressive-left, inextricably tied to the multinational corporate structure, has sought for decades; we now have it. We now have a new kind of warfare which has grown up under its auspices, its cause and effect. The people gain little in this new one world order and looking upon each nation, the way one used to view each nation's provinces, domestic states (like in the United States: Mississippi and New York) *one sees another outline.*

One can begin to see these other nation's neighboring as close as Fidel Castro's *fidelistas* were while waging war on Havana from atop the *Sierra Maestra* mountains; the new guerrillas range across the open borders of the borderless economic regime. They do not fight to defeat America, they fight to survive and with the likely vain hope of social reform, that is to say, seeing their world restored to a time when there was no empire, just independent sovereign nations whose destinies were not tied-up with our destiny; to the western and United State's destiny as sole hegemon and empire. Not to put too fine an edge on this argument, whether we choose to call these people terrorists or guerrillas, fanatics or soldiers, we are now having to face that their training and patience, skills and networks, cover the entire globe. One way of arguing this theory is to call these men a term used in the theory of war: revolutionary terrorists and military terrorists. In any case one finds substantial backing by specific nation-states.

How Shall America Fight

The question left unanswered in this analysis is how America intends to fight this global war? It seems that former Chairman of the Joint Chiefs of Staff, Retired General Colin Powell, President George Bush's Secretary of State, has found himself on the outs with many on Bush's staff. He seems to be the only one who understands what we are up against; said better, what is up against us. He wants to move slower than the hawks (and especially hawks who will not, nor ever have served in the military or combat), deliberate, but using all means necessary to engage the nation-states who are clearly a significant part of all this. It is my unsubstantiated view that Powell knows we are in a guerrilla war of much larger dimensions and not just chasing Osama bin Laden's terrorist network. He, of all men on staff, clearly sees the targets were of a distinct nature. Al Qaida may be what Bush says it is in some way, but clearly we are seeing the evolution of that organization and others not yet understood and maybe many still unknown altogether, into a worldwide guerrilla war targeting the United States for far more than its relationship with Israel.

In a lengthy study of war and what really qualifies as war, rather than terrorism, Donald J. Hanle teamed up with Yonah Alexander (general editor) to publish one of Pergamon-Brassey's Terrorism Library volumes during 1989. *Terrorism, The Newest Face of Warfare* looks at all the various forms of terrorism, state-sponsored, military terrorism, state terrorism, repression terrorism, etc., and finds many wanting where the defining characteristics leave them as not qualified definitionally as warfare. When Hanle gets to his section on revolutionary terrorism, his definition becomes that of pure guerrilla warfare. Military terrorism is war; guerrilla tactics used by terrorists is not. But state-backed, not just sponsored, clearly is a face of war. These distinctions become important and are not academic. How one fights terrorism is one thing, how one fights guerrilla warfare or revolutionary terrorism is another.

> The significance of these findings is obvious. To neutralize these forms of terrorism they must be treated as a form of war, and only by waging war upon them in accordance with the principles of war and combat is it possible to defeat this threat. Of course, given that military terrorism represents a military tactic

within the context of a larger war, it is not possible to talk about waging war against this form of terrorism per se. Rather, it is defeated in conjunction with defeating the enemy's conventional armed forces. Revolutionary and state-sponsored terrorism, however represent individual categories of types of war and can exist independently from other, larger forms of war. Consequently, engaging and defeating these can be achieved and require a specific mode of force employment to do so. (Page 237)

It is on this point that I fear President Bush has not informed the American people well at all. The impression has been left that we simply go country by country and round-up criminal elements just as though they are what Bush wrongly depicted them, like our *Mafia.* If these terrorists are in fact revolutionary terrorism like military terrorism, as in guerrilla war, then...

Defeating revolutionary terrorism poses particularly difficult problems in that the regime is waging war against an enemy that is operating in and among its own population. Consequently the chances of causing casualties among innocent civilians is very high unless only a minimum of force is employed in highly discriminate fashion. Defeating the revolutionary terrorists involves employing force in essentially the same basic manner as in conventional, classical warfare. Since the revolutionary terrorists are waging a total war against the regime and are an internal threat, the regime must wage total war against the revolutionaries. It is essential that the revolutionary terrorists' armed forces are destroyed, their "territory" is occupied, and their will to resist is neutralized. (Page 238)

Thus the inevitable course of events will, no must, evolve into all out war against the states themselves to eliminate the *war of the flea;* eliminate the guerrillas qua terrorists whose war this really is. Are Americans really being prepared by the administration to militarily occupy one or several nation-states' territory with ground troops over the long term?

There remains the multitude of other terrorists as well who had nothing (or substantially nothing, to do with the September 11, air attacks: Osama bin Laden, Al Qaida, Hizballah and Hamas, the latter two have already proclaimed that should President Bush invade Afghanistan and go after Osama bin Laden, "We (America) will have to contend with them as well." Should we go into Iraq to eliminate one source of state-sponsored terrorism, their military's guerrilla warriors and intelligence operatives, spread across the globe, do we simultaneously attack Libya, Syria, Iran and Lebanon for the same? Do we begin what will in essence draw other states into this conflict, like it or not; do we allow some level of what continues to look more and more like world war on several state's soil? Occupy each in turn, after defeating its military? Put into power those we would rather *do business with* than the existing power structure?

It is clear this President has much to deliberate, and he needs the time to evaluate every question, intelligence from the world over, every option short of war. Secretary Powell is right in cautioning these things. Americans are right to question every decision this President makes; question each move. Our freedoms dictate what we do as citizens; we were not granted a free press and free speech so we can discuss events and politics while enjoying peace-time prosperity. We have these freedoms so as to speak-out when the Congress or President decides on war. Nothing less should be expected from every American.

CHAPTER FIVE

The Hydra of Carnage
The Silk Road Strategy:

The bellum Justum Between Empire and Revolt

You can not spill a drop of American blood without spilling the blood of the whole world....Our blood is as the flood of the Amazon, made of a thousand noble currents all pouring into one. We are not a nation so much as a world; for unless we may claim all the world for our sire, like Melchisedec, we are without mother or father... Our ancestry is lost in the universal paternity... We are the heirs of all time, and with all nations we divide our inheritance.

—HERMAN MELVILLE

There is no escaping American business.

—LOUIS-FERDINAND CELINE

We Americans will find our honor or we will disappear.

THE *bellum justum* BETWEEN EMPIRE AND REVOLT

*The people no longer exist...*the people are missing.
—GILLES DELEUZE

*Fate has willed it that America is from now on
to be at the center of Western civilization
rather than on the periphery.*
—WALTER LIPPMANN

Introduction To Chapter Five

This may be the most difficult piece I will write, to date, on President Bush's war in Afghanistan. As most of you know, who have followed my work over these past twenty years, I read a great deal of philosophy; both for my own sanity but for a kind of perspectivism, as Nietzsche might put it. I have argued that the September 11th attacks were against Empire not just America per se. This chapter will try to address this more diligently.

Do we even understand the term *Empire*? If not, really fully grasp the significance of the phrase for the year 2002, how shall we grasp a revolt against that which we can not conceptualize? That most people throughout the world perceive the American hegemony as empire is not in dispute. That there is therefore an empire perceived is not in dispute. Every elite writer that endorses this new conceptual form of empire call it that. Zbignew Brzezinski, Dr. Henry Kissinger, Joseph Joffe and too many others to list have written millions of words on *America at the Apex* of Power. Kissinger recently asked if we were a "leader or empire, a bully or friend to the world?" Joseph Joffe stated that our queerly soft power is projected across the entire globe..."where the sun never sets."

Therefore it would behoove us to call it what its endorsee's call it...empire. And so I shall. This American-led, or rightfully altogether American empire, spans the globe. I will argue from that premise for two reasons, one, the perception of almost all our friends and allies is that this is an American empire, and secondly, every single enemy believes this to be true. Therefore, the only way is to question, to argue, what happened on 9/11/01 and why did it happen, those events that led up to the air attacks, not just the attacks themselves, but what "led up" to the attacks? Moreover, I shall finally answer the nagging question, "Why is it necessary for America, in behalf of Empire, to remove the governing Taliban regime from power in Afghanistan"? Get *Osama bin Laden*, fine, but international law scholars the world over have raised the question "How is it that President Bush believes he has the legal right to re-move a sovereign nation-state's governing body." As I pointed out in chapter one, he had no such legal rights. I shall explain below what the real political objectives are that underlie this grievous act; it is called *The Silk Road Strategy*.

I shall, as well, outline what a couple of bright authors, one Italian and an inmate at Rebibbia Prison , Rome, have to say about this Empire. I am going to spell out what a protracted guerrilla war will mean for Americans here at home and the world over. This war of attrition will inevitably, forever alter the American way of life and the American standard of living. Indeed, not even Christmas will bail-out the economy this year, nor likely next.

The Global Paradigm Shift

There has been, in philosophical terms, a paradigm shift of enormous proportions. The world is no longer the same. Americans are always, and ev-erywhere, perplexed by change; they just do not see what affects the rest of the world for better or for, more importantly, worse. Empire has morphed about us; from among us. American foreign policy initiatives have seen and guided the metamorphosis. How does one recognize such a paradigmatic metamorphosis?

> The paradigm shift is defined, at least initially, by recognition that only an established power, over-determined with respect to and relatively autonomous from the sovereign nation-states, is capable of functioning as the center of the new world order, exercising over it an effective regulation and, when necessary, coercion. (*Empire*, Hardt and Negri, 2000, pp 14-15, Harvard University Press)

In their volume, *Empire*, Hardt and Negri argue forcefully that empire not only exists, but one would be at a loss to describe the present world order without it. Empire just is. In their introductory chapters they spell out what they mean when they say empire.

> Every juridical system is in some way a crystallization of a spe-cific set of values, because ethics is part of the materiality of every juridical foundation, but Empire—and in particular the Roman tradition of imperial right—is peculiar in that it pushes the coincidence and universality of the ethical and the juridi-cal to the extreme: in Empire there is peace, in Empire there is the guarantee of justice for all peoples. The concept of Empire is presented as a global concert under the direction of a single conductor, a unitary power that maintains the social peace and produces its ethical truths. And in order to achieve these ends, the single power is given the necessary force to conduct, when necessary, "just wars" at the borders against the barbarians and internally against the rebellious. (Ibid., p. 10)

The just war, *bellum justum,* is the sole prerogative then of Empire. I shall proceed to capitalize Empire as the above authors do, throughout the remainder of my text for obvious reasons. The notion of right, either Kantian, Hegelian or Lockean (and many others) is here what we are expressing. Right is not rights, per se; rights will be granted by the Empire under its sole juridical (legal and jurisprudential) offering and assertion of *Right.* Hardt and Negri point out that there are two tendencies in the juridical notion of right: "...first, the notion of right that is affirmed in the construction of a new order that envelopes the entire space of what it considers civilization, a boundless, universal space; and second, a notion of right that encompasses all time within its ethical foundation." In essence, Empire presents its order as "permanent, eternal and necessary."

What we have here is a borderless world, for the first time in human history, created by communications and technology, that spans the globe. America is the only juridical force to maintain the peace, in its view. And indeed the peace was clearly broken. There is no argument against what President George Bush intends to do to those he allegedly has charged with responsibility for the September 11 air attacks; I shall not even pursue such a critique as what Bush will do is just that, war, nothing more, nothing less. To argue whether he ought to or ought not to...is moot. Empire claims all right to prosecute *bellum justum.* Empire claims all jurisdiction.

The process of globalization, primarily that of the few western democracies (less democracy in each, every day that Empire remains its support mechanism) and America predominates all others, is pressed forward primarily in the interests of productivity and very inexpensive labor throughout the world. Labor will become more important to this analysis at a later date but left for now without comment. Empire I would argue, along with Hardt and Negri, is the center, the very support for the process of globalization. Without Empire the nation-states would have to make legitimate what many of its own citizens, in every nation now, see as illegitimate. The people rallying in support of the air attacks on American soil are but a few of the vast numbers which are disillusioned, dissatisfied and disheartened over what this newest metamorphosis of Empire implies for their future. "Empire is emerging today as the center that supports the globalization of productive networks and casts its widely inclusive net to try to envelop all power relations within its world order—"...

> ...and yet at the same time it deploys a powerful police function against the new barbarians and the rebellious slaves who threaten its order. The power of Empire appears to be subordinated to the fluctuations of local power dynamics and to the partial juridical orderings that attempt, but never fully succeed, to lead back to a state of normalcy in the name of the "exceptionality" of the administrative procedures. (Ibid., p. 20)

To put this more in the context of recent events and the carpet bombing of Afghanistan, and maybe Iraq too, the imperial right exercised by the Empire is its exceptionality; it may do what it likes as it is the only entity that has the power to maintain peace and justice throughout the vast expanse of its holdings, in its view. The barbarians broke the imperial peace and the Empire shall render imperial justice.

> This kind of continual intervention, then, which is both moral and military, is really the logical form of the exercise of force that follows from a paradigm of legitimation based on a state of permanent exception and police action. Interventions are always exceptional even though they arise continually; they take the form of police actions because they are aimed at maintaining an internal order. In this way intervention is an effective mechanism that through police deployments contributes directly to the construction of the moral, normative, and institutional order of Empire. (Ibid., p. 38)

When the people suggest, peaceably, through partial juridical orderings of their own nation-state prerogatives, that the Empire roll-back to a time of normalcy (for them a return to when their own sovereigns conducted their own orchestras), the Empire uses its vast array of international governing organizations (IGO) to whip the dissenters into line; trade talks, treaties signed, fiscal interventions, and outright monetary (bribery) pressures are just a few coercive administrative techniques used. Should the dissent turn to rebellion, like here in America, with our own home grown "terrorists," the militia movement, coercion turns to force. Should foreign rebellion appear in confined specific nation-states Empire lends a hand without ruling out force in limited ways; Iraq, Somalia, Panama, Vietnam, Cambodia, Nicaragua, El Salvador, Columbia, Palestine, Libya, Cuba, Korea, etc.; that these are always called police actions rather than wars is not just semantics. Wars are fought with many tools; political warfare is no less warfare.

> Empires tend to perform most effectively in political warfare when driven by a militant, messianic ideology that complements and transcends the rational-legalistic framework of the nation-states within them. Such combinations of ideological and statist elements in an empire can create problems, indeed very serious problems, when an inherent tension between ideology and the state arises at the core of the imperial political vision. The outcome can be decisive, particularly for multinational empires. (*On Political War*, Paul A. Smith Jr., pp 12-13, National Defense University Press)

There has been a rethinking about when, why and how war-making is to be deployed in the world. Clausewitz remains the most significant contributor to the theory and practice of war. His great contribution included the concept that war was politics by other means. But for the new strategists in the United States defense related think tanks, including the National Defense University quoted above, the concept has evolved into something altogether new. In the recent issue of *Millennium,* (London School of Economics) Michael Dillon and Julian Reid discuss the new strategic thinking called RMA or the Revolution in Military Affairs. One of their conclusions bears reporting:

> Whereas for Clausewitz, war was the extension of politics by other means, for these new strategists the practice of war has become the extension of that form of wealth creation, which also operates around information as a generative principle and prized commodity. Successful organization of war mimics successful organization of profit....Just as successful organization for profit is dependent upon the radical relationality of effective network organization, so also is the successful use of lethal military force. Biopolitical economy is war pursued by other means. (*Millennium,* Vol.30 No.1, 2001: *Global Liberal Governance,* pp. 64-65)

Biopolitical economy is war by other means; the rest of the world understands this; the underdeveloped world, like Afghanistan for example, fully understands this. Here is a quote from Mujahid Sheikh Usamah bin Laden you will not read in most of the American censored press:

> *Declaration of war*: concerning the illegitimate presence of the American occupation forces in the Arab Peninsula: ...2) The inability of the regime to protect the country, and allowing the enemy of Ummah — the American crusader forces — to occupy the land for the longest of years...5) *Destruction of the oil industries*: The presence of the USA crusader military forces on land, sea and air of the states of the Islamic Gulf is the greatest danger threatening the largest oil reserve in the world. The existence of these forces in the area will provoke the people of the country and induces aggression on their religion, feelings and prides and push them to take up armed struggle against the invaders occupying the land; therefore spread of the fighting in the region will expose the oil wealth to the danger of being burned up....I would like here to alert my brothers, the Mujahideen, the sons of the nation, to protect this (oil) wealth and not to include it in the battle as it is a great Islamic wealth and a large economical power essential for the soon to be established Islamic state...(Usamah bin Muhammad Laden, Friday, 9/4/1417 A.H. [23/8/1996 AD] Hindukursh Mountains, Khurasan, Afghanistan. Source: Committee for the Defense of Legitimate Rights [CFLR] http://msanews.mynet.net/MSAN-EWS/199610/19961012.3.html)

Smith, quoted previously above, states that for multinational empires, the lack of a core imperial vision can cause problems for the empire as divisiveness sets in; "Such problems are not unmanageable, though; some empires have survived for extended periods while riven with ethnic and social contradictions. And yet a strong political warfare strategy against such empires may be spectacularly successful, as Anglo-American strategy was against Austria-Hungary in 1918."

> On balance, a large multinational empire still seems to require some form of potent ideological adhesive to hold it together. To dissolve that adhesive is the task of political warfare. (Ibid., *On Political War*, pp. 12-13)

That potent ideology is clearly Corporatism. Clearly, bin Laden and his Muslim brothers, the Mujahideen in Afghanistan, believe they have a legitimate war-making cause against Empire; one may call it "only" their perception but everyone knows perceptions are reality even for Americans believing President Bush's perceptions about reality. It might be prudent here to inject a truth that all history will attest:

> [Under these circumstances], it seems wise to assume that national leaders of all kinds, political and military, will feel compelled to fight wars with every intention of winning them. One should ask not whether leaders seek victory, but rather, how do they define victory and defeat. The question is paramount in political war. (Ibid., p. 28)

That we are faced with both a political war, for the hearts and minds of the have-nots throughout the world, today and only today mind you, the Arab people's hearts and minds, and now also a shooting war. These regions make up the great world order, the global neighborhood, the City State writ large.

Empire always looks upon the world as its great neighborhood. Nation-states become less states than international communities. Empire does not intervene with war-making powers but, instead, help police the neighborhoods where the rebellious are apt to disturb the administration of globalization; the administration of peace and justice. In the Empire's view it is not only warranted but accepted by every rational thinking person. Former President, Mr. Bush-Senior placed United States Marines in the streets of Los Angeles to "police" the community; Mr. Bush Jr. feels he must do the same now, the world over, to fight terrorism "wherever it is found." This is why Mr. Bush Jr. (wrongly) depicted the terrorists as akin the western mafias.

This is understood as moral intervention as much as anything else. Of course moral intervention is the first stage in what likely, and almost always, turns into military intervention. Americans no longer ask why America has lost every war since 1945? This is because these were not wars, these were police actions, and one can never really lose a police action, one can, of course, lose a war. A police action is used in behalf of Empire alone; war would be utilized in all-out fashion if America, as nation-state, were attacked, which it was not. The air attacks targeted, once again, *Empire's infrastructure*, right here in the United States.

> Today military intervention is progressively less a product of decisions that arise out of the old international order or even U.N. structures. More often it is dictated unilaterally by the United States, which charges itself with the primary task and then subsequently asks it allies to set in motion a process of armed containment and/or repression of the current enemy of Empire. These enemies are most often called terrorist, a crude conceptual and terminological reduction that is rooted in a police mentality. (*Empire*, p. 37)

Notice how America still has allies to "subsequently...set in motion a process of armed containment..." but other countries must stand-down in the face of the juggernaut, as their allies are not true allies but reneging on their promises to Empire, therefore subject to equal punishment if other less-violent coercive administrative techniques fail to convince. If any country announces it will not stand with America in its quest to rid the entire planetary system of Empire of its criminal elements, then that country is against the Empire? Not against America itself, because it was the Empire which was attacked and only incidentally America as America. Empire alone renders justice, in its view.

This is such an important point in understanding what and why the September 11 attacks occurred and what and why President Bush will prosecute as police action. The actual repression of these groups called "terrorists" when they have morphed right along with Empire into international urban guerrilla warfare, becomes clearer. We must continue to call them terrorists rather than guerrillas as the only enemy of Empire as language allowable is the criminal elements within the community (of nations). On occasion, President Bush has slipped-up while performing one of his unrehearsed adlibs, by calling the upcoming war a guerrilla war; immediately he catches himself and returns to the preferred semantics of Empire, a war on terrorism. This is done so it can never be implied that we are at world war with a revolutionary element within Empire, and without, at the margins of what were once nation-state borders, of the entire Empire itself. The equation runs something like this: terrorist = criminal (and we all hate criminals) guerrilla = revolution (and that would have to be explained).

The actual repression of these groups may not be as important as "criminalizing their activities and managing social alarm at their very existence in order to facilitate their control." Even though the attempt by Empire to control "ethnic terrorists" or "narco-terrorists" and their "drug mafias" clearly represents an expansive community effort to control the barbarians and rebellious. Community policing it is called here in America when focused upon American cities. This is principally what Empire does globally.

The "just war" is effectively supported by the "moral police," just as the validity of imperial right and its legitimate functioning is supported by the necessary and continuous exercise of police power." (Ibid., pp. 37-38)

Indeed, Hardt and Negri argue that the very legitimacy of Empire and its new power, "is in part based directly on the effectiveness of its use of force." Thus, as I have pointed out numerous times, in this view the September 11 air attacks were an attack by the rebellious, and successful rebellion is called revolution, so therefore the revolutionaries attacked the heart of the Empire; unfortunately for the Americans and so many others that died in the infernos, America is directly and inextricably merged with Empire.

This legitimacy is expressed in the *exercise of legitimate force* and is based upon the fact that its legitimacy is being constructed simultaneously while the use of force is being utilized. Said differently, the use of force makes the use of force legitimate.

Now is the Time of Furnaces

The police appears as an administration heading the state,
together with the judiciary, the army, and the exchequer.
True. Yet in fact, it embraces everything else.
Turquet says so:
"It branches out into all of the people's conditions,
everything they do or undertake.
Its field comprised the judiciary, finance, and the army."
The *police* includes everything.
—MICHEL FOUCAULT

Now is the time of furnaces, and only light should be seen.
—JOSE MARTI

Nation-states have been considered the primary source of the people's sovereignty for over three hundred years. The Peace of Westphalia is nearly always the historical point of demarcation for the formation and extension of nation-state prerogatives. Nations (of people) were represented by their governing bodies (States) and this configuration remains hotly debated among international relations theorists; whether they still exist is less important today than the heyday of the debates during the nineties. They exist, nation-states; that they are less important, is also true; that they still command abundant reserves of sovereignty has just become clearer as state after state rebuffed the American-led coalition (of states, of course) in its lone fight to defend Empire at any cost.

Empire tends to make each nation-state an instrument of its own. Each state has become, in effect, the record keeper of monies, commodities, goods and services and the very populations of each as they roam across borders looking for work or fleeing just and unjust wars. The nation-state is today the record keeper for Empire's process of globalization.

It is the multinational corporations that manufacture the products and in a very real sense manufacture the workers, which are sent hither and yon to produce the goods wherever the goods might be manufactured cheaper. The institutions like the International Monetary Fund (IMF) and World bank, the World Trade Organization, (WTO) as General Agreement on Tariffs and Trade, (GATT), the United Nations and NATO are the mighty regulators of the trade and commerce between the nation-states and in particularly peculiar ways see to it that the states record these flows properly and keep the trade routes open and accessible to all the various corporations. This process is not like an invasion, it is an invasion to others whose beliefs and practices, governments and cultures are not America's nor America's notion of Empire. "The Empires' institutional structure is like a software program that carries a virus along with it, so that it is continually modulating and corrupting the institutional forms around it." The nation-states are those other institutional forms being corrupted. The answer, said differently, to why they hate us? The transnational corporations distribute labor no less than commodities and services and information. But most important of all...money!

> The most complete figure of this world is presented from the monetary perspective. From here we can see a horizon of values and a machine of distribution, a mechanism of accumulation and means of circulation, a power and a language. There is nothing, no "naked life," no external standpoint, that can be posed outside this field permeated by money; nothing escapes money. Production and reproduction are dressed in monetary clothing. In fact, on the global stage, every biopolitical figure appears dressed in monetary garb. "Accumulate, accumulate! This is Moses and the Prophets." (*Empire*, p. 32)

And that is one "permeated" field "by money" most people throughout the world are left out of. Dr. Kissinger warned of the inherent envy global communications would engender against the West and America in particular. Envy is not that the have-nots want what the haves have, but that the have-nots would like nothing better than to see the haves get their comeuppance. The Empire is the creator, the support, of this process globally. Western monopoly capitalism is but the engine globally. Capitalism in its free enterprise mode has nothing to do with this Imperial mode of production, and the Left should get this correct if their analysis is ever to be correct. We are, then, looking at something never seen before globally. And only America and a few western states (Britain and France, Germany and Japan) have witnessed this phenomenon domestically. The Empire of productivity based on globalization, is attempting, wittingly or not, to remake the world over in its image.

The great industrial and financial powers thus produce not only commodities but also subjectivities. They produce agentic subjectivities within the biopolitical context: they produce needs, social relations, bodies and minds—which is to say, they produce producers. In the biopolitical sphere, life is made to work for production and production is made to work for life. (Ibid., p. 33)

Hardt and Negri compared this evolution globally to a "great hive in which the queen bee continuously oversees production and reproduction." The queen bee is Empire. These authors easily, it seems, anticipated significant struggles in Empire's future. Because Empire is not hierarchical as nation-states remain, but diffused over the globe, each international governing organization (IGO) resting in differing parts of the Empire's states. Struggles against Empire will take on a different hue, a different feel and sense of what is going on; thus, Mr. Bush erroneously identified this international revolutionary guerrilla warfare as simple terrorism. (I do not believe I am omniscient, I believe President Bush knows full well what we are really dealing with, he just cannot explain it to his subjects for fear they would declare, "no blood for Empire!")

Empire presents a superficial world, the virtual center of which can be accessed immediately from any point across the surface. If these points were to constitute something like a new cycle of struggles, it would be a cycle defined not by the communicative extension of the struggles but rather by their singular emergence, by the intensity that characterizes them one by one. In short, this new phase is defined by the fact that these struggles do not link horizontally, but each one leaps vertically, directly to the virtual center of Empire. (Ibid., p. 58)

It is here, I believe, America is going to get its hardest lesson. "To achieve significance, every struggle must attack the heart of Empire, at its strength." The fact that the world is its Empire, each and every struggle, in Hardt's and Negri's terminology, mine is today more aggressive, each and every attack by the global guerrillas, "does not give priority to any geographical regions," because Washington D.C. or Geneva matter equally as Tokyo or Saudi Arabia. But America is the thrust of first importance to every other existing nation-state and important city the world over. It was American elites who wanted to see this hegemony take place, applauded it as it extended its influence, and now its citizens must pay for their intoxicated overreach. America can be made secure?

On the contrary, the construction of Empire, and the globalization of economic and cultural relationships, means that the virtual center of Empire can be attacked from any point. The tactical preoccupations of the old revolutionary school are thus completely irretrievable; the only strategy available to the struggles is that of a constituent counterpower that emerges from within Empire. (Ibid., p. 59)

The authors have hit upon something that American scholars and elites have missed. The new face of warfare is not only terrorism, which remains true as well, but something altogether newer still; a global unification of global revolt against Empire, is the only thing that could work against the enormous reach of Empire's might. These isolated attacks at the heart of Empire, whether here in America or anywhere the Empire's reach affects the lives of the disaffected, will become the "maniacal focus of the critical attention of Empire." The authors, almost demurely note that these attentions "are the educational lessons in the classroom of administration and the chambers of government—lessons that demand repressive instruments."

The lessons that are being taught are not slights against terrorists, or insults at nation-state sovereignty, the lessons are becoming clearer: "The primary lesson is that such events cannot be repeated if the process of capitalist globalization are to continue." Right then, here we have the point. Nothing can be allowed to upset the Empire's process of supporting the globalization of the productive capital of monopoly capitalism. And if the furnaces must be lit, so be it.

Political Objectives of War

My central argument rests upon my premise, and maybe mine alone, that it is not only not in the interests of Americans generally, to see the American Republic slip away under the presence of an emerging Empire, even if American elites lead it, our laws and norms, based upon our specific Constitution precludes this evolution; claims it to be illegitimate. Unfortunately Empire can and will ignore the U.S. juridical form and pursue its own growth and will.

From the myths of power that historical anthropologists such as Rudolf Otto and Georges Dumezil employed to the rules of the new political science that the authors of *The Federalist* described; from the Rights of Man to the norms of international public law—all of this fades away with the passage to Empire. (*Empire*, p. 354)

No war is ever fought without political objectives. Even where there is an obvious act of war needing response, like the September 11 air attacks on America, other considerations have already been discussed for years or months before the act of war presented itself. Strategic planners, the analysts whose responsibility it is to achieve various political, economic, or social objectives of the state apparatuses are always "in" each and every decision needing to be taken. War is an especially popular rubric to operate under for achieving objectives long put on hold for whatever reason.

When Saddam Hussein seized Kuwait on August 2nd, 1990, after assurances from the American Ambassador, Mrs. April Glaspie, that "the United States does not get involved with nation-state's border disputes," he erred greatly. What other political objectives did then President George Bush (Sr.) bring to the table to accomplish, that war-making might provide an opportunity to achieve, where other political means precluded such maneuvers? There were several, although the President did not inform the public of these objectives; I, on the other hand, did inform the American people for the entire seven months prior to Bush's launching the air bombardments. One political objective, which was outlined in a task force report transcribed and authored prior to the April, 1990, meeting at the White House, was to utilize the United Nation's Security Council apparatus to disarm Iraq's conventional, biological and nuclear military capability in the region. Hussein's gullibility in believing Glaspie's statement, then seizing Kuwait, gave the White House the opportunity to achieve a political objective (disarming Iraq) it had outlined months prior to Hussein's blunder on August 2, 1990. Another political objective was to figure out how to convince the Saudi regime to accept a permanent U.S. military presence on Arab soil; something no Arab state could ever allow except under extraordinary circumstances. Hussein provided the circumstances to achieve an objective that could not be accomplished politically. I argued at the time, that the U.S. military presence would not be allowed to stand; one year, or ten, there would be a violent reaction, and I warned of this often at the time.

There were other objectives. One always must look at the "why" your government does anything; who stands to gain; in whose interest is it to do this or that. As FDR said, "nothing happens in government by accident." This is also where the naive fall into the conspiracy theory trap; connecting the dots or the "ah-ha" theory as it has been called.

But even the paranoid often get their facts straight. It is their interpretation that trips them up. President Bush Sr. did not go to war with Iraq to achieve the political objectives outlined above (knowing these objectives beforehand is in the nature of politics itself) but in planning what to do at the time, these objectives were tabled for operational planning and implementation. Brutally Machiavellian, true, but perfectly understandable when looked at through adult eyes.

President George Bush Jr. has faced the same operational and strategic planning, many of the very same planners and analysts on tap, from his father's reign, to set into motion any political objectives which have been on hold for various reasons regarding the region in question after the September 11, 2001 air attacks. I had been fortunate to have come into possession of a United States House of Representatives, Committee on International Relations, Subcommittee on Asia and the Pacific, transcript of a hearing held on Thursday, February 12, 1998. The contents explain many questions I have had since the beginning of the targeting of Osama bin Laden as the only apparent suspect in the attacks. I found it of incredible interest how this obscure little man, whose terrorist acts of the past he had nearly always claimed credit for, was not even listed or mentioned in most CIA and State Department documents as late as 1998, never indicted or named in most documents regarding the World Trade Center bombing of 1993, never looked at as the most dangerous man in the world...until September 11, 2001?

Suddenly "all roads lead to bin laden" and we want him "dead or alive." I remain convinced that even if some of bin Laden's contacts/soldiers had made contact with some of the alleged, and do let us continue calling these dead men "alleged," hijackers, there is still no supportable evidence that bin Laden masterminded the plot; Iraqi military intelligence agents had been meeting with these same individuals and many others in both Afghanistan and throughout Europe. But I have spoken to this issue elsewhere and shall let it stand...bin Laden had a hand in it. And maybe he did.

The question I had been unable to get any sufficient answer to (until now) was why has President Bush Jr. declared war on the Taleban (or Taliban) governing elite? International relations' scholars in Britain and Europe have been arguing vigorously that going after bin Laden is one thing, it is a police function and nobody can deny America's right to have him picked-up, arrested and brought to justice; even extraordinary means (a snatch-team) might be deployed "if" the evidence in fact points to him as masterminding these horrific deeds. But no scholar, with the exception of those under instructions by the American administration, has argued successfully that President Bush, and more to the point, the United States proper, has the right under international law, the United Nations, the World Court and 300 years of international norms (the normative relations between sovereign nation-states), to make removing the present seated government of a sovereign nation-state part of its effort to make war on terrorism. Please tolerate my redundancy.

No nation, not even one on a noble moral crusade, has the legitimate authority, the right that is to say, to intervene in any nation's sovereign affairs. And bombing the regime into the stone age certainly qualifies as intervention into the affairs of Afghanistan.

So here is my point: What, then, is the political objective of the present Bush Administration in bombing and its declared intent to remove the Taliban ruling party from office and installing one more favorable (more favorable to "whom" being the rest of the question) to the international community? Or the Afghan people? Or more favorable in some one else's interest? Below is the documentation which I now allegedly claim may be one of the other political objectives. (Later this is called coincidence when achieved or antecedent to the removal of the Taliban.)

HEARING ON U. S. INTERESTS IN THE CENTRAL ASIAN REPUBLICS

February, 12 1998

I shall quote at length from the hearing and with as little commentary as possible; the words spoken by those I quote are far superior to whatever I might add as garnish. I shall begin at the best place, the beginning, and allow one Mr. Robert W. Gee, Assistant Secretary for Policy and International Affairs, Department of State, to ask his rhetorical question:

To begin, you may ask why is the United States active in the region? The United States has energy security, strategic, and commercial interests in promoting Caspian region energy development. We have an interest in strengthening global energy security through diversification, and the development of these new sources of supply. Caspian export routes would diversify rather than concentrate world energy supplies, while avoiding over-reliance on the Persian Gulf. ... We have strategic interests in supporting the independence, sovereignty, and prosperity of the Newly Independent States of the Caspian Basin. We want to assist the development of these States into democratic, sovereign members of the world community of nations, enjoying unfettered access to world markets without pressure or undue influence from regional powers.

...We also have an interest in maximizing commercial opportunities for U.S. firms and for U.S. and other foreign investment in the region's energy development. In short, our interests are rooted in achieving multiple objectives. Rapid development of the region's energy resources and trade linkages are critical to the independence, prosperity, democracy, and stability of all of the countries of that region.

This gives you some idea of reference what the hearing was meant to address. The testimony continues in this vein, outlining several areas of policy objectives:

While we recognize the influence regional politics will play on the development of export routes, we have always maintained that commercial considerations will principally determine the outcome. These massive infrastructure projects must be commercially competitive before the private sector and the international financial community can move forward. Our support of specific pipelines, such as the Baku-Ceyhan oil pipeline and trans-Caspian oil and gas lines, is not driven by any desire to intervene in private commercial decisions. Rather, it derives from our conclusion that it is not in the commercial interest of companies operating in the Caspian States, nor in the strategic interests of those host States, to rely on a major competitor for transit rights.

...cooperating with Russia. Our Caspian policy is not intended to bypass or to thwart Russia. In fact, two key projects closest to fruition go through Russia, those of the Azerbaijan International Operating Company northern early pipeline, and the Caspian Pipeline Consortium from Kazakhstan through Russia to the Black Sea port of Novorossiysk....U.S. companies are working in partnership with Russian firms in the Caspian, and there will be future opportunities to expand that commercial cooperation.

...isolating Iran. Our policy on Iran is unchanged. The U.S. Government opposes pipelines through Iran. Development of Iran's oil and gas industry and pipelines from the Caspian Basin south through Iran will seriously undercut the development of east-west infrastructure, and give Iran improper leverage over the economies of the Caucasus and Central Asian States. Moreover, from an energy security standpoint, it makes no sense to move yet more energy resources through the Persian Gulf, a potential major hot spot or chokepoint. From an economic standpoint, Iran competes with Turkmenistan for the lucrative Turkish gas market. Turkmenistan could provide the gas to build the pipeline, only to see itself displaced ultimately by Iran's own gas exports.

...The United States has stressed the importance of achieving agreement on concrete project proposals among the relevant countries as early as possible. Along these lines, we have encouraged the regional governments to accelerate multilateral discussions with their neighboring States and with the private sector shippers through the establishment of national working groups. These groups have a critical role in resolving regulatory, legal, tariff, and other issues that will make the Eurasian corridor most commercially attractive

Thus we have the synopsis of the policy objectives of the United States government. Questioning Mr. Gee on his trip to Turkey, a key player in the region where the pipeline projects are being proposed, Congressman Bereuter asking what actions Turkey was prepared to take elicited this response.

They recognize that they need to take proper steps to reform some of their governmental infrastructure in order to make the environment much more commercially viable. Among other things, they are experiencing some difficulties in reforming some of their legal requirements relative to the privatization of the power generation market in order to allow private investment to come in, with the necessary guarantees of securing investment, to provide the gas market that would facilitate the transport of gas into Turkey.

...I did mention, without asking a question, the role of OPIC and of course the multilateral organization, MEGA. OPIC would facilitate American firms' participation. We would expect to see other countries do something similar in a worthy project. Is it essential to the Turkish Government that there be a multilateral investment guarantee agency or are they satisfied with simply the various developed countries that have such loan guarantee programs like OPIC, to provide them one by one under a competitive kind of environment?

When Mr. Gee was asked about Afghanistan he stated the following:

Perhaps the Unocal witness can give you more detail. I do understand that they do have an agreement with the government of Turkmenistan. They have also been in discussions with the various factions within Afghanistan through which that proposed pipeline would be routed. ...The U.S. Government's position is that we support multiple pipelines with the exception of the southern pipeline that would transit Iran. The Unocal pipeline is among those pipelines that would receive our support under that policy. I would caution that while we do support the project, the U.S. Government has not at this point recognized any governing regime of the transit country, one of the transit countries, Afghanistan, through which that pipeline would be routed. But we do support the project.

Mr. Berman then asked him, "I am thinking of how Uzbekistan, Kazakhstan-is this a pipeline for their use or is this primarily for Caspian Sea oil? Mr. Gee responded "It would be a pipeline generally for production from Kazakhstan and Turkmenistan, which is where most of the potential reserves are thought to be located. Mr. Bereuter questioned again, "There is an oil field in Kazakhstan, Tengiz, or something like that. Mr. Gee added, "The Tengiz oil field, yes." Mr. Bereuter: "Reportedly the world's largest known untapped field. That may be subject to dispute. It began to be exploited apparently most recently about 1993, I am told. How much have U.S. firms invested? Have they received any substantial return on their investment at this point"? Mr. Gee, responded with this important additional information:

...I believe that the transit route for that field is still under development. I don't know whether there have actually been sales of production from the Tengiz field. I am informed by our staff that there have been sales from that field. I can provide that information to you. We don't have it available today as to any specific volumes or monetary returns from that sale. ...According to our calculations, total foreign direct investment in Kazakhstan's oil and gas sector from 1991 through 1996 was approximately U.S. $2 billion. Total commitments for new, future direct investment in Kazakhstan's oil and gas development now stands at over U.S. $35 billion. The Tengiz field has estimated reserves of 24 billion barrels of crude oil and over 1800 billion cubic meters of associated natural gas. Oil production has slowly risen to its current level of approximately 160,000 barrels per day. Production is currently being hampered by limited access to export pipelines. Once the Caspian Pipeline Consortium pipeline is constructed, oil production from Tengiz is expected to increase to 750,000 barrels per day by 2010. Even at production of 160,000 barrels per day, the venture has been profitable. Tengizchevroil, the consortium producing the Tengiz field, reported profits of U.S. $80 million in 1996, up from only U.S. $1 million in 1995.

Professor S. Frederick Starr of Johns Hopkins University was the next to testify, stating with regard to the legislation put forward to implement the policy,...

In this progress toward formulating an American policy toward this region, it seems to me that the so-called Silk Road Strategy Act, H.R. 2867, goes further than any previous official act of the U.S. Government toward translating our principles with regard to this region into concrete action.

The next testimony is clearly the most important for any understanding as to why President Bush feels such urgent need to displace the Taliban governing party. (Keeping in mind that the only opposition to the Taliban is the Northern Alliance whose human rights and record of atrocities against the Afghan people makes the Taliban pale to insignificance.)

STATEMENT OF JOHN J. MARESCA, VICE PRESIDENT OF INTERNATIONAL RELATIONS, Unocal CORPORATION

Mr. John J. Maresca: Thank you, Mr. Chairman. It's nice to see you again. I am John Maresca, vice president for international relations of the Unocal Corporation. Unocal, as you know, is one of the world's leading energy resource and project development companies. I appreciate your invitation to speak here today. I believe these hearings are important and timely. I congratulate you for focusing on Central Asia oil and gas reserves and the role they play in shaping U.S. policy.

...I would like to focus today on three issues. First, the need for multiple pipeline routes for Central Asian oil and gas resources. Second, the need for U.S. support for international and regional efforts to achieve balanced and lasting political settlements to the conflicts in the region, including Afghanistan. Third, the need for structured assistance to encourage economic reforms and the development of appropriate investment climates in the region. In this regard, we specifically support repeal or removal of section 907 of the Freedom Support Act.

...Mr. Chairman, the Caspian region contains tremendous untapped hydrocarbon reserves. Just to give an idea of the scale, proven natural gas reserves equal more than 236 trillion cubic feet. The region's total oil reserves may well reach more than 60 billion barrels of oil. Some estimates are as high as 200 billion barrels. In 1995, the region was producing only 870,000 barrels per day. By 2010, western companies could increase production to about 4.5 million barrels a day, an increase of more than 500 percent in only 15 years. If this occurs, the region would represent about 5 percent of the world's total oil production.

...One major problem has yet to be resolved: how to get the region's vast energy resources to the markets where they are needed. Central Asia is isolated. Their natural resources are landlocked, both geographically and politically.

...The other project is sponsored by the Azerbaijan International Operating Company, a consortium of 11 foreign oil companies, including four American companies, Unocal, Amoco, Exxon and Pennzoil. This consortium conceives of two possible routes, one line would angle north and cross the north Caucasus to Novorossiysk. The other route would cross Georgia to a shipping terminal on the Black Sea. This second route could be extended west and south across Turkey to the Mediterranean port of Ceyhan.

...But even if both pipelines were built, they would not have enough total capacity to transport all the oil expected to flow from the region in the future. Nor would they have the capability to move it to the right markets. Other export pipelines must be built.

...The second option is to build a pipeline south from Central Asia to the Indian Ocean. One obvious route south would cross Iran, but this is foreclosed for American companies because of U.S. sanctions legislation. *The only other possible route is across Afghanistan, which has of course its own unique challenges. The country has been involved in bitter warfare for almost two decades, and is still divided by civil war. From the outset, we have made it clear that construction of the pipeline we have proposed across Afghanistan could not begin until a recognized government is in place that has the confidence of governments, lenders, and our company.* (my emphasis) ...Unocal foresees a pipeline which would become part of a regional system that will gather oil from existing pipeline infrastructure in Turkmenistan, Uzbekistan, Kazakhstan and Russia. The 1,040-mile long oil pipeline would extend south through Afghanistan to an export terminal that would be constructed on the Pakistan coast. This 42-inch diameter pipeline will have a shipping capacity of one million barrels of oil per day. The estimated cost of the project, which is similar in scope to the trans-Alaska pipeline, is about $2.5 billion.

...Given the plentiful natural gas supplies of Central Asia, our aim is to link gas resources with the nearest viable markets. This is basic for the commercial viability of any gas project. But these projects also face geopolitical challenges. Unocal and the Turkish company Koc Holding are interested in bringing competitive gas supplies to Turkey. The proposed Eurasia natural gas pipeline would transport gas from Turkmenistan directly across the Caspian Sea through Azerbaijan and Georgia to Turkey. Of course the demarcation of the Caspian remains an issue.

...Last October, the Central Asia Gas Pipeline Consortium, called CentGas, in which Unocal holds an interest, was formed to develop a gas pipeline which will link Turkmenistan's vast Dauletabad gas field with markets in Pakistan and possibly India. The proposed 790-mile pipeline will open up new markets for this gas, traveling from Turkmenistan through Afghanistan to Multan in Pakistan. The proposed extension would move gas on to New Delhi, where it would connect with an existing pipeline. As with the proposed Central Asia oil pipeline, Cent-Gas can not begin construction until an internationally recognized Afghanistan Government is in place.

...The Central Asia and Caspian region is blessed with abundant oil and gas that can enhance the lives of the region's residents, and provide energy for growth in both Europe and Asia. The impact of these resources on U.S. commercial interests and U.S. foreign policy is also significant. Without peaceful settlement of the conflicts in the region, cross-border oil and gas pipelines are not likely to be built. We urge the Administration and the Congress to give strong support to the U.N.-led peace process in Afghanistan. The U.S. Government should use its influence to help find solutions to all of the region's conflicts.

Congressman Bereuter then asked Mr. Maresca if, given the history of violence in Afghanistan, did he believe that a pipeline could be reasonably secured? Mr. Maresca said the following:

...First, on the question about Afghanistan, of course we're not in a phase where we are negotiating on a contract because there is no recognized government really to negotiate with. However, we have had talks and briefings with all the factions. It is clear that they all understand the significance for their country of this pipeline project, and they all support it, all of them. They all want it. They would like it to start tomorrow. All of the factions would like it to start tomorrow if we could do it...It's not going to be built until there is a single Afghan Government. That's the simple answer. We would not want to be in the situation where we became the target of the other faction. In any case, because of the financing situation, credits are not going to be available until there is a recognized government of Afghanistan.

Congressman Rohrabacher then added the following, "I am reminded of a joke where God is asked when peace will come to the Middle East. He says, "Not in my lifetime." I am afraid that this may well be true of Afghanistan as well. In fact, I am more hopeful right now, having just returned from one trip to the Middle East and another trip to Central Asia that there is a greater chance for peace between Israel and its neighbors than there is for peace in Afghanistan. And I know Afghanistan probably better than anyone else in the Congress. I hate to tell you that. But let me ask a few questions. So there will be no pipeline until there is an internationally recognized government and a government that is recognized by the people of Afghanistan too, I would imagine that you wanted to put that caveat on it. Right? It's not just internationally recognized, but it has to be accepted by the people of the country. Right"? *The following exchange took place and it is here that the parties make the point all too well:*

Mr. MARESCA. It depends on who you mean by the people. I assume that no matter what government is put in place, there will be some people who are opposed to it.

Mr. ROHRABACHER. I found something here. There seems to be a little attachment onto... there,... that may be a little more controversial than people understood when they first heard what you were saying. So the government doesn't necessarily have to be acceptable to the people of Afghanistan as long as it's internationally recognized? The current government of Afghanistan or the current group of people who hold Kabul, I guess is the best way to say that, and about 60 percent of the country are known as the Taliban. What type of relationship does your company have to the Taliban?

Mr. MARESCA. We have the same relationship as we have with the other factions, which is that we have talked with them, we have briefed them, we have invited them to our headquarters to see what our projects are.

Mr. ROHRABACHER. Right.

Mr. MARESCA. These are exactly the same things we have done with the other factions.

Mr. ROHRABACHER. However, the Taliban, who are now in control of 60 percent of Afghanistan, could you give me an estimate of where the opium that's being produced in Afghanistan is being produced? Is it in the Taliban areas or is it in the northern areas of Afghanistan? What about the haven for international terrorists? There is a Saudi terrorist who is infamous for financing terrorism around the world. Is he in the Taliban area or is he up there with the northern people?

Mr. MARESCA. If it is the person I am thinking of, he is there in the Taliban area.

Mr. ROHRABACHER. Right. And in the northern area as compared to the place where the Taliban are in control, would you say that one has a better human rights record toward women than the other?

Mr. MARESCA. With respect to women, yes. But I don't think either faction here has a very clean human rights record, to tell you the truth....I am not here to defend the Taliban. That is not my role. We are a company that is trying to build a pipeline across this country.

Mr. ROHRABACHER. I sympathize with that. By the way, you are right. All factions agree that the pipeline will be something that's good. But let me warn you that if the pipeline is constructed before there is a government that is acceptable at a general level to the population of Afghanistan and not just to international, other international entities, other governments, that your pipeline will be blown up. There is no doubt about that. I have been in and out of Afghanistan for 15 years. These are very brave, courageous people. If they think they are being stepped on, just like the Soviets found out, they are going to kick somebody back. They are not going to lay down and let somebody put the boot in their face. If the government that is receiving the funds that you are talking about is a government that is not accepted by a large number of people in Afghanistan, there will continue to be problems. You say you have had a positive relationship with all the factions. That is what you are presenting to us today.

Mr. MARESCA. We are hesitant too, Mr. Congressman. I appreciate the fact that you are a person well-read into these issues. I think you would agree with us that the international community needs to pay a lot more attention to this problem. We would like to see the international community focused hard on this problem and pushing for that kind of a peaceful resolution that you described.

Mr. ROHRABACHER. If I could just say just a couple more words. During the break, I did manage to take a swing through Central Asia that took me to Turkey and Azerbaijan and Uzbekistan, Turkmenistan, Kazakhstan. I, Mr. Chairman, agree with the witness. The most important thing we can do now is to try to get this region that's been isolated for so long into the global economy. There is so much potential there, wealth as well as the people there, are fine. They are the traders of ancient times. They could do very well in the global economy. I think Turkey is playing a very positive role there. It's not trying to dominate like it was before—earlier on they thought they might dominate the region. Instead, they are playing a very positive role economically and bringing those people into the world economic system. *So the subject of this hearing was well chosen. I do hope that, and I don't know if anybody else is going to get involved in Afghanistan now, but I would hope that people of the world focus a little more on these poor people. They helped us end the cold war. If it wasn't for the courage and the bravery of the people of Afghanistan, we would*

*still be in the middle of a cold war, spending $100 billion a year more
trying to defend ourselves from the Russians. It was their strength and
courage that broke the will of the Kremlin leaders. They decided that
they could not stand up to this kind of resistance among the people of
the world. So we owe them a lot. They are still suffering. This pipeline
will help them, if we can ever get it built. But in the meantime, we owe
it to them to help try to bring peace to Afghanistan. The rest of Central
Asia depends on it. Thank you very much.* (my emphasis)

End

Nobody will argue that bringing peace to the Afghan people is something
that ought to be done. But bombing their country into the stone age in an effort to capture Osama bin Laden, whether he was significantly involved in the
commandeering of the four airliners or not, seems somewhat odd. Moreover,
if one of the real political objectives is removal of the ruling Taliban party
from power, to replace it with another regime which will act more favorably
towards the Western and American multinational oil companies, then this is
something else altogether. We know from Mr. Gee's testimony above that this
is without question what the policy objective is. We also know from the proposed legislation, *The Silk Road Strategy* bill. H.R. 2867, that the U.S. House of
Representatives has been studying the problem and has also made this policy
objective an issue. We know what Unocal, Exxon, Pennzoil and Amoco (and
at least seven other foreign firms) want, and the testimony of Mr. Maresca
couldn't be plainer: they want the United States government to do something
about the regime in Afghanistan which is holding up the construction of a
trillion dollar pipedream.

Now, there can be no doubt that Empire is about to achieve this global
dream in behalf of Corporatism. There can be no doubt that millions of Afghans could die; thousands of American troops; thousands of Americans once
again when America is hit with another wave of guerrilla warfare. For once
the slogan of the Left rings clear, "No blood for oil."

But who is going to hear this message stated correctly? Who even listens
to the progressive-left any longer. They have no credibility. Anyone that raises
this issue in the media will be hammered with "conspiracy theorist," silenced
and ridiculed. But the facts are plain to see. This is the policy objective. This
is the answer to the simple but utterly profound question..."Why is America
trying to overthrow the ruling Taliban"? To punish them because they chose
not to turn over bin Laden? That never made any sense to international law
scholars nor the international relations crowd. But Americans did not hear
that debate because it was only carried in the foreign press (Britain primarily).

And what was, once again, that question? By what rule of law does America have the right to overthrow any sovereign government in any sovereign
nation-state? And now we know why President Bush, like his father before
him, decides what the rule of law is to be. Empire makes the rules, Empire

makes the laws. The Taliban are in the way of Empire's successful prosecution of economic hegemony, also known as globalization. The global regime of economic interdependence has decided the fate of Afghanistan. One recent scholar who has written numerous books and articles on military theory and Operations Other than War (OOTW) had this to say:

> ...Clausewitz did succeed in anticipating the crux of the problem in military preparedness or in war waging: the difference between making war subordinate to "policy" and allowing war to be submerged in "politics," in present day terminology. In war properly conducted according to Clausewitz's theory...the military arm would take its marching orders from the political head. But the obligation was reciprocal: the political head would not misuse the military arm for non-military objectives, nor assign it objectives obviously beyond its reach. (*The Politics of Warfare*, Stephan J. Cimbala, 1997, p.206)

Cimbala makes the point well, going on to say what so many of us tend to forget, "Many twentieth century wars found that this desirable relationship between force and policy never obtained." Clearly former President Bush Sr. carried out a signal political objective during 1990-91, that this writer at the time warned would never stand without a violent reaction. Bush Senior putting a U.S. permanent military presence on Saudi soil, "the two Holy places," of Islam, created Osama bin Laden. Now his son, President Bush Jr., like monarchs of old, is having to deal with both bin Laden and yet another outside commercial political objective, whereby the "political head" shall "misuse the military arm." I will stand today and tomorrow, should Mr. Bush Jr., under the Senior's advice and counsel, achieve the second objective and remove the Taliban from power and insert a government more acceptable to the "government, lenders and the company," Unocal, to quote Mr. Maresca's testimony. This political objective too will not stand; one, two or ten years from whenever it is achieved (if that is even possible, which I doubt today) the pipelines will be blown up and yet another round of civil war in Afghanistan will begin. Why? because just like in Saudi Arabia, the people themselves will not see a nickel's benefit from building the pipeline nor from exploiting Afghanistan's vast oil and gas reserves. Not even jobs over the longer haul, just as in Saudi Arabia, foreign labor will be brought in which will work cheaper than the domestic workers who were told they would have the jobs and see the financial gain right along with the political elite the American military presence might put in power.

Another problem with these kinds of objectives is that the President and his administration never informs the public about these objectives and often it looks like a reversal of policy in the middle of hostilities. "Limited wars can be vulnerable to politicization if their war aims and military missions undergo impromptu changes for which military leaders and publics are not prepared."(Cimbala, p.211) The author used the Korean conflict as example but here I shall use the Persian Gulf war. President Bush Sr. did not inform the public that his political objective was to leave Saddam Hussein in power after his nation's infrastructure and military capability was destroyed; the public assumed Bush would march to Baghdad and remove "Hitler" from power. He failed to achieve the objective the public thought *was* the objective, so we still hear the nonsense today, "We should have finished the job." But at the time some few of us were trying to inform the public, General William Westmoreland specifically working with myself on this effort, that that was not the objective at all. First, leaving Hussein in power was to keep Iran from overrunning Kuwait next, and second, the American ground forces did not have enough ammunition per man to fight a longer firefight than three days to a week. Cimbala euphemistically notes this as a "lack of logistical support," but at least made the point upon reflection. OOTW, are looked at below.

Some may now have a clearer idea of what I have tried to define as Empire versus the scenario that President Bush painted...why they hate us? And this is why they, and there are many more of them than just the Muslims in this particular region. This is why America will be hit again. This is why this little war will go on for years, if not decades. The international urban guerrilla warfare Americans face can only be understood in the light of Empire. It is not Americans the Muslims hate, but what Americans have allowed their government to do world-wide to others. I assure you, others throughout the world are asking what gives America the right to decide who rules in any country? The answer will not be forthcoming, and without their grievances addressed, the war of attrition shall certainly escalate. "Obviously, use of overwhelming firepower of the kind brought to bear in the 1945 Berlin operation (Afghanistan now, ed.) would not be appropriate for OOTW against Third World urban terrorists or insurgents. One cannot combat an insurgency by blowing up the very people and their resources that one has been invited to save from anarchy." (Cimbala, p.164) On the back cover is the map which was attached to the Hearing before Congress which I discussed above. (Or you may view it at, www.kcandassociates.org)

What does the future hold for American troops fighting an international urban guerrilla war?

War of Attrition

*It is often said that guerrilla warfare is primitive.
This generalization is misleading and true
only in the technological sense.
Guerrilla war is not dependent for success on the
efficient operation of complex mechanical devices,
highly organized logistical systems, or the
accuracy of electronic computers.
It can be conducted in any terrain, in any climate,
in any weather; in swamps, in mountains, in fields.
Its basic element is man, and man is more complex than any
of his machines. He is endowed with intelligence,
emotions, and will.
Guerrilla warfare is therefore suffused with,
and reflects, man's admirable qualities as well as his
less pleasant ones.
While it is not always humane, it is human,
which is more than can be said
for the strategy of extinction.*
—SAMUEL B. GRIFFITH II

The quote above is from Mao Tse-tung's translation and introduction by Samuel B. Griffith II. This "nice little war" President George Bush has set off in full deployment of, with our nation's most "complex mechanical devices" whose success is "dependent...on their efficient operation" and our "highly organized logistical systems" will, I fear, be found somewhat wanting. In Griffith's opinion, guerrilla warfare is misunderstood in that it is, "in fact more sophisticated than nuclear war or atomic war or war as it was waged by conventional armies, navies and air forces." (Introduction, p.7, *On Guerrilla Warfare*).

Guerrilla warfare is a war of attrition against its designated enemy, a nation-state, any authority, whether King or Prince,...or Empire. It is clear from another perspective too: Every significant guerrilla war has been won by the guerrillas; every significant attempt to defeat a guerrilla army with conventional forces has met with failure; the guerrilla needs his war to be protracted if he is to win. Winning for the guerrilla is not in every case the defeat of a specific governing political regime, it is an attempt to achieve some level of redress of grievances and social reform; the bettering of the lot of the people themselves from the abject poverty this new age has wrought upon the many for the benefit of the few.

The pain inflicted upon the enemy is characterized by what today is misrepresented as terrorism. America-as-Empire will have to face this sooner or later, but face it we will. The many have lost more ground since the fall of communism, not gained. The few, the Western few that is, along with their chosen despots in regions like the Middle East, have been the sole gainers in the equation; we all know this to be true and only the most self-absorbed materialistic reactionary would claim it is the have-not's own fault. It is the non-western have-nots which are to blame because they have not adopted our hedonistic materialism in exchange for their chosen beliefs and practices?

> At $15 to $30 per barrel, oil makes the Middle East a rich place. Times are changing in Saudi Arabia. "Per capita income exceeded $28,000 in the early 80s, matching that of the United States. The population of native Saudis has doubled since, to 14 million, while per capita income has sunk below $7,000. Unemployment, once unheard of, is now at 18%. A lot of young Saudis are being forced into unskilled (menial) jobs that they once felt were beneath them. There are 6-7 million expatriates (foreigners) working in Saudi Arabia now. The Saudis are increasingly resentful that the oil perks of the past are drying up." Into this bin Laden was born and is now operating.

> (Source: August 2001 in the New York Times, by Neil MacFarquhar, NYT, as appeared in S.F. Chronicle A13, Aug. 26.)

And once again we get a better understanding of why so many have-nots are angered that the Saudi Princedom, American oil companies and the purely Western multinational Empire gain the vast wealth and riches while the people themselves live under western supported and endorsed (members in good standing with the WTO) tyrannies like Kuwait, Saudi Arabia, and the Peoples Republic of China and others. It is here where we find the reason why America and its Empire will face this war of attrition. And what of nations like Afghanistan?

> Any proposition of a particular community in isolation, defined in racial, religious, or regional terms, "delinked" from Empire, shielded from its powers by fixed boundaries, is destined to end up as a kind of ghetto. (*Empire*, p. 206)

*   *   *

A war of attrition has been touched upon in both chapters *On War: September 11, 2001* and *A Study in the Theory of International Urban Guerrilla Warfare*. Here I shall look at what a war of attrition will mean, not only to the United States and our few, very few indeed, western allies; primarily Great Britain and precariously that of Russia. I will, as well, look at what terrorism will mean in the future for both U.S. security at home, but abroad as well.

One thing that became very difficult at the time of the September 11 air attacks, was purely definitional. President Bush in a couple of appearances seemed to slip up and while describing our upcoming air campaign against Afghanistan, calling upon the American people to prepare for a long "guerrilla" war; immediately acting as though he did make a semantic slip, he corrected himself, repeatedly referring, once again, to terrorism as the target. I shall not go into the difference between a guerrilla and terrorist; the choice of targets of the one versus the other; the explicit differences between a war with guerrillas and one with terrorists: I covered that, I hope at least, in the chapters above. Here, as part of this chapter I wish to confine my arguments to (whatever one chooses to call this war and call whomever we are at war with) two larger issues. First, the why America has been targeted and the collection of groups involved in the coordinated attacks of late and in the future.

The Guerrilla Campaign

> *The term "enforceability" means that law implies being forced, hence, "the enforcement of law is always deemed legitimate even if at the same time it is recognized as unjust."*
>
> —JACQUES DERRIDA

The CIA and FBI announced, immediately before the air bombardment began against Afghanistan, in their threat assessment that America will be hit again putting it at 100 percent; not 80%, but 100%. The campaign against Empire has as resources an almost unlimited supply of soldiers available to it. The level of anger, dissatisfaction hardly states it well, is enormous. Those individuals which make up such organized groups that already exist are significant where known; those individuals prepared to join any one of these is even larger; larger still is the number of subjects angered throughout the world whose lives have been swallowed whole by Empire with no way out. Recruitment will be quite easy. The targets of Empire quite endless. It remains a real question whether American forces can sustain Operations Other than War, OOTW.

> Slums and shantytowns from Monrovia to Mogadishu provide ample opportunities for insurgency and entrapments for the conduct of OOTW. Classic insurgencies were rooted in the peasantry and based in the countryside, following the Maoist and Maoist-derived models based on the successful Chinese (and later, Vietnamese) experiences. Today's insurgents can follow migrations into the growing numbers of large cities in the Third World, many located within territorial states that are themselves unable to provide security for much of their urban population. Concealment of insurgents and terrorists within a large urban population is easily accomplished. (Cimbala, *The Politics of Warfare*, p..160)

Cimbala and those I quoted in previous chapters demonstrate the difficulty of fighting a guerrilla war, an OOTW in military jargon. "The tactics open to insurgents in the more urbanized environment of the developing world, and in some of the less well-protected cities of the developed world, include disruption or destruction of electrical power and other energy supplies, of communications, of water and sewage, most important, of security." (Ibid., p.161) Clearly the United States has demonstrated its vulnerability with many of the developed world's less well-protected cities: New York and Washington D.C.; and these are the better protected cities. "...cities have become relatively simple targets that yield high dividends for low cost" for urban guerrillas and insurgents. (Taw and Hoffman, *Operations Other than War*, p. 228)

Boeing Company, Microsoft Headquarters and Weyerhauser offices just in the Seattle area, come to mind in Washington State. U.S. Nuclear power facilities are vulnerable to a small Cessna loaded with only its JP-4 fuel. Every major U.S. corporation has facilities and headquarters which have already been targets of smaller bombings throughout the United States; throughout the world simply extends the area of operation for the guerrillas that much greater. They can hit anywhere, anytime, with total impunity.

GE's immense tower in New York City was overlooked, in my opinion, only for lack of hijackers. This one company, above all others, is a significant global operation while being America's longest standing number one defense contractor. No company represents the process of globalization supported by Empire more than GE. In banking, Chase Manhattan, after its mergers and recent acquisitions, represents the private monetary hegemony of Empire like no other. Targets such as these are more numerous throughout the world than military bases and embassies combined. Any one company could be selected by a coordinated and sustained attack by guerrillas on every nation-state's soil until the company faced complete ruin. The process repeated endlessly over time.

> Rather than thinking of the struggles as relating to one another like links in a chain, it might be better to conceive them as communicating like a virus that modulates its form to find in each context an adequate host. (*Empire*, pp.51)

The Global Recession

The recession the world markets are facing is already here. The United States Stock Exchange and NASDAQ are now just simple indicators of what is coming world-wide. Interest rates are the lowest since the days of JFK and the money supply is cranked up to horrific levels. President Bush spends a few of hundred million dollars to send aid, uneatable food stuffs, to the refugees in Afghanistan, which they will rarely receive as the borders are closed or corrupted from all directions and Pakistan and Iranian troops will confiscate the stuff and drive back the refugees at gun point. All the while, that which does get through, the Afghans often destroy, fearing it is poisoned as the Soviets had done in the past. All the while Mr. Bush will have to spend, not 100 billions of dollars, but $500 billion if he even hopes to stave off the corporate crashes coming. Billions for corporate America, a few million for the innocent civilians we have turned out homeless once again in a bombing campaign which will bear little results.

I say little results because we are bombing a country already in the stone age. What more can they really effect? We are bombing bombed out cities and sending cruise missiles to strike at the sand and hillsides where nothing but lizards live. What will Bush accomplish? Nothing more than call-up new recruits from the world's Muslim populations and turn even more significant others into guerrillas the world over. More western (American) attacks=more guerrillas. More attacks=greater recessionary forces.

This is what a war of attrition is about. Attacking the infrastructure of Empire will, incidentally, devastate the U.S. economy as well as the world's. A recent look at the stock market found that 4,600 U.S. corporation's stock values went below $1 a share; the SEC had to revise their rule (nothing below $1 dollar) to allow these companies to remain listed. Companies like Cisco went from $68 a share to $11; further drops are to be anticipated. Most analysts were waiting for some kind of burn-off of the speculative bubble the American exchange had witnessed for a decade. Nothing burns-off speculation like a protracted war against an enemy that cannot be defeated. And no true guerrilla army has ever been eliminated by conventional forces without redress of grievances. And I do not believe a nation-state like this American state has the courage to even tell its subjects that this war of attrition is about the American-led Empire; they will continue to misinform (disinform) the public that it is radical Islamic fanatics alone we are dealing with. But the truth can never be concealed forever, not even for long.

Every lesser terrorist group will escalate their personal wars with their chosen enemies under such a global conflict, spreading ever more fear and unrest, more areas of operations to contain, more troops deployed here and there. This alone will undermine the American-led coalition as it withers away globally to protect its own domestically.

Gold has been touted by every analyst of late as the only safe place to protect one's wealth. I would not bet on such an outcome as the FDR confiscation came for precisely this reason. Individuals are not going to be allowed, especially middle- and lower middle-class Americans, to prosper during a global crises; to prop-up the global corporate structure is going to be the quiet (behind closed doors) and loud (within the beltway) clarion call to arms that will really be our day of infamy.

Should Saudi Arabia become embroiled in revolution along with Kuwait, or worse, a joint attack on each by Iran and Iraq, can the United States defend the Gulf region while prosecuting campaigns against Iraq, Afghanistan and then likely Syria and Libya? Nobody believes such a global campaign is doable and the British seem to be the only ones saying they will stay on board with Mr. Bush if this campaign enlarges to such dimensions.

Wall Street is bracing for this year 2002, and for as long as the guerrilla campaign lasts, for unprecedented corporate collapses in all industries, Enron just the beginning; takeovers by the largest firms, already bloated from two decades of mergers and acquisitions, will be the outcome. Further market share will slip into the hands of the largest monopolies and further centralization of every industry that matters will grow. The true beneficiaries of Empire will continue to benefit as the federal government transfers, shifts, billions of taxpayers dollars to the largest firms and selected industries; the American taxpayer and consumer shall once again be squeezed like a soggy lemon.

Unemployment will accelerate in the United States as well. Of this there can be no doubt. The largest corporations will lay off millions before the end of this year 2002 to add to the estimated 1.5 million new layoffs. And should this war go protracted which is what everyone now believes, the layoffs shall certainly continue for the foreseeable future. It is this writer's informed opinion that Bush & Company will defend the Empire regardless of how many American lives or jobs would be lost. The attempt at Empire preserves that which belongs to Empire; cannon fodder will not be the only cost; mall fodder is about to be counted amongst the casualties.

The idea which some self-interested self-important materialists have put forward in the media (I even received an e-mail to this affect) has been to "shop" our way out of this crisis. Buy American made products to help America? Can anybody still be this naive? Certainly not the CEO I received the e-mail from. There are no longer any significant made-in-America products. If Americans bothered themselves enough to stay informed they would have seen the news article in the Guardian the week before Bush launched. American flag orders were backed-up solid and hundreds of workers were being hired in one of the few growth industries due directly to this crisis; the flags are made in Red China of course.

Let us face reality. Many of America's largest firms and not so large, will no longer be working for their stockholders; they will be working for and taking instructions from their bank managers; the real owners of each firm will surface, willy-nilly, and make every significant survival decision; your bright little broker will be talking in his hat about investment opportunities as nobody will be able to guess what happens next.

Those greedy, and have never done without, subjects of the realm, will try to stock-up on silly things like toilet paper and bottled water; the American militia members will be scalping MREs like Madonna concert tickets. That would be *Meals, Ready-to-Eat,* for those hundreds of millions of Americans who have never served in their country's military over these past thirty-years that America has not fought in a real war. But that too could change if Bush decides American *mall fodder* must of necessity become *cannon fodder,* and we see selective service once again draft Wayne's World to occupy territories the Empire must hold if the Empire is to hold. One wonders just how many feminists will trade in their Big-Bar-Hair for the military buzz; trade-in their shopping bags for duffle-bags?

Oh yes, this could be a time of reckoning for all those American males whose sole purpose in life is "to rock," or be part of "a wave" over some insignificant football game. They could become part of a wave; in military jargon that would be a wave assault on guerrillas or the reverse; like Vietnam's Hamburger Hill, where my old Division, the 101st, lost thousands trying to take a hill nobody wanted or needed.

One good thing to maybe come out of this little campaign, but only if it lasts long term, then the good thing would worsen into pathology: the great American strut, the arrogant, can-do American attitude, that smug and unquestioned superiority to the rest of the world's people, might just get wiped off their faces; a little much-needed humility. But then, maybe not.

I fully realize these last several paragraphs were hard for some to swallow. But if America is to grow-up, and I have repeatedly stated in interviews that this is adult stuff, it needs to happen soon. President Bush's frowning and Tony Blair's sword rattling will only make things worse for those who must carry the war to the enemy. They hate us enough for being the weight, the power, the military might behind the Empire. We do not need to be seen as even more arrogant and self-righteous than we are already seen to be the world over.

The Other War of Attrition

Peace has become the miserable condition
of survival, the extreme urgency
of escaping death.

—HARDT AND NEGRI

My cherished idea is a solution for the social problem,
i.e., in order to save the 40,000,000 inhabitants
of the United Kingdom from bloody civil war,
we colonial statesmen must acquire new lands to settle
the surplus population, to provide new markets
for the goods produced by them in factories and the mines.
The Empire,
as I have always said,
is a bread and butter question.
If you want to avoid civil war,
you must become imperialists.

—CECIL RHODES

The other war, should this war go protracted as Bush seems intent on doing, will be that war at home. The guerrilla fights for change, social reform in his own land, to get the Empire out of his own land, to make those seen as the cause for their people's suffering to suffer as well. If the war were against a nation-state, a sovereign of whatever kind, republic, monarchy, democracy or dictatorship (as each can be as repressive as the others), the other war would be to see that the people within the regime rise up and overthrow it, if their grievances are never addressed. When the barbarians are at the gates of Empire, and they are, they would not mind seeing the regime most responsible fall, but that cannot be the goal; the real strategic outcome is not the fall of the United States of America; nobody believes the enemy, whatever we find ourselves calling them, and it certainly is not Osama bin Laden alone, envisions such an outcome.

No, the real objectives here, in my humble opinion, are to get the Empire off the backs of the people in those parts of the world where these guerrilla armies shall certainly continue to grow and flourish with the full support of their people. The only question remains, how long will our own elite defend the Empire at the expense of the American people, who by and large, also see so little benefit from its global reach. The social and societal disruption, the continued loss of life, continued loss of living standards, continued loss of income, jobs lost, companies failing, and taxation taking its toll in the future, civil liberties vanishing, all spell disaster for the Empire itself.

The billions of dollars President Bush has already earmarked for corporate bailouts will be paid for through inflation and taxation; the people always pay "in blood and coin." During the protracted Vietnam war the market was flat until two years after it ended. Without the continued productivity of the war, recession soon struck while interest rates went through the roof to 21-1/2 % to stave off the inflationary spike caused by the enormous deficit spending during and immediately after that little war (which most analysts today agree was closer to 25% per year). The cycles of downturns for the next fifteen years was horrendous if one was in business at the time. If one has a memory. Does everyone recall the wage and price controls and the oil shock? These are mere cause and effect and they will always appear.

There will be other attacks on America as sure as Mr. Bush prosecutes this war. The effect on the culture may be debatable in extent and duration, but that is all. In the long haul, maybe all this will make Americans of this land a better folk. We have now, for the first time in our checkered history faced an enemy on our own soil; the enemy breeched our protected air space; they can and will do it again. Americans, it is my estimation alone, will give up all their important liberties in exchange for a misleading and impossible security. There is no such thing in the real world called security; the whole world already knows this and most have little freedom today for that vacuous exchange already given into. But Americans do not read. They do not think about these troubles; they refuse to stop shopping and having fun. This is their life, their life must be perfect. This alone may be our greatest weakness in the face of an enemy who knows only too well that there is no security, no real fun in the real world, no perfect world. American's are really going to have very many bad-hair-days.

Addendum (October 16, 2001)

In an article by Adele Simmons, senior associate at the Center for International Studies, University of Chicago, to the Chicago Times (in Sept., but pre-Sept. 11, 2001) titled "U.S. : Make the World Go Away" suggests the U.S. "Exceptionalism" policy means "Rules do not apply to us." The U.S. under Mr. Bush Jr., and only 200 days into his administration, pulled out of the following international agreements:

Kyoto Protocol [U.S. pulled out. The solution at the Bonn meeting was that the Europeans offered solutions that saved the treaty. They were leaders.],

1975 Biological Weapons Convention;

Comprehensive Test Ban Treaty;

Land Mine Treaty;

1998 Rome Statute (U.S. position weakened standing of International court);

Convention on Rights of Child (Clinton Adm. did not ratify either);

Vienna Convention on Consular Rights; Anti-Ballistic Treaty;

Illicit Trade in Small Arms (Conference).

One interpretation of recent events (Sept. 11-pre.) is that the U.S.'s withdrawal from the treaties indicated to our enemies that we were alone and isolated. This is typically when predators attack. Another interpretation is that we were seen to be too proud in our defiance of world law, and so our enemies attacked.

(I would like to thank Professor Greg P. Smestad, Ph.D. Associate Editor of Solar Energy Materials and Solar Cells, and Professor of Environmental Policy Studies at the Monterey Institute of International Studies, for the above information)

CHAPTER SIX

National Treatment and
The World Trade Organization

*The truth of the political world
is what it is, apart from all opinion.
Such is the primary conviction of
an honest mind...*

—GEORGE SANTAYANA

*The internal "enemy," however,
the true "heretic" is more dangerous
than the avowed enemy or apostate.
A heretic transubstantiates the basics of the
official ideas. He must be better educated, more
devoted to his cause, more original and creative than
his antagonists. He attacks the deeply hidden
life-lines of the establishment,
he strikes at the vital nerve centers
of ossification.*

—MIECZYSLAW MANELI

NATIONAL TREATMENT

WHENEVER WE SPEAK TO THE ISSUES of world trade and world finance, we are speaking of **National Treatment** as defined within every International Governing Organization (IGO). National Treatment is the cornerstone of every *Agreement*. National Treatment is the very foundation of the World Trade Organization (WTO) and National Treatment was the centerpiece of the former Multilateral Agreement on Investment (MAI).

When we discover the definition of National Treatment in legal terminology within these agreements we find the following:

> Each Contracting Party (each Nation-State) shall accord to investors of another Contracting Party and to their investments, treatment no less favorable than the treatment it accords to its own investors and their investments with respect to the establishment, acquisition, expansion, operation, management, maintenance, use, enjoyment, and sale or other disposition of investments.

Definitions include language that specifically accords investors:... *the better of the treatment*, whichever is the more favorable to those investors or investments. Now this is crucial to any understanding of these agreements like the General Agreement on Tariffs and Trade (GATT), which is now the WTO, and any MAI type agreement.

Further understanding as to what is defined as investor itself, is of some importance: This definition includes the obvious... the natural person, the flesh and blood person that might invest in some country that is a signatory to these agreements and international bodies. But it also includes the following:

> ...a legal person or any other entity constituted or organized under the applicable law of a Contracting Party, whether or not for profit, (I repeat, whether or not for Profit), and whether private or government owned or controlled, and includes a corporation, a trust, partnership, sole proprietorship, joint venture, association or organization.

I am not going to focus on the further implications covering where these investors might invest in each of the nation-state's, or Contracting Party's, territory, land, internal waters etc., ... as we get the picture: wherever and whatever they choose to invest in, is the point.

They may buy public utilities, media outlets, technology firms, and automobile manufacturers. All they need is their *paperwork* in order. For those bored with this most important element of these agreements and their consequences I shall say it in plain English: The *Ford Motor Company* shall be treated as a full citizen of each of the 130 nations it invests in, with all the often hard fought rights and hard fought privileges of each natural person of that country. The paper person of *Ford Motor Company* becomes the operative flesh and blood citizen of any country it invests in. The paper person of any tax-exempt, non-governmental organization like, say, the *Ford Foundation*, becomes the operative flesh and blood citizen of any country it operates in.

The Paper Person is treated "the better" or most favored, wherever National Treatment is defined within the respective agreements.

Corporatism and the Corporate State never implied Democracy. The corporations, whether for profit, like *Ford,* or not for profit, like *Ford,* becomes the only true global citizens. And *Ford,* the former, and *Ford* the latter, become the true sovereigns.

This sovereignty and let us be clear here ...this power, and this is about power, exceeds even the expectations of Henry Ford himself. When, of the 100 largest economies of the world, 51 are corporations, we all must see the importance of this transformation. When, 45 percent of all global trade is intra-firm trade, between *Ford of Detroit* and *Ford of Bonn,* not between countries at all, the consequences are clear.

This is not about trade between countries as is so often thought when National Treatment is treated in the media, if it is treated at all. National Treatment in these agreements is about one thing ...one thing, Power, and therefore sovereignty. Just as progress has always been about one thing ...one thing, Progress for whom?

China and PNTR

A brief historical look back at the process by which China gained accession into the WTO might prove useful. One must be dismayed by what has gone on in this country, in the media, in the House of Representatives, regarding this most fundamental transformation of our own country and its sovereign people and its sovereign representatives. Congress is not authorized to delegate these powers to the WTO, and rest assured, PNTR's passage under H.R. 4444, (Permanent Normal Trade Relations) in behalf of China (and Ford), was always the necessary step to bringing China into the WTO's Protocol of Accession, with full standing in world trade. Even while it had, at the time of this writing during 2000, not been passed in the Senate under S-2277, the Clinton Administration's negotiators were pressing for China's accession into the world body before the end of the year 2000; ignoring the Senate vote altogether and granting China accession may not be entirely illegal but once again, under our tattered Constitution only the Congress may negotiate trade with foreign nations. By the end of 2001, with both Houses frozen under Bush's glare, China was afforded accession.

China receives National Treatment just like Ford. China's publicly owned or controlled entities become American citizens in America just like Ford shall become a Chinese citizen in China. Both become sovereign global citizens over and above the less well treated citizens of each other's nations. Now that China gained its Protocol of Accession to the World Trade Organization, it can easily soften or ignore the provisions as the WTO body itself and has yet to agree to any such additional encumbrances. In fact, the terminology throughout the text of H.R. 4444 was this: WTO Members this, WTO members that ...wherever there exists each and every dispute.

A quote from the text:
Under **TITLE IV**, Subtitle A, Review of Membership of the People's Republic of China in the WTO...under **Sec. 401**. REVIEW WITHIN THE WTO - It shall be the objective of the United States to obtain as part of the Protocol of Accession of the People's Republic of China to the WTO, an annual review within the WTO of the compliance by the PRC with its terms of accession to the TWO. (This appeared in both H.R. 4444 & S-2277)

Everywhere in the media, at the time then, after the vote, we read that what China was really interested in is importing U.S. investment, not U.S. goods. And of course we knew this going all the way back to the early 1990s when China was the leading borrower at the World Bank during 1992 and 1993 and other years as well. The United States has, since 1992, been the number three or four supplier of Foreign Direct Investment in China from the private sector, behind Hong Kong, Taiwan and Japan.

In a recent issue of *The National Interest* Zbigniew Brezinski would go even further: Knowing H.R. 4444 passed even before the vote was in, (the journal had already gone to press) Brzezinski was even then calling for China to be brought into the G-8 (formerly the G-7 until Russia gained a place) making it the G-9. After admitting that "the forum is no longer a forum for democracies nor a conclave of the most advanced economies," since the inclusion of Russia,. quoting Brezinski further, then a

> Similar political expediency, therefore, should dictate the inclusion of the economically much more dynamic China, with the G-9 thereby becoming a more genuine global power forum. That would propitiate China's quest for status while also enhancing its stake in the emerging global system.

Corporatism and especially global corporatism never implied democracy, as I have stated often. And here we have it made clear. And let us make this clear to those 237 China lobbyists that voted for H.R. 4444 - the WT0 and the G-9 are about power not freedom, power not democracy, power not trade. The WTO will clearly enhance the power of some at the risk of others. U.S. private banks and all lending institutions will gain further access to the lucrative investment opportunities. The multinational corporations shall gain immensely as shall their stockholders.

National Treatment and Ralph Nader's Endorsement

We must draw further attention to the notion of National Treatment for the multinational corporations, which, as I shall point out below, even Ralph Nader and Lori Wallach of *Public Citizen* unwisely and irresponsibly defend. Only by denying National Treatment to these same corporations, which would de-fang this supposedly *evil menace*, in Nader's and Wallach's view, could Wallach and Nader effectively put forward any proper argument against Corporatism and its global base, the WTO. What of the American citizen? the American worker? From the *U.S. News and World Report*, which also declared victory before the votes were cast (even to correctly predicting the Ayes at 237, though they missed the nays by only four), and bears repeating: "China is more interested in importing U.S. investment, not U.S. goods."

Investment in China, and there is more Foreign Direct Investment (FDI) going to China now than anywhere in the world, which may go somewhat to explain their 70 billion dollar trade surplus with the United States, and explain their booming economy while not even one percentage point can point to gains for American workers. It does not take a genius to understand what happens when three quarters of a billion (of the 1.3 billion population) brand new fresh faced young Chinese enter the international labor pool, and they will not be working at AFL/CIO wage levels Mr. Sweeney, but ordered to work. They will work in industries in China, financed by western investment in China, producing products in China, manufacturing American multinational corporation's products in China; so Chinese enterprises, joint ventured with American firms, can sell what they made to Americans.

Their labor pool is easily twice the size of the entire United States' population. That is if we add our aging population and our wee toddlers, who are today begging Grandpeasants to buy them stuffed animals made in China.

Nader and Wallach: The Artful Deceit

And where were the protests against Permanent Normal Trade Relations with China? Where was the protest that passing nondiscriminatory status meant nothing whatsoever unless and until China is granted its Protocol of Accession into the WTO? There was none because nobody actually read the infamous H.R. 4444. Not even *the Avant Guard* of the progressive-left that protested the WTO in Seattle and Washington D.C.

When Ralph Nader's band leader Lori Wallach of *Public Citizen* was interviewed by the journal *Foreign Policy* she was asked this question: "You want to prevent China from joining the WTO"? - Her answer?

No. Basically, our goal is to prevent the granting by the United States of permanent most-favored-nation trading status to China.

So Nader and Wallach want China in the WTO but they do not want China to receive permanent nondiscriminatory trade status. Their argument is so convoluted it is no wonder Nader & Co. disappeared during the last few weeks before the vote, ending any lobbying efforts against H.R. 4444. They could not oppose PNTR without interfering with China's guaranteed accession into the WTO, the *quid pro quo* of H.R. 4444. It seems Nader may have read the bill after all, but failed to get Wallach a copy before her self-aggrandizing ambitious interview with *Foreign Policy*. I say that because Nader's other group *Global Trade Watch* and its Deputy Director, Michael Dolan, opposed House Joint Resolution 90, which would have withdrawn America from the World Trade Organization. He suggested in an E-mail that the sponsors of HJRes. 90 were part of a *conspiracy orchestrated by the corporate WTO Killers* (his words not mine). Dolan stated he wouldn't support HJRes 90 and the *red-herring strawman ambush* by the *WTO-Killers!* (his words not mine). Although these progressives opposed the WTO in street protests, gaining for themselves much notoriety and funding from *the Ford Foundation*, which supports the WTO, they want China in the WTO: they did not want permanent trade status for China but opposed opposing WTO status which would **only** then grant China permanent trade status? People this confused should really be ignored.

During the interview with Wallach in *Foreign Policy* she was asked about her vision, and I use the word very reluctantly, of an alternative trade regime, she oddly noted this:

> I would keep the notion of National Treatment, the notion of competition between countries without discrimination based on where something is made, but I would eliminate all these subjective decisions that have been patched onto the trade system.

There is, of course, nothing more subjective than National Treatment. Here we find the country's main progressives, Nader, Wallach and *Public Citizen*, endorsing the very thing they have, for years, claimed they are opposed to — the corporations becoming ever more powerful, in the face of declining democratic institutions? But it really is not such a strange set of bedfellows when one understands that not only *Ford Motor Company* gains global sovereignty, but *The Ford Foundation* as well. And the *Ford Foundation* is the non-governmental organization (NGO) that funded the NGO *Public Citizen* in their protests against the WTO in Seattle and elsewhere. Indeed, Wallach admits this during the interview while endorsing National Treatment. So with some clarity of vision one finds *Ford, Ford and Public Citizen* all being granted National Treatment, that is to say, Nader, Wallach and Henry Ford III all become the global sovereigns right along with GE and ATT etc., and who could refuse such an offer as that? Intoxicated with her own rhetoric and being a smart, sassy, and strong progressive woman, who better to reign as global sovereign.

*   *   *

House Joint Resolution 90 was at the time something we must reconsider now more than ever. We need hearings, not red-herrings, now more than ever; granted, HJRes 90 failed, and H.R. 4444 was passed, as did S-2277; it is never too late to rewrite badly written unconstitutional law. It is never too late...but I may be wrong.

Because...it couldn't be clearer what they voted for in the House of Representatives. We have already voted for an annual review of the status of China in the WTO with that vote ...and *we did this with China not even in the WTO at that time.* Clearly the fix was in for China over at the WTO and 237 Representatives, 164 Republicans and 73 Democrats, voted for precisely that. They became merely lobbyists for China.

After the vote on Permanent Normal Trade Relations (PNTR) was cast, articles appeared in the *Wall Street Journal, U.S. News & World Report, The National Interest*, etc., each author proclaiming the victory and pointing out the alleged losers and probable winners. Admitting that the trade negotiations (referred to as *the deal*) were in fact worked out at the World Trade Organization rather than via the customary procedures (Trade Representatives, State, Congress and Commerce Departments, etc.), it is clear now that PNTR was the necessary *deal* for getting China into the world body. Representatives attached additional measures and pork before they would consider its passage; this was not included in the actual negotiations over China's role, as Congress had no say in those negotiations.

The Arguments about Sovereignty

At the time PNTR was being voted on there were numerous arguments in the media about sovereignty of the nation-state. I shall leave these in this chapter for the historical record, as the fact is, they will be made again when further trade deals are in the offing. In the articles that appeared at the time most of the authors utilized sources to argue that the state was not through as a political unit, that the state was stronger than ever, that the nation-state remains the true and only arbiter of interdependence and the process known as globalization. Kenneth N. Waltz clearly believes that the state remains the process, and that globalization is merely the newest version of procedures long understood in International Relations Theory. Waltz quotes sources I have used, but in an extremely abbreviated form, in my opinion, not just to make his case, but to eliminate these sources from our discourse, as they no longer are valid in his view.

The sources he quotes at length to argue his case are those of authors that we might consider, say, of the popular genre, rather than those scholars arguing the real issue itself. That issue being, is sovereignty an issue? is sovereignty being diffused over International Governing Organizations (IGOs)? Is sovereignty of the nation-state slipping away? Nobody of merit argues sovereignty of the nation-state has not been affected at all, it has, but argue instead that it is not as relevant as before or during the Cold War; after the Cold War everything has changed, so we are calmly informed.

To some degree that is my argument. Everything has changed except the disingenuousness of the dialectic on domestic and foreign affairs. To argue *only* whether the state is losing sovereignty is to miss the mark: to argue *only* whether the state remains the most powerful institutional body that actually decides important issues, including trade issues, misses the mark; to argue that globalization is not as comprehensive, not as encompassing, not as threatening to state sovereignty, well, misses the mark. We know national sovereignty is being diffused over to, into, international bodies; NATO, the United Nations and the World Bank may be the better examples, especially where security issues are in the forefront, or bailouts and humanitarian aid. But the application of those examples' terminology to trade issues is blatantly erroneous. Using the language of security issues to argue economic globalization and interdependence muddies the waters, not distills.

Quoting excessively from Thomas Friedman's book *The Lexus and the Olive Tree,* Kenneth N. Waltz in the Spring 2000 issue of *The National Interest,* first points out Friedman's argument then demolishes it: to barely paraphrase - The herd (of investors) do not threaten the state by simply moving assets around the globe electronically, as states, and particularly the United States, intervene often to bailout countries devastated by such global actors. Good argument. But even though I would argue the same, because it remains an accurate depiction of his closed argument, I would stress something else subsequently ignored.

Here is my problem: If one argues the sovereignty issue one is decried as a protectionist of the Pat Buchanan ilk, and ugh! we don't want that slung upon our special suit: or one is appropriately scuttled for being a left-protectionist like the *new Nader* and ugh! that cannot be easily washed off either. Both of these points were elaborated upon in the same issue of *The National Interest* by Lawrence Kaplan. Almost everyone follows these arguments in this fashion.

Here is my point: Globalization and interdependence are not the same thing except in security matters, not trade matters. No amount of interdependence between nations, between nation's trading with each other, creates any loss of sovereignty. Nations have always been interdependent, and arguably as interdependent as ever in the past. Interdependence in trade does not threaten sovereignty. Only when the regime of trade and interdependence creates a new kind of authority can sovereignty be considered threatened. Michael Williams, an International Relations theorist, regards globalization as being distinct in its effects from those of interdependence or integration, in that

> ...increased transactions will not in themselves pose a problem
> to sovereignty unless it can be demonstrated that new authority
> patterns have emerged or are nascent in this process.

Today nobody can argue that the WTO does not create a new authority pattern for the United States and the Congress of the United States, whose authority over trade matters is, or was at the time, still reserved to Congress alone. A power argued by some, including the Supreme Court, that cannot be allocated or discharged by Congress to some other body or authority.

Clearly the WTO hashed-out the deal on PNTR and Congress was then allowed to vote on the matter. But Congress did not negotiate the deal, did not author the deal, did nothing except vote on the deal. And their vote for permanent trade relations did not go into effect, as I have pointed out before, until China was granted accession into the world Trade Organization. Let me give another quote.

> Globalization is not simply about the diminution of sovereignty in the sense of the state's ability to manage its own affairs. More fundamentally, it is about the reconstitution of sovereignty 'pari passu' with reshaping of the state itself.

In the above quote Ian Clark in his new book *Globalization and International Relations Theory*, Oxford University Press, makes his point further regarding what is happening to state sovereignty, as it is "the shadow-play of the transformations that the state is currently undergoing." Clark goes on suggesting a triangular interrelationship between the concepts of sovereignty, statehood and globalization, all three, "of necessity, are synchronized in their movements."

Stephan Krasner in the volume *International Rules* goes into more detail by explaining global regimes as functional attributes of world order: environmental regimes, financial regimes and of course trade regimes.

> In a world of sovereign states the basic function of regimes is to coordinate state behavior to achieve desired outcomes in particular issue-areas .... If, as many have argued, there is a general movement toward a world of complex interdependence then the number of areas in which regimes can matter is growing.

But we are not here speaking of changes within an existing regime whereby elected representatives of free people make adjustments to new technologies, new ideas and further the betterment of their people: the first duty of elected representatives is to look out for their constituency. The World Trade Organization does not represent changes within the existing regime but an entirely new regime. It has assumed an unprecedented degree of American sovereignty over the economic regime of the nation and the world. Then who are the sovereigns? Is it the people, the *nation* in nation-state? I do not believe so. I would argue that who governs, rules: who negotiates, rules: who decides, rules: who negotiates, decides and rules, is therefore sovereign. And the people of America and their elected representatives do not rule nor govern at the WTO but corporate diplomats (a word decidedly oxymoronic). I have included this section below for history; those not interested may, of course, skip over it.

The History of the Senate Vote on Permanent Normal Trade Relations with China
S-2277

According to the Bureau of National Affairs *WTO Reporter*, French President Jacques Chirac said October 23, 2000 that nearly all the remaining issues keeping China from entering the World Trade Organization during that year had been ironed out. Chirac stated, "We do feel that accession could take place before the end of this year." Chirac was also the president of the European Union. Also reported was the date of November 2, 2000 for the latest round of negotiations with China and the WTO. This working party session was hopeful all issues could be resolved and China granted permanent status as a full member of that world body. This was taking place at the request of the Clinton Administration of the United States, even though the U.S. Senate had as yet not voted on S-2277, which would grant Permanent Normal Trade Relations (PNTR) with that country. Clearly the American people had no say; the House voted in favor of H.R. 4444, granting PNTR to China, while the majority of Americans were opposed. Now without the Senate vote in place the Administration had moved ahead with pressing for China's accession in the WTO which would grant the same thing without the Senate vote, a vote which would and did come, but come after the fact, making the vote moot, the issue settled.

The House vote on Permanent Normal Trade Relations with China passed the House of Representatives by a wide majority. Yet 197 members voted against the measure. Far more than anyone expected. Those members that voted against the measure were not against trading with China, were not against improved relations with China, and nobody wants to see China not become more democratic, free, prosperous and become a true member of the world community of nations. Congressman Jack Metcalf stated at the time "I along with the others that voted with me on this were and are in favor of trade, we never proposed sanctions and tariffs, never proposed restrictions and protectionism. I argued that regulating trade with foreign nations falls clearly under the enumerated powers of Congress; I argued then, and still, that bi-lateral negotiations are the way to deal with each nation. I argued against delegating these most important powers, which should never be delegated, to some international governing organization such as the World Trade Organization, an organization which clearly governs. Which clearly governs. But governs without the legitimacy granted this Congress by our unique Constitution." (Stated with the author on the Jim Bohannon Show, May, 2000)

Many that voted on H.R. 4444, the House version of S.2277, never bothered to read nor fully understood the bill. Had they read it they could have made different arguments for and against it. The Senators faced the same conundrum. Even while voting for permanent relations, they were voting for non-discriminatory treatment; while voting for no annual review, they are voting for National Treatment; while voting to open up China's economy, they concede China already has full access to the US. The vote was about language and dates, about looking out for American citizens and American business here at home. This vote should not have been about, and only about, American multi-national, trans-national, global corporations, and what they want.

Look at the language Congressman Jack Metcalf used and understand why I left this in this chapter of the book. These points were his words:

· *Permanent Normal Trade Relations* are not even granted after your vote in favor of it until the date of accession into the World Trade Organization. Congress did not negotiate, that is to say, regulate, trade with this foreign nation - the WTO did. And only when China meets the WTO's standards of conduct, only when what the WTO wants is achieved, does your vote mean anything at all. A vote which may not even matter as the Administration has moved their schedule ahead for this November 2 with China's accession in any case, thus maybe before Congress even reconvenes. This is the quid pro quo of all time. America delegates another small piece of its once unique Constitution to another unelected governing group.

· *Non-discriminatory treatment* applies, not to China, not to the Chinese people, not the Chinese government. It means US corporations, many which no longer even see themselves as American, but some special mythical global citizenry. It means these corporations want to be treated with non-discrimination while opening facilities of their own on China's vast soil. And Chinese firms, public and private, shall be granted the same on our soil.

· *National Treatment*, the legal terminological cant that describes the above, is a two way street without annual Congressional review. Once China gains accession into the World Trade Organization, this Congress, and our unique Constitutional mandate to regulate foreign trade, is forever relinquished. The WTO allows China non-discriminatory status here in America. Not the Chinese Government you say? yes, that part of the Chinese governing body that represents state-owned, for profit enterprises. China's corporations, private and public, must be treated as equals with American citizens that own and operate private businesses. They shall be allowed to buy businesses, acquire businesses, merge with business, just as any American citizen can, with full citizenship legally approved. Not by Congress, but WTO approved. (Cong. Metcalf during House debates,and two interviews with this author, May- November, 2000)

True, Americans that own American companies may do the same in China under WTO guidelines. That would be presumably the Forty Industrials and the thirty largest high technology firms. Once again **Corporatism** gains its foothold in another targeted market. But this shall do little to help smaller-large American firms to compete with massive state-owned enterprises - both American-based and now Chinese.

These issues are about American citizens; about American's well-being; about all Americans that own and operate businesses and corporations here in America. This applies equally well to British, Belgium and French citizens. These decisions taken in Congress are not just meant to improve the well-being of those majestic monopolies that mitigate and manipulate each nation's sovereignty. We are making the world safe for Corporatism.

We seem to be able to only speak to these issues of trade under the legal language offered up to us in legislative legalese. We speak of fairness and level playing fields - for the monopoly multinationals; we speak of better products for the consumer - made by monopoly multinationals; we speak of gaining access to the vast Chinese consumers, 1.3 billion strong, but it is not some sentimental "Us" referred to, not citizens of any one country, but the same monopoly multinationals.

We stand by and witness the truth everyday. More and more products are made in China. More and an ever greater percentage of multinational's products are manufactured in China. More and more American jobs quietly slip away now to Indonesia, now to China. No, we cannot say it has *completely* happened yet — we said at the time "look, Alan Greenspan says we have nearly full employment." But we know who isn't counted, who remains permanently unemployed and we thus know what the future has in store for more workers working, when American multinationals finally get what they want in China. Boeing is ultimately headed for China for manufacturing.

That is the only reason the *workers* argument falls on deaf ears in both Houses of Congress. We can only hear what we want to hear. We have less vision in Congress than the homeless.

We need to become Earwitnesses; we need to hear what we cannot yet see; we need some little vision to see consequences that are constantly clouded by words, words, words.

CHAPTER SEVEN

Medieval Multinationals: Law Merchants and Corporate Governance

*When in the fascist and various authoritarian
states the persons of the "duce," "caudillo,"
"presidente," or a "maximus leader," are
surrounded by special protocol and
ceremony, when, they are
proclaimed "saviors," "brightest," and
"noblest"— that means that political
culture is in full retreat.*

—MIECZYSLAW MANELI

LAW MERCHANTS AND CORPORATE GOVERNANCE

THE GLOBAL MARKETPLACE. We hear a great deal about this these days, especially where the Internet is concerned and IT, information technology. This is all new and therefore all for the good. We never question any longer whether what is new is in fact better; never question, that because this new global regime seems new to us, that it is the collective we, that may be naive.

As the new year came upon us, during the year 2000, we had discovered many great and new things; growth and productivity was up; unemployment was down; wages, while not down, they were not up either. Stocks were up, except for the losers with each dramatic correction. And then we hear of the triumph of our system over the stodgy communist failure; we won—they lost. We still call this the post cold-war period, the end of the worst phase of contemporary history. And like the period immediately after World War Two, we collectively relaxed and enjoyed our new found prosperity. And we believed all was good because all was *new*. Then 2001 came along and everything above took a turn.

Not to sound alarms, but one really needs a more adult take on these things. A little less enthusiasm for this new world; a little more understanding of what is new in reality and not so new after all.

Here are few really new developments that we can agree on; they are new that is:

· Of the 100 largest economies in the world, America being the largest, 51 are now multinational corporations. You see that is new!

· 45 percent of all global trade is *intra-corporate trade*, that between Ford of Detroit and Ford of Bonn. And this is new.

· The United States government has ceased to submit so much as an enquiry into the fantastic state of mergers and acquisitions between enormous corporations and other, often just as enormous, corporations. Indeed, other than the rare and arbitrary Anti-Trust action, like Microsoft, we no longer care what firm monopolizes which industry. The *Fortune 500* is rapidly becoming the *Fortune 300*. Which goes some distance towards understanding the first *new* development — where 51 behemoth corporations are larger than all but 49 nation-states! And this is very new indeed.

· One more new development that really is not entirely new, but we are today at least entirely aware of it as citizens. Just about every member of every Administration's Cabinet, from Secretary of State, to Vice president; Labor and Treasury; Energy and Education; Defense and of course Commerce — are posts filled exclusively from the pool of elite corporate directors and CEOs. In the rare cases where undersecretaries are not drawn *from* the elite they are later, upon leaving government service, drawn to *Wall Street*.

These are just a few of the new things taking place globally and here at home in the US; whether these are good things? history shall certainly be our judge. Now I should speak to another new development that I am sure most of you think is indeed *new*. We have diffused United States and Britain's sovereignty over to, into, a fair number of multilateral agencies. The United Nations Security Council, OECD, the World Bank and the IMF; and the newest international governing organization, or IGO in IR lingo, or International Relations terminology, is the most important of all — the WTO. The World Trade Organization.

I am not a fan. I know that most readers think it is a good thing, the WTO, or not think about it at all; it shall, so the argument goes, bring peace and prosperity to all citizens in all nations where it now governs. Where it now governs. The WTO governs trade and trade relations between nations. Not the Congress of the United States; not the elected leaders of some 130 other nations; not the people of any nation which by all reason ought to remain sovereign.

But is this good because it is new? Now a history lesson is in order. The very concept we are seeing develop throughout the world where trade is concerned, is the privatization of law; the privatization of enforcement of nation-state law; the privatization of the legal means by which each nation might have looked out for its own citizen's well-being. And while this is not the way each of us has long understood the legal aspects of trade and commerce, both domestically and internationally, this is not new.

There have been roughly three periods whereby trade and commerce was regulated. Legal historians have identified these phases in evolution of trade law as follows:

1. The medieval phase from about the eleventh to sixteenth centuries, and
2. the middle period from about the seventeenth to nineteenth centuries, and
3. the third phase with the past twentieth century to date, the globgalization period.

I have already touched upon a few areas in above chapters which are considerably *new* in this present phase. And we could spend a great deal of time praising our success and exciting prospects, but I hesitate to add to the already abundant back-slapping going on in the halls of Congress and on television. If only we all felt as good about the future as Alan Greenspan and George Bush Jr. I would have little need for this reminder. They like all that they see. They like the Corporatism they embrace. They would like to be seen as responsible for all they look out and view throughout the world. And indeed, history may find them in part (along with Clinton and Bush-Sr.) responsible for the future.

But let me remind you of the second period mentioned above. It was the period dated from the seventeenth to nineteenth centuries; the Peace of Westphalia might ring a bell for IR scholars. But what we really saw in this period, was when the people threw off the yoke of oppression from monarchical rule. It was the beginning of enlightenment in all aspects of life; it was the dawning of the new age of freedom and democracy's great dream. It was, in short, the beginning of the modern era. I shall primarily look at only America's.

The people discovered their sovereignty; they elected their representatives; the elected representatives obeyed the people's Constitution; the people were free to trade and trade with anyone they so chose. As long as their trade was not a violation of other people's rights, both inalienable and codified; both positive and negative rights.

And how were the rights of each nation's citizens protected? For the first time in history when individuals traded with each other, or with companies or corporations, public or private, their rights were guarantied by the State. The State represented the people. A State, that is to say, the people elected, appointed and sought to place their grievances with. The State in *Nation*-State represented its people in Nation-*State*.

And the nation-state represented their people in claims against foreign individuals and companies; foreign trade meets state representatives. Also, those elected representatives could seek in behalf of its citizens, restitution and satisfaction through the people's courts. You do business with American citizens and you may face American justice in American courts. This was the new era of rapid industrialization and the defense of free enterprise. Competition replaced the ancient guilds and overlords of archaic monarchical injustices. No more arbitrary courts and inquisitional tribunals! No more Star Cambers! And with this, liberal internationalism was born.

Corporate Governance

Today we see all around us the dawning of the newest phase in liberal international trade relations. The new *Global Regime of Economic Interdependence*, as our own elite like to refer to it. And with this new global regime we find the evolution of the newest forms of managing this enormous international trade. We see, then, the budding growth on every stem of commerce between nations — the new multilateral governing bodies. The flower of the nation-state, its sovereignty that is, is said to be enhanced by each nation's participation in these new regimes of order and discipline. America has enhanced its national sovereignty by its very membership in the World Trade Organization, we are solemnly assured. Here are two authors, Abram Chayes and Antonia Handler Chayes, in their new book *The New Sovereignty*.

> Traditionally, sovereignty has signified the complete autonomy of the state to act as it chooses, without legal limitation by any superior entity. The state realized and expressed its sovereignty through independent action to achieve its goals. If sovereignty in such terms ever existed outside books on international law and international relations, however, it no longer has any real meaning.

It is arguable, from a purely academic view, that U.S. sovereignty, defined as in the above, never really existed; this is something I find empirically false and quite misleading. But we can leave this argument aside. Here is why the authors might have concluded the above before-hand, it helps make their preconceived conclusion seem more methodological:

> Our argument goes further. It is that, for all but a few self-isolated nations, sovereignty no longer consists in the freedom of states to act independently, in their self-interest, but in membership in reasonably good standing in the regimes that make up the substance of international life. To be a player, the state must submit to the pressures that international regulations impose.... When nations enter into an international agreement, therefore, they tend to alter their mutual expectations and actions over time in accordance with its terms. (Ibid.)

The authors spend considerable time making their argument, but their experience as international lawyers was admittedly in the regime of arms control, where I think their argument holds great weight. Why? Because it is in fact *States* that make up the regime negotiated and it is each *State's representatives* that in fact negotiate what the regime itself might decide is an enforceable decree. This makes fairly logical sense. But the authors go on, like so many in our government, to make the leap of logic, using the compliance regime of security issue's terminology, and apply it to the international trade regime.

It is this convolution of terms, language, wrapped into trade issues, that I fear shall one day get us all in very deep waters. Waters already very murky.

The argument is not all words. But the key words are these: *Dispute Settlement Regimes*. The mechanism of dispute settlement is a necessary vehicle for nation-states to implement in settling those areas in many agreements and treaties, that give rise to conflict. War avoidance can never be a bad thing. But let us look closely at what dispute settlement mechanisms really are when applied to the trade regime rather than the security regime. When applied to corporate governance within trade regimes.

The dispute settlement regime in each trade agreement now, and particularly at the new World Trade Organization, is nothing less than the

> ...adoption of international arbitration as the chosen method for resolving international commercial disputes. Today, private international trade disputes are resolved predominately through international arbitration, as opposed to adjudication in national courts of law. Indeed, arbitration has replaced adjudication as the norm for resolving international commercial disputes.

This, from *A. Claire Cutler* in a past and important issue of *Millennium*.

I am of course, as was Cutler, stating the obvious. We know this has been brought into place. But do remember who is facing arbitration rather than

adjudication in our domestic courts of law. It is not, as is often stated wrongly, America bringing an action in the dispute settlement regime against, say
Mexico. Mexico does not trade commercially with America. Mexico may buy
tanks and small arms from America, through our Pentagon programs, but
Mexico does not trade with America commercially, Ford trades with private
or public Mexican firms, and the reverse is true; although I should be remiss
in not noting again that some 45 percent of all international trade is between
Ford and Ford, GE and GE, etc. It is private firms seeking arbitration through
the WTO's dispute settlement regime under the shelter of a lost American
(and other country's as well) sovereignty. And it is the WTO that decides the
fate.

Why is this distinction so important? Because what we have done here,
besides delegating authority over the regulation of foreign trade to this private body of unelected officials, is take what was formerly public legal authority, public law, as administered via each legal court system, and placed it
into the private realm of Corporatism: Which is to say, *Corporate Governance*.
Corporations really like this idea of policing themselves without the messy
legal mechanisms of each nation's courts; in each nation's jurisdiction; within
each nation's sovereign right to protect their own citizens' rights from these
same corporations. One cannot help but notice, labor has no such private
means to address these same corporations, when they have a dispute they
might like settled. Let me let Cutler make the case for Corporate Governance.

> The use of private means to resolve disputes between commer-
> cial actors evokes images of medieval merchants who, traveling
> from market to market, 'carried their law, as it were, in the same
> consignment as their goods, and both law and goods remained
> in the places they traded and became part of the general stock
> of the country.' Medieval commercial disputes were settled by
> merchant juries who sat in courts of 'pie powder.' The law ap-
> plied was called the law merchant, lex mercatoria,...The law
> merchant evolved as a distinct and autonomous body of law
> regulating the activities of merchants who were granted signifi-
> cant immunities from local laws and regulations.

It can hardly be argued that this "striking resemblance" between the present dispute settlement agreements in our new trade regime and that of medieval practices is, well, beyond dispute. The boundary between the public
and the private spheres is shifting, as matters previously regarded as public
are today being delegated to private actors. This is how *David Kennedy* in the
Harvard International Law Journal put it:

> The regime of 'private international law' sustains trade rules
> about property and contract, mechanisms to stabilize jurisdic-
> tional conflicts while liberating private actors to choose forums,
> and ad hoc mechanisms of dispute resolution. The dominant

players are private traders, and to a far greater extent than even the most laissez-faire national system, they legislate the rules that govern their trade through contract.

They legislate the rules. The private corporations and their elite corporate diplomats make the rules that govern their own corporate activities and practices. This is no affair to be taken lightly. During the GATT accords and every other negotiated trade or investment regime in the international arena, there are the *Negotiating Groups* (made up of predominantly international lawyers and trade specialists drawn from the private sector); there are *Expert Groups* (made up of industry experts drawn from corporations' boards of directors and CEOs); there are *Advisory Groups* (drawn from the same corporations' private trade specialists). All this is mounted by the *Contracting Parties* to each agreement, made up of each nation's public officials, like trade representative (made up of each nation's talented specialists drawn from the corporations' private stock of former directors, trade experts and corporate lawyers).

A Zone of Irresponsibility

We have therefore seen international economic activity removed from the sphere of public accountability and even public scrutiny. The corporations that make up this trade regime, negotiated the trade regime, consulted the trade negotiations and are the regime *players* themselves, have insulated their commercial activities from challenge. *Stanley Hoffman* (hardly a leftist) in the journal *Foreign Policy,* regarding precisely this new distinction between the public/private legal realms, called this a creation of a *zone of irresponsibility.*

It is this zone of irresponsibility that ought to have concerned everyone during all these different negotiations; this zone of activity is where the public aspects of private activities are unregulated and unaccountable (except for those areas that come under dispute between one corporation and another, or between corporations and another nation-state). But of course, as I have just pointed out, the language of the dispute settlement mechanism, lifted from the compliance regime of arms control, is a creature of private Corporate Governance; the private corporate elite themselves: which effectively removes their private activities from public scrutiny. It, in fact, shields their private activities from public law. This can only succeed in further consolidating *Corporatism as an ideology.*

This so-called *Freedom of Contract* is

> ...a delegation by the state to individuals of the power to enter into binding contracts according to self-determined terms: private arbitration is regarded as a logical and necessary corollary of this power...

This quote is from author *Bernardo Cremades.* Private arbitration replaces public adjudication.

We are not witnessing the hegemony of the United States *per se;* we are not seeing the End of History; we are not waiting for the future New Order. And what has arrived upon the scene in international affairs, commercial trade relations and the global regime is the binding and consolidation of *Corporatism,* which is an ideology. And the process is *Corporate Governance.*

Corporatism rests sheltered in the private sector. Corporate Governance is thus seen as being rightfully removed from political jurisprudence. But the hegemonic ambitions of Corporatism's elite are clearly in the public sphere as this volume has begun to demonstrate. And it is clearly supported by a public elite that rotate in and out of government and the corporations seemingly at will.

The new *Lex Mercatoria,* the new rule of the **law merchant** in international commercial relations, is therefore not so very New after all: *In fact, it is positively Medieval.*

CHAPTER EIGHT

Oil and Sovereignty
In Whose Interests?

America is in Danger.
Already, increasing military
weakness and confusion about foreign
and defense policy have encouraged the development
of powerful hostile states and coalitions
that challenge the interests and security of the
United States....without American support
the friends of democracy and human rights will cry in vain
for protection against the forces of repression...these forces
will continue to identify the United States as the source
of a modernization that threatens them,
as the propagator of values they find evil and abhorrent,
as their principle enemy.
—DONALD AND FREDERICK KAGAN
While America Sleeps, 2000

Each man, each nation, each vested or ideal interest,
must unflinchingly assert itself;
all concessions, co-operations or federations
being, in the logic of life,
either roundabout ways of serving extant interests,
or the inception of some new particular organism,
which will substitute its own interests
and loyalties for those which the
dying organism imposed.
—GEORGE SANTAYANA

OIL AND SOVEREIGNTY

Organized hypocrisy is the normal state of affairs.
—STEPHAN D. KRASNER

Introduction to Chapter Eight

IN THIS CHAPTER I AM GOING TO ARGUE two important points. The first section has to do with the sovereignty of nation-states and whether the rules and normative behavior of states still apply in a world where there is but one great power, that of the United States. As the one grand hegemon does America have to follow the rules of international relations? Does international law even mean anything if Empire is either in place or being put into place? Or is *power* the only measure today where in the past *interests* and *rules* were often prime considerations? International sovereignty and nation-state sovereignty are today argued as distinct and separate ways of viewing the concept. In any case we must start where most international relations (IR) scholars begin: The Peace of Westphalia some 300 years ago. Westphalian sovereignty is the way most nations' governments judged other nations. Today recognition of one state by another, or by a group of others, is judged to be a valid approach; which really only means the most powerful states judge whether another weaker state is really a legitimate state, a legal state in the juridical sense. Empire implies the end of Westphalian sovereignty. This is the argument then, whether President George Bush Jr. has any legal right to bomb Afghanistan at all. If the United States had any evidence that the nation-state of Afghanistan and the ruling Taliban had anything at all to do with the September 11th air attacks, or anthrax, or anything at all, there would be justification for retaliation; but the Taliban and the nation-state, whatever else one might think of the regime, did not have anything to do with the attacks. Mr. Bush has never even hinted that they did; he only argues that they did not turn over the alleged suspect Osama in Laden. There is no court in the world nor here domestically that would hold that the United States has this right to attack the regime, the sovereign nation-state of Afghanistan (as sovereign as Saudi Arabia with no worse human rights record than that regime) because it has not "extradited" the individual in question; since the individual in question has not been lawfully indicted, tried nor convicted, he remains un-extraditable by any legal system let alone one which has no extradition treaty with the US. If sovereignty is nothing but "organized hypocrisy" as Stephan Krasner has stated, then what rule of law applies? Is non-intervention into another state's territory then a myth?

In part two I shall look more closely at who stands to gain by the war in Afghanistan, a war prosecuted almost entirely by the United States alone, with Great Britain going along but placing few troops and fewer aircraft in the region. The rest of the western world is just watching and there really is no coalition regardless of what an obedient mass media parrots from White House press releases and the vague rhetoric from a president hell bent on bombing the Taliban into submission, something no thinking person believes he will achieve. The Silk Road Strategy of the mid-1990s has been discussed some in my chapter *The Hydra of Carnage,* and is here not only delineated in greater detail, but "who" has lobbied for the policy and the revision of other policies, such as the Freedom Support Act's Section 907, and its removal (See Appendix One), is understood fully.

One cannot understand the Bush objectives without a fuller understanding of the Caspian Sea and region taken as a whole; and the nation-state of Azerbaijan in particular has to be specifically identified. Indeed, this war may have more to do with Azerbaijan than Afghanistan. It has been Azerbaijan which has been the primary focus of much of the United States' policy formulations, as shall be shown. *In whose interests?* (Benjamin Cohen's title of his book on international financial institutions) is of utmost importance. Interests lie at the bottom of everything any nation-state does; in the case of Empire, commercial interests lie at the bottom of everything as every Empire is a commercial empire. Imperialism has always and everywhere been about resources and shipping lanes, airspace and industrial linkage, mining and oil, forests and seas. In short, wealth; that is to say, money, mammon, the new God.

The half-wit cynic will smugly mutter "everybody knows that" and write-off this treatise as not noteworthy given his signal wealth of knowledge and vast life experience; but what is really the case is that he is too arrogant and lazy to understand anything at all. And every war needs to be understood, not just stared at like Internet pornography. I am not writing and researching this for the smug and self-righteous America-firster. I am not offering any insight for the crackpot conspiracy theorists on the left who can only recite slogans like "no blood for oil." I am, in complete honesty, writing this but for two reasons: history, always, for one; and secondly...to get my own mind around the Empire's first Holy War and the real political objectives which will one day be proclaimed as a consequence, an outcome, an entirely coincidental effect not planned at all but somehow miraculously achieved for the betterment of all mankind. This is the bill of goods we here in America will be sold five years hence, and we here in America will likely believe it. Americans, above all else, love their "silver linings."

I rarely offer any thanks in my written works, but this case is very different. I would not have been here to research this period were it not for my client base over these past six years. The paradigm shift to the far right in America since 1992, but clearly present much before then, has made public discourse almost impossible. The progressive-left self-destructed by not cleaning out its foul dingy basement. All that is left of the left are tree-huggers and new-age gurus. On the far right, self-righteousness has grown worse right along with militia deadbeats; anti-Semitism has actually found a rebirth. But the real killer where public debate and dialectical discourse is concerned is the utter ignorance of the vast majority; ignorance breeding arrogance, nobody can tell this mob anything. as they pretend to know all; pretend to care, teary-eyed when appropriate; pretend, with sentimental displays now the norm and a heightened patriotism which scarcely hides the racism and hate. This is not an America Thomas Paine would find familiar. This is not one I find familiar, although I really do know better. This is America's becoming; becoming who we are. If sovereignty is organized hypocrisy then Empire is organized hypocrisy writ large.

Chapter Eight Part One

Even the most modern armies are poorly
suited to wage war in mountain regions.
...even large numbers of modern warriors
can be fought to a standstill by
poorly-armed but mobile
mountaineers doing battle on their own territory.
Any government that thinks it can bludgeon
mountain people into submission is
engaging in a most destructive
form of self-deception.
—S. FREDERICK STARR

S. Frederick Starr, quoted above, closed his article in the Fall 2001 issue of *The National Interest*, titled *Altitude Sickness*, with this:

> We may blame the terrorist, drug dealer, local warlord, the farmer who raises coca or poppies, the head of an old style mining firm that exploits equally the land and its people, or the regional governor who steals from the public till. But spending time and money hounding down every one of these purported villains will not improve the lot of most mountain folk. A fresh crop of villains will quickly emerge to replace those who are displaced. (*Altitude Sickness*, p.99)

It is here that I shall begin to look at the question of sovereignty, ours as well as Afghanistan's, and oil, of course oil. Mr. Bush had already decided it was in America's National Security interest to remove the Taliban from power for political objectives he has yet to inform the public: The Silk Road Strategy. I began informing the public regarding the Caspian Oil Initiative, the Silk Road Strategy, and my arguments regarding sovereignty on KLOS radio, Los Angeles (The Frank Sontag *Impact Program*, October 15th, 2001). The paper subtitled The Silk Road Strategy, *The Hydra of Carnage*, was released on our website October 1st, 2001. I shall here describe the past some, and the future, of Afghanistan for two reasons: one, I believe in the long term

Mr. Bush shall fail miserably in Central Asia, and two, this will surely not be the last attempt by this American- led Empire to impose its will on other sovereign states made up of various nations (of people). One sees Afghanistan surrounded by Turkmenistan, Kazakhstan, Uzbekistan and others...but let us, for now, call these countries what they are about to become, language is important: Unocalistan, Mobiloilistan, Exxonistan, and Gettyoilistan. The last one is added because almost fifty percent of Getty Oil is now owned by the Russian firm Lukoil. China will become a player in the future as well, but for the most part I shall leave China out of this present section. This effort at an American-led western Empire supporting globalization is becoming more articulated in the world's press even if not in the general American media. An example of a few comments that got through during Mr. Bush's recent trip to the Asian Conference (ASEAN), mid-October, 2001, is becoming the norm in developing countries.

President, Mahathir bin Mohamad, of Malaysia, met with Mr. Bush at his hotel in the center of Shanghai, and the Malaysian leader used the occasion to complain that the war in Afghanistan was taking innocent Afghan lives. (Interestingly, the White House allowed photographers to record the meeting [so a smiling Bush could claim that Mohamad supported the coalition against Afghanistan], but banned the reporters who usually ask a few questions at the outset of such of a meeting.) When Mr. Mahathir bin Mohamad emerged to give a speech to business executives, the same group Mr. Bush addressed earlier in the day, he did not mention terrorism. But he did "level a strong blast at the forces of economic globalization that Mr. Bush had just hailed to the same audience."

"If I had a billion U.S. dollars, I suspect I too would be very committed to a fully globalized world without any barriers and without any constraints on what I can do with my money and how I can make even more money,"...mocking the group's commitment to free trade. (*New York Times*, October 20, 2001)

And so here is where I shall begin a longer analysis of what can only be understood as war as the extended energy politics in the region. Not their politics, not the politics of "the people" in the region, but the politics of Empire; American and foreign oil companies seeking to assure themselves a secure world supply of crude, by the crudest means conceivable, war.

Professor William Maley is a professor at the School of Politics, University College at the University of New South Wales in Australia. (He has written widely on Afghanistan, and edited *Fundamentalism Reborn? Afghanistan and the Taliban*, 1998.) Here is what he noted in a recent article prepared and posted on the Council on Foreign Relations' website. (I do not think it will appear in any other form such as *Foreign Affairs* journal.)

In October 1995, the US corporation UNOCAL and the Saudi corporation Delta Oil signed a memorandum of intent with the government of Turkmenistan, which anticipated the construction of a gas pipeline through Afghanistan to Pakistan. When the Taliban took Kabul, a UNOCAL Vice-President, Chris Taggart, reportedly termed it a "positive development." However, for both UNOCAL and the Taliban, the relationship proved frustrating. For the Taliban, the relationship with UNOCAL delivered neither revenue nor wider American support. Their expectations were extremely unrealistic: according to Rashid, they expected "the company which wins the contract to provide electricity, gas, telephones, roads-in fact, virtually a new infrastructure for a destroyed country." From UNOCAL's point of view, the Taliban proved unable to deliver the level of security which would be required to permit such a project to go ahead—and given the vulnerability not only of the pipeline itself but also the expatriate staff who would inevitably be involved in its construction, that level of security is extremely high. As a result, according to another UNOCAL Vice-President, Marty Miller, "lenders have said the project at this moment is just not financeable," and in August 1998, the company suspended its involvement in the project following US Tomahawk cruise missile strikes against alleged terrorist training camps operated in eastern Afghanistan by Osama bin Laden. In the face of these problems, the Taliban sought to maintain lines of communication with one of UNOCAL's competitors, the Argentinian company Bridas, but ultimately that avenue proved unrewarding as well and, the Taliban's hopes of securing a free revenue stream through bargaining with major multinational consortia simply slipped away.

When the Taliban took Kabul, they had high hopes of support from America. Understandably, as it was the Taliban that helped end the Cold War for the west and America in particular; it was their efforts that halted the Soviets' efforts in the region. In October 1995, the U.S. Ambassador to Pakistan reportedly accompanied General Naseerullah Babar in a convoy of trucks which entered Afghan territory from Quetta, a move which could only have been interpreted as a calculated insult to the Rabbani Government. Staff of the US Embassy in Pakistan had made no secret of their animosity towards the Taliban's predecessors, and the US Assistant Secretary of State for South Asia, Robin Raphel, had just a month earlier, according to Maley, demanded that Iran "should stop supplying Kabul." In a fatal subordination of foreign policy to commercial interests, the US Administration was also sympathetic to Unocal's ambitions for the region. Maley further notes that the State Department's acting spokesman, Glyn Davies, remarked that "the United States finds nothing objectionable in the policy statements of the new government, including its move to impose Islamic law." An Afghan-American commentator with the RAND Corporation who had served in the upper echelons of the State Department and the Department of Defense even went into print to argue that it was time for the United States to reengage in Afghanistan, maintaining that "the departure of Osama bin Laden, the Saudi financier of various anti-U.S. terrorist groups, from Afghanistan indicates some common interest between the United States and the Taliban."

To further aggravate the U.S. relationship with the Taliban there was the bombing of the embassies during 1998. Maley brings these events into some further clarity.

> The bomb blasts on 7 August 1998 which devastated the US Embassies in Kenya and Tanzania were blamed by US intelligence sources on Bin Laden, prompting the Tomahawk missile strikes on his training camps in Afghanistan two weeks later. This led to an upsurge of anti-American sentiment on the part of the Taliban and their Pakistani backers from the Jamiat-e Ulema-i Islam, and ultimately the promulgation by President Clinton on 6 July 1999 of an Executive Order freezing all Taliban assets in the USA and banning commercial and financial ties between the Taliban and the US.

As the piece pointed out, this led up to the some eighty Tomahawk cruise missiles being launched at Bin Laden in an attempt at rather exaggerated revenge. Of the eighty-some missiles launched at Bin Laden, forty failed to detonate in the mountainous regions; Bin Laden, as was recently reported during October 20th and 21st, throughout the world's press, sold many of these missiles for tens of millions of dollars to The Peoples Republic of China, in tact. (Source: *Claims that China paid Bin Laden to see Cruise Missiles*, By John Hooper in Milan, Saturday October 20, 2001, The Guardian, UK)

This has of course exacerbated the environment whereby American oil companies quite simply are not allowed to operate in Afghanistan; this has been a problem since 1996. According to former Department of Energy's Robert W. Gee, Assistant Secretary for Policy and International Affairs, he stated it thusly during the February 1998 hearing on the Silk Road Strategy Bill, H.R. 2867:

> ....Perhaps the Unocal witness can give you more detail. I do understand that they do have an agreement with the government of Turkmenistan. They have also been in discussions with the various factions within Afghanistan through which that proposed pipeline would be routed. The U.S. Government's position is that we support multiple pipelines with the exception of the southern pipeline that would transit Iran. The Unocal pipeline is among those pipelines that would receive our support under that policy. I would caution that while we do support the project, the U.S. Government has not at this point recognized any governing regime of the transit country, one of the transit countries, Afghanistan, through which that pipeline would be routed. But we do support the project.

After the September 11, 2001 air attacks on the World Trade Center and the Pentagon, *Foreign Affairs* journal made the newsstands with this article written prior to that date: *Caspian Energy at the Crossroads* by Jan H. Kalicki. Kalicki argues in his summary:

> The Caspian basin holds enormous oil and gas deposits that could play a critical role in the world's economic future. But getting them out of the ground and onto the market requires overcoming formidable political and geographic problems. For its own sake as well as that of the region's, Washington should do whatever is necessary to ensure the emergence of secure and independent routes for Caspian energy to reach the outside world.

This was the very same argument Mr. John J. Maresca, Vice President for International Relations, Unocal Corporation, made three years earlier during the hearing mentioned above; after discussing proposed pipelines to run north and west through Turkey and under or across the Caspian Sea he argued for another pipeline route.

> The only other possible route is across Afghanistan, which has of course its own unique challenges. The country has been involved in bitter warfare for almost two decades, and is still divided by civil war. From the outset, we have made it clear that construction of the pipeline we have proposed across Afghanistan could not begin until a recognized government is in place that has the confidence of governments, lenders, and our company. Last October, the Central Asia Gas Pipeline Consortium, called CentGas, in which Unocal holds an interest, was formed to develop a gas pipeline which will link Turkmenistan's vast Dauletabad gas field with markets in Pakistan and possibly India. The proposed 790-mile pipeline will open up new markets for this gas, traveling from Turkmenistan through Afghanistan to Multan in Pakistan. The proposed extension would move gas on to New Delhi, where it would connect with an existing pipeline. As with the proposed Central Asia oil pipeline, CentGas can not begin construction until an internationally recognized Afghanistan Government is in place.

How important to the United States National Security is this, as seen by the policy makers of Corporatism and the Empire that globalization rests for its support? It is called a secure energy policy initiative which requires some form of legislation. And as Dr. Greg Smestad pointed out in a recent contribution:

> This week, (October 2001) the Senate Energy & Natural Resources Committee will take up energy infrastructure security with hearings and markup of a yet to be written bill to address

national security and energy needs. The committee's goal, says Chairman Jeff Bingaman (D-N.M.), is to have a free-standing legislation ready for action right away working on a comprehensive bill with a markup seen for mid-October, and the senator now says he expects to have the committee complete energy legislation in the next few weeks. Bingaman's opposite on the committee, Sen. Frank H. Murkowski (R-Alaska), ranking minority member, has prepared an outline of what he would like to see in an infra-structure bill: the Homeland Energy Security Act of 2001. It includes drilling in the Arctic National Wildlife Refuge, which Bingaman opposes, and support for nuclear power and clean-coal technologies as well as electricity reliability and pipeline safety components. (Source: E-mailed to our KC&A offices: Contributed by Greg P. Smestad, Ph.D., Associate Editor of Solar Energy Materials and Solar Cells, and Professor of Environmental Policy Studies at the Monterey Institute of International Studies in an article *Pressure Mounts for Energy Bill,* Chemical and Engineering News, Oct. 8, 2001, Government & Policy, p. 23).

The California energy crisis has caused many Americans to care very little how we achieve energy security; indeed, Californians would vote in the high 90 percentile to bomb all Arab nations into the stone age if they were convinced their gasoline prices would not go up while driving their gas guzzling Sports Utility Vehicles. The elite thinkers and policy makers have taken note of the problem recently. In a press release from the Council on Foreign Relations' website, the topic gained greater importance. The title of the release and the study groups' mission statement was..."Recurring Energy Supply Shortages Could Result in a Nationwide Crisis if an Energy Policy isn't Developed Soon," (...warns the independent task force report of Rice University's James A. Baker III Institute for Public Policy and the Council on Foreign Relations, New York, NY, April 10, 2001.) The report is titled, *Strategic Energy Policy: Challenges for the 21st Century.*

Arguing that there could be more California(s) in America's future unless the U.S. government adopts a long-term, comprehensive energy policy now, the press release from the James A. Baker III Institute for Public Policy of Rice University in Houston, makes the following statements: (One does wonder what they mean by "independent.")

Given the capital-intensive nature of the energy industry, such energy woes could worsen before they get better, the study notes. Americans should therefore brace themselves for more California-style electricity problems and seasonal shortfalls of natural gas and heating fuels, as well as occasional spikes in regional gasoline prices. The experts note, however, that the situation is not a sign that the world is running out of energy resources. Rather, the situation finds its roots in chronic under-investment and soaring energy use. The report, signed by 51 experts with widely different backgrounds and perspectives on the problem, believes that President Bush has an opportunity to begin educating the public about this reality and to start building a broad base of popular support for the hard policy choices ahead.

The report itself warns that the United States now faces the consequences of not having had an energy policy over the last several decades. The task force concludes that "there are no overnight solutions to the energy supply and infrastructure bottlenecks facing the nation and the world." The bottlenecks are those that periodically occur in, say, the Persian Gulf. Which is the *raison d'etre* for the Silk Road Strategy; i.e., isolate Iran and Iraq from the world markets and diversify sources away from the Persian Gulf using the proposed pipelines to circumvent the two countries above, and bring the Caspian region's states into the oil producing collection of countries. It is, interestingly, assumed without argument that America and the west will never diversify energy "needs" itself, nor explore non-fossil fuel forms of energy.

The task force, chaired by Edward L. Morse, a widely recognized authority on energy at Hess Energy, and assisted by Amy Myers Jaffe of the Baker Institute, noted that both Democratic and Republican Administrations have allowed energy policy to drift despite its central importance to the domestic economy and to the nation's security. In particular, energy policy has underplayed energy efficiency and demand management measures for two decades.

The report also notes that a spike in oil prices preceded every American recession since the late 1940s and that despite the obvious pattern, successive governments did nothing to craft a coherent and visionary national energy policy.

The task force warns that what lies ahead now are agonizing policy tradeoffs between legitimate and competing interests. Among those tradeoffs, the task force states, is whether Americans are willing to compromise their hunger for cheap energy to achieve their increasing demand for cleaner energy and a cleaner environment.

Ironically, the economic boom of recent years has exacerbated the potential for an energy crisis. Strong growth in most countries and new demands for energy have led to the end of previously sustained surplus in hydrocarbon fuels. What with the war and the looming ever larger of a global recession, is the thinking now to force the Taliban from power and place in their stead a regime which will be considered more favorably by the economic community and lenders for the oil companies? Clearly the answer is yes.

The report argued (again, it was published prior to the September 11, 2001 air attacks and the ensuing war in Afghanistan) that as a result, the world is now precariously close to using all its available global oil production capacity. If an accident or other disruption in production occurred — whether on the

Alaskan oil pipeline, in the Middle East or elsewhere — the world might be on the brink of the worst international oil crisis in three decades. The situation in oil markets is compounded by shortages of other forms of readily available clean energy in the U.S., including natural gas and electricity in certain localities.

The authors stated it in this rather childish (for such experts) fashion, "The situation is, by analogy, like traveling in a car with broken shock absorbers at very high speeds, such as 90 miles per hour,...As long as the pavement on the highway is perfectly smooth, no injury to the driver will result from the poor decision of not spending the money to fix the car. But if the car confronts a large bump or pothole, the injury to the driver could be quite severe."

What is important for this present analysis of the political and commercial objectives being pursued, using war as the means, is this: oil field production capacity limitations today in the Middle East mean that the U.S. can no longer assume that the oil-producing states will provide more oil at will. Moreover, it is not politically desirable for the U.S. to increase its dependence on a few foreign sources. Thus the need to increase capacity from the Caspian region's states, Azerbaijan, Turkmenistan, Kazakhstan and Uzbekistan; landlocked that they are, thus the serious and immediate need to get pipelines into production to carry the product through Afghanistan south and Turkey to the west.

The task force states that the Bush administration, while not responsible for the current problems, needs to make some hard policy choices to secure the energy future of the United States. A comprehensive energy policy that combines supply, demand restraint and environmental objectives is required, the report concludes.

The Baker Institute/Council on Foreign Relations independent task force report was offered on the eve of the final deliberations of the administration's energy task force headed by Vice President Dick Cheney. It was argued that any viable energy policy will need to cope with the following important and often conflicting foreign policy issues:
· U.S. policy in the Middle East;
· U.S. policy toward the former Soviet Union and China;
· The fight against international terrorism;
· Environmental policy;
· International trade policy, including the U.S. position on the European Union energy charter;
· NAFTA;
· Foreign aid and credits.

This last one is the Silk Road Strategy itself, and the argued need to remove or amend Section 907 from the Freedom Support Act, which disallows American government backing, support that is, for the many oil companies wanting to enter the region's lucrative potential markets, and altering other sanctions legislation. (See Appendix One)

In describing the nation's policy choices in creating a national energy policy, the task force report emphasizes a tough bottom line: "When it comes to energy, the American people cannot achieve both a painless present and a secure future." Painful for whom?

The report states that if the current administration tells it like it is to the American people, the U.S. would be taking the first step in years toward achieving a much-needed national energy policy. While the report says "telling it like is," to the American people, making war in Afghanistan was not their foremost thought, nor likeliest choice, but then the opportunity did present itself after all. And opportunism is the hallmark of Empire.

What is included in the steps, as policy itself, is not outlined? The Silk Road Strategy reported in my previous chapter, *The Hydra of Carnage*, was to begin a process of altering existing sanctions legislation against, primarily, Afghanistan and Azerbaijan, so as to facilitate lender's financing and oil exploration and pipelines in the region. Removing the Taliban from power is seen by Mr. Bush as one of the primary objectives; most analysts and reporters outside the United States have argued there is no legal nor moral precedent to do so; that there is no evidence that the Taliban had anything to do with the September 11, air attacks on America's political infrastructure and the Empire's economic symbol, the World Trade Organization's (WTO) World Trade Center (WTC), nor any foreknowledge of the attacks, makes their argument fairly solid. But that will not stop the Empire's leader Mr. Bush. I shall argue this further below, but a brief note on another topic is too important to place in the appendices.

Companies are paying protection money to terrorists

Stephanie Dexter of Wilmington, Dela.,
opted last month for a GMC Yukon XL (12 mpg, city).
She believes Americans have a right
"to do what we want and buy what we want.
Isn't that why we're fighting?"
(REPORTED MSNBC NOV.19TH, 2001)

As an aside, in an article by Paul Peachey, October 1, 2001 it was reported (finally, what so many in the security field already knew) that, "Campaigns waged by terrorist organizations are being partly financed through protection rackets that extort money from respected large corporations across the world." Preachey makes these important points.

> Oil companies in South America and Middle Eastern airlines are among those paying to prevent their businesses being damaged, according to the magazine Forbes Global. It claimed timber companies in South-east Asia have also made protection payments and until recently, a Jewish-owned bank was paying

off the Lebanese Islamist group Hizbollah. An executive in the financial division of a state-owned oil company in southern Europe claimed that donating money to Islamic groups was a cost of doing business in the Middle East. He said: "I have been more and more worried about these transactions over the last seven or eight years, because friends in our government's secret service have told me that a number of these intermediaries have direct links to terrorist organizations."

Americans are likely to agree with this war as self-interest is our major philosophical moral imperative. Americans think their gasoline and heating oil prices will remain low and there is, therefore, no other financial burden on either making war or making policy. They shall be proven wrong on both counts, the "people" always pay; the Empire's identifiable commercial entities pay little or nothing when it can be postulated, without the public's knowledge, that these are National Security issues; energy is now under that fanciful title. Jan I I. Kalicka lays out the future: Americans will pay in tribute if not cash for their oil.

Although increased tariffs or decreased investment returns could cover moderate cost overruns, both the United States and Turkey should be prepared to subsidize any excess costs that would be commercially unsustainable. Already, Ankara has guaranteed to cover construction costs in Turkey that exceed $1.4 billion. Washington could make a similar guarantee by agreeing to subsidize construction and other risk insurance for the pipeline's corporate sponsors to be issued by the Overseas Private Investment Corporation. Although it would be far better to base pipeline development on purely commercial terms, the strategic importance of alternative, independent transportation routes for Caspian energy is great enough to justify government intervention as a last resort. (Jan H. Kalicki, *Foreign Affairs*, September, October, *Caspian Energy at the Crossroads*, p.131)

Below is some text which one finds amusing if one keeps his sense of humor. The organization which Kalicki and others have suggested ought to be enlisted to subsidize the cost overruns for the benefit of the oil companies and their engineering and fabrication firms is the Overseas Private Investment Corporation, (OPIC) part private, part public, with guarantees and insurance through government lending institutions. Peter S. Watson is the current CEO of OPIC. From his biography published by OPIC we find this: "Peter S. Watson, prior to becoming President and CEO of the Overseas Private Investment Corporation, was Counsel to Pillsbury Winthrop, L.L.P., in the firm's Washington office, advising on international business and trade policy matters. *He also served as Senior Advisor to Armitage Associates, L.C. "* We shall discover below just how much Richard Armitage Associates, L.C. lobbied in the Caspian region in behalf of the oil industries and their off-shoot construction firms during 1993 through 2000, before the whole bunch, it would seem, were appointed to high public office (now implementing their own policies); former Armitage Associates personnel include former deputy secretary of defense Richard Armitage now Deputy Secretary of State under Secretary of State Colin Powell; Peter S. Watson above, now CEO of OPIC; Lincoln P. Blumfield now Assistant Secretary of State for Political-Military Affairs; many others are looked at below where conflict of interest would apparently be an issue. But I am getting ahead of myself. What this really specifies then, is this: Corporatism reigns at the most obvious and highest level of our government commercial nexus.

This is Corporatism by definition. Of the Empire's 100 largest economies in the world, America being the largest, (including these major oil companies) 51 corporation's economies are larger than all the nation-state economies with the exception of the top 49. The American people will pay for the war, the recession, the corporate bailouts, the energy when it is short in supply, the energy when the construction begins for exploration and the building of the pipelines; Americans will pay forever to protect the finished pipelines as it will be argued forever that it is a National Energy Security issue. The future pipelines will be blown-up regularly in Azerbaijan, Afghanistan, Pakistan and India. Americans will pay in blood and coin. They will just never be aware in their utter ignorance of it as inflation and their taxes go up, and taxes always go up. Kalicki argues that these "strong, coherent" policies by the United States "toward the Caspian region could bolster world energy security as well as regional stability and independence." (Ibid., p.134) While he may be correct on the first point, world energy security (paid for righteously by U.S. taxpayers), the latter two points are problematic at best, as we shall certainly see below.

International law and State Sovereignty

> *A month ago, in his address to Congress,*
> *President Bush said the war will not end*
> *"until every terrorist group of global reach has*
> *been found, stopped and defeated."*
> *Last week, before setting out for China, he said:*
> *"So long as anybody is*
> *terrorising established governments*
> *there needs to be a war."*
> *This mission is not creeping;*
> *it's positively galloping.*
> —MATTHEW ENGEL, THE GURDIAN, UK;
> *Wednesday October 24, 2001*

In an article with the lengthy title, *Issues of International Law and Politics in the Caspian in the Context of the Turkmenistan-Azerbaijan Discussion and Fuel Transport* by one Yagmur Kochumov, it was argued that little is really new to the recent events in the Caspian region. It has long been sought for the energy reserves either known to exist or in the past thought to exist. The last great find in oil reserves, it should be recalled was the North Sea discoveries twenty-five years ago. The Caspian region is said to be substantially larger than the Alaska fields, (See hearing transcript above and my chapter Hydra of Carnage). Kochumov put it this way.

> History seems to be repeating itself. One need only remember that in 1903 Rockefeller planned to lease and then buy the Baku oil fields. In 1919 Churchill was concerned that "Allied strategic control of the former Russian empire cannot be reliable if the northern Caucasus and the Caspian area are not under the control of western powers." [1] During World War II, Germany developed long-term projects for the development of the Caspian's oil riches.

The current focus on Caspian oil is characterized by a direct interest not only in Baku oil, but also in the fuel and energy potential of the entire region. Kochumov says this "is attributable to opportunities to satisfy the growing demand of all countries for energy resources and to future pricing mechanisms on world hydrocarbon markets. The current situation has necessitated the development of an effective model for long-term cooperation and international legal tools to satisfy the interests of all littoral states." The solution, that is to say, to the problem, of the Caspian's status, (whose status approved by whom is never questioned?)..."is largely determined by the economic and geopolitical interests of the states, transnational companies, major industrial/financial groups, organizations, and environmental protection movements."

But Kochumov is no apologist for the Western-led Empire and he closes his historical discourse with a subtle warning few in the United States are today prepared to listen to.

> The opportunity to use pipelines as a tool for accomplishing political goals or a political or economic dictate must be entirely eliminated. The process of globalization in international economic relations requires the development of an International Convention on the treatment of and the guarantees of the functioning of trans-national pipelines. Turkmenistan sees this as one of the most important challenges of the 21st century and, according to available information, is ready to act as a cosponsor of the appropriate UN documents.

This bears repeating in the face of Mr. Bush's declared intent to remove the sovereign regional ruling Taliban regime from power. "The opportunity to use pipelines as a tool for accomplishing political goals or a political or economic dictate must be entirely eliminated." But this use of the proposed pipelines is precisely what the American administration is doing. Using Turkmenistan and Uzbekistan to launch their attacks on Afghanistan while using the vicious Northern Alliance to help achieve the objective is horrendous. The Taliban may not be acceptable to the American regime, the Empire, the oil companies and their lenders, and even to the so-called international community. (Which community internationally is always the most powerful nation-states, which decide who live and who dies: Global Triage was the name I gave this Empire some seven years ago.)

One author, and hardly a peace protestor from the ranks of Mr. Ralph Nader's silly Volk, Lt. General William E. Odom, Ret., wrote a piece titled, *The Caspian Sea Littoral States: The Object of a New Great Game?* His concern was that America felt it could secure the region from threats to our national security interests and energy interests specifically, by whatever means were deemed necessary. He called it the Great Game.

> Security in the Caspian Sea region has emerged with surprising force in policy debates in Washington, and claims are made sometimes that it has parallels with previous struggles for hegemony in this area. I do not intend to add a new contribution to the debate revolving around the region, Rather, I want to make some modest clarifications, particularly on the issue of why the United States is extremely ill-positioned to deal with regional security problems in the Caspian.

Below are Odom's lucid arguments regarding the so-called threats in the Caspian region. In particular his comments regarding what constitutes a weakened regime and how this comes about should be required reading at the White House.

Caspian Regional Threats

Suppose that I throw a rock through a window
and the window breaks. Then suppose an observer says,
"the glass broke because it was brittle."
The implication seems to be that brittleness broke the glass,
but consider it for a moment. Did brittleness break the glass?
Not at all. It was brittle before I threw the rock,
and it did not break earlier.
Obviously the rock broke the glass.
Brittleness is a disposition or condition, not the cause.
In military security language,
"threats" are potential causes,
and "vulnerability" is the proper label
for a disposition that threats may exploit.

—William E. Odom

Threats to the Region

Lt. General William E. Odom is concerned with threats in the classical sense but threats to whom is not overlooked. Nor does he forget what is a cause of specific conditions and what is a threat. Mr. Bush argued that fanatical Islam is the threat in the region.

> If we are concerned with the security of this region, we must properly identify and distinguish between threats and vulnerabilities, not confusing the latter for the former. Much talk about threats to the region has clearly been off the mark precisely because it has confused conditions or dispositions with causes.

The Threat of Oil Revenues

Before I give Odom voice to these concerns we must go back to the Caspian's leading advocate for pipeline production and intervention in the region by the United States. In Jan H. Kalicki's recent article noted above in *Foreign Affairs* journal *Caspian Energy at the Crossroads*, he states this important point (but we feel wrongly). (Ibid., p. 121)

> Located at the crossroads of western Europe, eastern Asia, and the Middle East, the Caspian serves as a trafficking area for weapons of mass destruction, terrorists, and narcotics—a role enhanced by the weakness of the regions governments. With few exceptions, the fledgling Caspian republics are plagued with pervasive corruption, political repression, and the virtual absence of the rule of law. Even if they can muster the political will to attempt reform themselves, the attempt will fail so long as they lack the resources to build strong economic and political institutions....The cooperative development of regional energy reserves and pipelines—independent of their huge neighbors to the north and south—thus represents not only a boon for the United States and the world at large, but also the surest way to provide for the Caspian nation's own security and prosperity.

One sees that Kalicki believes that by developing the Caspian region's oil reserves and the necessary pipeline structures, these nations will find security and prosperity. Security for whom and prosperity for whom? is never argued. But other authorities are more forthright about what happens to nations and their people, that develop their one vast resource and especially oil. Lt. General William Odom, Ret., argues differently.

> A [fourth] factor falls into the threat category because of the deleterious effects it will almost inexorably have on several regimes. As some of these states succeed in exporting significant amounts of oil or gas, large revenues will pour in. Anyone

familiar with the history of Peru knows what a state's dependency on commodity exports for revenues does to the strength of the regime. It keeps it weak. The regime has no incentive to compromise with social, economic, and political interests that resist its power. This is true because rulers do not have to tax individuals and business at the local level. Oil exports are particularly dangerous in this respect. Nigeria's history over the past two decades and recent developments in Venezuela are cases in point. The Shah's fall in Iran was in no small part abetted by dependency on oil revenues for state income. The fragility of all the Persian Gulf oil producing regimes is conspicuous, and the oil price boom in the 1970s weakened Saudi Arabia's internal tax system noticeably, imposing serious problems when the price bust came in the 1980s.

This last point Odom makes regarding the Persian Gulf states is very important as most fail to see the difference between the people of, say, Saudi Arabia, and the Sheikdom's Royalty, as to who gains. I pointed this out in the chapter, *The Hydra of Carnage*, and it bears repeating here.

At $15 to $30 per barrel, oil makes the Middle East a rich place. Times are changing in Saudi Arabia. "Per capita income exceeded $28,000 in the early 80s, matching that of the United States. The population of native Saudis has doubled since, to 14 million, while per capita income has sunk below $7,000. Unemployment, once unheard of, is now at 18%. A lot of young Saudis are being forced into unskilled (menial) jobs that they once felt were beneath them. There are 6-7 million expatriates (foreigners) working in Saudi Arabia now. The Saudis are increasingly resentful that the oil perks of the past are drying up." Into this bin Laden was born and is now operating. (Source: August, 2001 in the New York Times, by Neil MacFarquhar, NYT, as appeared in S.F. Chronicle A13, Aug. 26.)

The threat to the region's governance and stability is their dependence upon oil as their main resource. The prosperity that Mr. Kalicki, Mr. Bush and Mr. Tony Blair claim shall come to the people of the region is a mirage; to the Royalty, whether a Monarchy or duly elected tyranny, is another thing altogether; let us not mix this up. The "people" will receive little benefit. To paraphrase George Santayana, "All government is Monarchy."

Imperialism's rebirth?

The citizen who sees his society's
democratic clothes being worn out
and does not cry out
is not a patriot but a traitor.

—MARK TWAIN

There are those today arguing for raw Empire, Imperialism as such, as was administered by Great Britain during its imperial period. There are too many American elite to name. (I have written for over twenty years on this particular issue.) Now, in a very recent article in the British Guardian this was expressed favorably in no uncertain terms.

We have to call it by its real name. Political globalization is a fancy word for imperialism, imposing your values and institutions on others. However you may dress it up, whatever rhetoric you may use, it is not very different in practice to what Great Britain did in the 18th and 19th centuries. We already have precedents: the new imperialism is already in operation in Bosnia, Kosovo, East Timor. Essentially it is the imperialism that evolved in the 1920s when League of Nations mandates were the polite word for what were the post-Versailles treaty colonies.

The future of Afghanistan must, if the war is successfully prosecuted, be very similar indeed to those states currently under this kind of international colonial rule. Nothing else will do. Contrary to popular arguments made in the 1980s, imperialism is affordable for the richest economy in the world. (Niall Ferguson is a professor of history at Oxford University, *Welcome the new imperialism—The US must make the transition from informal to formal empire.* Niall Ferguson, Guardian, Wednesday October 31, 2001)

There is a very real push here in the United States as well. President George Bush Jr., heeding a previous call from his father to enact existing emergency legislation and executive orders, has moved dangerously ahead. The domestic protections against the use of U.S. military against our domestic population will be purportedly overthrown by Bush; adding to this, suspected terrorists, defined as illusively as what constitutes pornography, will now be tried by a United States military tribunal, on U.S. military bases anywhere in the world.

—A handful of U.S. senators and some in the Bush administration are calling for changes in a 150-year-old statute, known as the Posse Comitatus Act, that keeps the military out of the business of domestic law enforcement....The notion of amending the act first surfaced last month, when Sen. John Warner, R-VA., wrote the secretary of defense asking his department to "re-examine military doctrines," including Posse, to "enable our active duty military to more fully join other domestic assets in the war against terrorism."...Deputy Secretary of Defense Paul Wolfowitz, testifying before the Armed Services committee, said he "strongly agrees" with Warner on the issue. (Kelley Beaucar Vlahos, *Lawmakers Debate Sending in the Troops — at Home*, Friday, November 09, 2001)

– President Bush signed an order Tuesday that would allow for the trial of people accused of terrorism by a special military commission instead of civilian courts, The Associated Press has learned....The order, signed by Bush before he left for Crawford, Texas, gives the Bush administration another avenue to bring the Sept. 11 terrorists to justice, said White House counsel Albert Gonzales. "This is a new tool to use against terrorism," Gonzales said in a telephone interview. (*By Ron Fournier* AP White House Correspondent , Tuesday, November 13, 2001)

These military tribunals have the sympathetic effect of simultaneously allowing President Bush to try, say, bin Laden without revealing publicly that he really has no solid legal evidence against him. He can be tried on just the fact that he has publicly declared America the enemy and that would be enough for a military tribunal to execute him. We would simply never know if the evidence against bin Laden was fabricated to achieve political objectives Bush is simply not prepared to reveal. Indeed, it is hard to not see in this decision that this may have been one of the primary motivations for the executive order. Donald Rumsfeld stated as much when he said,, regarding the secret tribunals and Mullah Omar and bin Laden, "They are the reasons for these tribunals." And this is only the beginning; Empire cannot be launched unless the domestic population can be absolutely controlled. Not just terrorists, but any who would argue that Empire, or the imperialism suggested by Niall Ferguson above, should *not* be the norm, will come under special scrutiny; debate stifled, protest eliminated in all its forms. The concept of Empire implies Corporatism as ideology. Indeed, the one implies the other whichever one might come first. One scholar had this to say when Corporatism as ideological fertilizer of our system here in America takes root.

America is a 'liberal' polity. By that I mean almost everyone in the American tradition—Ronald Reagan as well as Bill Clinton—believes in the classic nineteenth-century freedoms; freedom of speech, religion, press—the Bill of Rights. Recall also that this hallowed addendum also includes freedom of assembly, of petition, and of association. These provisions stand in the way of a corporate ordering of society where, [recall], group rights take precedence over individual rights and a group's juridical personality must be recognized by the state before that group can participate in the political process—i.e., can assemble, petition, and associate....This liberal tradition—the belief in democratic, individualistic, free, and representative government—is so strong in the United States that almost everyone believes in and accepts it. No other alternative political system (communism, authoritarianism, fascism, corporatism) is acceptable. So if corporatism is ever to find a foothold in the United States, it has to come in through the back door, disguised and by stealth, and be called 'liberalism' rather than 'corporatism.' (Howard J. Wiarda, *Corporatism and Comparative Politics: The Other Great "Ism"*, 1997, p.132)

We will hear more from the above author below, but suffice to say for now, his theory of how corporatism will come to America is more valid now than when he wrote.   Corporatism is the ideological framework of Empire and globalization is its foundation and support. The one thing some of us, who have argued that we were in the throws of Corporatism since 1945, had always stressed, and Wiarda stressed as well, was the need for a crisis to bring it all to fruition. Not just any crisis, one the one hand, the Persian Gulf, the Los Angeles riots, the Oklahoma City bombing of the Murrah P. Federal building by a known militia affiliated cell member, could only further the foundation-building for a future fully corporative state. The air attacks of September 11, 2001, are, on the other, a perfect crisis; with full Gallup Poll support registering a whopping 88-96% public vote in favor of bombing Afghanistan and the overall war, it seems well assured.

First, corporatism is clearly related to crises—the war industries boards of World War I and II, the depression of the 1930s, the perceived Bolshevik threat, and the political challenge of lower class and/or guerrilla groups in Latin America and elsewhere in the 1960s. Crises and challenges tend to force governments to tighten up, to look for control mechanisms—such as corporatism—by which they can manage potentially threatening groups. (Ibid., p.157)

Now that we, here in the United States as infrastructure to Empire, have been hit by a guerrilla group on our homeland, there is little to stop corporatism from locking down on civil liberties, unleashing the full power of the police-state, and bringing corporatism to Corporatism. Empire is on the move, and Mr. Bush is launching it. Oddly enough it was a Russian author which looked at U.S. citizens giving up "temporarily" their civil rights so as to feel more secure here at home. In the English language edition of *Pravda*, the author makes this lucid point as reminder.

Ordinary citizens, scared by terrorist threats, are ready to "temporarily" give up their rights to address new challenges....Unfortunately, they do not know that all things temporary eventually becomes standing. The US administration explains this by saying that only this way it can successfully counter terrorism. It may be so. An example taken from out recent history can corroborate this. The Stalinist political machinery operated without a hitch in the USSR. Among the arrested "spies" and "saboteurs" were millions of innocent people. Who was guilty and who was not? How can one find the right criterion of the selection, and who is to conduct it? ....Fighting terrorism is not a matter of one day or one year. Yet, when it is over, the rulers will be highly tempted to leave it the way it is.(DMITRI LITVINOVICH, PRAVDA, Russia; *THE TREE OF FREEDOM HAS FADED FOREVER* , 2001-11-01)

Westphalian Sovereignty and International Law

No other just cause for undertaking war can there be excepting injury received.
Hugo Grotius,
de Jure Bella ac Pacis libri tres

Never yet has a government declared that is was resorting to war only because it felt at liberty to do so, or because such a step seemed advantageous.
HANS KELSEN

The question comes down to this: is Afghanistan and Azerbaijan sovereign nation-states in the classical sense of the term? The starting point for all IR studies is the Peace of Westphalia of 1645. The Westphalian system, granted to each nation absolute sovereignty within its own territory, territoriality it is called, and proscribed any other nation-state's sovereign from intervening in that nation's affairs. Non-intervention was the key to defining sovereignty; autonomy. Arguably autonomy is the same key for understanding the Westphalian system. It seems I should be remiss in not quoting the United Nations, which has tried to claim the sole right to prosecute or authorize war, since its signatories signed on with the international body

...it would appear that such matters (war) would now come within the purview of the United Nations so far as they constituted a threat to international peace and security. Article 2 (4) of the United Nations Charter strictly enjoins members from 'the threat or use of force against the territorial integrity or political independence of any state.' (Morris Greenspan, *The Modern Law of Land Warfare,* P. 626)

From every corner, war has been seen to be valid only if the sovereign state in question had been attacked another sovereign state. This is called a delict in jurisprudence, that is, the conduct of a state which is held to be illegal. The response to a delict can be reprisal. In lay terms, if the Taliban of Afghanistan attacked America, America has the right to defend itself; should war be that act of reprisal, for the delict, it is *Bellum Justum,* a just war. The ruling Taliban of Afghanistan, and not even Mr. Bush nor Mr. Blair have argued otherwise, never attacked America; they had no foreknowledge of the attacks; and even if Bin Laden had a hand in the attacks, harboring Bin Laden (who is without indictment or conviction) without any legal extradition procedures under our own domestic laws, not to mention international law, nor Afghanistan's, precluded the attacks on Afghanistan.

> The coercive act is [therefore] either a delict, a condition of the sanction—and hence forbidden—or a sanction, the consequence of a delict—and hence permitted. This alternative is an essential characteristic of the coercive order called law.....International law is law in this sense if a coercive act on the part of a state, the forcible interference of a state in the sphere of interests of another, is permitted only as a sanction against a delict and the employment of force to any other end is forbidden—only if the coercive act undertaken as a reaction against a delict can be interpreted as a reaction of the international legal community. (Hans Kelsen, *The Nature of International Law,* in *International Rules,* Edited by Robert J. Beck, et al, Oxford University Press, p. 61-62, 1996)

Kelsen goes on to argue that if international law is seen to be either sanction or delict, then international law is law in the same sense as national law. But clearly Mr. Bush and the United Nations is not interested in international law at all. There is no justifiable reason for this massive intervention into the affairs of Afghanistan with the sole exception of interests, not because a delict was perpetrated against the United States by Afghanistan. The capture of the criminal elements in any and all countries for terrorist acts can alone be justified under international law and the use of the vast machinery of international criminal arrest and prosecution (Noriega of Panama comes to mind). Many authors, including Kelsen, in other works questioned whether international law was even law. Hans Kelsen argued later in the above volume that international law bore some resemblance to primitive law and this bears quoting at length.

> In its technical aspects, general international law is a primitive law, as is evidenced among other ways by its complete lack of a

particular organ charged with the application of legal norms to concrete instances. In primitive law the individual whose legally protected interests have been violated is himself authorized by the legal order to proceed against the wrongdoer with all the coercive measures provided by the legal order. This is called self-help. Every individual takes the law into his own hands. Blood revenge is the most characteristic form of this primitive legal technique. (Kelsen, Ibid., p.71)

If Kelsen's views and others like him are correct then Mr. Bush is going some distance proving the point quite well; the prosecution of this war against a state which did not attack the interests nor the sovereign territory of the United States has been done an injustice. And a rather primitive form of injustice as well. This amounts to an individual attack of blood revenge. Which is why I might add so many Americans are going to go along with it or worse, (using an American slang term) going to *get off on it*. Again, if there were such proof that bin Laden had a hand in it, there are a multitude of means to bring this *individual* to justice; there are literally hundreds of means available and the entire world would have backed all those means necessary. But none of those means would achieve the other political and commercial objectives desired by the present Bush Administration. Only the removal of the ruling Taliban from power and the installation of "a regime acceptable to the international community, the oil companies and their lenders" (I am quoting here from the February 18, 1997 hearing on the Silk Road Strategy, Mr. Maresca of Unocal) can achieve those objectives. And that, then, would place America in the awkward position of having committed the delict, rather than Afghanistan. So where does that leave us as Americans who uphold the United States Constitution and as patriots might find that our own government, purportedly representing our personal values, betrayed them and has acted on the impulse of raw commercial self-interest and Empire and prosecuted an illegal act, a delict, against another nation-state? And maybe there is no answer but the human conscience; we each must decide for ourselves what kind of country we presently do, and in the future may, have to live in.

H.L.A. Hart, a legal scholar every lawyer must cut his teeth on, has summed it up well in the same volume I have quoted Hans Kelsen in.

To the innocent eye, the formal structure of international law lacking a legislature, courts with compulsory jurisdiction and officially organized sanctions, appears very different from that of municipal law. It resembles...in form though not at all in content, a simple regime of primary or customary law. Yet some theorists, in their anxiety to defend against the skeptic the title of international law to be called 'law,' have succumbed to the temptation to minimize these formal differences, and to exaggerate the analogies which can be found in international law to legislation or other desirable formal features of municipal law. Thus, it has been claimed that war, ending with a treaty whereby the defeated power cedes territory, or assumes obligations, or accepts some diminished form of independence, is essentially a legislative act; for like legislation, it is an imposed legal change. Few would now be impressed by this analogy, or think that it helped show that international law had an equal title with municipal law to be called 'law'; for one of the salient differences between municipal and international law is that the former usually does not, and the latter does, recognize the validity of agreements extorted by violence. (Hart, *Legal Positivism*, in *International Rules*, p. 89)

And this is where the reader may find himself giving-up, as it were, about taking a stand for one's principled belief system, or to defend the United States against not just bin Laden, if he were guilty, but against the massive abuse of power by our own President and a Cabinet made up of men, not unlike a brotherhood, clearly acting in their own self-interest as shall be proved below within this text. If there is no international law, there is only primitive law, then international rules, whatever else they may be, are not the same thing as law; so if we cannot call international law "law," then we are left with a Nietzschean will to power and we all must go along or be crushed ourselves. This also implies, then, there is no such thing as a sovereign; no personal sovereigns like those of us brought up to believe that "we" as citizens are the true sovereigns here in America; no sovereigns such as another sovereign nation-state; no sovereign United States either. Only Empire shall lay title claim. With that we continue to explore this notion of sovereignty.

Today it is argued that there are other forms of sovereignty like international sovereignty and interdependence sovereignty, which we shall explore below. The Peace of Westphalia system today is considered anachronistic if not downright silly.

The standard approaches to the study of international relations, and politics more generally, suggest three general kinds of explanatory variables—power, interests and ideas—suitably defined and elaborated of course to deal with specific issues. In the extreme, constructivist arguments suggest that only ideas matter, realist arguments that only power matters, and liberal arguments that only interests matter. No one of these explanatory variables can by itself provide an account of the conditions under which sovereignty is more or less consequential. (Stephan D. Krasner, Ed., *Problematic Sovereignty*, P.323)

Unlike Westphalian sovereignty, international sovereignty is decided by other state's regarding another's legitimacy. That is to say, should the one great hegemon alone, or with several other powerful states, decide that a particular regime is not legitimate, in their view, then it is neither a sovereign state nor are its rulers sovereign. Recognition then, is an important element in our understanding. Stephan D. Krasner puts it this way:

> Whether international legal sovereignty and Westphalian sovereignty are honored depends on the decisions of rulers. There is no hierarchical structure to prevent rulers from violating the logics of appropriateness associated with mutual recognition or the exclusion of external authority. Rulers can recognize another state or not; they can recognize entities that lack juridical independence or territory. They can intervene in the internal affairs of other states or voluntarily compromise the autonomy of their own polity. (Krasner, *Sovereignty, Organized Hypocrisy*, p.7)

In a telling statement Krasner argues that "Westphalian sovereignty has frequently been compromised because autonomy has clashed with competing principles and disparate interests in an environment of asymmetrical power." (Ibid., p.228) That the United States is clearly one state which wields asymmetrical power over all other nation-states is not questioned any longer. Recognition of another state's sovereignty is decided by the most powerful states; this has always been true, it can be argued, whether it ought to be true may just be an academic exercise. Krasner points out that "Recognition has been extended to entities with attributes other than those conventionally associated with sovereignty." Taiwan and Hong Kong as well as the PLO (U.N. observer status) come to mind. But also, regarding sovereignty, [It] "...has been denied to governments in territories that possessed these attributes." Namely a juridically independent territorial entity which claims its right to rule without outside intervention in its domestic affairs. Krasner suggests that new rules can be (simply) invented if the old rules interfere with the execution of a given policy, especially by a more powerful state over the protests of the weaker. We will see below in Part Two that the Bush Administration has been *recognizing* the Taliban and in fact *negotiating* with them since early February 2001; up until five weeks before September 11, 2001, Bush considered the Taliban a "stabilizing force in the region." and had "wished to consolidate the position of the Taliban" so as to get at the oil and gas in the region. He simply changed his mind when negotiations did not achieve what the Bush Administration wanted (commercial interests and pipelines in exchange for a different governmental makeup in Afghanistan). Krasner does not argue whether this reinventing the rules "ought" to be true, it just is what is done.

> The rules of sovereignty, like rules that have existed in any international environment, do matter, especially if political leaders cannot agree, or use coercion, to create alternatives. Prevailing rules make it easier to do some things and harder to do others. But they are not determinative. New rules can be invented. (Krasner, *Problematic Sovereignty, Explaining Variation*, p. 343)

Clearly Mr. Bush has simply denied that the ruling Taliban, whatever the Afghan people might think, have any legitimate standing in international relations, therefore Mr. Bush has decided it is not a sovereign state; if not sovereign then the rules of Westphalian sovereignty may be violated at will. Krasner does point out that the other kind of sovereignty, international sovereignty, "has been more widely honored because interests and rules have been more congruent." (Ibid., *Sovereignty—Organized Hypocrisy*)

When it was in United States' interests to train and arm Osama bin Laden and the Taliban the rules dictated then, there was a congruence (of interests); when U.S. interests changed, the U.S. changes the rules and incongruence occurs in the international relations between the Taliban, Osama Bin Laden and the United States. It is therefore, purportedly, the lack of congruence in interests that gives Mr. Bush the legal right to bomb and remove the Taliban from power; some of the interests are outlined in part two of this text. It matters little what any court, domestic or world, has ruled, as the most powerful states, including the United States simply ignore rulings regarding themselves, that they do not agree with. Indeed, it was once said by Justice Cardoza, that "there is no such thing as international law," and "law may just be literature" after all. But I feel compelled to point out the following: In the words of one U.S. Supreme Court decision, that

> Every sovereign State is bound to respect the independence of every other sovereign State, and the courts of one country will not sit in judgment on the acts of the government of another done within its own territory. (The case is *Underhill vs. Hernandez*, quoted in *Oppenheim's International Law*, 1992, pp. 365-67)

With the process of globalization and the voluntary compromising of sovereignty that every nation-state must do when signing-on with the some 1,500 agreements of international governing bodies (WTO, IMF, World Bank, etc.), it is harder to give the concept of sovereignty its rightful place any longer. But, the many newly independent states (NIS) in the Caspian region, having spun off, like so many others, from the Soviet Union's hegemonic collapse, is particularly important to these states. Nationalism and identification with the State itself is maybe the only way these nations can survive; if they are allowed to go their own way, or the way dictated by yet another hegemon, is what is being played out on the present stage of history. And does the newest grand hegemon have such rights to decide. Krasner argues they always did.

> But rulers might also choose to reconfigure domestic authority structures in other states, accepting their juridical independence but compromising their de facto autonomy, a policy that does violate Westphalian sovereignty. Stronger states can pick and choose among different rules selecting the one that best suits their instrumental objectives, as the European powers did during the era of colonialism when they "resuscitated

pre-Westphalian forms of sovereignty" such as protectorates and subordinate states. (*Sovereignty*, Ibid., p.6)

Then it hardly should surprise anyone that American hegemony and intervention into the internal affairs of otherwise recognized (and previously by America) sovereign states might be construed as a revival of imperialism's colonialism. Has Mr. Bush not tossed out the very concept of Westphalian sovereignty in the case of not only Afghanistan, but it is explicit in his statements to the surrounding states, that "if you are not with us you are against us?" The American hegemon of Empire has announced to the world that a pre-Westphalian system is now in place and if your state sovereign is not aligned with the unipolar power of the United States your state is merely, and at best, a tributary state, a protectorate, a subordinate state, and at worst, the enemy of all civilization. There is little room to maneuver when Empire rules. And the interests of Empire are always commercial.

> The norm of autonomy, the core of Westphalian sovereignty, has been challenged by alternatives including human rights, minority rights, fiscal responsibility, and the maintenance of international stability. Moreover, in the international system principled claims have sometimes merely been a rationalization for exploiting the opportunities presented by power asymmetries. (Ibid. p.8)

Stephan D. Krasner is no absolutist, he simply points out the way it is, has been, and probably shall continue to be in international relations. He is fully cognizant of the fact that sovereignty is consistently violated. Coercion and intervention are such markers.

> Coercion and imposition involving issues of autonomy are violations of both international sovereignty and Westphalian sovereignty. Both coercion and imposition leave one of the parties worse off. The weaker actor would not have accepted an outcome inferior to the status quo ante if it were not faced with the threat of sanctions, possibly including the use of force. In the most extreme case, the target could be eliminated. coercion and imposition violate a basic norm of international legal sovereignty, which is that states have the right to act voluntarily. Rulers would never voluntarily accept an arrangement that leaves them worse off. (*Sovereignty and its Discontents*, p.27, in *Sovereignty*)

Krasner understands power. The powerful, the one which initiates the coercion is often in absolute control. "The initiator must have overwhelming power, the ability to determine life or death, figuratively and sometimes literally, of rulers in the target entity" (state or would-be state). Clearly this power is often military in its makeup. In the case of Afghanistan this is all too true.

But Mr. Bush is using other forms of coercion in the surrounding region to gain, not approval, but non-complaint, no interference from the other actors in the region. Sometimes it involves the initial recognition of the governing elite of one or more states if not the state itself. This is what Mr. Bush is doing with Uzbekistan and Turkmenistan and of course Azerbaijan. Bribery and promises of business and investment in their state's infrastructure. But it is more.

> Already powerful states have engaged in imposition by conditioning recognition on the target's acceptance of conditions related to domestic political structures. Rejection would mean that the target never becomes an actor. The status quo is an option, but the status quo, an absence of international recognition, would leave the ruler without a state to rule. (Ibid.)

For our analysis, Krasner added this significant contribution. Non-recognition does not completely eliminate the rulers of the target state from conducting its affairs, witness Saddam Hussein's Iraqi recovery, but it adds an element of uncertainty. "Ex ante they may not be able to predict how particular governments or national court systems will respond to an unrecognized government. Multinational firms might be more reluctant to invest." (Ibid., p.16) It is here that non-congruence of interests with the United States appears and therefore the rules have changed for Afghanistan and Azerbaijan (not to mention all the surrounding states), this is the outcome. (See Appendix One below)

In Whose Interests?
Chapter Eight Part Two

Azerbaijan International Operating Company (AIOC)

Exactly who stands to gain by the Caspian region being developed into an oil and gas producer or pipeline transit country for the oil and gas produced by the other states in the region? Who gains specifically, by name, is the question? One can easily see how Exxon and Unocal shall gain, and gain greater then even the Saudi Royal family does in Saudi Arabia. Can we, by due diligence, ascertain a few names of individuals which have long wanted to see the region opened-up to benefit United States energy interests? One needs to look back to discover such a thing, as the present often hides the past in a veil of mist and lack of interest. We tend to see events like September 11, through eyes deluded by the present rhetoric. An analyst, researcher that is to say, must read everything, past, present and look to the future. We found this of some interest given the present players in the Bush Jr. Administration's roster. And remember, the following individuals were no longer part of the

168 The Hydra of Carnage

United States government at the time; they were part of the oil and gas, banking and lending, and consulting industries which would gain specifically by
the opening of the Caspian region's reserves. They were, then, *lobbyists* for
their personal interests and that of the multinational corporations represented; i.e. Corporatism proper to Empire.

> Among those newspaper articles on American interests in Cas-
> pian oil and Azerbaijan, perhaps the most revealing, in terms of
> the emerging foreign policy consensus on the region was titled,
> "Former Top U.S. Aides Seek Caspian Gusher," and appeared
> in *The Washington Post*. The article described the activities of a
> prestigious group of former high-ranking U.S. government of-
> ficials who were directly involved in the oil rush in the Caspian
> and in shaping U.S. policy towards the region. The article states,
> "These men come from different parties and different past ad-
> ministrations, but they are working together for policy chang-
> es that they say are needed to put U.S. companies on an equal
> footing with foreign competitors in Azerbaijan." The article
> mentioned specifically two former National Security advisors,
> Brent Scowcroft and Zbigniew Brezinski, former White House
> Chief of Staff John Sununu, former Secretary of Defense Richard
> Cheney, former Secretary of State James A. Baker III, and former
> Secretary of the Treasury Lloyd Bentsen. The lobbying and pub-
> lic affairs efforts of these individuals in support of U.S. policy
> towards Azerbaijan were described as "intense" and have cer-
> tainly been instrumental in influencing the opinions of current
> U.S. policy makers. (Source: *A NEW STAGE IN U.S.-CASPIAN
> SEA BASIN RELATIONS*; CENTRAL ASIA No. 5 (11) 1997 by
> James MacDougall)

Mr. MacDougall is not remiss in going even further in his take on the
region. Looking at 1996-7 he states that, "Over the course of the last year both
the U.S. academic community and a number of policy analysis organizations
or 'think tanks' have sharpened their focus on the Caspian basin, particularly notable among them is *The Heritage Foundation*, a conservative think tank
whose chief mission is to provide foreign policy advice to the U.S. Congress.
In addition to publishing regular policy analysis on the Caspian region, *The
Heritage Foundation* hosted a banquet in honor of SOCAR Vice-President Il-
ham Aliyev during his visit to Washington in February 1997." (Ibid.)

The fact is that even in the academic community where endless discussions often seem the norm, the circumstances for a more rigorous study of
Central Asia and the Caucasus are being created. In many universities, un-
dergraduate and graduate students alike began their fall semesters with opportunities to take new courses related to the Caucasus and Central Asia. At
one leading Washington-based university a Central Asia Institute has been
formed to conduct research and inform public policy. MacDougall goes on

with his argument with this important item at the time. "Earlier this year, the Institute's Director (S. Frederick Starr) published a thought-provoking article on U.S. policy towards the countries of the Caspian basin." One need not remind the reader that it was S. Frederick Starr who testified in the February 18, 1998, hearing of the following year on The Silk Road Strategy. MacDougall continues,

> The appearance of Deputy Secretary of State Strobe Talbott at the Central Asia Institute to deliver a major foreign policy speech on Central Asia and the Caucasus illustrates the close relationship between government officials and academics in shaping consensus on U.S. foreign policy issues. Mr. Talbott's speech, delivered on July 21, 1997 restated the point made by Mr. Berger in March, underscoring the importance the United States attaches to Central Asia and the Caucasus. Coming as it did, one week before the visit of Azerbaijan President Heydar Aliyev to Washington, the speech was an acknowledgement that a new stage in U.S. relations with the countries of the region, particularly Azerbaijan, has begun. (Ibid.)

Clearly we have an elite who believe they can not only lobby the government itself for policy changes in any region of the world, lobby for personal financial, and commercial interests, but with sufficient patience, rotate back into the same governance structure to implement the very same policies previously lobbied for. Keep in mind that several of the individuals in the above piece were part of the Senior Bush's Cabinet during the Persian Gulf War, or were in Clinton's Cabinet first term, or were in Bush Sr.'s, Clinton's, and now Bush Junior's as well. Truly these elite are the only true international *global citizens*. Former NSA, Brent "Scowcroft, for example, was paid $100,000 in 1996 by Pennzoil Co. for consulting on special international projects," according to the firm's latest annual report. The former Bush adviser also earned a $30,000 board of director's fee from the company, which is a partner in the **Azerbaijan International Operating Company** (AIOC), the main foreign oil consortium in Azerbaijan." (Ibid., and the Washington Post article dated July, 6, 1997, Page A-1).

> AIOC, in which American firms (Mobil, Unocal, Exxon, Pennzoil) have a 40 percent stake, is a client of the law firm of (former secretary of state for Bush Sr.) James A. Baker III, while (current Vice President) Dick Cheney is chairman of Halliburton Inc., an oil services firm operating in the Caspian fields.... (Former Chief of Staff to Bush Sr.) John Sununu's management consulting firm, JHS Associates, [is expected to] (did) sign a major contract with the Azeri government during a U.S. visit next month by President Geidar Aliyev, according to Azeri sources. At a gala dinner here for visiting Azeri Prime Minister Artur

Rasizade in May, several hundred U.S. businessmen savored Caspian caviar and rubbed shoulders with Azeri visitors. Featured speaker Sununu, just back from the Azerbaijan capital of Baku, flattered the dignitary and expounded on Azerbaijan's strategic importance...."— "(former secretary of treasury, Clinton) Lloyd Bentsen is a shareholder in Frontera Resources, an oil services company working in Azerbaijan. Frontera is chaired by fellow Texan William H. White, a former Clinton deputy secretary of energy. (Former national security advisor, Carter) Zbigniew Brezenski is a consultant to Amoco, another AIOC partner promoting Azerbaijan's cause in Washington. An Amoco spokesman confirmed that Brzezinski advises the firm on Caspian oil matters but declined to disclose his fee. Along with those Washington powers, an assortment of only slightly lower-ranking former officials have descended on the Baku oil frontier. They include former representative Charles Wilson (D-Tex.), who is working with an energy developer, and former assistant secretary of defense Richard L. Armitage (today Undersecretary of State, under Powell), whose consulting firm is helping U.S. companies in the region. Adding a sense of intrigue, former Maj. Gen. Richard Secord, chief covert operative for Oliver L. North in the Iran-contra scandal, reportedly had been sighted in Baku. (Source: Washington Post, *Former Top U.S. Aides Seek Caspian Gusher*, July 6, 1997, p. A-1, by David B. Ottaway)

Dick Cheney, who joined Halliburton in 1995, said, "I have greatly enjoyed working with the worldwide family of Halliburton employees and customers during my employment with Halliburton. Having worked closely with Dave Lesar and the Halliburton management team over the past five years, I have great confidence for the future success of Halliburton." Dave Lesar, who replaced Cheney (2000) commented, "Halliburton has immensely benefited from Dick Cheney's leadership and the worldwide respect he commands. Together we have established corporate strategies that will remain in place and continue to lead Halliburton in the future." Clearly this is truer than ever.

There are several others in the present Bush Jr. administration who have long histories in the oil industry besides Bush himself and Cheney and the others noted above. These others need to be considered as well. Ms Condoleeza Rice, Bush's National Security Advisor, was with Chevron Oil from 1991 - 2000, as a manager; Secretary of Commerce Donald Evans and Secretary of Energy, Stanley Abraham both worked for Tom Brown, another oil giant, according to authors Brisard and Dasquie in their new book titled "Bin Laden, the forbidden truth" (Published in France, November 2001; see below for other revealing facts by these authors.) Dr. Henry Kissinger was hired by

Unocal to specifically lobby for the Afghanistan pipeline route into Pakistan and India.

Regarding Richard Armitage, it is generally believed that Mr. Armitage actually served in the Central Intelligence Agency (CIA) till 1978 and from 1976, after a cover resignation from the CIA, worked for some private companies of the CIA, which were being used by it for covert actions in Indo-China. "His critics had alleged in the past that he was the author of the idea of using heroin to weaken the fighting capability of the communists in Indo-China and then in Afghanistan; though the late Le Comte de Marenches, the head of the French External Intelligence Agency under Presidents George Pompidou and Giscard d'Estaing, had claimed that it was he who had given this idea to the Americans with specific reference to Afghanistan." Whether it was Armitage or not who gave the idea to the American government, it was used; and it is Armitage, Cheney, Wolfowitz, back in public life to prosecute what they had lobbied for in private life. Kissinger, Brzezinski, and Scowcroft and others are what makes-up the Defense Policy Board to advise on the prosecution of the war, and what they, as well, lobbied for in private life.

Threat to the Region?

*The irresponsibility of this is breathtaking;
the pressure on Pakistan alone could
ignite an unprecedented crisis across the
Indian sub-continent.
Having reported many wars, I am always struck
by the absurdity of effete politicians eager
to wave farewell to young soldiers,
but who themselves would not say boo to a Taliban goose.*

—BY JOHN PILGER, FORMER MIRROR
chief foreign correspondent

Given that, we shall return to Mr. Bush Jr.' s present policy statements and further reality checks. Mr. Bush claimed that the fanatical Muslims were exclusively responsible for the September 11, air attacks; he further claimed that they hate us because they hate the very institutions of liberty, they hate our freedoms, they hate our Christianity. He could then claim that the real threat in the region are fundamentalist Islam. He is waging a war on al-Qaida and the terrorists which follow Osama bin Laden; "All roads lead to bin Laden," Bush has been quoted as saying. But is fundamentalist Islam the threat to the region? Lt. General William Odom sees it somewhat differently.

As a tentative judgment, I suggest that Islam is a cultural disposition, not a threat, but possibly a vulnerability. The seven decades of secularization in Central Asia and Azerbaijan will retard but probably not permanently preclude the revival of

Islam. Whether its politics will be radical is likely to be determined by how the dictators treat it. If they treat it as a threat and repress it brutally, it will turn radical. Thus we may want to call Islam a vulnerability, but we should not see it as a threat to the region. (Ibid., below)

What Mr. Bush is about to set in motion in the Caspian region is precisely what will create the threat to the region, not the other war round. In fact, it is hard to imagine anything but a dictatorial regime of some various shade to control the region after Bush attempts to remove the Taliban from power. Only an authoritarian regime will be able to make the region safe for the oil pipelines. The Taliban, as Bin Laden stated the first week of November 2001, will simply slip into the mountains and continue the guerrilla war from there against the Americans and whatever puppet regime we place in power. Given our newly approved tyrants export wealth from oil and gas, pipelines and power will destabilize the region further, not the other way round. General Odom continues his elaboration on just this point:

> In the Caspian Sea littoral states, pouring wealth into the hands of weak governments could destroy them, or at least prevent them from making significant progress in state-building. This threat is far more serious for these regimes than Russian imperialism. Yet it is the most difficult and the threat least likely to be addressed by effective Western strategies. (Lt. General William E. Odom, USA, Ret., William E. Odom is the *Director of National Security Studies at the Hudson Institute* in Washington, D.C.; He served as a Director of the *US National Security Agency*.)

In another article of related interest titled, *The Relationship Between Internal Cohesion and External Sovereignty in Central Asia and the Caucasus* the author makes a similar point although one falling upon deaf American policy maker's ears.

> Neither Russia nor the West will find any advantage in a repetition of a Great Game in Central Asia and the Transcaucasus. No hegemon has the capacity to solve the problems involved in the nation-building process of Eurasia's deeply divided societies. As we have seen, their lack of internal sovereignty has been a basic motive both for the establishment of authoritarian regimes and for the support of a hegemon, be it Russia or the West. It is doubtful that either method is appropriate for increasing popular loyalty to the state and avoiding the eruption of violent social, ethnic or regional conflicts. (Dr. Bruno Coppieters, Centrum voor Politicologie, Vrije Universiteit Brussel)

Nothing can be said to be written in stone, and I am not arguing that Mr. Bush is willingly out to, willy-nilly, destroy the nation-states in the region just to satisfy our western and specifically American hunger for fossil fuels. I am not saying Mr. Bush is only, and exclusively, setting out to benefit solely the American oil companies like Unocal, Mobil, Exxon and Pennzoil, whose commercial interests, and in securing those interests, they would make U.S. taxpayer's responsible. I am not, further, stating that Mr. Bush will agree, as will the next president and Congress, to tax the American people to insure the bloody venture. But I am saying, there seems to be a single-mindedness here that is problematic in outcome to a rather great degree. The ambitions of the United States is comparable to that of Great Britain during its period of imperial expansion. Britain was warned then by Edmond Burke:

> Among precautions against ambition it may not be amiss to take one precaution against our own. I must fairly say, I dread our *own* power and our *own* power ambition; I dread being too much dreaded....We may say that we shall not abuse this astonishing and hitherto unheard of power. But every other nation will think we shall abuse it. It is impossible but that, sooner or later, this state of things must produce a combination against us which may be our ruin. (Burke, *Remarks on the Policy of the Allies with Respect to France*, The Works of Edmond Burke, Boston: Little, Brown & Company, 1901, Vol. 4, p.457.)

"Iran, Zaire, Guatemala, Chile, Indonesia, Greece, Panama, Australia, Haiti... we're real good at toppling regimes. But just collecting your basic data about who's up to what in the U.S. and what not, that's not our strong suit... if the U.S. needed to swoop in and take out Colombia's current government, man, we could have that done by the weekend."
CENTRAL INTELLIGENCE AGENCY DIRECTOR GEORGE TENET, LANGLEY, VA

In the recent Fall issue of *The National Interest*, author Owen Harries suggests now that America should heed the same warning (which it clearly has not, in retrospect) as above; regarding America's preoccupation with the business of the world, economic, policing every corner, exercising a level of hegemony the world has never seen, cultural and other nation's governance, Harries stated this:

> What we have seen has been a pattern of indiscriminate and irresolute—but unrelenting—busyness, of interfering and lecturing, of a promiscuous though largely ineffectual use of force and of sanction. It is a pattern of behavior that is alienating an increasing number of states and that, if persisted in, will ultimately be dangerous for the United States.(*The Anglosphere Illusion*, p. 136)

It is the weak state that will find cooperation with other states like itself, find common cause with terrorist groups and guerrilla armies from everywhere, from anywhere; it is this process which the United States has ignored where not even Great Britain, in their heyday, did. Harries noted that if America, as the newest effort at anglophile hegemony does not pay heed to these warnings for "prudence and restraint,"— "not faith in American exceptionalism," saying that it is those "qualities and only those qualities...that will in the long run enable the United States to avoid the usual fate of assertive hegemons." (Ibid.) Weak states do not cause disorder as Mr. Bush has suggested; this is the so-called reason to rid Afghanistan of the Taliban. (Other commercial objectives aside?) Here is how this pertains to the Caspian region presently in consideration.

> Weak states do not actually "cause" disorder, violence, and war. Rather they are vulnerable to the actors that cause such things. We find two types of weak states in Central Asia and the Caucasus. The first is the struggling democracy, or those states that tried to follow the democracy path in the last years of perestroika and immediately after the collapse of the Soviet Union. They are Georgia, Armenia, Azerbaijan, Tajikistan, and Kyrgyzstan. In all of these cases but Kyrgyzstan, the Russians took advantage of the open political processes there to create chaos, applying a divide and rule strategy to retain Moscow's influence. Kyrgyzstan has been an exception, probably because Kazakstan and Uzbekistan did not want a civil war there and nipped the KGB's mischief in the bud in the Fergana disorders in 1990....The second type of weak state includes the dictatorships Kazakstan, Uzbekistan and Turkmenistan. In these cases, local communist party leaders changed their labels, became nationalists, kept control, and therefore, were able to keep the Russians from stirring up conflicts which they could then pretend to manage as so-called "peacekeeping" endeavors, the pattern in Tajikistan, Georgia, and for a time in Azerbaijan. Aliyev has moved Azerbaijan toward this type, just as Akayev has done in Kyrgyzstan. It allows them to keep the Russians out, but it brings other problems. (Ibid., Odom's article above)

Regional Power Politics

In the region we have seen the lobbying efforts of a close knit group of powerful former government officials, many from the Defense Department of past United States' administrations. These unregistered foreign lobbyists would secure the region in the interests of Empire and Empire's imperial industrial base, AIOC one of the primary players in the region. These men while no longer in office gained enormous power as CEOs, directors and legal counsel for the largest firms. The names were given above and it is here that I must point out how serious this lobbying effort ("intense" it was called at the time) was to these men. As I traced their names individually I kept coming across an acronym unfamiliar to me: USACC. Richard Armitage, Zbigniew Brzezinski, Henry Kissinger, John Sunnu, Lloyd Bentson, James A. Baker III and Dick Cheney; these names were precisely those named in the *Washington Times* article mentioned above. Every name was repeated on the USACC roster. In fact the last six were the *only* six listed as the Honorary Council of Advisors under Officers. Each was listed as advisors to the United States Azerbaijan Chamber of Commerce. Richard Armitage was listed on the full Board of Directors of the same USACC. This led me to take a closer interest in the one player, lobbyist, former Secretary of Defense under President Bush Sr., and the man that prosecuted the Persian Gulf War, and now arguably prosecuting the Caspian regional war: Dick Cheney.

*   *   *

Most know that Cheney was the CEO of Halliburton Company since 1995 resigning Nov. 2000 when named Vice-Presidential candidate. I looked at past press releases of Halliburton on their website archives (one thing one can count on with corporations is their bragging rights) there were many but this one and the next tell enough of the story. (Others were included in my Appendix Six to the origianl paper, and there were many others.)

HALLIBURTON SUBSEA OPENS CASPIAN MARINE BASE

ABERDEEN, Scotland—Halliburton International Inc. and KASPMORNEFTELOT (KMNF), the marine division of the State Oil Company of Azerbaijan Republic (SOCAR), have entered into a 12-year contract for a marine base and associated services to support Halliburton Subsea offshore construction activity in the Caspian region. Halliburton Subsea is a business unit of Halliburton Company's (NYSE: HAL) Energy Services Group.

Halliburton has gained enormous power in the region with Dick Cheney's lobbying efforts as CEO and as an Officer of the United States Azerbaijan Chamber of Commerce. But it was pipelines that were the major consideration where both Azerbaijan and Afghanistan are concerned. More was uncovered within the same archives.

AIOC GIVES BROWN & ROOT THE GO-AHEAD ON MAJOR CASPIAN PROJECT

DALLAS, Texas (August 11, 1997) - AIOC (Azerbaijan International Operating Company) has issued Brown & Root a letter of intent relating to the award of a contract to provide engineering design and procurement services for Phase 1 of the Full Field Development of the GCA (Guneshli Chirag Azeri) offshore fields in the Caspian Sea. The development is likely to center on a single processing platform plus two drilling and wellhead platforms for up to 80 wells. Also included in the design and procurement work scope are: infield pipelines; main oil and gas pipelines to the Sangachal onshore terminal approximately 200 kilometers away; expansion of the onshore terminal; and up-grading of the main export pipelines from Azerbaijan to ports on the Black Sea in Russia (Novorossiysk) and Georgia (Supsa) – the Northern and Western Routes respectively.

As one can see Brown & Root is one of the more significant global build-ers of pipelines throughout the world, and one can go to their website to see the region's they range over. But the Caspian region and Azerbaijan and Af-ghanistan are what is important for the present analysis. Brown & Root is a division of Halliburton Company as is Halliburton Energy Services. This is important to point out now, as when Brown & Root receives contract awards to build the pipelines which must run through Azerbaijan and Afghanistan few journalists will even know that it was Dick Cheney who headed Brown & Root and not just Halliburton alone. And that it shall be Dick Cheney who reaps untold millions by removing the Taliban from power and placing into power a government, once again, the international community, Unocal and AIOC and their lenders will recognize. An important point needs to be brought out now rather than later: I do not today need to *prove* a Conflict of Interest case against Dick Cheney. Conflict of Interest laws are written to preclude any "apparent" conflict, any "appearance" of "potential" conflict of interest. This is the same criterion which precludes a judge from sitting at the bench in a trial where there is even some doubt that he may have an interest in the outcome. These laws are enforced (in the past) very seriously. It will be up to Dick Cheney to prove he will not gain, nor his family and financial associates, financially by the prosecution of the war and removal and replacement of the ruling Taliban in Afghanistan. Indeed, five years from now, should Cheney return to the private sector or retirement, how will one (or who) seek evidence then, should he have gained financially right along with the Bush family?

*   *   *

Corporatism and International Law

This is raw Corporatism and even more raw Empire in the making. A word on Empire's Corporatism is in order. Corporatism is the guiding philo-sophical ideology of Empire and globalization is the process that supports it. Regarding the above analysis of those very gentle-men, regardless of Party, which have moved in and out of government from the private sector, lobby-ing in behalf of their own private corporate interests into positions of power that effectively give them the opportunity to execute that same policy, other scholars have seen this as clearly as I.

[Hence], the United States was treated at the ideological and policy level to a debate for and against corporatism, while at the level of practical politics both parties had their own set of supportive corporatized interests ("strap hangers," we will call them) who road the Washington Metro into and out of administrative positions depending on which party was in power at any particular time. In other words, the Democrats had a whole raft of corporate interests that came into government when they won elections, and Republicans had their own (though smaller) raft of interest groups that accompanied them into office. (Howard J. Wiarda, *Corporatism and Comparative Politics*, 1997, p.146)

The case was made by Wiarda that when the government was divided, as under Reagan with a Democratically controlled House and Senate, the same held true but for different reasons, arguing that the "famous 'gridlock' or 'logjam' that engulfs Washington, in other words, is not just a result of the clash between the parties or between the White House and Congress but of an even larger, cultural, ideological, and interest-based conflict that characterizes the competition of the two parties' respective corporatized hangers-on as well." This point is important for understanding Empire as well as our present corporatized regime domestically. The above names which lobbied in behalf of the oil industries in the Caspian region came from both parties and several had served in both Republican and Democratic administrations. As an aside, Corporatism, and I always capitalize it as it is an ideology no less effective and permanent than the other two great idea based ideologies, or isms, Marxism and liberalism, and is the vehicle by which both labor and environmental groups, feminists and gays, business and financial interests all make their way into the body politic understood as corporatism as process. Each does not any longer want to see the system fundamentally changed, there are no socialists or Marxists seriously out for revolution, the feminists and gays right along with, and specifically Ralph Nader's octopus-like organizations, environmental and civic groups want a seat at the table of Corporatism; they are, each one, prepared to give up specific liberties to gain acceptance, positions of power, and funding at the trough of big government, big business and big labor. Corporatism sucks everything into its vortex.

A U.S.-style corporate state has arrived unsung, unheralded, and almost never mentioned. The emergence of corporatism has to do with the parallel emergence of Big labor, Big Agriculture, Big Business, Big Universities, Big Defense, Big Welfare, and Big government, all operating in a symbiotic relationship....Among its implications are the merging of the public and private sectors, the delegation of public power to private-interest associations, and the increased central government consolidation of economic and political power. (Ibid., pp. 147-148)

This is why there is no serious challenge to the "Industrial Interests" of Big Business, like the oil and pipeline lobbying seen above in this argument. Ralph Nader wants a seat at the table; they, or I should say his, groups like *Public Citizen* do not want to see the *World Trade Organization* abolished and have always and every time, denounced any individual or group, Senator or Congressman, who proposed America pull out of the WTO. (See the chapter titled *The WTO and National Treatment: Ralph Nader's Endorsement*) Nader's agent at *Public Citizen*, Laurie Wallach, which had most to do with organizing the past 1999 Seattle WTO protests and elsewhere, has publicly endorsed National Treatment for the multinational corporations operating throughout the world. This effectively grants full citizenship rights to each paper company in whatever nation-state it operates in. The hypocrisy on the part of Nader & company, and his are money-making companies, is clear when one understands Nader is not opposed to the Coporatism he helps to create (and helps to finance with his own personal investment dollars) but in fact stands to gain precisely the same "status" as global citizen of their own non-profit corporations as do the for-profit corporations. And there are other groups that are "in" on creating corporatism as Wiarda points out above. Indeed, everybody is "in" today; there are no groups on the outside except those that do not matter as the State/Media nexus does not recognize them and therefore they have no voice, no right to assemble, no right to the media, no first amendment rights at all. It is this understanding alone that can give one a clear picture why there is so little protest against president Bush's "Jolly Little War." Everyone today is in, on the take, stand to gain, by Empire's success.

> Note how far beyond interest-group pluralism the United States had come. This was no longer just interest-groups vying for political influence. This was interest-groups operating within the system, operating from inside, being incorporated into the state system of cabinet ministries and other agencies....This merging and blurring of private groups and public agencies is what corporatism...is all about. Moreover, such a blurring of the private and the public tends to produce corruption, special favoritism, and the serving of private interests over the public weal. (ibid., p.140)

We shall here take note of another special interest group which wants a seat at the table of Big Government's Corporatism and the residual power that Empire brings to the table. The feminist movement is not without their hypocritical strap-hangers.

The so-called Women's Issue:
A most hypocritical "strap-hanger."

*The world of criminals, generally speaking,
is not and cannot be tolerant.
But political criminals must be
intolerant not only for personal
but also political reasons.*

—MIECZYSLAW MANELI

Mr. George W. Bush and Tony Blair blared it from the rooftops: The Taliban mistreat their women; girls are not allowed to go to school after a certain age; women must wear clothing unacceptable to Hollywood's raw styles;
women cannot be self-reliant and tough, smart and sassy...like the phony fem-
inist-driven nonsense we see on so many new movies that come out of Hollywood these days, the female action-hero. Are we to believe that suddenly
American women, in any significant numbers at all, ever gave a damn what
happens to any other women other than themselves?

This is one area that some are concerned less with, but I think it wise to
point out how what seems, at the time, a proper protest regarding a proper area of concern, can aid in the destruction and wreak havoc for the very
people the protestors would claim they were trying to help. Never mind that
when most American's protest, it has little relationship to the thing protested
in favor of or in disfavor of. It is, most often, individuals intoxicated with
their own words, self, and the belief that because they had a thought, one
small, and often very small indeed, concept, it is akin to a religious revelation
of "THE TRUTH." While the political far-right religious elements are well-
known enough, the political Left in America is highly susceptible as well to
this kind of myth-making and disingenuousness.

When I hear that a Hollywood celebrity is directly involved in any protest, I grab my wallet, and immediately find myself more concerned than ever
about the truth (as an essence needing deliberate protection), and whether anything I might hear should be given weight; this is not cynicism but
personal real life experience speaking. Those who make just way too much
money, have way too much free time on their hands, tend to think that due
to their luck, and marginal talents (talent in one area like singing, or being
funny, does not make one an expert on humanitarian nor geopolitical affairs)
and a recognizable mug, they "ought" to speak out on something, anything.
The wives of over-paid popular folk-heroes especially get caught-up in this,
due to the age-old coattail effect. When their efforts wreak havoc on the very
people they claimed they cared so much about? ...they fall as silent as the
dead ones they helped kill-off. Their guilt never surfaces and apology is never
forthcoming. The dead Afghan women and children, the starving women and
children refugees, the wanton destruction of these women's homes, has been,
in part, due to an extraordinary racial hatred raising its ugly head towards

peoples and cultures we understand not at all. The ruling Taliban regime of Afghanistan has been the target of extraordinary bigotry, much hatred and racism, bias and nonsense. Nobody is saying the regime is not a tyranny, but a tyranny unlike the seventy some odd tyrannies the world over? Worse than the Saudi regime? worse than the Al Sabah family? China? No, the fundamental difference is the Taliban are poor tyrants, the others are rich. And the American progressive-Left rarely, if ever, attacks rich foreign tyrants.

Here is what one account of the Taliban and the current carpet bombing and killing of women and children had to say prior to the war on Afghanistan. It should be pointed out here as well, the Northern Alliance which Mr. Bush has allied our forces are worse by far than the Taliban ever were; the neighboring countries' ruling dictatorships from where we are presently launching our Great Game, are equally tyrants.

> The Taliban came on the world scene at the wrong time for their own good. In the early 1980s, Afghan groups with similar attitudes to women—for example, the Hezb-e Islami of Gulbuddin Hekmatyar—were funded with few qualms by the US Administration. But by the mid-1990s, the global strategic situation was radically different as a result of the collapse of the USSR, and new agendas of social awareness were being pressed with increasing vigor. The UN International Women's Conference in Beijing in September 1995 confirmed an agenda radically at odds with that of the Taliban, and a dense network of women's groups had formed to give effect to that agenda. Indeed, the failure of the Taliban to secure recognition or Afghanistan's General Assembly seat reflected in part the effective lobbying of those groups (which also put pressure on UNOCAL to distance itself from the Taliban). The Feminist Majority Foundation under Eleanor Smeal took a strong lead in such action, with support from American celebrities such as Mavis Leno and Lionel Richie, and their position was bolstered by the release in August 1998 of a damning and widely-publicized report from the Boston-based Physicians for Human Rights entitled The Taliban's War on Women. For these groups, the response of their own governments to the Taliban's demands for acceptance became an important symbol of those governments' seriousness about gender issues and (in contrast to what might have been the case had the rulers of a resource-rich state such as Saudi Arabia been under fire) there were no compelling reasons for the governments to ignore this domestic pressure.

There is no reason why the Bush Jr. regime will ignore these helpful and ultimately rewarding pressures against the Taliban now although the Bush regime had as recently as five weeks before September 11, 2001 recognized the Taliban as "a stabilizing force in the region." How many women will have died in our carpet bombing of Afghanistan? How many children? But the *Feminist Majority Foundation* led by Smeal with the help of Jay Leno's wife, will not decry these deaths as these were women which did not join their peculiar crusade nor even likely would have agreed with it in any numbers. The majority that makes up Smeal's taxpayer funded *minority* movement will only care about those women that are of like mind. Will the Afghan women be better off under the Bush and Blair appointed dictators? not likely. Are the women who lost their children better off? certainly not. Are the women who lost their Taliban husbands? By Mavis Leno's standards, certainly.

> Kill another fetus now...we don't like children anyhow. (Leonard Cohen, CD *The Future*)

Will the Afghan women who lost their lives be seen as martyrs? Afghan women in burkas were visible fighting along-side their Taliban husbands against the Northern Alliance insurgents and our own US Special Forces. How may of these "terrorists" were killed defending their country? I am sure that most American feminists will say we cannot blame Ms Smeal and Ms Leno for what Bush has decided to do. But one would be remiss in forgetting that Smeal & Company (and it is a money making company) lobbied against Unocal's acceptance of the Taliban. "In whose interests?" has many ways of treatment. The Leftist women who would deliver a death blow to men and women, Janet Reno-like, of foreign cultures (whose values are their own), which do not agree with their very peculiar western petty bourgeoisie middle-class progressive leftist's personal values, are equally to blame when wars are prosecuted against their chosen devils. That this was not what they intended to see happen is pure sophistry when one knows they remained not the least vocal in opposing the carpet bombing. The act of claiming sufficient power to have a seat at the table of Corporatism, this women's movement so-called, should be no less proud than Unocal and Dick Cheney in the carpet bombing of Afghanistan they have all taken part. They, these American feminists in particular, and the American Left in general, have said nothing, for the most part, against the war; leaving men more principled like Bill Maher, on *Politically Incorrect*, to squirm while a guest (to defend his few statements against the war) on none other than Mavis Leno's hubby's *Late Night*. A hubby which did nothing to defend Mahr's right to say what he wishes on his own program? A hubby with some thirty or more, gas guzzling, exotic automobiles; his little greedy hobby, which must, of course, consume just how much in fossil fuels?

While Mr. Bush bombs and kills more Muslims, killing Muslim women's husbands and fathers, and leaving Afghan women dead as well, in the hundreds if not thousands, during Ramadan, Mr. Bush holds a gala event for Muslims at the White House! The pragmatic Arab diplomats and Persian diplomats which attend, seek a seat at the table of Empire just as the Saudi Royalty has for decades.

> Last night, Bush wished "a blessed Ramadan" to 52 Muslim
> diplomats who came to the State Dining Room for a tradition-
> al Iftar dinner, which breaks the daily sunrise-to-sundown fast
> during Islam's holy month. Bush had refused calls from some
> Muslim leaders to cease hostilities in Afghanistan during Ra-
> madan, which began Friday (Nov. 17th, 2001)....The guests in-
> cluded the Palestinian National Authority's representative in
> Washington, Hasan Abdel Rahman, and the Saudi ambassador
> to the United States, Prince Bandar bin Sultan.(Cited in *Bush De-
> fends Order For Military Tribunals, President Hosts Ramadan Iftar
> Dinner*, By Mike Allen, Washington Post Staff Writer, Tuesday,
> November 20, 2001; Page A14)

But there was another group of pragmatists (defined properly as oppor-
tunists) attending the several day's gala celebrations. Women, and none too
few man-haters of various stripes, attended as well. Seeking a seat at the table
of Empire's corporatism, these hypocritical few (which by no stretch of the
imagination represent the mass of women at all, just their own self-importance), intoxicated with hearing their own loud, bleating voices, endorse the
killing of the husbands and fathers of Afghan women and children. These
deaths are clearly better for these "oppressed" Muslim women, according to
these depraved bigots, than to live with a belief system these few upper-class
wealthy western white-girls do not share. This same principle was applied at
the Branch Davidian compound in Waco, Texas, under the full legal authority
and responsibility of, then Attorney General, man-hating, Ms Janet Reno: the
women at Waco were better off dead than living with a heterosexual, religious, gun-owning male. The same women lobbyists noted above make their
glorious presence felt once again.

> In a continuation of the administration's global campaign to
> highlight the oppression of Afghan women by the Taliban re-
> gime, Secretary of State Colin L. Powell met at the Eisenhower
> Executive Office Building yesterday with a spectrum of women
> that included Christian radio host Janet Parshall and feminists
> Eleanor Smeal and Mavis Leno....Bonnie Erbe, host of PBS's "To
> the Contrary," said women who usually disagree rose to praise
> the administration for the campaign. "The Democratic wom-
> en had to give them credit, because they're doing something
> very atypical and something that takes a lot of guts," Erbe said.
> (Ibid.)

I would add that it indeed takes a lot of guts, and "gall" to make such an
appearance appear to be something charitable and decent. "...rose to praise
the administration for the campaign," indeed. We are seeing the rise of hatred
and bigotry, racism and inflamed passions, over issues clearly manipulated
in the State/mass media nexus for their own rating's gain. This is what one
respected Afghan woman had to say about our peculiar American-brand of
feminists:

General Suhaila Siddiq, 60, sighs with exasperation at Western feminists and their obsession with the burka, the all-enveloping veil whose forcible use symbolized for many outsiders the Taleban's oppressive rule.

"The first priority should be given to education, primary school facilities, the economy and reconstruction of the country but the West concentrates on the burka and whether the policies of the Taleban are better or worse than other regimes," she says dismissively. "Let these things be decided by history."

She believes that the burka, which was worn long before the Taleban and still is by most women around Kabul, is not the battlefield upon which to fight their war. (West's feminists under fire from female general, From STEPHEN FARRELL IN KABUL, November 28, 2001)

Moreover, this hatred displayed everywhere, veiled as patriotism or caring activism, will bring only greater hatred of Americans in general by many oppressed people throughout the world. Mr. Bush's defense of his prosecution of this *delict* against Afghanistan shall find America facing further reprisals and further attacks on our soil; Americans will never be truly safe anywhere in the developing world after these events run their course.

Historical Perspectives: Similarities of Process

The full story of this Administration's manipulation of events surrounding the September 11th air attacks may never be known. As with the Persian Gulf War of 1990-91, which Bush Sr. played out, much is hidden. Like father like son, Bush Junior's real political objectives are never admitted to. Meetings taken at the White House during April, 1990, prior to the August 2nd, 1990 invasion by Iraq into Kuwait, told the real story, still not widely understood. Bush Junior's administration officials had taken meetings since February 2001, with the Taliban, and just five weeks before the air attacks of September 2001, during that August. These meetings outlined what was to come in Afghanistan should the Taliban not accept U.S. terms of a coalition government. That the terms were rejected and the carpet bombing carried out is a fact/truth few are today prepared to accept. But they are true facts nevertheless. To point out once again,...

....until August, the U.S. government saw the Taliban regime "as a source of stability in Central Asia that would enable the construction of an oil pipeline across Central Asia," from the rich oilfields in Turkmenistan, Uzbekistan, and Kazakhstan, through Afghanistan and Pakistan, to the Indian Ocean.

Until now,..."the oil and gas reserves of Central Asia have been controlled by Russia. The Bush government wanted to change all that." But, confronted with Taliban's refusal to accept U.S. conditions, "this rationale of energy security changed into a military one,"..."At one moment during the negotiations, the U.S. representatives told the Taliban, "either you accept our offer of a carpet of gold, or we bury you under a carpet of bombs," Brisard said in an interview in Paris. (*Published on Thursday, November 15, 2001 by the "http://www.ips.org/" :U.S. Policy Towards Taliban Influenced by Oil - Authors*, by Julio Godoy, Paris)

In their book titled *Bin laden, la verite interdite* ("Bin Laden, the forbidden truth") authors Jean-Charles Brisard and Guillaume Dasquie, revealed a great deal more. Both well-known intelligence analysts, were present for many of the meetings. At the time of the meetings prior to September 11, 2001, the authors claim the U.S.

...government of Bush began to negotiate with the Taliban immediately after coming into power in February. U.S. and Taliban diplomatic representatives met several times in Washington, Berlin and Islamabad. To polish their image in the United States, the Taliban even employed a U.S. expert on public relations, Laila Helms. The authors claim that Helms is also an expert in the works of U.S. Secret services, for her uncle, Richard Helms, is a former director of the Central Intelligence Agency (CIA). The last meeting between U.S. And Taliban representatives took place in August, five weeks before the attacks on New York and Washington, the analysts maintain. On that occasion, Christina Rocca, in charge of Central Asian affairs for the U.S. Government, met the Taliban ambassador to Pakistan in Islamabad.... government's main objective in Afghanistan was to consolidate the position of the Taliban regime to obtain access to the oil and gas reserves in Central Asia. (Ibid.)

Those reading this account of these meetings by the two reputable French authors will argue that this constitutes no proof, no evidence of Mr. Bush's wrong-doing, no evidence that these clear political commercial objectives are the real objectives for the war, that bin Laden was simply the means to that end. While it is true that these facts, "standing alone," cannot make a legal case, any more than the facts assembled against the known terrorist bin Laden have made a case against him for involvement in the September 11, air attacks. But taken with all the other abundant evidence assembled here and in the five previous papers (all with substantial appendices) on these events this author alone has published, the case is sufficient to call for a complete Joint United States House-Senate investigation into these matters. The account the authors present in their well-documented book bears investigation. Coupled with the data collected in this book alone there is a *prima facie* case already built. Here is how the article's reporter concluded his original piece, noting one of the author's interview on French television around November 1st, 2001:

Representatives of the U.S. Government and Russia, and the six countries that border with Afghanistan were present at these meetings," it (the book) says. "Sometimes, representatives of the Taliban also sat around the table." These meetings, also called "6+2" because of the number of states (six neighbors plus U.S. And Russia) involved, have been confirmed by Naif Naik, former Pakistani Minister for Foreign Affairs. In a French television news program two weeks ago, Naik said during a "6+2" meeting in Berlin in July, the discussions turned around "the formation of a government of national unity. If the Taliban had accepted this coalition, they would have immediately received international economic aid."

"And the pipe lines from Kazakhstan and Uzbekistan would have come," he added. Naik also claimed that Tom Simons, the U.S. representative at these meetings, openly threatened the Taliban and Pakistan. "Simons said, 'either the Taliban behave as they ought to, or Pakistan convinces them to do so, or we will use another option.' The words Simons used were, 'a military operation,' " Naik claimed. (Ibid.)

Americans are even less interested in the truth of these findings than they were over a decade ago regarding the findings of this author, and many others, about similar meetings and policy formulations already decided upon long before past President Bush-Senior's administration sought to bomb Iraq into the stone age. In fact it was outlined and planned to do just that, had Saddam Hussein not gone along with the deal offered him at the time. Boring as it might seem to draw this analogy here, I shall reprint the policy formulations below. It all began with the Palestinian peace process. To quote directly from the White House, April, 1990 meeting:

The Trilateral countries could assist a possible peace process, as well as helping to reduce the dangers to their own interests deriving from a renewal of inter-State conflict in the Middle East, by pursuing issues of non-proliferation of chemical, biological and atomic weapons and of conventional disarmament in the region, as well as of limitation of arms sales to the areas. The extent to which peace in the region is currently endangered by past sales, both legal and illegal, of armaments and of technology cannot be exaggerated. (*Task Force Report: the Israeli-Palestinian Issue*, The Washington, D.C., Plenary Meeting of the Trilateral Commission, April 1990, p.74. See also the Triangle Paper report itself number 38, p. 32, issued May 1990)

This meeting of the infamous Trilateral Commission (much argued among conspiracy theorists still) did take place; it was hosted by then President George Bush-Senior at the White House. Admitting that "The arms

producing countries in the industrial world as well as the Soviet Union, some
of its former satellites, and China share responsibility for this," they hypocrit-
ically failed mentioning the presence for decades of American arms sales to
many countries in the region by the United States itself, especially to Iraq; this
is understandable, as Iraq is singled out in the same text.

> In particular, the development both of nuclear weapons and
> chemical weapons in the region would scarcely have been pos-
> sible without access to Western materials and technology, and
> there has been a notable failure to face up to the fact of, and
> the implications of, these leakages to both Israel and to Arab
> States such as Iraq. Peace and stability in the Middle East will
> be difficult to ensure without a major international initiative de-
> signed to undo this damage—an initiative which may now be
> more readily achieved by agreement between East and West as
> a result of greatly improved climate of international relations.
> (Ibid.)

This was the argument to intervene in the region and set up a permanent
military presence to ensure stability in the Persian Gulf in the State of Saudi
Arabia; the Soviet Union has collapsed and its presence was no longer a threat
to the region. It was no longer a threat to Western and particularly American
hegemony in the region then either. America under Mr. Bush Senior decided
American hegemony was the future for the Middle East. Of course, it is common knowledge now that it was precisely this permanent military presence
in the two Holy Lands of Saudi Arabia that set Osama bin Laden into motion
after America had trained him and his followers along with the Taliban to
stop Soviet expansion in the Central region of Afghanistan. The report goes
on to say this:

> Accordingly, urgent action should be taken to initiate linked
> nuclear, chemical and biological disarmament, control and ver-
> ification measures in the Middle East. This is a matter which
> might appropriately be considered by the U.N. security Council
> in view of the serious threat to peace now posed by the prolifer-
> ation of these weapons. (Ibid.)

Urgent action by the U.N. Security Council and the seemingly (at the
time that is) ability of then President George Bush Sr. to simply pick up the
phone and form an instantaneous coalition of western powers to attack Iraq
after August, 2nd, 1990, is now easily explained, as I did during the period in
question. Bush already had all the respective western powers lined up after
Senator Robert Dole's April 1990 mission to Iraq failed to get resolution on
the question of Iraqi disarmament. Saddam Hussein simply said no, he would
not disarm unless Israel did so as well. Of course Israel was not asked to disarm. The western powers that made up Bush's immediate coalition are specifically those European nation-states which make up the Trilateral Commission

itself: i.e., all of Western Europe, North America and Japan (Which is what the word "Trilateral" means in the organization' name)

It is only in the context of those meetings during April and after Robert Dole's failed mission to Iraq, that Ambassador to Iraq, Ms April Glaspie, and her remarks to Saddam Hussein during June and July of 1990 make sense. Saddam Hussien asked Ms Glaspie what America's position was on the border dispute between Iraq and Kuwait? It was a long-standing dispute over who owned the strip of land between the two States and the separate very real dispute that Kuwait was "slant drilling" into Iraqi territory using newly developed technology of the Kuwaiti-owned Al Sabah family's private firm, *Santa Fe International.* Glaspie's response to Hussein was "that America would not get involved in Middle Eastern border disputes." Saddam assumed wrongly that this left him free to resolve the situation with his own means. Many analysts saw these developments as Saddam Hussein having been clearly hoodwinked ("The Green Light" it was called) into invading Kuwait and was duly shocked when President George Bush Sr. declared Hussein a "Hitler."

I would be failing to do my job by not pointing out, as an aside, that the company *Sante Fe International,* owned 100 percent by the Al Sabah family of Kuwait had on its board of directors former President Gerald Ford (the President that appointed George Bush Senior to Director of the CIA), General Brent Scowcroft (at the time Bush Senior's National Security Advisor) and Roderich Hills (husband of Carla Hills, Bush Senior's Trade Representative).

One does not need to see conspiracy where policy formulations stated earlier in the same year, even just weeks or months before-hand laid out the political objectives. That the political objectives laid out earlier are fulfilled using war or conflict as the means is simply a von Clausewitzian understanding of the way the real world works, i.e., war is politics by other means.

Chapter Eight: Summary and Concluding Remarks

*In fear and trembling, have they finally
realized of what man is capable—
and this is indeed the precondition
of any modern political thinking.
Such persons will not serve very well as
functionaries of vengeance.
This however, is certain:
Upon them and only upon them, who are filled
with a genuine fear of the inescapable guilt
of the human race, can there be any reliance
when it comes to fighting fearlessly,
uncompromisingly, everywhere against the
incalculable evil that men are
capable of bringing about.*
—HANNAH ARENDT,
"Organized Guilt and Universal Responsibility"

There is periodically, in all of history, the resurgence of empire-building; there are always those which believe they have the right, and certainly the will if they have the actual power, to build a greater vision of the state, the regime, the world itself; this is not knew. I have argued for decades now that there are those elite on both the left and right, Republicans and Democrats, business monopolists and academic hegemonists which all agree: they are special, their special insights, their exaggerated self-importance always called "enlightened self-interest," as though those of us which disagree are less enlightened rather than just less important or less powerful. That these hegemonic ambitions bear fruit on occasion should shock no-one; that these men, and there are plenty of ambitious women to boot, will try for Empire is not even questioned by intelligent reasonable people. The only question, the only real debate is whether they can achieve it, and for how long can they maintain it, should they achieve it.

The only question I take any time with, as the above is the academic debate, is this—they will try. It simply is irrelevant whether they achieve their ambitions; what matters to the rest of us, less enlightened as we are, is that these enlightened few will most certainly try. What chaos they bring to the world in these efforts is what real world history always records, later, true, rather than sooner. George Santayana had this to say on authority:

The Revival of Authority

"A sense of brotherhood with all forms of existence, however strange, whether it comes through spiritual insight, or through an initial sympathy, such as in the joy which children take in animals, implies security in one's own being; the child does not yield an inch of his own ground out of consideration to his pet's wishes, nor is a clear spirit tempted at all to forego its intellectual dominion and whoop with the savages or burrow with the worm. On the contrary, what chills this natural sympathy and suggests the preposterous desire to impose human morality on nature or human logic on God, is the sense of insecurity in oneself. Terror does not create the gods; but it creates the mania to humanize them. And the same terror creates the passion for regimenting other men, and compelling them to think and to act as we do.

A truly lordly spirit, or a truly humble one, perfectly content and sure of itself, would love to be surrounded by giants and dwarfs, by persons of all nations and moralities: without contaminating one's own soul, they enlarge its field and add to the gaiety of nature. But unfortunately it is seldom given to an incarnate spirit to be safe: its food and air, if not its inner resolution, are always being filched away from it, or poisoned. Nature is overcrowded with seeds: you must trample on others to make room for yourself. This is the reason why on earth there is a recurrent ambition to establish universal empires, religions, or systems of thought. Terror, and uneasiness at being oneself, are at the base of it; as now-a-days we all dress alike, because each of us is ashamed of his looks. Uniformity is our refuge from nullity. No brave and spontaneous organism would put forth such a claim: but a dreadful consciousness of weakness—and inferiority—drives us to abolish all differences, and to hide our ugliness, and bolster up our illusions, by imposing them on other people; or (what comes to the same thing) by adopting theirs." (*George Santayana*, Physical Order and Moral Liberty, 1935)

Authority, and the "recurrent ambition to establish universal empires," always is attempted by those inferior individuals which are uneasy "at being oneself," face the terror of it each day, and in their effort to overcome it, overcome themselves one might say, they feel the drive to establish their power over all others. For the elite then, to bolster up their own illusions, they would find "imposing them on other people," the only way to live with their own "dreadful consciousness of weakness—and inferiority." The masses, feeling even more weakness and inferiority than the elite they secretly admire, and admire even more when ruthless and criminal, must adopt the elite's own illusions as their own. Patriotism and all its often terrible manifestations, traits, like xenophobia, bigotry and hatred for others not like "us," has a great appeal to the neurotic and fearful. Empire can only be brought about in a world of base materialism and fear of losing what one has gained through acquisitiveness and avarice.

Only a characterless people would honor terror by their own regime while denouncing the wrath of those which find themselves crushed underfoot by the latest grand hegemon. Leviathan always creates its own enemies.

Empire itself implies the cause of revolution and guerrilla warfare against that which is seen as all-encompassing, all-knowing, all-powerful. It is now the American people, weaned-off liberty and honor, who simply cannot see what is happening all round them. It is Americans and our sham democracy that has created a people which will give up all liberty, but not, as in the past philosophical arguments, in exchange for security alone; it is their childish belief that someone wants their stuff, or to deny them more stuff, cheaper stuff, toys and playthings.

> *Every child tenaciously wants to keep all his possessions*
> *and will jealously resist every attempt at an encroachment.*
> *The youngest child will obstinately cling to his*
> *privilege of being spoiled as the baby.*
> —RUDOLF BIENEFELD,
> *Justice in the Nursery*

CHAPTER NINE

Strategic Analysis Afghanistan's Afghan Arabs

Globalization has diffused economic and technological power around the world....and globalization also has the potential of giving rise to a gnawing sense of impotence as decisions affecting the lives of millions slip out of local political control.

DR. HENRY KISSINGER
America at the Apex: Empire or Leader?

Suffering, hardship, impatience at the structure of society, with hatred and envy of those supposed to be more fortunate, are ancient inevitable sources of rebellion and of slow perpetual revolution in the world; but such unrest, when combined with mystical exaltation and ambiguous prophecies about another world destined to soon appear, takes on the character of a positive delusion and a devastating fanaticism.

GEORGE SANTAYANA

STRATEGIC ANALYSIS

THE TALIBAN'S WITHDRAWAL INTO THE MOUNTAINS and the dispersion of the so-called Afghan Arabs throughout the worlds' regions (from where they originated), is making Afghanistan an ineffective base for militant Muslims. Many foreign-born members of al Qaida and the Taliban, cut off from their infrastructure and under attack from Northern Alliance Afghans and U.S. forces, have long left the country. A number of these guerrillas will attempt to return to their home countries -- or go to others not under U.S. bombardment — and resume militant activities. (Source, StratFor November 15th.) Additionally, it is now known that all of the hijackers allegedly having been of the nineteen identified by the FBI were all in the United States legally with only a few having overstayed their visas (Associated Press and INS reported). That all of these, only now understood as, terrorists (today called terrorists, but prior to that none were on any State Department watch list as having committed any crimes), is a significant development where any thorough analysis is concerned. This office argued from the beginning (when briefing Federal Law Enforcement intelligence personnel on September 11, 2001 @ 9am Pacific Coast Time) and during numerous media interviews, that we are not dealing with terrorism in any classical sense, but a new level of "international urban guerrilla warfare." (See Chapters Two and Four.) It was then stated, "look at the nationalities of the suspects and their supporting network." That these skilled operatives of the 9-11 incidents came from maybe six different nation-states is significant. One of the so-called worst of the first Afghan captives, shipped on January 11th, 2002, to Guantanamo Bay Naval Base, Cuba, was a British citizen. That many, if not most, of the original nineteen were "clean" and without any previous known illegal activity, passports were valid, will make the apprehension of others that much more difficult.

Analysis

The process which has brought the war in Afghanistan to its current point (as of this original writing Nov.20th-30th, 2001) has not been fully disclosed to the public. Pieces of evidence slowly coming to fruition will give analysts fits for years to come. One thing of recent significance is that the Bush administration, again, beginning in February 2001, had intensely engaged the ruling Taliban in negotiations regarding their future in the region right up until five weeks before the September 11, air attacks. Administration officials stated until that time that the Taliban were seen as a "stabilizing force in the region" by Washington and offered them recognition and financial aid packages based on the specific offers from Washington. This period of recognition has not been admitted to publicly but has been widely reported in the foreign press, primarily the French and British. (Chapter Eight above *Oil & Sovereignty*.)

This will undoubtedly be seen as a betrayal by the ousted regime and Osama bin Laden's forces.

It is these kinds of effects, consequences that is, of the bombing, that shall create a long-term problematic for doing business globally and American tourism worldwide. We shall be well-remembered by Muslims everywhere. A map on our website demonstrates how far and wide the refugee *Afghan Arabs*, as they are called, will be disbursed. When the world believes it has returned to normal, these dispersed guerrillas will strike again, both at the United States and the symbols of global hegemony like the World Trade Center (WTC) and the World Trade Organization (WTO). (See *Foreign Affairs*, William Perry, *The Next Attack*: Nov./Dec. 2001.)

Some 50 Filipinos suspected of training with al Qaida in Afghanistan have started slipping back into the Philippines through mostly Muslim-dominated islands in the south, according to immigration authorities cited by the *Philippine Daily Inquirer*. A Philippine government source told the paper the suspected terrorists began arriving soon after the Northern Alliance started overrunning Taliban strongholds in Afghanistan. By January, Mr. Bush had sent 600 US Special Forces to the Phillippines to begin another Afghan-style war. By February 3rd, 2002, Europeans were angered by this, and Mr. Bush's *State of the Union* speech, where he characterized Iran, Iraq and North Korea as an "axis of evil." Europeans at a major defense conference "expressed fears [Saturday] that President Bush is bypassing the NATO alliance in waging the war on terrorism -- a sentiment that Deputy Defense Secretary Paul Wolfowitz summarily dismissed." according to reports. A German delegate, Stefan Kornelius, (foreign editor of the influential Munich newspaper *Suddeutsche Zeitung* summed it up for many of the other delegates, asking Wolfowitz, "If the main lesson learned is that the U.S. needs to engage in flexible coalition-building, what do you need NATO for?" Wolfowitz replied "We will consult with other countries,...the events of September 11th have made this a case of national self-defense....We don't need NATO in the Phillippines.... We didn't need everyone in Afghanistan." One of our own retired generals, Wesley Clark (former supreme commander of NATO), who attended the conference, stated "There's a substantial animus about the [president's] speech." Karl Lamers, foreign policy spokeman for the conservative Christian Democratic Union party in the German Bundestag, argued that the US should, "bring us in on the planning of the strategy" for the war on terrorism...."It cannot be that you plan on your own and then we trot along afterwards." Mr. Lamers protested." (Source, Richard Whittle, *The Dallas Morning News*, Sunday, February 3, 2002, P. 10A.) Clearly Mr. Bush's "going his own way" is beginning to rile many significant allies, as well as enemies abroad. It will begin to seep into the body-politic here in America as well. The Phillippines will not be the last country where Afghan Arabs turn-up; not the last country Mr. Bush wants to invade.

The Taliban's retreat over the past two months has made Afghanistan a much less effective base for militant Muslims. Many foreign-born members of al Qaida and the Taliban have left the country, although many won't get past Pakistan or even the Afghan border. Still others will be apprehended when they arrive in their home countries, but some, and very many at that, will slip through the cracks and resume operations. The CIS countries have jointly announced their co-operation with the west. (Caspian News Agency 11/30/01) The Taliban's position in Afghanistan has been upended, with the group losing control of about 70 percent of the country. Taliban loyalists who were not surrounded in Kunduz or Kandahar have predictably taken to the hills to begin a more guerrilla-style war. Other members of the country's majority Pushtun population, of which many were only marginal Taliban sympathizers to begin with, have simply switched loyalties to the Northern Alliance. But many of the Taliban's foreign fighters are not ever going to surrender. These fighters, known as "Afghan Arabs," include not just Arab nationals but also (as noted already) Filipinos, but includes Chinese Uighers, Indonesians, Malaysians, Bosnians and Chechens. Some have lived in Afghanistan since the 1980s while others moved in once the Taliban took control. Estimates of their number range from 10,000 to 25,000. (Strategic Forecasting) Many will remain in the region to fight on against the newest ruling puppet regime the United Nations, but in all seriousness, the United States has placed in power. The Taliban have vowed to fight this new regime with the same tenacity as they fought the Soviets. They must be taken seriously. Some 5,000 Taliban soldiers with over 500 tanks and APCs have escaped and are hiding throughout Afghanistan's villages and hills; they had attacked US convoys by January. Russia will not stand by and watch the United States decide which parties rule in this region as will be shown further below. Mr. Bush selected as interim president Mr. Hamid Karazai. Why?

Mr. Hamid Karazai has a long history of contacts with both the CIA and Pakistan's Inter-Services Intelligence service, known as ISI, according to Bill Gertz (Geostrategy-Direct.com, 12/14/2001). Gertz goes on to argue that "The connections are said to be the reasons Karazai was the candidate most acceptable to the United States and Pakistan." Which is properly why the remnants of the Taliban, the Afghan Arabs and the people themselves of Afghanistan may find the new regime totally unacceptable; among other reasons already pointed out in the above chapters. Karazai and several of his brothers own restaurants in Chicago, San Francisco, Boston and Baltimore. Although a native of Kanadar, Karazai spent most of his life in Quetta; he has residences there and in Islamabad and Peshawar. His ties to Pakistan originated with his relationship to former ISI Director Akhtar Abdur Rahman Khan and date from the early 1980s. According to Gertz "Karazai met the late CIA Director Bill Casey when Casey made one of his numerous trips to Pakistan during the U.S. covert operation to back Mujahideen rebels against the Soviet Union during the 1980s." The Taliban were of course part of that rebel force as was Mr. bin Laden. As an aside, Bill Casey's then Special Assistant, Herb Meyer, has filed (as of this writing) to run for the seat in the Second Congressional District of Washington State for the 2002 elections. Which is just what the government in the United States is sorely lacking, more former CIA operatives in the Congress, along with bus drivers and wrestlers, to back Mr. Bush's policies.

With all of this in mind, the region which borders on the larger Caspian Sea region will for years to come be a source of destabilization and terrorist activity and guerrilla warfare. But increasingly the area will be more isolated as well. While the Russian media has been consistently reporting the potential long-term destabilization effects it has been largely ignored by a seemingly obedient American press. This will change over time as further issues below become common knowledge. The most significant issue which shall come to light soon enough will be the U.S. politico-commercial objectives in the region. The Silk Road Strategy as it is called.

The Northern Alliance, it is now well known, which Mr. Bush's administration has chosen to align itself with, has a far worse human rights record than the Taliban. The Northern Alliance has also asked the British and Americans to leave Afghanistan causing a split in its own force network. These various warlords will war with each other and with the now splitting-up forces of the Taliban: a war of all against all. The members of Osama bin Laden's forces, on the other hand, will be enlivened and more dedicated than ever. Proof of everything they have been told about America by bin Laden and others, will be seen as verified if not prophesized. Indeed, as pointed out in chapter four above, bin Laden "needed" and the international guerrilla movement (although not created by bin Laden, certainly now inspired by him) needed the massive counter strike against Afghanistan to gain credibility in their guerrilla war. It is the *reason for being* of guerrilla warfare, to induce precisely such a massive retaliation. One would have thought someone might have informed Mr. Bush and Mr. Blair of this first ground rule premise of guerrilla war. Guerrillas are always devoted to their cause and their leaders.

Part of their devotion may be attributed to religious fervor, but some of it is likely due to fear of reprisal from vengeful Afghans. Hundreds of foreign fighters have reportedly been executed by Northern Alliance troops since their advance and campaigns against the guerrillas (the Northern Alliance were regularly and wrongly called guerrillas in the western press). The mass executions and brutality has been denounced by the Bush administration but this is sheer sophistry and pointless and was fully expected by all serious analysts.

Afghanistan is no longer the ideal base for extremist groups that it once was. Training camps, munitions depots and communications equipment have all been destroyed, along with the government that sheltered extremist fighters. These factors have forced many Afghan Arabs to leave the country. A similar situation existed in the early 1990s, after the Soviets left Afghanistan and Kabul's communist regime crumbled. Large numbers of well-trained Afghan Arabs discovered they weren't especially welcome in the country, and many returned to their home states.(Stratfor)

These returnees formed the core of extremist groups such as the Egyptian

Islamic Jihad, the Abu Sayyaf in the Philippines and Algeria's Islamic Salvation Front. Some of these extremists returned to Afghanistan once the Taliban took power while others joined Osama bin Laden's alleged al Qaida group. It should be pointed out that the al Qaida group has been almost mythically enlarged in the eyes of the world the way the mafia has been by Hollywood to a generation of movie goers. But the disparate groups which do work together and have been since about 1982 (Chapter Four), exist, and reprisals against Americans must be predictably assumed. Indeed, it has already begun, it is just that many of the attacks have been thwarted by security services in their new heightened state; a heightened state which cannot continue forever, once relaxed (with now expectant attacks eminent), is precisely when the next real attack shall certainly occur.

Although at the time during the war itself it was argued that a "similar exodus may be attempted now (November),..." It was argued by some analysts that "getting out of Pakistan isn't easy. Northern Alliance loyalists and Pushtun turncoats are combing the hills while U.S. and British special forces are manning roadblocks throughout the south. Escaping north means braving the desert in southern Turkmenistan, army troops in Uzbekistan,... (and Russian border frontier guards from Tajikistan to Armenia)... Human smugglers can breach the Iranian border, but the Tehran government is decidedly anti-Taliban." (StratFor). I, at the time, and I still do not agree with the depth of this argument, although certainly it will be true in many cases. In any case, the best option may be eastward through Afghanistan's 1,500-mile border with Pakistan. But despite a multitude of routes, this option is no longer as simple as it was three months ago. Pakistan has reinforced its border with 20,000 soldiers and is likely using the recent $80 million in U.S. aid for equipment such as sensors and night-vision gear. (This has not been verified)

The network of Afghanistan's canals underground which have been used for centuries to bring water to this arid land are now used as an underground virtual highway (footpath and crawlspace in other cases) that only the experienced and trained guerrillas know well; the very experienced know every route which can be traveled. These will be used to exit and used again to return. It is most likely that any future regime in Afghanistan will face horrendous opposition for decades to come. Pipeline security, what can be made believable when built and insured primarily by American taxpayers, will be an effort in futility. Why? Things get marginally easier for militants upon their arrival in Pakistan, as the Taliban have a significant support network in the country. Sea routes out of Pakistan — the most common and anonymous method of transportation — are now being patrolled by the U.S. Navy, with warships searching merchant vessels leaving the country. (*Evening Standard*, a British daily).

Given enough time and money, and with the general chaos in Afghanistan and Pakistan, it can be assumed that perhaps no more than 2,000 to 5,000 Afghan Arabs will escape to their home countries. These fighters may find shelter in numerous areas: Morocco, Algeria, Egypt, Jordan, Saudi Arabia and the other Persian Gulf states, Lebanon, Syria, Turkey, Russia (Chechnya), Yemen, Pakistan, Uzbekistan, Tajikistan, western China, Malaysia, Philippines, Indonesia, Bosnia, Sudan and Somalia. President Bush has revealed the week of November 20th, that Somalia, Yemen and Sudan were targeted next after Afghanistan falls; hints at a late January date were profoundly optimistic, but Mr. Bush has the habit now of going his own way regardless of what world opinion says.

It has been argued that "most of the Middle Eastern states have extensive internal security apparatuses, capable of monitoring and intercepting returning extremists. A handful of fighters may be able to slip into each nation, but large-scale returns are unlikely." (Strategic Forecast) We think this may be too pessimistic an appraisal if Mr. Bush does continue to bomb other states as he now claims is his intent. Especially if he decides to move against Iraq and Syria, both of which the Hawks, which dominate the Bush National Security process want to see. This will further reduce the support from these countries and many may even have to begin turning a blind-eye where specific returning guerrillas are concerned. In fact someone has done just this where Mr. bin Laden is concerned.

In Asia, both Malaysia and China have strict internal security. Conversely the Philippines and Indonesia are relatively easy to penetrate; Indonesia has lax border security and the southern Philippines is the site of a large-scale Muslim insurgency. But relatively few Afghan Arabs are Asian, and non-Asians would be highly conspicuous.

According the StratFor, November 2001, "Somalia, Sudan and Chechnya are realistically the two areas where significant numbers of Afghan Arabs could set up camp. Their relatively close location to Afghanistan and already unstable situations would make it easier for large numbers of fighters to remain undetected. All three should expect to see significant inflows." This will make the Mediterranean region less hospitable to American business ventures. This will make the war against the new regime in Afghanistan by the guerrillas that much more assured.

In any event, an extremist rise in most of the various host countries should be expected as the evacuation from Afghanistan continues for years to come. The guerrillas can hide for long periods of time in the mountains of Afghanistan and not attempt to leave, now that the bombing has virtually ended. Then slip out at their leisure. Then these fighters will return with experience, training and a renewed network of contacts in other countries. The returnees will likely not take direct orders from bin Laden, al Qaida or the Taliban. Communications will be monitored, and the al Qaida network appears to be in some disarray. But wherever they end up, the fighters will adapt their skills and ideology to the local context and exploit existing political or military rifts. In most cases, these actions will be consistent with al Qaida's interests, and violence against host governments, foreign, and especially American businesses, or U.S. military personnel, should be expected. It is without question, this war will go on for years to come, maybe decades to come.

One side effect of this dispersal may be the foundation of a second network of Islamic extremists. Just as the Soviet war against Afghanistan — and the subsequent scattering of fighters — produced a worldwide network of extremists, the American war in Afghanistan will produce a secondary network, one that will not be centered around Osama bin Laden, but centered around an anti-American focus like never before.

Taliban Withdrawal Was Strategy, Not Rout

It was reported during November at the time "In less than a week, Taliban fighters have been swept from most of northern Afghanistan, including the key cities of Mazar-e-Sharif, Herat, Kunduz, Taloqan, Bamiyan, Jalalabad and the capital Kabul. How did a force that only two months ago controlled most of Afghanistan get swept from the battlefield so quickly, and is the battle over? Evidence suggests it has only just begun."

Analysis

"Northern Alliance troops moved into Kabul on Nov. 13, less than a week after launching an offensive that has swept the Taliban from most of northern Afghanistan. The Northern Alliance now controls the key cities of Mazar-e-Sharif, Herat, Kunduz and Taloqan, all located astride vital supply routes into neighboring countries. Popular uprisings have reportedly ousted the Taliban from Bamiyan and Jalalabad, and there are even reports of anti-Taliban Pushtun forces marching on Kandahar. On the surface it appears a lightning offensive by the Northern Alliance — supported by U.S. aerial bombardment — has shattered the Taliban army in a matter of days. But have the Taliban been defeated? An examination of the Taliban withdrawal suggests the group has intentionally surrendered territory in the interest of adopting tactics more amenable to its strengths." (Sources: Strategic Forecast, November 15, 2001 *The Guardian* and *The U.K. Independent*.)

The United States now must face what every guerrilla warrior wants, a ground war on their territory; a protracted war is the only war a guerrilla army can ever hope to win. I stated at the time "This office only hopes that Mr. Bush and Mr. Blair have not been led into a Custer-like war; have not taken the bait to fight a guerrilla war where nobody is likely to be the winner. A guerrilla war is not fought with victory foremost in mind. The guerrilla fights with but one primary objective: To survive."

This was an important aspect completely ignored in the American press and certainly Mr. Bush would never discuss it. The towns abandoned have no strategic importance to the Taliban, nor anybody else; they cannot even be called pre-industrial towns. To abandon these primitive bombed-out facilities has only propaganda value to the western forces; virtually only Americans in the world will believe this matters one whit. The war was always destined to be fought as a guerrilla war within the territories and mountains, arid wastelands and urban centers of far more developed nations as the war's zones of attack. The targets will be western international and global targets and this war will last for well over a decade; by January 15th, 2002, our own Pentagon admits this, as Secretary Rumsfeld begs for greater defense dollars to fight a war which will last "six years or more."

If the United States and its allies misread the Taliban withdrawal as a rout, they will find themselves locked in a nasty guerrilla war in Afghanistan. Worse, that war is likely to spread well beyond Afghanistan's borders, as the core of Taliban and al Qaida forces in that country seek to secure their supply lines and capitalize on their strengths and their opponents' weaknesses. America proper will be hit again.

Western Political/Commercial Objectives

Reasons for long-term terrorism are many but, again to repeat, one significant area overlooked is the recent standing recognition of the Taliban regime as the Afghanistan sovereigns, by the Bush administration until five weeks before the September 11, 2001, air attacks. This will always be seen as a betrayal by the Taliban refugees and guerrillas as well as all members of Osama bin Laden's groups.

> When Pakistan ditched its ally, the Taliban, in September, and sided with the U.S., Islamabad and Washington fully expected to implant a pro-American regime in Kabul and open the way for the Pak-American pipeline. But this was not to be. In a dazzling coup, Russian President Vladimir Putin stole a march on the Bush administration, which was so busy trying to tear apart Afghanistan to find bin Laden it failed to notice the Russians were taking over half the country...The wily Russians achieved this victory through their proxy Afghan force, the Northern Alliance. Moscow, which has sustained the Alliance since 1990, re-armed it after Sept. 11 with new tanks, armoured vehicles, artillery, helicopters and trucks. The Alliance's two military leaders, Gen. Rashid Dostam and Gen. Muhammed Fahim, were stalwarts of the old Communist regime with close links to the KGB. Putin put the chief of the Russian general staff, Viktor Kvashnin, and the deputy director of the KGB, in charge of the Alliance. During the Balkan fighting in 1999, the hard-charging Kvashnin outfoxed the U.S. by seizing Pristina's airfield, thus assuring a permanent Russian role in Kosovo. (Source: By Eric Margolis, Nov. 25th, 2001 *The Toronto Sun*)

Now, Kvashnin, has done it again. To the outrage of Washington and Islamabad, Kvashnin rushed the Northern Alliance into Kabul, in direct contravention of Bush's dictates. The Alliance is now Afghanistan's dominant force and, in the face of Bush-led multi-party political talks in Germany, the weekend of November 24th, the Northern Alliance styled itself the new sovereign government, a claim fully backed by Moscow. The conference was moved to Bonn from Berlin for security reasons.

> Burhanuddin Rabbani, the leader of the Northern Alliance, has rightly called the conference a "symbolic" effort to establish a broad-based government as past attempts over many decades to impose peace on Afghanistan have proved fruitless. Undoubtedly, too, it will turn into a media circus....Iran, Afghanistan (Northern Alliance), Russia and to some extent India have formed their own agenda, and everything is likely to follow their program, while the interests of the main investors in the drama - the US, Britain and Pakistan - have been reduced to virtual observers. (Source; November 23rd, Asia Times, *Talks promise only hot air:* By Syed Saleem Shahzad.)

The pipelines Mr. Bush and western oil consortiums want must run South through Afghanistan. With the Russians (and Chinese?), the pipelines shall run North and East, which is of course the real "silk road" route. Has Mr. Bush seriously blundered, as Mr. Margolis suggests? This we shall have to wait and see. The question remains who will control the vast oil and gas reserves in the region? The Russians and Chinese or the American-led western Empire? Does this put us in the grip of a new Cold War? And should the outcome turn to confrontation with the Russians and possibly the Chinese, what effect will this have on the global economy, not to mention the American economy, staggering under what is beginning to look more and more like a coming deflationary cycle of recessionary proportions...if not worse? That the Russians are on the move along with the Chinese in the region is not under dispute; a quick search of the sources available such as the *Caspian News Agency (CNA)* and Azerbaijan's News Service *Azerinews.com* one finds activity ongoing such as the press briefing below at the time. I have listed these with their proper dates to demonstrate that while Mr. Bush and Mr. Blair were raving on about their victories other sources facing a somewhat differing reality were reporting other goings-on. These stories were only, as far as I am aware, reported by myself during interviews on KLOS/KABC radio in Los Angeles on the Impact Program (Host Mr. Frank Sontag) and in my original working papers which prepared the way for this volume. Bear with me, these lengthy and important wire service releases are left fully intact.

CASPIAN NEWS AGENCY

LUKOIL will take part in Baku-Ceyhan project in case of receiving approval of Russian government
Caspian News Agency, Thu 22 Nov 2001

> Moscow, November 22, 2001. (CNA). LUKOIL Russian Oil Company will take part in the construction of Baku-Ceyhan oil-pipeline in case if it is made certain of profitability of this

project and receives government's approval, Vagit Alekperov, the president of LUKOIL, stated at the press conference organized within the frames of Oil of Russia – Present and Future International forum, started today in Moscow. According to Alekperov, on November 23 the representatives of LUKOIL and TransOil will get acquainted with new surveys of the experts of Azerbaijani International Operation Company (AIOC) on Baku-Ceyhan project. Thus, LUKOIL can soon make clear for itself the issue about its participation in the project, however, the final decision by the heads of the company will be coordinated with the Russian government.

20:25 28.11.2001/ Russia/Oil/PSA/Summit

Kalujny will take part in Russian energy summit PSA 2001: investments to XXI century Moscow, November 28, 2001. (CNA). The Russian energy summit On Production Sharing Agreement (PSA) 2001: investments in XXI century will take place December 10-11 of 2001, in Moscow. Special Envoy of the Russian President Victor Kalujny will take part in the summit. Initiators of the conference informed CNA that intermediate results of the work on formation of efficient managing and legal infrastructure of PSA will be concluded. The sides will also create preconditions for dynamic growth of investment activity in oil and gas sphere in various regions of Russia, on the Caspian Sea in particular. The heads of the Russian and foreign oil and gas companies, banks, largest industrial enterprises, heads of federal bodies of local self government, Russian lawmakers etc. will take part in the conference. Moscow's international oil club and Oil and Gas Vertical organized the summit with assistance of CWC Associates company and Ministry for Economic Development and Trade of the Russian Federation. It is the second such Forum, the first one - PSA 2000 - was held last fall in Southern Sakhalin.

15:58 10.12.2001/ Kazakhstan/President/oil/transportation
Foreign investors prefer oil transportation from Kazakhstan via Iran to Persian Gulf, Kazakh President considers Astana, December 10, 2001. (CNA). The Foreign investors working in Kazakhstan consider most profitable to transport oil via Iran to the Persian Gulf, the Kazakh President Nursultan Nazarbayev said a briefing in Astana. "This is not only my opinion, but of companies working in Kazakhstan including the US ones," the head of the state stressed. The President reminded that the maximum capacity of the CPC oil pipeline recently put into operation amounts at 48 million tons per year and this route would

be loaded by the raw materials from the Tengiz field. At the same time the exploitation of the world largest Kashagan field will start at the end of 2005. "In 2015 the export possibilities of Kazakhstan are forecasted at the level of 150 million tons of oil, and up to 80 billion cubic meters of natural gas will be extracted in passing," Nazarbayev said. The President noted that various vectors of oil pipelines are important for the state, that's why Astana "supported the Baku-Ceyhan oil pipeline." The Kazakh leader also mentioned the possibility "of handing up to 20 million tons of oil from Kazakhstan to Baku via the Caspian Sea without oil pipeline construction" exists. Besides, Nazarbayev mentioned "we have a contract on oil pipeline to the West China." On the whole, the President concluded, "we are interested in many opportunities." -OK-

16:11 05.12.2001/ Russia/oil/conference

Perspectives of Russian Oil Industry Development international conference opened in Moscow, December 5, 2001. (CNA). Perspectives of Russian Oil Industry Development international conference opened today, December 5, in Moscow. At the forum's opening ceremony the first deputy of Russian Energy Minister Ivan Matlashov said the main aim of the conference is preparation for the 17th World Oil Congress. CNA reports that representatives of Russian Energy, Foreign, Economic Development and Trade Ministries, heads of leading oil companies, including LUKOIL, Rosneft, Zarubezhneft and others, take part in the forum. -OK-

17:49 05.12.2001/ Russia/oil/strategy/Caspian Sea

Russian energy strategy foresees implementation of large projects in Caspian region: Moscow, December 5, 2001. (CNA). According to the Russian Energy strategy, series of large projects will be implemented in the Caspian region till 2022, senior councilor of Russian Foreign Ministry Stanislav Jhiznin said at the conference called as Perspectives of Russian Oil Industry Development. He mentioned one of such projects would be the oil main construction. The diplomat said despite Europe is the central market for Russia, "later on our state intends expanding its market infrastructure." According to the Russian Energy strategy, the market developing will go in the eastern and southern directions. So, Jhiznin stressed the Central Asian and Caspian regions are "the most prior and attractive ones for investors." -OK-

12:25 03.12.2001/ Azerbaijan/oil/exporters/CIS/Alliance

Azerbaijan supports Kazakh initiative on establishing Alliance of CIS states - oil and gas exporters

Baku, December 3, 2001. (CNA). Azerbaijan supports the Kazakh initiative on establishing Alliance of CIS states - oil and gas exporters in contrast to the OPEC, president of the Azeri State Oil Company (SOCAR) Natig Aliyev informed CNA. He added the CIS state-members, extracting and exporting hydrocarbons, should carry out the coordinated policy. The Kazakh President Nursultan Nazarbayev declared the same idea. He suggested establishing the Alliance of oil and gas state-exporters with participation of Kazakhstan, Russia, Azerbaijan, Turkmenistan and Uzbekistan. Nazarbayev said the new Alliance would serve in contrast of the OPEC in oil and gas spheres, and the principal role in it should be played by Russia. -OK-

12:09 03.12.2001/ Azerbaijan/AIOC/contracts

AIOC signed contracts on constructive works within Stage-1 of three Caspian oilfields exploitation

Baku, December 3, 2001. (CNA). The Azerbaijani International Operating Company (AIOC) signed recently six main contracts for USD 750 million on Stage-1 construction works concerning Azeri Caspian oilfield exploitation. The consortium press release reads that the Stage-1, approved in August 2001 by the AIOC shareholders, is estimated at USD 3.4 billion: USD 1.1 billion will go for construction works, USD 1 billion - for Azeri field drilling. The rest of the funds should be spent on purchasing equipment and establishing reserves, insurance and project managing. AIOC signed contacts with several companies: with the McDermott company - on construction of upper units of the drilling platform on the Azeri contract area and laying down the underwater gas pipeline from the field to shore terminal, with the Bouygues Offshore company - on construction of the foot block, piles and bedplate for drilling, with the Emtunga International company - on construction of accommodation hulks on the drilling platform, the Saipem company - on transportation and installation work, and the Eiffel company - on delivering the drilling module of the platform.

The AIOC president David Woodword informed CN about USD 75 million would be invested in modernization of Azeri constructive and sea units within Stage-1. Extraction of the first portion of oil from Stage-1 is scheduled for first quarter of 2005, and by this time Baku-Tbilisi-Ceyhan oil pipeline will have been put into operation. -OK-

16:04 04.12.2001/ Azerbaijan/oil/BP/prospecting

BP company intends resuming oil prospecting on Inam offshore structure

Baku, December 4, 2001. (CNA). The BP company intends resuming prospecting drilling on the Inam offshore perspective structure in the first half of 2002. BP representatives informed CNA the drilling work held up due to high pressure in the bed in August 2001 would resume after coordination the Istiglal drilling unit operating schedule. Till March 2002 this floating semisubmersible drilling unit will be used by the Exxon Mobil company on the Nakhchyvan perspective structure on the Caspian Sea. -OK-

12:15 05.12.2001/ Armenia/Ukraine/cooperation

Ukrainian company to take part in Iran-Armenia gas pipeline construction

Yerevan, December 5, 2001. (CNA). Administration of the Intercontact Ukrainian company received reliable guarantees of investments' protection "at the highest level," the honorary president of Intercontact, people's deputy of Ukrainian parliament Aleksander Edin said after negotiations with Armenian authorities for purchasing the controlling interest of the Nairit-1 close jsc.

Recently Aleksander Edin and the deputy of Ukrainian Minister of Industrial Policy Aleksey Golubev met with the Armenian Prime Minister and parliamentary Speaker. They were also received by the Armenian President Robert Kocharian. Armenian presidential press service informed CNA the Ukrainian guests emphasized Armenian attraction for business, while stressing the internal political stability in the state and prudential approaches of the Armenian government to industrial development. The Armenian President mentioned the economic policy of Armenian government is aimed at creation of new workplaces.

During the meeting with Armenian President the arrangement on Intercontact's participation in Iran-Armenia gas pipeline construction, particularly a 40-km part of the main on the Armenian territory, is reached, Edin informed journalists. -OK-

According to CSA's regular daily briefings, which this office subscribes to, there are ongoing CIS (Commonwealth of Independent States) meetings at every level of each government. These meetings included discussions regarding the re-establishment of some governmental body in Afghanistan. The ten-year anniversary of the CIS was held in Moscow, as are all the other on-going meetings every year. Russia is increasingly the largest single trading partner with every country, including now Azerbaijan (as of the period September through January 2000-2001), according to CNA. It is becoming clear that not only is Mr. Bush not going to solve the problems in the region, the problems are increasingly being brokered by Moscow. In a recent December (2am) CNN interview former Hoover Institution fellow and former editor of the Washington Times, now editor at United Press International (UPI), Mr. Arnaud deBorchgrave, argued that Mr. Bush may have brought on a new Cold War over the energy issues surrounding not only the critical Caspian region, but the entire outstretched areas including Russia and China and Georgia.

Additionally, the Chinese have had a decade's lead in doing for the region what the western powers completely neglected to do at all. The Chinese have been financing and helping to build the infrastructure of these neighboring states; agribusiness, hydroelectric, textile mills and mining ventures of every stripe. (CNA reports Nov.2001.) The United States and its western partners have only, and exclusively, been trying to control the region's oil and gas; typical of Empire, its interests rest with control and power, of less interest, what happens to the region's people and governments thus exploited. This is no post-Marxist analysis, this is simply the history of the region to date and makes perfect sense. The Russians and Chinese have to live with these bordering states and every conflict in their region stands to spill over into their own territories' (especially their Muslim populations) people. What happens in these regions regarding oil and gas exploration and the much needed transport system of pipelines has been virtually the "only" serious concern of the west and the United States in particular. This neglect and effort to isolate Iran and Russia out of the oil markets will prove to be a dismal failure. A new Cold War may indeed be in the offing.

Opium and Heroin

Now that the Taliban are retreating to the hills and across borders, to fight again their long standing guerrilla war with an imposed regime from without their country, Mr. Bush and Mr. Blair must rewrite another piece of history. The Taliban, presumably out of an effort to appeal to the new Bush Jr. administration for recognition during the now well-known negotiations during 2001, but as well, to see their people fed, had in fact banned the entire production of opium during 2000/2001. One must recall Mr. Bush's charges immediately after the September 11, 2001 air attacks, that Afghanistan was (still) the leading nation supplying heroin to the world. Bush-Senior's, almost single-handed Drug War, in America and the world, since the 1980s, was a reminder that this is the greatest evil a president can offer-up to rally a majority of American white, middle-class drug-users, to support a war (on drugs or any other kind of war). But was the rhetoric true? It once was, as Afghanistan was aided in its production of opium and heroin by the United States and

France in its war with the Soviet Union from about 1980-on. But this was no longer true by March 2001, well before 09/11/01. The Taliban had banned all opium production!

> "We did a great job, and now it is time for the world community to respond." says Maulvi Amir Muhammad Haqqani, an Islamic scholar and head of the Taliban's drug control group in Jalalabad, Afghanistan, a major opium hub. "This is an urgent situation for our farmers. They are looking for something else to meet their needs, like fertilizer and seeds to start over." (*The Christian Science Monitor*, p.9, April 3, 2001)

Not everyone believed the Taliban meant what they said, but looking at what they did from about January through April, the *Monitor* reported that "Bernard Frahi also had his doubts. As regional director for the United Nation's Drug Control Program, he had been involved in negotiations with the Taliban for years, and had seen only minor results. But now that UNDCP observers have surveyed some 85 percent of the country's known opium-growing areas, he is confident that Afghanistan's opium ban is legitimate." Mr. Frahi added, "The first year, in 2000, they only decreased opium by 10 percent, and we said it's not enough. Now they've banned it outright. What are we going to say to that?...we have to recognize it as a major result."(Ibid.)

In a country where farmers had often used opium as a currency this was remarkable. The shift to wheat and other crops though had hurt the farmers in particular, especially in trying to repay loans, but it was beginning to feed their people, something opium did not do. The ban predictably wreaked havoc across the land and America and the UN was asked for aid for the transition to other crops, seeds and fertilizer. But as I have already pointed out above, the Bush administration and the west in general, does not now, nor will it in the future, care what happens to the people of Afghanistan. Only when the deal is met over oil and gas reserves in Afghanistan, and more important still, transit pipelines to transfer Caspian regional oil and gas, will there be anything like real assistance to the country. That Mr. Bush Jr. failed to recognize and admit, after September 11, 2001, these efforts and successes on the part of the Taliban, tells us a great deal about this President here in America. Indeed, he loudly and repeatedly stated they were "still" the largest producers of opium and heroin when this was entirely untrue. The ban on opium production did not demonstrate the Taliban's good-will? Of course it did, and had some to do with Mr. Bush's administration arguing, up until August 2001, that "the Taliban were a stabilizing force in the region," recognizing the regime during negotiations throughout 2001, as the legitimate governing sovereigns.

Maulvi haqqani, the Taliban drug control officer in Jalalabad, says that any rumors that the Taliban would reverse the ban are fabrications, and that in any case, the Taliban government decree won't change its opium decree." Because it is a religious decree. "We are all Muslims and our country is Muslim...and when the authority of a Muslim land asks the community to obey a religious decree, even if they are starving or facing a difficult situation, they have to obey and they have to be patient." (Ibid.) What is Bush going to say to this? Well, we already know, he will say what he has been saying, and Mr. Blair repeats sheep-like, "We all know they lie." But the United Nations said this is true, not the Taliban. Presumably, the UN lies as well.

This does not make me any the happier that Mr. Bush Jr. has lied about more than he has been truthful about; it is my duty as a sovereign, a sovereign citizen, guaranteed the right to speak, organize, and write, and be found in print in a free press, to speak-out against anything which will diminish my country's proper governing. We are not empire, at least not supposed to be; not a state of tyrannical measures to achieve global economic hegemony, at least not supposed to be; not a nation of people, which must learn to "watch what we say from now on," as White House *Press Lord* Ari Fleischer stated, at least not supposed to be.

This book is but the finale of my long present career, both working in, and actively working outside of, this government, for some thirty years. It will hopefully, as well, be a part of my further *becoming*.

END OF BOOK ONE.

PART II

CHAPTER TEN

Foreign Affairs Affects Domestic Policies

To the extent that non-Westerners see the world as one, they see it as a threat.
—SAMUEL P. HUNTINGTON

...globalization has encouraged the re-emergence of particularist identities.
—J. A. SCHOLTE

Globalization creates new forms of hegemonic power which threaten cultural differences.
—A. LINKLATER

Citizens should not be permitted to observe how laws or sausages are made.
—PRINCE BISMARCK

Firms may lobby for policies that shelter them from foreign competitors, generate monopoly rights, or exempt them from taxes. The task of policy makers, legislators and civil society is to ensure to the greatest extent possible that such rent-seeking behavior is controlled and filtered through institutions that limit the risk of capture by the powerful.
—B. HOEKMAN, M. KOSTECKI
The Political Economy of the World Trading System

FOREIGN AFFAIRS
AFFECTS DOMESTIC POLICY

REPRINTING THIS ESSAY HERE SEEMED APPROPRIATE as well as those which follow; there is much to be learned by a glance back, history that is to say, and as well, the events of September 11th have a history in our American foreign and economic policies globally. Mr. Bush and presumably Mr. Blair would deny this outright, but denials of this sort can only be meaningful to the ignorant and biased; in America that would include the far right as any war anywhere seems to find its support there; indeed the American genre of Christians, which make up America's hinterlands and wealthy suburbs alike, are the often the prime supporters of war-making as they have been throughout our history. I have made no changes in the original text below.

*   *   *

Those informed on issues of importance will find this article redundant if not trite. The Cold War *was* foreign policy. The North America Free Trade Agreement (NAFTA) *is* foreign policy. Many things that the citizen finds dull and complex are things that affect the very future, indeed the existence of those same citizens.

The Cold War was (some would say still is) a foreign policy formulation the direction of which was dominated by national security perceptions. The latter, the NAFTA, while additionally a foreign policy initiative with security overtones, is primarily pressed forward by the transnational corporate interests, State Department and Commerce Department perceptions about the new world after the collapse of the Soviet Block.

That isn't to say NAFTA, and GATT (General Agreement on Tariffs and Trade) were not pressed forward during the Cold War era with security concerns less notable; security, or national interests in the abstract, was clearly on the minds of the GATT participants at the 1947 Geneva Accords, as now.

Without being the least dramatic, most of what has happened to the United States on the domestic front is directly attributable to foreign policy initiatives that altered forever how Americans live and therefore view their world.

Separating the real affects of change and the general perception of what has happened can be difficult. I have chose, for reasons unimportant for this topic, to speak directly to the people via the technology available for over a decade; radio talk programs with listener participation were not the invention of Ross Perot nor has Perot given it its impetus. It has been a powerful voice for a long time, from stopping congressional pay raises (which were then passed later after a due period of time so apathy would again set in), to getting term limits on representatives in several states.

Unfortunately, simultaneously, talk radio has elevated opinion to the status of fact. Bertrand Russell did say technology was a double-edged sword.

Foreign Policy

Pointed out in the article *Trading American Interests* in *Foreign Affairs*, was Alfred E. Eckes' precise statement that for 45 years every president has..."-consciously subordinated domestic economic interests to foreign policy objectives." In the United States we have a two-party system, but more than that we have two distinct groupings of citizens that make up what we (rather narrow-mindedly) refer to as the left and right (I will not here refer to them in Dr. Kissinger's terms, the lunatic left and the radical right, although HK is not without some accuracy). I must raise the issue to aid an understanding why there may be so little interest in foreign policy.

Given the fact that the U.S. government has "sacrificed thousands of domestic jobs to create employment and prosperity in the non-communist world." (Eckes)...one would have thought American citizens would become enlivened to the world around them.

On the right, the fear, if not blind paranoia, of the communist threat left little room for informed discourse. On the left, the ignorance, if not willful rejection of anything to do with economic, industrial or banking issues, rendered the left moot on the question. A dichotomy of some note is the left's perception of themselves as socialists (within our capitalist system's benefits) precludes them from addressing issues of business or trade at any level above slogans. NAFTA is only discussed within the parameters of environmental concerns and labor's working conditions: sort of placing NAFTA or GATT within the politically correct paradigm. On the right — well — they think Bill Clinton is a communist selling Yeltsin (now) "the rope."

In any case, since 1945, the U.S. government has aided in the shift of millions of jobs overseas in an effort to attract allies and contain communism. While the Cold War may be over there is no question that because of the above reality U.S. based multinationals found themselves even more aggressively seeking jobs and trade globally. Borders began making little sense to the global corporation as the world was their marketplace and the United States was just another market, albeit the largest.

As Eckes points out, it was not just labor intensive industries such as footwear manufacturing that fell victim to foreign policy views (a loss of 148,000 jobs just since the '73 Kennedy Round GATT agreement), but also,

> similar considerations influenced decisions affecting high wage industries producing automobiles, steel, and consumer electronics, among others. (Eckes, FA Vol. 71 No.4)

Too many perceptions about what is and what has been happening within the domestic economy are patently misleading. Issues such as GATT and NAFTA are in the forefront of the debate over perceptions as opposed to a debate over fundamentals or accurate fact-based analysis.

The perception that NAFTA or GATT require a one for one (equalized) reduction in tariffs is quite simply untrue. The goal in the out years (for some items on the tariff schedules up to a decade) are complete tariff reductions to zero by all parties or states. That's the projected goal. But in the short term, about five years average, the real reciprocity is less. Even with that fact in hand it becomes harder to convince citizen or expert that in the not very short term, real damage to the economy and jobs is an obvious reality. How much and how many are the only real issues.

As a given, Eckes points out, the history and as such the probable short term reality. Regarding GATT and NAFTA:

> ...from the standpoint of U.S. workers and producers, such deals lack commercial reciprocity.

And this:

> America's current economic problems have roots in those one sided trade policies. A series of unilateral and non-reciprocal concessions have contributed, cumulatively, to a demise of domestic manufacturing and to the loss of production jobs. (Eckes, FA Vol. 71 No. 4)

History is clear, the GATT and the NAFTA are going to bring about great changes in our domestic economy. The perception of the projected good the dropping of trade barriers will achieve, in the years after the projected short term losses is an understandable gain. It is harder for the citizen qua worker to be reassured of such a future. Eckes necessarily addresses this.

> The ...Uruguay Round and the promise of a North American Free Trade Agreement all may mesmerize and motivate Washington policy makers. But in the American heartland these initiatives translate as further efforts to promote international order at the expense of existing American jobs. (Eckes, FA Vol. 71, No. 4)

From 1981-90 Eckes was a commissioner and chairman, 1982-84, of the U.S. *International Trade Commission*, so one hopes his views are not seen as those of a conspiracy theorist's paranoia.

To those American heartlanders of which he speaks the reality is that they need only be late one month on a house payment to begin the paperwork for a foreclosure. Perceptions aside, reality is a quick kill in the job market. Eckes, who will probably never face the potential "pink slip" in his pay envelope, is quite right to point this out.

There are more perceptions versus reality that too must be addressed. One such perception is the — again potential — future market Mexico offers to U.S. producers and the potential (again in the out years) for the creation of new export jobs for Americans. The argument should be put thus: Given the present administration, and the past one also, their argument is that indeed in the years ahead export job creation will outnumber job losses in other sectors of the economy. Are we to assume therefore that all shall remain the same over the next decade and *only job creation* is the substance of the argument?

No greater advocate of NAFTA itself than M. Delal Baer, director of the *Mexico Project* at the *Center for Strategic and International Studies*, Washington D.C., makes it obvious that the future can never be more than speculation. All things considered the following remains fact and history.

> In 1982, when Mexico nearly defaulted on its debt, the fate of more than one U.S. banking giant hung in the balance. Main Street U.S.A. lost more than 300,000 export jobs as the Mexican economy nose-dived in the 1980's, and in this period millions of Mexicans crossed the border illegally looking for work. As Mexico's recession ground on, U.S. policy makers contemplated the nightmarish implications of a destabilized Mexico for border security and American commitments around the globe. (Baer, FA Vol. 70, No. 4)

For foreign policy makers a stable Mexico can be achieved through the passage of NAFTA. Clinton's recent (Sept.'93) proposals to strengthen our border controls flies in the face of reality. Open borders for *goods* but not *people* is going to be a tough sell to everyone with the sole exceptions of Rush Limbaugh and Pat Buchanan. If Mexico nose-dives again only full military deployment could stop the flow from Mexico of illegals.

The 1980's was the period, one must remind the reader, that Eckes points out the U.S. lost more than just Baer's estimated 300,000 due to the Mexican crisis. Eckes states it was from the date of the concluded *Kennedy Round* tariff cuts in 1972 that,

> coincides with the beginning of a twenty-year decline in domestic earnings and manufacturing jobs. In 1991 American workers earned average weekly wages 20 percent below 1972 levels. Meanwhile the textile and apparel industries lost over 600,000 jobs, while steel and automobiles sacrificed another 500,000 positions. (FA Vol. 71,No.4)

This all took place over the twenty-year period since 1972 with one serious debt crisis in Mexico during the early 1980s. The totals are over 2 million jobs in 20 years.

One cannot but be reminded that particularly U.S. automobile manufacturers have been in Mexico since the first Ford assembly plant in 1925. General Motors and Chrysler both entered Mexico only ten to fifteen years later according to Laurence Hecht and Peter Morici in their article in the *Harvard Business Review*:

> Since the 1960's, the low wages found in Maquiladoras - factories near the U.S. border that use Mexican labor to assemble products for export - have been a major lure. GM alone owns

214 The Hydra of Carnage

48 maquilas, which employ 50,000 Mexican workers. (Hecht/
Morici, HBR, July/August '93, pg.33)

Interesting to note also in the Hecht/Morici article is the fact that these
(2,000 total) maquiladoras account for some 45 percent of Mexico's exports to
the United States.

It is hard to figure how making, what are privately negotiated trade arrangements (such as the maquiladoras are, between Mexico's regime and U.S.
corporations) wide open for use for all comers is going to create a boom in export jobs in the U.S. We are clear what it will do in Mexico - Hecht and Morici
have already shown that.

Hecht and Morici also state the increase in "manufacturing compensa-
tion in Mexico is currently about 14% of U.S. levels and will probably rise to
about 20% by the end of the decade." This is not a manifold shift to disposable income for Mexico's workers. So exactly where do we see the potential
90 million consumer market for U.S. produced goods we keep hearing about
in the U.S. media?

Hecht and Morici clear that up also. In the same article in *HBR*, the authors headline a section as follows: *Ninety Million Consumers or Nine?* (pg. 36)
The area discussed is the ability of the future Mexican worker to be able to
purchase the products of the purported export boom on the U.S. manufacturing side. It is the "sharp disparity in Mexican incomes - and whether incomes
will rise fast enough to support a particular product," that the authors feel,
"business planners must take into account."

Bill Clinton should take this disparity into account as well. The authors
point out the reality we face.

About 10% of Mexico's current population is wealthy, 45% are
middle class, and the rest are undeniably poor. Although wages
are clearly rising, the Mexican middle class doesn't have much
disposable income. And after the economic collapse of the early
1980's, many Mexican workers are now earning much less than
they did ten years ago. (Hecht/Morici, HBR, July/August '93)

With nine million Mexicans wealthy enough to take advantage of American products it isn't hard to imagine that they already have. That leaves us
with not only the Eckes' nonreciprocal agreement short term, but the *Ninety
Million* really isn't even the Hecht/Morici *Nine*. Where is the bargain?

This author believes in Free Trade. But I am not mesmerized by the idea.
Taken as a given that the foreign policy objective is to create a stable democracy on our border, is this the time to do so? Is our own democracy stable
enough to stabilize a worse-off Mexican one?

October 9, 1993, the Labor Department reported (Associated Press) that
the seventh straight monthly decline in manufacturing employment was off-
set by a big gain in service jobs, but analysts complained many of those service jobs were low pay or part-time.

In September of 1993, jobs in the manufacturing sector fell by 18,000, with 11,000 of the lost jobs held by middle-managers and the rest by production workers. This continued decline in manufacturing jobs, the Labor Department goes on to say,

> pushed total manufacturing employment down to 17.69 million, the lowest since January 1965. (AP Oct. 9th, 1993 NYT's)

Again, as in 1950, we are faced with an admirable foreign policy initiative of seeing that stable democracies flourish throughout the post Cold War world. I am certainly in favor of both stability and democracy. But the recorded cost since 1972 must be reversed. Another twenty-years of what we must see as observable trends going on during 1993, with an explainable 20 year history, is not speculation. It is rational projection of the GATT's and the NAFTA's consequences. If this administration ignores this history, that is so recent, former Chairman of the Senate Finance Committee, Senator Long's 1972 warning to Dr. Henry Kissinger will be heard again.

> If we trade away American jobs and farmers' incomes for some vague concept of a 'new international order', the American people will demand from their elected representatives a new order of their own, which puts their jobs, their security and their income above the priorities of those who dealt them a bad deal. (Quoted in Eckes, FA vol. 71, No.4)

It doesn't seem many are listening to any rational arguments against GATT or the NAFTA agreements. As the editors of the *New Republic* stated : (Oct. 11, 1993)

> With each passing decade, the line between domestic and foreign policy becomes more blurry. (Which one is NAFTA?)

Without question it is both but driven by the same moral vision of the Cold War. As this article attempts to demonstrate, *Foreign Policy Affects Domestic Policies*, and not unusually for the worse.

But the argument for the agreements are vague and speculative. The arguments against them have been polemical, not historical, nor factual. Perceptions seem to rule reality. And I think we shall move on to further analysis about just such vague perceived truths that hide a reality often quite different.

The perception that the U.S. trade deficit is the best indicator of U.S. economic health may also be misleading. The trade deficit has soared once again to a projected $110 billion for 1994. Reasons why bringing the trade deficit into balance is not a cure-all are many, but the strongest argument is, according to Cowhey and Aronson in their article *A New Trade Order* (Foreign Affairs,Vol.72 No.l).

> Foreign investment flows are only about 10 percent of the size of world trade flows each year, but intra-firm trade (for example,

sales by Ford Europe to Ford USA) now accounts for up to an
astonishing 40 percent of all U.S. trade.

The point is becoming clearer. The transnational corporation has placed
itself above the economies of nation states. While GM and Chrysler lay off
workers in Detroit (75,000) they are, at one and the same time period, opening
some of their largest factories in Poland with a $2.8 billion investment. The
layoffs seemingly and tragically will affect GM, Ford, or IBM to the less-informed. But that is not the whole story. The corporate world is today a borderless one. The long term benefits to this world economy and specifically the
corporations representative of it are many. We need not go into them here.

National security interests were obvious during the Cold War. It could be
spelled out easily with rhetoric about communism and nuclear war. Sacrifice
was easy for Americans given this perception of a credible enemy and threat
scenario.

With communism a less viable threat and no longer the glue holding public perceptions together, the U.S. Government must find another enemy credible enough to be believable. As William McNeill in *Winds of Change* states,

> The situation we face in the United States as the Cold War
> winds down and the arms race peters out is that some new
> balance among all the special interests and social groupings
> of American society will have to be contrived. (*Foreign Affairs*,
> Vol.69 No.4)

While McNeill does not elaborate much outside the abstract he does give
us an idea of what sort of contrivance may work.

> That calls for the sort of political process that went into the re-
> definition of the role of the federal government after World War
> II. Debate then centered upon what the United States ought to
> do overseas to contain communism. (McNeill)

In thinking about "what ought to happen at home" (McNeill), we are
again in the area of speculation. But it is becoming clearer if we follow the
thinking through. That means following the public pronouncements of the
President, congressional leaders and business leaders; we can then get some
idea what foreign policy perceptions will be a driving force in the future.
What constitutes the future threats to national security, or simply national
interests, is the equivalent to the cold war rhetoric of the past.

National Interests

Here we find the threat of terrorism and economic threats from a powerful Japan and EC (European Community) has loomed large. Larger still is
the perceived threat that illegal drug traffic poses to U.S. national security.
Environmental concerns too vie for top billing.

While it is true that ethnic blocks and groupings of former states into regional groupings for economic gain could constitute a threat of sorts, an ICBM they are not. Nor will Americans pay much heed to a threat from the former Yugoslavian Serbs and Croats killing each other. Without the perception that gas prices will rise because of a group's actions or inflation will spiral, Americans care little what happens globally.

Strange isn't it, that what has affected American's standard of living, inflation, recessions, and job losses more than anything, was the policy formulations of foreign affairs and their implementation through trade agreements such as GATT, yet today's Uruguay Round of the GATT and NAFTA are hidden in a cloud. A recent Gallup poll put the level of ignorance at some 70%.

In looking at the leads given us by the spokesmen most listened to, the drug war sounds like the qualifier for Cold War style policies. Theodore C. Sorensen, *Rethinking National Security* in *Foreign Affairs*, seems sure of it.

> I believe our national interests are truly threatened, for example, by the invasion of our country by illicit narcotics from Latin America, Asia and elsewhere. (FA Vol-69 No.3)

Sorensen goes on to include environmental pollution as a threat and adds that the government should,

> be careful about conferring undefined yet undeniably far-reaching powers of national security on every law enforcement or military official engaged in combating either of those evils, with their potential impact on the *individual liberties* and business freedom of virtually every American, lest we gravely harm the values and institutions that the very concept of national security is intended to protect. (Ibid.)

It seems Sorensen, in the summer of 1990 when his article appeared in *Foreign Affairs*, was unaware that the institutional erosion of many significant values, not to mention constitutional rights were negatively impacted because of exactly those national security concerns of the drug war. I will only cite Executive Order 12333, P.L. 99-570 and P.L. 100-690 as examples as well as shock incarceration, euphemistically called boot camps, in Bush and Clinton crime initiatives. Our institutions and values have been altered decidedly by the above initiatives. There are more on the table, (S. 995 '93).

Nobody can argue that a goal of America should be "the peaceful enhancement of democracy around the world" (Sorensen), provided that that policy doesn't simply continue the loss of U.S. jobs overseas as the means to that end. That was clearly the means used since Truman to achieve similar goals in the past 45 years as Eckes points out.

Sorensen's argument that of "the two basic national security goals for the new multipolar era," one) the above democracy enhancement, and two) "the preservation of this nation's economic effectiveness and independence in the global marketplace" begs the question.

Has it not been , since 1947, the goal of the U.S. Government due to national security interests of *containment*, to intervene in that marketplace? Has not that intervention by foreign policy initiatives as applied through the institutions of the GATT (as well as the World Bank, the Agency for International Development and the XM Bank) been a cause for exactly that harm to American individual liberties, business freedom and job losses overseas?

Unless we re-define what we mean by national interests and pose the question as Benjamin J. Cohen did, in the title of his work on International Banking and American Foreign Policy - *In Whose Interest?*, we are truly left with a paradox.

If the standard of living of Americans dropped, in real (inflation adjusted) terms, some 20-25 percent since 1973 in great measure due to the implementation of the GATT agreement's *Kennedy Round* as Eckes asserts can we really be talking about GATT's continued reforms being in America's national security interest?

George A. Carver in his article *Intelligence and Glasnost*, in *Foreign Affairs*, goes even further than Sorensen above. Carver believes the redefinition of national security *is* a national security agenda.

> Over the next few decades, not only will traditional concerns change and new ones arise, they are also likely to coalesce in potent, unprecedented combinations. During this period, for example, America's greatest challenges may not come from across any ocean lying to its east or west. Instead they may well come from the south, in a manner that obliterates such tidy classical distinctions as those between foreign and domestic affairs. Unrest in South and Central America and Mexico, the ramifications of drug abuse and narcotics traffic, the pressure of immigration — much of it illegal — and attendant pressures for biculturalism and bilingualism could easily strain America's democratic polity more severely than any time since the Civil War. (FA Vol.69 No.3)

While Carver may be right in the abstract or ideal, one cannot help but analyze the above rather ominous note. Why, for instance, is bilingualism and biculturalism a threat? Throughout the world from Libya to Japan, in every country of Europe (the EC) many, if not most, people speak one or more languages other than their mother tongue. Cultural distinctions abound in every country except those few that are homogeneous to the extreme. America has in fact been the leader in meltdown of cultural distinctions, languages and race, yet Mexicans and Californians (whatever defines a Californian escapes me) are at risk living together according to the notions of Carver.

Why, as another assertion of Carver's, is illegal immigration, and now with President Clinton's August 1993 agenda of legal immigration, seen as a threat? "We can police the world but not our own borders", Clinton appealed to Americans. Has Bill Clinton seen the Pat Buchanan light on this issue? Has

Clinton succumbed to xenophobia? Or is the reality, that NAFTA will pass the congressional hearings only if Mexicans are kept in Mexico earning one-tenth of what they would if working in an identical factory in California? Is it that *National Health Care Reform* has no chance if immigrants are included as beneficiaries?

Whenever I hear the appeal to national security concerns made by those influential enough to be taken serious I grab my wallet. Whenever the appeal is couched in drug war rhetoric I grab my civil rights. Can it be, as Carver believes, that the drugs in our culture are cause for alarm to the degree outlined by Carver below?

> Finally, no matter what else happens in the years immediately ahead, America's government — including its intelligence community — will have to grapple with the conceptual and organizational challenge posed by the extent to which traditional, jurisdictional-defining distinctions are being eroded: not only foreign versus domestic, but also economic versus political, military versus civilian, intelligence versus police responsibilities, federal versus state and local responsibilities, private versus public or governmental and, even in the foreign affairs field, friend versus foe. (FA Vol.69 N0.3)

While we may dismiss Carver's statements as his own desire to see the intelligence community expanded in the new era, we cannot dismiss our sense of it that too many see in the cold war's end, a need to expand the power and reach of government rather than reduce it. Carver would re-define it altogether to include closing the breach between State's rights and Federal reach; the long held distinction between the roles of domestic law enforcement and use of federal, U.S. Military, ground troops domestically; between the Central Intelligence Agency and the police powers. Each area of which would forever alter the relationship between the governed and those governing; between the people and their government.

As often as I have weighed these very issues in my professional life I cannot bring myself to conclude that cocaine is the equivalent of an ICBM, or that Mexican immigration equals a ground invasion by former Soviet and East Block nations. If the former Cold War was reality, then the argument of Carver's — that Mexicans and drugs require an even greater expansion of power projection capabilities to include re-defining traditional jurisdictions — is blatantly exaggerated.

Congress is listening to the new threat scenarios. In a recent crime bill Congress pleaded to fight the drug war, "by the principles that energized and sustained the mobilization for World War II." (HR-4079)

Conclusion

This turning inward against our own citizens and potential citizens by an ever more centralized federal government can only result in a more authoritarian regime. As technology advances with direct subsidies, *Federal Telecommunications System 2000* (FTS 2000); indirect incentives, tax breaks, R&D subsidies; total agenda rhetoric and the Information Hi-way, it does not require a crystal ball to project the outcome. In a recent Commerce Department Study it was enthusiastically stated that the above (FTS 2000 primarily) could..."bring about the futurist's dream of a cashless society."

Coupled with the passage of NAFTA and the Uruguay Round of the GATT, and the creation of the World Trade Organization (WTO), the future seems set in stone. No one area of foreign affairs, such as NAFTA, can be viewed in isolation from the other areas simultaneously being put forward. Each touches all the others. As each of these foreign policy objectives become policy the changes on the domestic front will be profound.

This will spell a significant loss of *National Sovereignty* for the United States. As Walter B. Wriston points out in *Technology and Sovereignty, (Foreign Affairs*, Vol.67 No.2) "Today we are witnessing a galloping new system of international finance," and "The entire globe is linked electronically, with no place to hide." Money matters are without question a matter of foreign affairs. Nearly half of the NAFTA agreement is about international financial integration, though this is lost on the citizen.

While the futurist is pleased, Washington and *National Security Agency* planners know that that future also means that the homeless, illegal aliens, drug users and drug dealers as well, are going to be in an untenable situation. A cashless (and coinless) society with *only* a debit and credit card as the medium of exchange will mean panhandling, begging, theft and the underground economy (cash-based) will come to an end. The then felt need to house these folks and reorient them to the new way of life is seen as priority.

The homeless must have work of some sort even if it is painting rocks on an abandoned military base. All must work in some manner so as to transfer to their unit of account electronically their newly defined wages or welfare. Mexicans must remain in Mexico. Cash sales, whether babysitting, lawn mowing, or drug buying will, (must), end in the new era.

Many will see the above as a positive sign, others will feel less uplifted. Neither is my concern for this article.

My concern is only to inform the uninformed that to ignore the foreign policies of our government, the foreign alliances of our corporate agenda and the objectives of national security perceptions is to live in a fool's paradise.

Things are going to change. Everyone knows that. To see the future, even the near future, requires only that one reads well the foreign (as well as domestic) policy objectives of one's own established powers. Follow the perceptions to their stated conclusive goals and one will be less surprised than the common herd.

Foreign policy affects domestic policy. History is not about to repeat itself as so many would claim by the slogan. Foreign interests are today so connected that the web of technology alone makes a new and distinct future not just probable but a certainty.

It can be understood only with the aid of foreign affairs study and a clear eye about its affects on domestic policies.

CHAPTER ELEVEN

Gulf War Illnesses
A Retrospective

*Given the effect of war in eliminating
many of the most able and courageous elements of
the population, there would seem better
reason for suggesting that it tends
to reduce a state's capacities over the
long term than that it will increase them.*
Evan Luard
War in International Society

*We learned to wage war because it made sense
in terms of the kind of world we lived in.
That is far less true today.
Nevertheless we fought because we were
able to fight. We crafted weapons.
We demonstrated aggression, both among
ourselves and against other species.
Our loyalty to our culture could be manipulated
through mechanisms such as religion
and our urge to reciprocate,
which also compelled us to seek revenge.*
—ROBERT L. O'CONNELL

GULF WAR ILLNESSES A RETROSPECTIVE

DURING AUGUST 1997, CONGRESSMAN JACK METCALF (R) WA, requested the *Government Accounting Office*, GAO, to look into the possibility that Gulf War-era veterans may have received vaccine inoculations to protect them from anthrax, which may have contained the adjuvant squalene (pronounced sk-wa-leen). Several researchers, including the respected Dr. Robert Garry at Tulane University, discovered squalene antibodies in the blood of many of the vets they examined.

Troops refusing to be inoculated with the anthrax vaccine have been punished. Others have complained of so many and varied symptoms, Gulf War Syndrome has been renamed Gulf War Illnesses. Clearly, with so many veterans ill (well over 100,000), with symptoms so slight some have been accused of hypochondria while others are so ill they are in wheel-chairs, this should be a high priority. Many have been diagnosed with *Lupus* and white males over fifty just do not get this particular malady.

Dr. Garry *et al*, finally got their article published in a respected medical journal. The article has raised the hackles on the important officials at the *Department of Defense*, DOD, and some scientific experts within the circle of chemical and biological weapons defense and the medical research facilities whose mission it is to find vaccines for such threats. Anthrax was the greatest threat posed to our troops during the Gulf War.

Hearings were held by the *Committee on Government Reform* during October 3, and 11, 2000. Congressman Metcalf was called to testify and submitted his final report to the Committee. As the *Metcalf Report* demonstrates, the GAO and Metcalf's office, were virtually alone in the simple request that Dr. Garry's test for antibodies be replicated to confirm or deny his findings; discover if, indeed, squalene antibodies are present in these very ill veterans; and if confirmed, discover how squalene antibodies came to be present in their blood? And finally, was squalene present in some of the vaccine batches prepared for the troops inoculated against anthrax? Squalene, at the time, was an experimental adjuvant, non FDA (*Food and Drug Administration*) approved, used to enhance the potency and accelerate an immune response from a given vaccine.

The DOD has repeatedly denied ever using squalene in any vaccines. The most recent denials are so frivolous they cannot be considered seriously. Like this one: *"Squalene can be found in shark liver oil, cosmetics and the human body produces squalene itself."* This clumsy rebuttal has been used since the beginning, three years ago when GAO began their investigation, and was the recent widely quoted denial on October 3, 2000. The press, other than the Chicago Tribune, universally quoted this rather silly rejoinder. (Why silly? While it is true that one form of squalene is found in human tissue, the human body does not produce antibodies to what is natural to itself — or we would all be dead.) Importantly omitted from press accounts has been this, that squalene can be synthetically manufactured, and in this form is highly toxic to humans. And it is toxins, as I shall demonstrate below, that are the question, as to make an antitoxin one must of necessity make a toxin.

In any case, DOD denials now fall on deaf ears as the GAO and Congressman Metcalf's *Special Assistant* Mrs. Norma Smith, have compiled enormous documentation that squalene has been used and used often by DOD, and experimented with well before the Gulf War. It is in fact used in a number of specific vaccines as the GAO finally discovered. Used, at times, even while not FDA approved. Which goes some distance to explain why DoD continues to deny its use today. In fact, according to the GAO's **Record of Interviews** from investigator Kwai Chan, DOD officials repeatedly lied to the investigators regarding their own research, only admitting to it after the GAO investigators showed them the public record. In three cases the very DOD scientists which did the research itself denied it outright when first asked, only admitting to it later. DOD, even when presented with such hard evidence, continues to deny ever having used squalene; denials which, as I shall get to below, are sounding hollow and absurd.

To be fair, the Gulf War never went as smoothly as we have repeatedly been told. And I feel this must be understood now, so as understand why some actions may have been taken, errors made, contaminated batches of vaccines or any number of things that may be responsible for the Gulf War Illnesses, may have happened. So be patient, a bit of history is in order before the issue can be clear.

Gulf Deployment A Logistical Nightmare

Over those three years since Congressman Metcalf requested the GAO look into the Gulf War Illnesses of veterans and era-veterans, he has repeatedly stated how disappointed he was in the response he received: "I am disappointed with the DOD in particular and the many branches and agencies inextricably tied to Defense where biological and chemical weapon's threats are taken so seriously." Further developments have come to my attention and I think a little background is needed. After all, the Gulf War is beginning to get those gray hairs around the edges like the Vietnam War.

Rather than offer my own opinion on some of this I shall quote from documents I reviewed from Metcalf's office which they received over the period of their own three year investigation, which closely followed that of GAO.

One source I looked at closely was the AFEB, the *Armed Forces Epidemiological Board*, and minutes from their meetings. The important time frame of February 28 and March 1, 1991 gives a real sense of the problems the Pentagon faced and the chaos surrounding the Gulf deployment. This is crucial to understanding just what may have happened and why; when we do discover what happened regarding the troops themselves, there will be less of a desire to try to *see some heads' roll*. Rather, maybe some help will be forthcoming for the Veterans, many which are getting worse by the day.

The meeting from which I shall quote, and elaborate upon, took place at the *U.S. Army Medical Research Institute for Infectious Diseases*, Ft. Detrick, Maryland. It is here that the best and brightest in the military's medical community gathered during Operation Desert Storm to discuss what had been done to date during Operation Desert Shield and the ongoing hostilities with Iraq. It is my contention and many experts and analysts at the time concurred, due to geopolitical objectives we were not informed of, President George Bush quite simply deployed our troops much too quickly. The United States, including the DOD, were not prepared logistically to support our troops adequately with such an enormous deployment over such a short period of time. Ammunition for our ground troops was in short supply, airstrips had to be improved or made from scratch, the sheer number of support personnel was staggering as well as Reservists and National Guard units called-up. Several former *Joint Chiefs of Staff* Chairmen testified to this prior to the hostilities. General William Westmoreland (Ret.) even went on radio programs with me at the time and made this case (his personal letter, which I received a first draft to prepare our joint interviews, is to be found in the *Congressional Record*). But here is what Major General Richard Travis said at the AFEB meeting on March 1st, 1991:

> ...we are going to be back in the exact same situation that we found ourselves in in August, (1990) and there isn't a soul in this room or in the world that would have predicted in August, and I had a lot of anthrax vaccine, but no one would have predicted that we were going to have 500,000 troops on the ground, and civilian populations or rich governments that wanted their entire populations vaccinated.

General Travis was commenting at the time regarding the short supply of vaccines to inoculate our troops with. Every vaccine and infectious disease was discussed by the many experts. From botulism to influenza, the needs had to be met. Anthrax is the one we must focus on. We must single out the short supply, and how the needs were met to inoculate our troops against the Iraqi anthrax capability, with an eye to the necessities and mentality at the time.

Why were the troops not vaccinated for anthrax until January 7th, 1991? According to Captain Parsons of the AFEB,

> ...the main reason the vaccine wasn't started was because we didn't have enough of it, and the question is, who do we give it to first among our own forces, and does giving it to our forces create problems in terms of the other allies we have. They were asking for it. ...So you know, it was really a tremendous geopolitical question that emerged.

Colonel Tomlinson's reply is important.

I think what he wanted to point out was that, in the future, that MRDC needs guidance on, number one, how much should we have in the stockpile, how much should we have to give our current troops.... But as we went ahead with that recommendation it was get all you can, as fast as you can, and nobody put a number on it. And that is what they are asking for now.

I have quoted these sources to give you a sense of the urgency created by the logistical nightmare the Gulf War deployment created. Decisions had to be made militarily, logistically and medically. It was a time of war. And so, as Captain Larry Laughlin stated, "I would just comment that Desert Shield/ Desert Storm has become a program effort....in war time epidemiology."

Captain Laughlin is candid in his remarks. He was then with NMRI, *Naval Medical Research Institute,* which among other things worked closely with our *Naval Forward Laboratories,* (NFL), which he praised because *"there is no substitute for getting with the boys."* He rightly observed at the time that you have to infiltrate the action if you are going to find out what's needed. And research was needed. And here is where we again get a sense of the urgency of mission the military was faced with; quoting once again Captain Laughlin:

...in dealing with these sorts of circumstances, the word "research" spooks people. You've got to make yourself useful to them on a day to day basis, and that was the approach that we took. We were prepared to take care of non-research issues for the moment for the possibility of bleeding 1,000 Marines.

Now please bear with me on this, as this is not in the *Metcalf Report,* nor did any of this get out with the Gulf War Hearings of October 3rd, 2000. Major General Richard Travis was as forthcoming in this 1991 March 1st meeting as the others:

A question was raised yesterday, "When did you vaccinate?" We began putting vaccines in arms on the 7th of January. When did the Board tell us to vaccinate? in October. It took that long from the decision until January, because there is no where in the entire DOD structure someone that will tell me what to do here....I will tell you that I have enumerable vaccines on the shelf, in X, Y and Z numbers. I cannot give you a rationale for the numbers. Clearly, with anthrax, we were caught short, and so, that began a problem that went all the way to the National Command Authority to decide what we were going to do in that particular situation, and how we were going to do it.

General Travis then pleaded with the Board to help him get with the Intel Community, the Joint Chiefs, Doctor Mendez, and others, including someone or agency named *"purple,"* to tell him what they were going to do in the long term. The frustration fairly lifts off the pages of the transcript. General Travis then goes on:

> Implicated in this is the entire industrial base. I don't need much of an industrial base if every arm is going to have every vaccine that we have, but I need a significant one if I'm going to store thousands or millions and millions of dollars of vaccines.... And so, hopefully, out of this we get this put into place, we get the imprimatur of the civilian academic community, we, in-house, get our arms around what we call the "laundered money," or whatever, and maybe in time it will go away. Don't know. In point of fact, we did have vaccine, we did have it against the major threats that were in the area, we just didn't have enough.

It was troubling to read this man speak so passionately about the need for more anthrax vaccine for our troops when he could not get the U.S. industrial base to help out. He referred to this as *"a major industrial base problem, a problem because of indemnification issues, because of no commercial market issues, even for the Third World."* The fact that the military's vaccine program *"is driven by commercial concerns..."* was mentioned during one of the recent GAO interviews with Colonel Carl Alving, the Pentagons top adjuvant specialist (whom we shall look more closely at below). But the point is clear, unless there is a commercial market for the major pharmaceutical firms to peddle their product, they find little incentive to produce sufficient amount of anything 'just' for U.S. troops. Their concern for the risk involved with novel vaccines using questionable adjuvant formulations (indemnification) is more understandable. The re*assurance* of in*surance* was lacking where liability is concerned.

It was not just that General Travis could not get the cooperation from any of the major pharmaceutical companies, and the recent GAO investigation did bring this out several times, but because civilian agencies and private firms are not looking for the same diseases that Defense is. And Anthrax was the big one at the time. The geopolitical decision had to be made based on the political objectives of the Administration — the National Command Authority: The President of the United States and his immediate Cabinet.

And General Travis knew the risks posed right there at Ft. Detrick; we all remember the horror stories of the alleged AIDS program. Well in part, at least the part about Ft. Detrick doing AIDS research, was true. General Travis points this out and that the research had to be shut down. Now comes Anthrax and Travis is faced with the same fear of public reprisal. Let me quote him one more time:

> And, I want, although you understand that to make an antitoxin I've got to make a toxin, I need to get out of the toxin business in this laboratory, because there are people that will misrepresent us once again, because they have for so long thought, you

know, you guys are doing stuff in there that you are not supposed to do, and I need to get out of that very quickly.

It is clear that General Travis at Ft Detrick was making toxins so as to make antitoxins. We know that he was involved, along with many others, in anthrax research during the Gulf War period. And often this research is classified because the threat is classified as well. Colonel William Bancroft noted this.

As development of a countermeasure for an infectious disease progresses, it is transitioned into advanced development, and the advanced development is not in a usual laboratory, but is under the responsibility of the United States Army Medical Materiel Agency, which is located here at Fort Detrick, and their job is to test and evaluate the countermeasures in humans, that is, to see that they are tested.

This has, by way of history, been an attempt to put what follows and the *Metcalf Report* into some perspective. We deployed 650,000 troops to a region against an enemy known to have chemical and biological weapons. But our troops were not able to be properly vaccinated against this threat due to time constraints. Again, the vaccine we had in short supply required a regimen of six shots over eighteen months. There was no time. These officers just quoted and many others interviewed since made it clear: If we were to protect our forces from anthrax, a new vaccine, or a boost in the performance of the present vaccine was needed. And we now know that squlaene (which is highly toxic) was looked at and tested as an adjuvant. This was war. It is hardly inconceivable that something was done out of the ordinary with what the FDA calls *Investigational New Drugs* (IND), drugs not fully licensed by the FDA but utilized on an experimental basis.

Is it more conceivable that we would have inoculated troops with a vaccine that would not have protected them? Or just not inoculated them at all because the FDA had not approved of a specific adjuvant that would have boosted the vaccine and protected the troops a the time?

Experimental Vaccine?

Over the past months I have gone through all the documents gathered by Metcalf's Special Assistant Norma Smith and the GAO and came across a document from the Department of the Army — *Documentation Guidelines for Anthrax Immunization*: dated — 9 July, 1991. A mere four months after the testimony I have just reported upon above. It said the following:

Soldiers in Southwest Asia Theater of Operations during the time frame 1 January through 16 February 1991 were ordered to receive the anthrax immunization which was the only **"secret"** immunization given in theater.

Why would the troops receive a vaccine which was the "only secret immunization given in theatre?" if the vaccines were FDA approved and would have in fact *protected the troops*? If everything was on the up-and-up why the need for secrecy at all? It wasn't secret from the Iraqis as they wouldn't have known in any case. But it was secret from the troops that received the vaccine, and secret until this document surfaced through the Metcalf and GAO investigations.

During the investigation the GAO uncovered an article in the journal *Infectious Disease Clinics of North America* by authors Russell and E. Takafuji, during March 1990, which stated that the *"United States military immunizes its forces with experimental limited use vaccines for special situations"*. E. Takafuji is Colonel E. Takafuji, United States Army MRMC. He was, as well, a participant in several recent GAO enquiries regarding the use of adjuvants in anthrax vaccines during the Gulf War. He stated during one such interview on September 11, 1998, *"The questions raised by the independent researchers are going to come back to DOD."* And so they have.

The independent researchers are again, the highly respected Dr. Robert Garry and colleagues, from Tulane University, who prepared a paper published in the journal *Experimental and Molecular Pathology* titled *Antibodies to Squalene in Gulf War Syndrome*. It is still causing controversy at DoD and Ft. Detrick. And it was based upon their work and a great deal of other material, that Metcalf requested GAO to investigate the matter in the first place. It has been years now of stonewalling, contradiction and obfuscation. But the GAO and Metcalf's staff persisted, and as the *Metcalf Report* demonstrates, there is smoke here, and some little fire.

Again, Dr. Garry and colleagues discovered squalene antibodies in ill Gulf War-era veterans. The sickest vets seem to have the largest count of antibodies. Dr. Garry has filed for a patent on his ASA assay [test]. The very idea that Dr. Garry has discovered such a finding has brought only angry responses from otherwise reasonable scientists; the haste with which the DOD and the AFEB dismissed Garry's findings is somewhat startling. Yet in their June 22, 2000, AFEB report, clearly designed to discredit Garry's findings, we read this conclusion:

> Therefore, the AFEB has little confidence that the patent-pending ASA assay actually measures antibodies to squalene, though we cannot entirely eliminate this possibility.

All Congressman Metcalf asked, and all the GAO ever recommended, was that DoD verify Dr. Garry's findings or conclusively refute them by replicating the tests. This would cost some few thousands of dollars. The GAO has reported that DoD and other agencies have spent over $121 million treating and examining Gulf War veterans and WRAIR (Walter Reed Army Hospital) are supposedly treating veterans with antibiotics and aerobics therapy! We are, in very real terms, dancing around the issue! And we still have no commitment to replicate Dr. Garry's work. Even the AFEB recommended the very same. Let me quote their final remarks regarding their criticism of Garry's paper:

Whatever the paper's flaws and since the AFEB cannot exclude the remote possibility that the authors have identified a laboratory means of distinguishing persons with possible Gulf War Syndrome from all others, replicability becomes the major unresolved issue....the AFEB feels that the symptom list in the Garry, Asa paper is a good starting point...Therefore, we recommend that a suitable test of replicability be done in cooperation with the authors ...

Nothing could be clearer: *replicability is the major unresolved issue!* It is time the testing get done. The veterans do not have any more time. We have wasted too much of that invaluable commodity already.

In closing, I must cite one last, very recent finding at the Metcalf office. They received a letter from the FDA dated March 20, 2000. It said in part the following:

Very limited testing of Anthrax Vaccine, absorbed, conducted by CBER (the FDA's Center for Biologics Evaluation and Research) in 1999 determined that there were only trace amounts of squalene in the lots tested....CBER tested in its laboratories the two lots mentioned in the article (FAV020 and FAV030) for squalene....Due to the inability to detect trace amounts of squalene parts per million, CBER developed a test to detect the substance in parts per billion.

The language *"detect* only *trace amounts of squalene"* puts the matter to rest. The very lots tested were the lots identified in an article published in *Vanity Fair* which discussed for the first time Dr. Robert Garry's research. With all the denials from DoD that there was never any squalene used in any of their Gulf War anthrax vaccines, we can now pose the question somewhat differently. We now must ask, and on October 3rd, Chairman Dan Burton of the House Committee on Government Reform has demanded further investigations by GAO to resolve this question, exactly why, and how, has even *trace amounts* of squalene been found in the very lots of Anthrax Vaccine known to have been used on Gulf War troops? Dr. Garry might suggest this could explain the squalene antibodies found in some of his patients. Certainly one Dr. Dorothy Lewis, *Baylor College of Medicine*, thought so. In a letter to Congressman Metcalf she noted that the test used by the FDA was a "much more sensitive technique" than the one used by DoD, adding the important point, the real issue:

...is whether squalene in parts per billion was added to the vaccine preparations given to the military, as well as whether this concentration could alter the immune response. ...it is possible that very small amounts of a biologically active product could induce an immune response, either to the molecule itself or it could boost immune responses to other agents in the mixture.

What Dr. Lewis did not speak to, because of its obviousness, is this, — what she described above is precisely why an adjuvant would be added to the mixture! She also added that further research was needed to respond to the findings [of both Dr. Garry and now the FDA]. And this argument is becoming ridiculously redundant.

Only the US Congress can get the answer to these questions. Burton's Committee report titled *Accountability of DoD, FDA and BioPort Officials For the Anthrax Vaccine Immunization Program* (AVIP), closed with these remarks:

> Bottom-line: Institutional tendencies to protect policies and the chain of command have promoted a seriously questionable force protection initiative instead of protecting the troops that are the object of the policy. In the meantime, ill troops are abandoned, healthy troops are punished, and the integrity of the military institution is tarnished. External from the DoD, this smear campaign on our militaries' integrity occurred through false testimony to Congress and inaccurate reporting to the American media. Internal within the DoD, an aggressive propaganda campaign of subtle misrepresentations and half-truths to the nation's subordinate military commanders and troops has replaced the trust and integrity essential to command. Clearly, the Congress recognizes that the DoD "did not intend to mislead or confuse people," initially, but regardless, DoD officials must now immediately and unilaterally end the AVIP, care for the inoculated ill, and expunge all punishments. Otherwise, Congress will be compelled to intervene, exercising its oversight authority and responsibility as the elected legislators for the American people.

In closing, I must admit that I always have little faith in most institutions; they are precisely as good or bad, deceptive or honest as the individuals that make up its body of personnel. There are too many individuals in this country (awash as we are with really terrible television programming like *Cops*, and unrealistic movie-making where some rather attractive young gal [reporter] defeats yet another smarmy male) which make up a disillusioned populace, thinking it is more important to *see some heads roll*, find the malevolent male (often enough in uniform) and see him fry.

What ought to matter is but the truth: if an unlicensed adjuvant (squalene) found its way, for obvious reasons during war, into some of the DoD's batches of anthrax vaccine, in order to protect the troops in theatre against a known threat, knowing they would have been completely vulnerable *without* the adjuvant, it is only important to discover this, replicate Dr. Garry's assay (test), and find an antidote to treat the veterans. It really does not matter whether

Colonel this or *Doctor that* did *this or that.* Unless *Col. this* is **presently** stone-walling the efforts above described. They were under orders no differently than the troops sent in harms way. Another Colonel North we do not need. Only CNN needs that, what with the little Cuban no longer in the news.

CHAPTER TWELVE:

Project Badger 1990
and the Illusive Colonel Alving

And I will war, at least in words (and—should
My chance so happen—deeds), with all who war
With thought;—and of Thought's foes by far most rude,
Tyrants and sycophants have been and are.
—DON JUAN, IX, XXIV.

Democratic governments suffer from the same
disadvantage as decent people do; they can
never profit from a pact or alliance
with criminals or organized "indecency."
—MIECZYSLAW MANELI

PROJECT BADGER 1990

THIS CHAPTER IS HEREIN INCLUDED for obvious reasons along with the above chapter. It will give the reader some idea of the kinds of questions raised behind the closed doors of a US representative's office which never see the light of day publicly. The issue of one Colonel Alving was the topic often regarding the Gulf War Illnesses investigations which Congressman Jack Metcalf undertook for several years. This is, in part, what was discovered about the illusive and uncooperative Colonel. The allegations which may be derived from this investigation are mine alone and not those of the Congressman.

Colonel Carl Alving M.D., stationed at Walter Reed Army Hospital, is considered the world's foremost expert on adjuvants and their applicability. During and immediately before the deployment of Operation Desert Shield, (ODS), there were questions only he could have answered. The GAO investigators noted above in chapter eleven, looked into these questions. I must cite *Special Assistant* Norma Smith of Congressman Jack Metcalf's office during 2000, for her thorough compilation of GAO's many *Record of Interview* documents I have drawn on below.

During March 30, 1998 GAO interviewed Donald Burke, Director of AIDS research for DoD during the Persian Gulf War. During the interview Burke stated he had decided not to get involved with biological weapons defense issues at that time. In his AIDS work he admitted to experimenting with MF59 (an adjuvant containing squalene). The only substance authorized at the time for use as an adjuvant was "alum" and it was destructive to HIV proteins. After noting his cooperation with the *National Institutes of Health* (NIH), he recalled several studies he was involved with including one with 300 subjects getting MF59...he also suggested GAO speak with Col. Carl Alving about DoD research.

On April 6, 1998 GAO investigators did interview Col. Alving for the first time. When questioned about vaccines that were used during Operations Desert Shield/Desert Storm (ODS), he opened his statement saying, "...he didn't know anything about ODS and the vaccines that were used. He is a researcher, and an expert, but not in the policy loop."

Given his world-class expertise, GAO wondered why he was not consulted. He admitted that he was contacted prior to the Gulf War regarding whether he could develop an anthrax vaccine on a crash basis. He noted that Walter Reed Army Hospital's Research facilities (WRAIR) had the manufacturing capability but that Ft. Detrick did not. ..." (He) could have done it in three to six months but he never received a follow-on phone call to formally authorize the work. If asked, he could have done it, but would have recommended MF59 for anthrax because Chiron had the manufacturing capacity and the desire to market it." There was further talk about different firms other than Chiron (Ribi, and Hunter), as these were the adjuvant leaders at the time. He was asked about the use of Liposomes to develop an anthrax vaccine (something he is an expert in) but he stated the tests had failed the criteria set for monkeys with a single shot, which he called, "...An absurd criteria. But commercial considerations may have driven the criteria."

In a final notation in one of GAO's *Report of Interview*, the investigators stated again their belief that "...commercial links appear to be crucial to the course of DoD vaccine R&D."

In the GAO report, Investigator Kwai Chan reported in a section titled *DoD officials were less than forthcoming about their role in Gulf War decision making*, said this "...Carl Alving was not included in our meetings at WRAIR where he worked, nor even mentioned as someone we should interview." When they finally did interview Col. Alving above and pressed him, he elaborated further that he "...had been called by someone from the army's biological warfare defense program at USAMRID [*United States Army Medical Research Institute of Infectious Diseases*], who asked if he could develop a new, more potent anthrax vaccine on a crash basis to use in the Operation Desert Shield. (He) worked on it and thought he could do it, but no one ever called him back." He wouldn't say who called him, nor answer why he never simply called them back himself, since "he worked on it and thought he could do it." Thus, he at first stated he had no involvement as "he was not in the policy loop," but when pressed he admitted involvement but minimized that involvement.

[But] on April 19, 1998, GAO interviewed Dr. Anna Johnson-Winegar, *Director Environmental and Life Sciences*, and a key participant at the time in *Project Badger* (Tri-Service Task Force) established September 9, 1990, whose mandate was to determine and investigate ways to increase production of biological warfare vaccines. The discussions were wide-ranging and interesting, according to Johnson-Winegar, regarding the scientific issues involved in improving troop vaccines. "But there was not much data. Carl Alving was our in-house adjuvant expert, and a participant in our discussion. We discussed using liposomes, but (they) didn't have enough. You have to go to war with what you have, not novelties that don't have your full confidence."

During *Project Badger* discussions during the early months of ODS, Johnson-Winegar admitted to the GAO, "Discussion of adjuvants was limited. Its one thing to discuss interesting phase 1 research, quite another to apply it to short-term shortages. In the long run they can be of potential use. But scientific inference doesn't lead to immediate military operations. Some in the group were willing to 'jump out and use everything'." Johnson-Winegar refused to say who advocated the latter. It is almost inconceivable that Col. Alving, their in-house expert and participant in discussions, failed to note that he had been called upon before *Project Badger* was even established, to produce precisely what they were there to determine: "ways to increase production of biological weapons vaccines"; and he thought he could have done it in three to six months.

Where safety issues for the troops were concerned, Johnson-Winegar noted this important point from that time period. "There was little discussion of long-term safety issues. They were thinking short-term and immediate. Generally inactive vaccines don't have a problem. They used inactive antigens. But there were a lot of discussions regarding GMP [Good Manufacturing Practices] issues." Because anthrax vaccine is stable up to twenty years if kept at the right cool temperature they initially had this problem to deal with. According to, again, Johnson-Winegar, "...For instance, they had trouble finding the exact same fermenter. Getting approval for a new one could take FDA 30 months. They went ahead and started production with it and got retroactive approval." Retroactive approval for a fermenter but not for the adjuvant for a new vaccine? Why would they need the new unapproved FDA fermenter if they had no new vaccines?

During the last three years (1997-2000) while Dr. Robert Garry *et al*, published their peer-reviewed article in the respected journal, *Experimental and Molecular Pathology*, and Congressman Metcalf requested GAO to investigate the use of squalene in DoD's anthrax vaccine, it is not surprising to find Col. Carl Alving at the head of every attempt to discredit Dr. Garry's research through the last AFEB report, stonewall the investigations, and even place scurrilous false information regarding Garry's work anonymously on DoD's Anthrax Vaccine Inoculation Program (AVIP) website. This last was removed only after Congressman Metcalf (once again) wrote Secretary of Defense Cohen pointing out the errors posted on DoD's website. Col. Alving talked Dr. Garry out of an early draft of his article, citing scientific interest and colleague neutrality, then posted his scathing attack *before* Dr. Garry published. This unethical act alone is something just not done to a *peer*; that is why one waits for the article to a-*peer* in a *peer*-reviewed journal.

It is clear from the GAO's *Report of Interview(s)* and the year 2000 *Metcalf Report* as well as the later hearings of October 3, 2000, there was nothing less than an effort to stonewall all investigations into the use of squalene or any other non-approved adjuvant in anthrax vaccines. It is clear some such adjuvant other than alum, had to be found that would have enhanced the potency and improve the time-lag of the inoculation protocol of six shots over eighteen months. That we had a shortage of existing anthrax vaccine in any case (a vaccine that would not have protected the troops given the deployment time frame) made the military objective imperative: Jump out and use everything!

Which only makes sense. To inoculate our troops with our existing anthrax vaccine, the "only secret vaccine given in theatre," (see full article), that would *not* protect the troops would be tantamount to treason. To give them a doctored vaccine that would protect them — but may have "long-term safety issues"-- may in retrospect seem medically seriously flawed, but not militarily out of the question.

Given *Project Badger's* important and at the time classified mandate to "determine ways to increase production of biological weapons vaccines," it is highly unlikely that they failed to do so. Failure to protect our troops from Iraq's known anthrax capability during ODS would have been out of the question and political suicide for the *National Command Authority*. And we know from the AFEB minutes of their meeting on March 1st, 1991, it was the NCA that had made the uncomfortable and probably dangerous decision needed. But we were at war.

Colonel Carl Alving M.D., was not called to testify before Burton's Committee on Government Reform on October 3, 2000. The main-stream press reported right off the DoD press release, wholly ignoring Congressman Metcalf's testimony; ignored the *Metcalf Report* entirely; sand-bagged all testimony except DoD spokesmen; reported only a few private veteran's complaints regarding their illnesses. Using quotes from several DoD spokesmen after the testimony, we have been treated to the same absurd rebuttals as we have heard for over three, then, now five years. The silliest one being: "Squalene is produced in the human body, shark liver oil and cosmetics." Therefore, nobody should be surprised to discover it in either the anthrax vaccine, which it was (see article) or in the blood of veterans, which it was, (see article) or presumably in anyone else's blood for that matter, which it has not.

If one never heard the testimony, read the GAO report, *Metcalf Report*, or the Garry article, one could conclude along with Col. Alving, that only conspiracy theorists find smoke. But nobody ever said they found squalene in veteran's blood — they found squalene *antibodies!* We know squalene is naturally found in the human body — but the human body does not create antibodies to fight off what is natural to the human body — we would all be dead men walking if that were true. But the human immune system does fight off toxins (which is precisely the job of an adjuvant's toxicity) — whether synthetically created squalene or some enhanced adjuvant version that would be toxic to humans: Thus the antibodies. "You have to make toxins to make antitoxins" (General Travis, Ft. Detrick).

Instead what do we see? We see a vitamin and antibiotics program at Walter Reed and Naval Health facilities. We see $121 million spent, some $20 million misallocated improperly according to the GAO report, to date with no improvement of even one single veteran. But DoD will not spend the few thousands of dollars to replicate Dr. Garry's assay and test. And finally, we see veterans doing *aerobics* to treat their symptoms.

It is here the mainstream press either ignores the issue, or cares so little about military personnel that to watch them die off, one at a time, just really does not matter that much. The press was contacted often from Metcalf's special assisstant, Norma Smith and myself. The story was sqwashed even at *Soldier of Fortune* magazine. (Mr. Bush Jr. was then running for President.)

CHAPTER THIRTEEN

Conspiracy Theories and
The Obedient Major Media

*It is a truism among political scientists
that while it is not possible for the media
to tell the population what to think,
they do tell the public what to think about.*

—BEN H. BAGDIKIAN

*The devastation that we have lately seen in the world
was due to an attempt at establishing ruthlessly
a particular national and social order;
it was not an inhuman revulsion against artifice
but an inhuman insistence upon artifice
and upon political unison.*

—GEORGE SANTAYANA

*Every day, all across the land, behind tightly
locked doors, millions of Americans are
watching other Americans stalking,
harassing, raping, and killing each
other on TV....It makes us more likely to buy locks,
watchdogs, and guns for protection;
...want more money spent on crime, drug abuse,
and national defense; and most ominously,
consent to our own and other's repression
in the name of security.*

—SONIA SHAH

THE OBEDIENT MAJOR MEDIA

WE ALL SHOULD BE INCREASINGLY CONCERNED over how so many authors, researchers, analysts and even television talk show hosts (Bill Mahr, *Politically Incorrect*), who have taken a position contrary to that of Mr. Bush Junior's views or those of Britain's Mr. Blair, on the imperial war-making in Afghanistan, are harangued for stating it. Those who bring to light the likelihood that there are other political and economic objectives which readily explain the raw aggression on Mr. Bush's part to remove the ruling Taliban (again, who had nothing to do with September 11, 2001) from power in Afghanistan, are being ridiculed and often, like Mahr, threatened with losing their jobs. Anyone bringing to light the obvious objectives, the vast oil and gas reserves and the needed pipelines, very specific, or maybe selected, reporters and editors nation-wide, sometimes world-wide, lunge upon the speaker with an concerted diatribe which truly astonishes one not used to being called names. The names one gets called? Conspiracy Theorist.

One of the very first articles appeared in the online magazine *Slate* (owned by Microsoft) written by Anne Applebaum; it was simply dismissive of anyone who raised the oil issue. She simply stated it was absurd to raise it as, "America had not even paid any attention to Afghanistan prior to September 11, 2001." Clearly she was dead wrong and most thinking people now know this. But that is not the point as I am sure she knows this too by now. It was her response when I e-mailed her just a note saying simply there are always more than one political objective in every crisis, including wars. Her response was, surprising to say the least. Her one line e-mail in response fairly leapt from the screen, "And I suppose you think Bush planned the air attacks on the WTC!" Well, no, I thought, but that was certainly an odd response.

Now *Conspiracy Theorist* is not just any old name to be called. Ask Oliver Stone what the intent really is. As an aside, I personally told Oliver Stone, when he asked me how long would the attacks go on (him being called a conspiracy theorist in the media) over his great film (a movie, it was a movie) JFK?..."Forever." was my response, "and long after you are dead." This epithet, and that is what it has evolved into, is used to silence, discredit, evoke fear in the reader (that they are being misled at the least by the ignorant, or worse, conned by the slippery smarmy wily anti-Semite), and finally, it is meant to forever silence this particular individual. It is used to end any dissent against the new regime of corporate empire, American-led. Interestingly, here in America this epithet is most often slung about by the so-called progressive-left and left-leaning mainstream media. (These were the specific ones attacking Oliver Stone as well.) It was Oliver Stone during an interview with Robert Downey Jr. for his documentary *The Last Party*, who stated there were only some 23 major corporations that dominated the main stream media.

Oliver Stone saw what was developing in his own industry where companies like Disney wanted to control ever greater outlets of all sources of media.

> Modern technology and American economics have quietly created a new kind of central authority over information—the national and multinational corporation. By the 1980s, the majority of all major American media—newspapers, magazines, radio, television, books, and movies—were controlled by fifty giant corporations. These corporations were interlocked in common financial interest with other massive industries and with a few dominant international banks. (Ben H. Bagdikian, *The Media Monopoly*, Introduction, pg. xiv, Beacon Press)

Oliver, at the time of JFK's massive success was caught completely offguard by the outpouring of organized hate, ridicule and the words "conspiracy theory" were attached to all of it. One analyst has identified this as *ritual defamation*. (Laird Wilcox, *The Watchdogs: A Look at Anti-Racist Watchdog Groups*) As stated, it was in concert with the mainstream media that the progressive-Left media joined in, sealing the fate of Oliver Stone and anyone that admitted to knowing him or arguing in his behalf, as I did at the time; I was simply added (one paragraph, completely out of context in an article in the *Nation*, where Alexander Cockburn called me, along with the standard fare, a para-Bircher?) Neither Oliver, nor I, was ever called by phone by anyone in any of the media outlets, mainstream or left-wing, during these few years it went on.

Only the very strong-willed can survive this withering verbal denunciation.

This needs some explaining. First, it is not just the suggestion on your part, that someone, anyone, might be involved in some level of misdeed, a group acting in concert, some few seeking to fulfill their own personal ambitions through what the elite like to call "enlightened self-interest." You see, that would entail naming names if one had such data, and naming names in America is just not done in polite company. The American progressive-left, which ceased being progressive about the time Sidney Hook departed this life, has always been terrified of naming names. One could attack big oil, big corporations and even big banking, as long as nobody was ever named by name. Attacking capitalism is one thing but attacking, or pointing an accusing finger at a capitalist himself, in name, is utterly taboo.

This can be explained by the notorious cowardice on the part of most active American leftists; but that is not a sufficient explanation. Attacking capitalism by attacking "all business operations" as evil free enterprise clearly benefits, the distinct from free enterprise, monopoly capitalists, that fund, finance and often call the shots of many progressive-left non-governmental organizations. Thus, during a critique, one *cannot* actually name Mobil Oil's principle directors, CEOs or major shareholders. These are the very men that decide to fund, say, Ralph Nader's *Public Citizen* and the *Institute for Policy*

Studies (IPS). But attacking Mobil Oil, or the Ford Foundation, as an institution (this is wisely called a Chomskyan "Institutional Analysis") is okay as one is attacking then, all free enterprise, the devout enemy of every social democrat and democratic socialist. Never defining the monopolist or monopoly capitalist as apart from the free enterprising spectrum is the key to this part of the progressive puzzle. *Corporatism* as ideology could not survive without the aid from this silence and dissembling from the progressive-left here in America. The rest of the "Left," globally, I have left out of these statements as they do not act in this manner, it is peculiar to the United States.

In many ways and through benefiting financially, the American progressive socialist (in name only) left is the same as "monopoly" capitalism. It should surprise few in America that the left has won many aspects of its personal political agenda within the confines of the present corporate government; a seat at the table they call it; Republican and Democrat administrations notwithstanding. The enemy of both the present corporate-state government and the progressive-left would be *free enterprise capitalism.* The smaller large private companies are struggling not to be taken over (in the media it is over) by yet another forced merger and acquisition strategy of one of the monopoly giants. So when the Left cries "no blood for oil," they cannot say no blood for Dick Cheney's oil, Richard Armitage's oil, Bush Senior's oil, or James A. Baker III' s oil, or Paul Wolfowitz's, or Condoleeza Rice's, and on and on *ad nauseum.*

Although clearly people stand to gain from the sale of oil and the building of pipelines; institutions do not stand to gain, as institutions are paper things, *people* spend money, things are the vehicles for *people* to gain from. And people collude to gain more than their share even if they do not conspire; conspire would be illegal and done in secret, and nobody here, least of all this writer, is charging any illegal activity other than within our conflict of interest laws. Nothing was done in secret as the archives and this book has demonstrated; all was and remains wide open to those who ever cared to know. And clearly most journalists just do not care to know what the American and British government and corporate monopolists have been doing these past ten years since the Persian Gulf maneuvers.

But there is more to it than even that. That only explains the progressive-left's less than enthusiastic support for an all-out verbal assault on the operators operating in the Caspian region presently. This does not fully explain why the mainstream media, the New York Times and the T.V. networks, also join the attack using the epithet "conspiracy theorist" against all who suggest there is something more going on than "get bin Laden." The mainstream media are monopoly corporations no different than Mobil Oil. The owners and directors are the same men, as often as not, sitting on the same several boards today, tomorrow holding office in the U.S. Cabinet. This will surely dampen criticism.

Regarding the monopoly corporate power of the 50 American media giants Professor Ben H. Bagdikian notes the problem well.

The problem is not one of universal evil among the corporations or their leaders. There is, in the output of the dominant
fifty, a rich mixture of news and ideas. But there is also limits,
that do not exist in most other democratic countries with private enterprise media. The limits are felt on open discussion of
the system that supports giantism in corporate life and of other
values that have been enshrined under the inaccurate label "free
enterprise." (Introduction, pg. xiviii)

An important point made here is giantism (although it is quite rare for
any American academic to argue that these giant corporations bear no resemblance to "free enterprise," I thank Mr. Bagdikian for his rare candor) and
may be the clue why the mainstream American media is reluctant to report on
what other heads of giant companies are doing as it is, as well, as Bagdikian
points out, these giants that advertise with the media giants especially where
one giant owns the media outlet. That is to say, the rise of mass advertising
by giant monopolies, whose advertising cost can only be afforded by other
giant corporations. *The Media Monopoly,* Beacon Press, 1997, is a fine read on
the subject.

Mass advertising has ordained that each city in the United
States that has a daily paper will have only one and that most
cities will have none....In the last two generations, during the
rise of mass advertising, the merchants have wiped out much of
their former competition, the small enterprises like corner gro-
cery stores and locally owned department stores. (Ibid., pg. 120)

We call this the *Walmart* syndrome, but Disney, Safeway, MSNBC, or Microsoft would due as well in each area they dominate and often the one, say,
Disney, also dominates in another market, ABC. Bagdikian is no conspiracy
theorist, it is what it is, the reversal of all past Federal Trade Commission
(FTC) and Justice Department's enforcement of its Anti-Trust Division's mandate to protect free competition; today their revised mandate, evolving since
1975, is only to protect the consumers receiving a quality product produced
by often only one giant monopoly corporation. These monopolies grow today
by mergers and acquisitions rather than producing new wealth by its own
expansion. Free enterprise is quite dead in America. Corporatism now rules
the government and the marketplace, so-called. And the power of the media
helps to protect it from dissent.

The power of the media to preserve the status quo is especially
effective because formal censorship is rare, because the media
often exposes corporate and government abuses, and because
the press so frequently proclaims itself as free. Hidden in each
of these dimensions is a set of political, cultural, and economic factors that guide our free press away from the kind of informed debate that is symbolized by our national commitment

to freedom of the press. (*Dissent, Injustice, and the Meanings of America*, Steven H Shiffrin, Princeton, 1999, pg.109)

If you want to ever, in your lifetime, become a reporter at one of the major papers (ambition abounds in the newsroom), one must follow the lead of the major league paper's editorial elite. If you ever expect to have a column of your own you had better not name names; certainly not names which today hold high office, tomorrow are back on the boards of directors of the inter-locking corporate network and whose private power is no less than their public power. What can a reporter really do in the American press?

> There is another paradox in American journalism, a seeming contradiction between heightened standards of news and a worsening deficiency. The country's newspapers and broadcast stations are rapidly, if unwittingly, abandoning a vital need of their audience. They are literally redrawing the map of American news. (Bagdikian, ibid., pg. 218)

It is the democratic process that Bagdikian sees as the big loser, and he is right. I owned a weekly newspaper for several years. I have worked for one congressman and have worked on several campaigns as well from all three parties (Libertarian the third). The public needs to be well-informed in America because our system is fundamentally different than a parliamentary style system. Only the American media can provide such vast and disparate news directly to the public. But it selects and filters the news based on what a few major papers and network television anchors say and write. As Bagdikian notes well, "Combining journalism with advertising and marketing ultimately will destroy the integrity of the news," (pg. 233). American voters need to know who said what, where and why more than most. There is little effort to do this any longer; since O.J. there is nothing sensational they will not do, all the while ignoring what is real and really important. The most important news of all, the monopoly media story?

> But for logic and common sense to emerge from the democratic process, the public requires adequate information. Other themes of this book suggests that when it comes to the issue of the media's corporate power, the media have never permitted news and commentary to make their corporate power a subject of common knowledge, let alone of public debate. (Ibid., pg. 225)

If the story is not endorsed by the New York Times, or at least several of the other, supposedly, newspapers of record, then it doesn't make the wire service at all. Many major papers have their own wire service that less magnificent papers must subscribe to. So if, for instance, the New York Times does not cover this story or that, the Seattle Times and Seattle Post Intelligencer does not, therefore, cover that story either. The marketplace of ideas is systematically being diminished. This is what Shiffrin notes about the marketplace idea:

The marketplace analogy was an elegant turn employed in a good cause, but there is no excuse for elevating it into a guiding framework. Free speech is an important principle, but there is no reason to assume that what emerges in the 'market' is the best test of truth. Societal pressures to conform are strong, and incentives to keep quiet about corruptions of power are often great. What emerges in the market might better be viewed as a testimonial to power than as a reflection of truth. (Ibid., pg. 6)

Should a story like the one below show up somewhere, or if someone like this writer e-mails the story to some paper or media outlet, they will not touch it. Even though some one isolated reporter may froth at the mouth in earnest to do so. Take for instance this story that appeared on CNA , the *Caspian News Agency*'s news service.

Kazakh President started official visit to US

Astana, December 19, 2001. (CNA). The Kazakh President Nursultan Nazarbayev started his official visit to the US. Kazakh Foreign Ministry's press service informed CNA that in Washington D.C. the Kazakh leader would meet with the US President George Bush, vice-president Richard Cheney, Defense Minister Donald Rumsfeld and CIA Director George Tenet. During meetings the sides intend discussing issues of bilateral cooperation and Kazakh participation in the international antiterrorist coalition. Signing series of documents, including the memorandum on energy partnership between Kazakhstan and the US, which can be the ground for long-lasting strategic partnership. Within the visit Nazarbayev will visit New York and Houston and hold meetings with the UN General Secretary Kofi Annan, US ex-president George Bush-senior and the former US State Secretary James Baker. The Kazakh President will also visit the place of the tragedy of September 11 and make a signature on the memorial wall devoted to the victims of terrorist attacks. The visit will be completed on December 22. -OK- ("CNA/ www.caspian.ru")

Now that was news, don't you think? The president of the largest nation-state in the Caspian region, a nation land-locked but oil rich; a nation which needs the pipelines proposed since 1996 in American legislation and by private interests, more than any other Commonwealth of Independent States (CIS) nations; a nation that just cut a deal with the Russians (December 2001; see chapter nine above) to run pipelines north into Russia and west into Turkey, comes to the United States the very week of Christmas 2001 to work out a deal on an *energy partnership* with Mr. Bush Junior. Meeting not only with Dick Cheney (former Caspian region oil lobbyist and CEO for Halliburton Oil and Brown & Root [pipeline builders of the world] who was "intensely" active in the region from 1996-2000) but with George Bush Senior (Former Zapata Oil CEO, and consultant to the Carlyle Group) and James A. Baker III (legal counsel for both the Carlyle Group and Azerbaijan International Operating Company, AIOC). AIOC is the single largest oil consortium in the entire region. Carlyle is one of the world's largest builders and defense contractors. Meeting with private citizens outside of the government?

And I would be remiss in repeating that James A Baker III, Dick Cheney, Richard Armitage (Armitage Associates Ltd. has consulted and lobbied in behalf of AIOC since 1992) and Paul Wolfowitz (leading academic promoting the region in Washington since 1992). These along with Dr. Henry Kissinger, Zbignew Brezenski and Condoleeza Rice among others all having been lobbyists in the region prior to taking public office directly with, or now consulting, the present administration.

On December 31, 2001, the United States named as special envoy to the interim government of Afghanistan a former aide to the American oil company Unocal, Afghan-born Zalmay Khalilzad. This tells you how important the pipeline has always been in the administration's plans and political objectives. Mr. Khalilzad was the man who outlined the Unocal proposal to the ruling Taliban during 1996-1997 and was instrumental in presenting the 2001 negotiations. Nobody knew of Mr. Khalilzad's activities because he was appointed not to the State Department or Commerce Departments where he would undergo Senate approval but under Condoleeza Rice with National Security where no Senate approval is carried out.

On May 23rd, 2001 the White House announced the appointment of Zalmay Khalilzad to a position on the National Security Council as special assistant to the president and senior director for Gulf, Southwest Asia and Other Regional Issues. Khalilzad was, as well, a former official in the Reagan and the Bush-Sr. administrations. After leaving the government, he then went to work for Unocal.

At the risk of further redundancy nearly everyone named above, with the exception of Khalilzad and the two Bush gentlemen proper, were on the Board of Advisors to the USACC — the *United States Azerbaijan Chamber of Commerce*, which as pointed out in chapter eight above had taken the lead in developing the entire Caspian region's oil reserves and the much needed pipelines. But according to the American media that just means these men are well-endowed with enlightened self-interest, correct? True enough.

Adding to everything already outlined above, these same men by name, plus too many others equally recognizable, (like William Bennett) set up the non-profit public information institute, *Project for A New American Century*, (PANC), which did very little since its founding other than lobby for the oil rich Caspian region and particularly regarding the removal of the Taliban from power in Afghanistan so as to place into power a "regime more acceptable to the international community and the oil companies" scrambling over the region. And yes, I mean each and every single one of these men and women named above, each working for, lobbying in behalf of, on the board of directors of, in the pay of, the very same oil concerns and/or non-profit lobbying firms and organizations whose purpose was to claim the region; each, by name throughout 1992- 1996 through 2000 on the board of Advisors of the USACC and PANC as well. Only the time element precludes finding numerous other fronts with these same men's names using various vehicles to achieve objectives both personal and public. What defines conflict of interest in the law is a question needing an answer now more than ever.

According to the American mainstream media elite this is all presumably just not relevant to the present events taking place in the Caspian region. The meetings taken here in the US with the presidents of the CIS nations in the region to discuss *energy partnerships* with their respective nations too is irrelevant. That Secretary of Defense Donald Rumsfeld left Armenia and Azerbaijan the week of December 16th, 2001 announcing the removal of Section 907 of the Freedom Support Act, is therefore, presumably a coincidence or perceived as a lucky consequence of the war effort rather than part of the original political objectives. (It was slated to be voted on Dec.24th, 2001). A press service announcement below appeared on January 15, 2002:

CNA Brief Newsline

15:00 15.01.2002/ Azerbaijan/US/relations/Ambassador

Official Washington intends making 2002 "shock" in developing relations with Azerbaijan:

Baku, January 15, 2002. (CNA). The US President George Bush and State Secretary Collin Powell intend making 2002 "most effective" in developing relations between the US and Azerbaijan. At the meeting with the Azeri President Heidar Aliyev the US Ambassador in Baku Ross Wilson said the higher Washington administration assured him of this fact during the diplomat's vacation in December-January. Wilson mentioned this is closely bound up with perspectives of settling the Karabakh conflict and abolishing Section 907 to the Freedom Support Act. "President Bush is optimistically disposed and considers till end of this year the Karabakh problem should be solved," the Ambassador said. He also noted in the nearest 10 days the group of the US diplomats will arrive in Baku to hold the conference with Azeri officials on cooperation in the economy sphere. Besides, the US military experts are to visit Azerbaijan and to hold talks on military cooperation.

These same men hold the region in the palm of their hands, now that they are back in power. All having served in the former Reagan, Clinton or Bush-Sr. regimes.

If one is going to be charged with being a conspiracy theorist, why not name the names, all the names of those who gain? Why not make the theory a fact-based hypothesis? Conflict of interest laws are nothing to sneeze at. One is (supposedly, if the law was enforced) not to gain financially while serving the government in areas of interest where one had been serving in the private sector. In my opinion, why not accept the charge of "Collusion Theorist" and empirical-fact purveyor? Empirical evidence must be refuted by empirical evidence. "Aristotle said 'To say of what is that it is, or of what is not that is not, is true.' This is perhaps the first expression of the *correspondence theory* of truth: True propositions tell it like it is, or in other words, for a proposition to be true is for it to correspond with the facts. It is important to realize that this is a platitude that nobody denies." (Simon Blackburn and Keith Simmons, *Truth, Oxford Readings in Philosophy*, OUP, 1999, Pg.1)

Name-calling is just that Mr. Blair, a smear no different than the New Left's heckler's veto from the sixties which is now back on campuses, only now led by the radical right supporters of Bush's *jolly little war*.

*　　*　　*

Conspiracy Theories ?

In a recent article in the British press, Mr. Tony Blair joined the chorus of denouncers of his Anglo-American elite circle of friends. The article was titled **Blair shames war weasels**. It read in part as follows:

> ANGRY Tony Blair named and shamed Left-wing newspapers yesterday for wobbling over the war on terror. The Prime Minister published a dossier to mark 100 days passing since September 11. It listed the Allies' military, diplomatic and humanitarian successes so far and hailed "acts of unity, tolerance, bravery and responsibility" in the face of the terrorism threat. But in a clear swipe at wobblers and doubters, the Premier also detailed "10 media views which have proved to be wrong". They included:

> **JOHN** Pilger in The Mirror on October 29, who claimed "the war against terrorism is a fraud".

> **ROBERT** Fisk in The Independent on November 11, who suggested Osama bin Laden "hasn't put a foot wrong" and that "things are unfolding pretty much as he wanted".

> **GEORGE** Monbiot in The Guardian on September 18: "The closer you look, the weaker the case against bin Laden becomes." **SUSAN** Sontag in US magazine The New Yorker on September 24: "If the word 'cowardly' is to be used, it might be more aptly applied to those who kill from beyond the range of retaliation, high in the sky, than to those willing to die themselves in order to kill others." (www.thesun.com.uk)

The dossier — entitled 100 Days, 100 Ways, 100 days of fighting international terrorism- once again purportedly gave further evidence of bin Laden's guilt. And I must state once again, redundancy is a plague on my house, even should bin Laden come forward and claim credit (which he has not done, period), that has absolutely nothing to do with removing the ruling Taliban from power which the new Bush Administration had recognized as the legitimate power in Afghanistan during negotiations which ran from February 2001 until five weeks before September 11, 2001. The Taliban was the recognized governing body as is evidenced by those very negotiations. It also has nothing to do with removing Saddam Hussein of Iraq from power. Likewise Somalia, Sudan, Syria, Cuba....

Blair's dossier went on by highlighting that since the toppling of the Taliban, women can work and study while music, games and TV are no longer banned. And of what importance is this Mr. Blair? Does this include, besides the lucky few who may now tap their toes to a bit of punk or be glued to the tube like the brain-dead youth in America, does this include the thousands of women who died under the worst bombardment in history of one of the poorest countries on earth by the richest?

The article continued by stating "Mr. Blair's anger at certain media coverage of the Allied campaign was demonstrated by the decision for European Minister Peter Hain to launch the report at a conference inside Downing Street. The dossier took a second swing at Robert Fisk for another article in **The Independent**. It also rapped Madeleine Bunting in **The Guardian**, who said the conflict would become like Vietnam, and Natasha Walter in **The Independent**, who said Afghan women's interests would be ignored. Also criticized were Arundhati Roy in **The Guardian**, a **Daily Mail** editorial and Seamus Milne in **The Guardian**." (Ibid., The Sun)

Mr. Hain slammed "excitable speculation at almost every point" of the war, saying: "Everything has been done in a careful, systematic way." Peter Hain warned that new terror bases would spring up in Afghanistan and "disintegration, conflict and instability" would ensue if the West turned its back on the country. And that is not the point either Mr. Hain. The critics are critics because it is both their right and *duty* to criticize; and specific to the United States, it is the *duty of every citizen* to critique their government, not only in peace time, but most important of all, dissent in time of war. If the free speech and free press doctrine of these past short centuries means anything it is that.

Mr. Blair was not the only one to make the case that dissent was just intolerable any longer. In *The National Interest*, which is normally an excellent quarterly, we find this extraordinary expose regarding those of us that are reluctant to "get into line," or "watch what we say from now on," as White House Spokesman Ari Fliescher stated regarding his personal attempt to silence *Politically Incorrect's* Bill Mahr. Here is one newspaper man's recent comments:

> The whole world is obsessed with America's panache, economic might, and popular culture, and it takes note of its military power and high culture. Envy being the energetic force that it is,

much of the world outside the United States, abetted by the carriers of the great liberal death wish within, want America to behave, in Richard Nixon's phrase, like "a pitiful helpless giant." If it does, the influence of lesser states and peoples is magnified, and guilt and shame of the minority of Americans who are in fact anti-American is appeased. These forces, for the good of all civilized people, must not be appeased. They must be severely disabused. (The National Interest, *What Victory Means*, Conrad Black, Number 66, Winter 2001/02, pg. 157)

Clearly I would be included as one of those "Americans who are in fact anti-American," needing to be "severely disabused," so that "for the good of all civilized people" I would not "be appeased" in my "great liberal death wish" from "within" this "high culture," and presumably should be overwhelmed by my "guilt and shame," for not being equally "obsessed with America's panache." Where did this guy come from?

From *Hollinger International, Inc.* as its Chairman of the Board and serves as chairman of the editorial board of *The National Interest*. Its holdings in the media include The *Chicago Sun-Times* (and some 104 papers in just Illinois, with others in California, Washington and Indiana), *The Jerusalem Post* (and fifteen others in Israel), *The Spectator* (and some fifty others in London alone, Great Britain), and Canada (thirteen papers). It is nice to know freedom of speech and freedom of the press is doing so well in these states and countries.

The Demise of Dissent

This gives one pause; too many Americans provide us with such examples of arrogance and pompous boasting, it is no wonder the world, in reality, holds Americans in such low regard. Being obsessed with the US "Popular culture" means only that our cancer is spreading, much to the demise of anyone familiar with the Hollywood crowd's nihilism and utter decay. But obsessed may be the correct term after all, just not to be assumed in a positive reflection.

The First Amendment has a special regard for those who swim against the current, for those who would shake us to our foundations, for those who reject prevailing authority. (Steven H. Shiffren, *Dissent, Injustice, and the Meanings of America*, Princeton, 1999, pg.10)

Shiffren makes the argument well in his great book; it is dissent which is one of the "meanings of America." Without dissent, club opinion rules. Without dissent any president may become an Imperial leader. Without dissent there is no free press, no free speech. If there is any meaning to what it is to be an American it is the right, and duty to dissent, always, all the time.

Well-informed dissent would be ideal, that is what I try to practice; but it is not a requirement, one need not be correct to dissent, as one still retains the right and duty. As Shiffren points out elsewhere "...if the political speech and model protects anything, it is attacks on the political establishment...." and if the government can silence "those who attack societal customs and traditions..." it must not stand "just because society hold its beliefs and symbols dear." (Ibid., pg.11) In other words, dissent should be, ought to be, "encouraged"! Shiffren makes a powerful and undeniable argument.

> The dissent model assumes that in large-scale societies powerful interest groups and self-seeking politicians and bureaucrats are unavoidable. Injustice will always be present (although its severity can vary). Dissenters and the dialogue that follows will always be necessary. On this premise, dissent has important instrumental value. So, of course, does democratic dialogue. Indeed, the dissent model would hope that dialogue would ultimately be spurred by the presence of dissent. In this respect the dialogue model and the dissent model run together. (Ibid., pg. 17)

Shiffren understands that this model barely exists and making the argument for free speech is not sufficient: "Necessary as the stock argument may be, the existence of the First Amendment as a cultural symbol masks the extent to which dissent is discouraged and subordinated." (Ibid., pg 26)

But specifics are in order regarding how little the mainstream media is allowing dissent from the Bush/Blair-led ridicule campaign under way. Here I should like to continue with just how far the criticism of any dissent has gone in just the United States. In another article in *Slate* the critique of any dissent took on a rather deliberate tone. The article was titled **Pipe Dreams,** The origin of the 'bombing-Afghanistan-for-oil-pipelines' theory, By Seth Stevenson—(Slate Online magazine, Posted Thursday, December 6, 2001). It began with this:

> A theory making the rounds on the Internet, on the airwaves, and in the press claims that the bombing of the Taliban has nothing to do with a 'war on terrorism' but everything to do with the oil pipeline the West wants to build through Afghanistan. Where did this theory start, and how did it spread?

The California energy company Unocal seriously pursued building an Afghanistan pipeline in the 1990s, but back then the theorists, such as this <http://www.brown.edu/Departments/Anthropology/publications/AFGHANConflict.htm> Middle East specialist in 1998, argued that the West was *propping up* the Taliban in hopes that they would cooperate on building a pipeline. On March 8, 2001, a think-tanker and former CIA analyst noted in a *New York Times* op-ed that "[i]n 1996, it seemed possible that American-built gas and oil pipelines from Central Asia could run through an Afghanistan ruled by one leader. Cruelty to women aside, we did not condemn the Taliban juggernaut rolling across the country."

Now let me explain something. As Mr. Stevenson named each piece, he included the website address to click on so the reader could see for himself the truth of what he was charging these authors with, that being "conspiracy theorists." He wrote "The beauty of conspiracy theories is that even the most contradictory evidence can be folded into a new conspiracy theory. For example, after the events of Sept. 11, the pipeline conspiracy theorists spun 180 degrees from ... *We're supporting the Taliban so we can build a pipeline while we pretend we don't care about their links to terrorism (and, to a lesser degree, their cruelty to women).* To ... *We're bombing the Taliban so we can build a pipeline while we pretend we care about their links to terrorism (and, to a lesser degree, their cruelty to women).*" He then goes about naming all the conspiracy culprits:

> The turnaround can be tracked within a single news agency. On Oct. 7 of this year, right before the U.S. bombing began, Agence France-Presse wrote up the old theory <http://sg.news.yahoo.com/011007/1/1jz0k.html>: "Keen to see Afghanistan under strong central rule to allow a US-led group to build a multi-billion-dollar oil and gas pipeline, Washington urged key allies Pakistan and Saudi Arabia to back the militia's bid for power in 1996." Just four days later, AFP wrote <http://sg.news.yahoo.com/011011/1/1k8no.html> that "experts say the end of the Islamic militia [the Taliban] could spell the start of more lucrative opportunities for Western oil companies." Nearly all sites pushing the newer theory point to two pieces of evidence:

> 1) This <http://www.eia.doe.gov/cabs/afghan.html> U.S. Department of Energy information page on Afghanistan, updated September 2001, which espouses the pipeline idea but says Afghanistan is too chaotic for it to work. 2) This <http://www.house.gov/international_relations/105th/ap/wsap212982.htm> 1998 testimony by a Unocal vice president to the House Committee on International Relations, in which he states that a pipeline will never be built without a stable Afghan government in place.

Stevenson goes on to query, "How did the new theory spread? After the Sept. 11 attacks, no one says anything oil-related for a respectable mourning period. Then, in the cover story of its Sept. 21-27 issue, *L.A. Weekly* makes the case that 'it's the oil, stupid.' The piece doesn't mention the pipeline specifically, but soon after, someone else does. On Sept. 25, the *Village Voice's* James Ridgeway and Camila E. Fard write <http://www.villagevoice.com/issues/0138/ridgeway.php> that the 9/11 terrorist attack 'provides Washington with an extraordinary opportunity' to overthrow the Taliban and build a pipeline. Ridgeway fails to make the direct link to Unocal, though. On Oct.

1, we see the whole theory come together <http://www.indy media.org front. php3?article id=69078&group= webcast> on the Web site of the Independent Media Center." This article links to both the Unocal testimony and the DOE page and says they 'leave little doubt as to the reasons behind Washington's desire to replace the Taliban government.'" After this, so Stevenson argues, "the floodgates open. The theory never evolves much—it just gets passed around." Stevenson then uses the vehicle of chronological order to further make his allegations. I must quote this at length as the web addresses are fundamental to my argument.

> *Oct. 5:* An India-based writer for the Inter Press Service says Bush's "coalition against terrorism" is "the first opportunity that has any chance of making UNOCAL's wish come true." The story is reprinted the following day <http://www.atimes.com/global-econ/CJ06Dj01.html> in the *Asia Times*.

> *Oct. 10:* The *Village Voice*'s Ridgeway makes his claim in stronger terms <http://www.villagevoice.com/issues/0141/ridgeway2.php> but still doesn't mention Unocal.

> *Oct. 11:* A Russian TV commentator says oil is the real reason for the war. In a transcript from Russia's Ren TV <http://www.cdi.org/russia/175-7.cfm>, the commentator refers to Unocal.

> *Oct. 12:* An essay on TomPaine.com <http://www.tompaine.com/news/2001/10/11/index.html> and another by cartoonist Ted Rall <http://www.uexpress.com/tedrallviewru.cfm?uc fn=1&uc full date=20011012&uc daction=X&u c comic=ru> both join the chorus.

> *Oct. 13:* The Hindu, an Indian national newspaper <http://www.hinduonnet.com/thehindu/2001/10/13/stories/05132524.htm>, asserts that the pipeline, not terrorism, is driving the U.S. bombing. The *Hindu* quotes the DOE page and adds the point that both President Bush and Vice President Cheney are "intimately connected with the U.S. oil industry."

> *Oct. 14:* The *Washington Times* reports that a Taliban ambassador says the war is more oil than Osama. Also, the International Action Center (an anti-militarism site) runs the Unocal theory <http://www.iacenter.org/nowar_oil.htm>.

> *Oct. 15:* An essay at the libertarian site LewRockwell.com makes the Unocal case <http://www.lewrockwell.com/orig/sardi7.html>. The following day it's reprinted by Russia's Pravda <http://english.pravda.ru/world/2001/10/16/18147.html> and posted in a Yahoo! newsgroup <http://groups.yahoo.com/group/decani/message/61065>.

Oct. 19: Green Party USA gets in on the fun <http://www.
greenparty.org/afghanbomb.html>.

Oct. 23: Britain's *Guardian* quotes the Unocal testimony and
says that while the United States is in part fighting terrorism, it
"would be naive to believe that this is all it is doing." Pakistan's
Dawn reprints the essay <http://www.dawn.com/2001/10/25/
int15.htm> two days later.

Oct. 24: The *Guardian* strikes again <http://www.guardian.
co.uk/waronterror/story/0,1361,579401,00.html>, writing that
any pipeline would require the creation of a stable government
and that "[t]his, it can be argued, is precisely what Washington
is now trying to do."

Oct. 25: Britain's Channel 4 says the pipeline is "an important
subtext <http://www.channel4.com/news/home20011025/
Story04.htm>" to the war.

Oct. 29: The cover story of the Britain's *Daily Mirror* screams,
"This War Is a Fraud <http://mirror.icnetwork.co.uk/news/
allnews/page.cfm?objectid=11392430&method=full>." Mean-
while, the BBC says the pipeline theory is in the air and recaps
its basic points, but then dismantles it <http://news.bbc.co.uk/
hi/english/world/south_asia/newsid_1626000/1626889.stm>.

The pipeline theory has continued to bounce around, showing up on every "progressive" Web site out there. It ran in the Syrian daily *Tishrin* on Nov.
29, from which it was picked up on Dec. 2 <http:/www. frontierpost.com.pk/
afghan.asp?id=3&date1=12/2/2001> by Pakistan's *Frontier Post*. It may never
die.

Stevenson then begins to ask the question only such a wise and thoughtful man would, then giving us his thoughtful answer: "Why does the bomb-
ing-for-pipelines theory hold such appeal? For the same reason the support-
ing-the-Taliban-for-pipelines theory attracted so many: There's evidence that
points in that direction. Unocal *did* want to build a pipeline through Afghanistan and *did* cozy up to the Taliban. Bush and Cheney *do* have ties to big oil.
But theories like these are ridiculously reductionist. Their authors don't try to
argue conclusions from evidence—they decide on conclusions first, then hunt
for justification."

There is only one reductionist here and it is Stevenson. He closes with
what can only be a sentence set out to ingratiate himself to the monopoly
corporate structure (he works for Microsoft) and the White House: "What's
absurd about the pipeline theory is how thoroughly it discounts the obvious reason the United States set the bombers loose on Afghanistan: Terrorists headquartered in Afghanistan attacked America's financial and military
centers, killing 4,000 people, and then took credit for it. Nope—must be the

pipeline." A clever closing but he fails to make the argument, in my humble, researched, thirty-years experience as an analyst, and former newspaper publisher, and reputed terrorism expert, opinion. First nobody, least of all Osama bin Laden has taken credit for anything at all and any such interpretation of edited tapes from the White House say nothing of the sort. But as one goes to each website listed in the above article, and I suggest the intrepid reader do so, one discovers Stevenson makes the argument "for" the pipeline theory, not against it; he simply hopes the lazier reader will simply take for granted that all these citations prove *his* theory and not refute it. But that is something the reader must pursue on his own.

To suggest that in the monopoly corporate structure, of which *Slate* online magazine is part of, one finds these are always and everywhere hierarchical, which cannot really be denied, but those within the structure must try. If for nothing else than to live with their own self-deception. Sheffrin's argument suggests we as a people ought to promote, as a social value, dissent. His argument rests on some "reasonable assumptions" to "combat injustice." "America is not a land of perfect equality. Hierarchies exist throughout the society, in both political and nonpolitical realms. It would be possible to assume hierarchies are perfectly just, but any such assumption would be a fantasy. Similarly improbable would be the suggestion that all hierarchy is inherently or mainly unjust. But often hierarchies are often generally or partially unjust for many reasons." It is a fair representation of power relationships and what, I would argue today, is what is taking place in the political and economic realms in America. Using Sheffrin to make the case, "People who exercise substantial power in hierarchies are prone to act in their own self-interest and are in a position to be effective. Even if they do not see themselves as acting in their own self-interest, they will often tend to see things in a biased way that operates to their advantage." (Ibid., pg.91)

I would only add, as this is as important, to the advantage of their circle of friends, who later, when conditions change, may reward the individual for his services to the brotherhood. Such as when Mr. Dick Cheney was rewarded for his service as Secretary of Defense when he prosecuted the Persian Gulf War during 1990/91 for Mr. Bush Senior, which benefited big oil interests, with being named CEO and President of Halliburton Energy and Brown and Root; later to be rewarded by being named Vice-President of the United States to George Bush Junior; then, again, being rewarded for his lobbying for big oil interests (the afore mentioned Halliburton and Brown and Root) with a golden parachute of $20 million. Now with Dick Cheney prosecuting the war on Afghanistan and the Caspian region with, subsequently Brown and Root pipelines and (among others) Halliburton's oil and gas exploration "moving right along" as they say, we must wait to see what "operates to [his] advantage" once leaving office again...by Cheney simply tending to see things "in a biased way."

"Moreover, power in one hierarchy has a tendency to spill over to other arenas in unjust ways." (Ibid., pp. 91-92) Is there such evidence coming to light? Mention once again, of a recent volume published in France is in order. Coupled with the evidence herein compiled by your present author, I think the redundancy is needed; even if not, I like to do it a lot.

I shall simply continue below with what became serious news on CNN sometime after Mr. Stevenson made his argument in *Slate*. One doubts he has the humility to openly state, in *Slate*, that he may have been quite simply in error; most journalists never can admit error, he will simply sweep it under his desk and go on writing about other things he knows so little about. He must have, maybe, felt a slight twinge of conscience when CNN reported the following in transcript:

AMERICAN MORNING WITH PAULA ZAHN Explosive New Book Published in France Alleges that U.S. Was in Negotiations to Do a Deal with Taliban Aired January 8, 2002 - 07:34 ET

PAULA ZAHN, CNN ANCHOR: Time to check in with ambassador-in- residence, Richard Butler, this morning. An explosive new book published in France alleges that the United States was in negotiations to do a deal with the Taliban for an oil pipeline in Afghanistan. Joining us right now is Richard Butler to shed some light on this new book. He is the former chief U.N. weapons inspector. He is now on the Council on Foreign Relations and our own ambassador-in- residence — good morning.

RICHARD BUTLER, FMR. U.N. WEAPONS INSPECTOR: Good morning, Paula.

ZAHN: Boy, if any of these charges are true...this is really big news.

BUTLER: I agree.

ZAHN: Start off with what your understanding is of what is in this book — the most explosive charge.

BUTLER: The most explosive charge, Paula, is that the Bush administration — the present one, just shortly after assuming office slowed down FBI investigations of al Qaeda and terrorism in Afghanistan in order to do a deal with the Taliban on oil — an oil pipeline across Afghanistan.

ZAHN: And this book points out that the FBI's deputy director, John O'Neill, actually resigned because he felt the U.S. administration was obstructing...the prosecution of terrorism.

BUTLER: Yes, yes, a proper intelligence investigation of terrorism. Now, you said if, and I affirmed that in responding to you. We have to be careful here. These are allegations. They're worth airing and talking about, because of their gravity. We don't know if they are correct. But I believe they should be investigated, because Central Asian oil, as we were discussing yesterday, is potentially so important. And all prior attempts to have a pipeline had to be done through Russia. It had to be negotiated with Russia.

Now, if there is to be a pipeline through Afghanistan, obviating the need to deal with Russia, it would also cost less than half of what a pipeline through Russia would cost. So financially and politically, there's a big prize to be had. A pipeline through Afghanistan down to the Pakistan coast would bring out that Central Asian oil easier and more cheaply.

ZAHN: But let's come back to this whole issue of what John O'Neill, this FBI agent...apparently told the authors of this book. He is alleging that the U.S. government was trying to protect U.S. oil interests? And at the same time, shut off the investigation of terrorism to allow for that to happen?

BUTLER: That's the allegation that instead of prosecuting properly an investigation of terrorism, which has its home in Afghanistan as we now know, or one of its main homes, that was shut down or slowed down in order to pursue oil interests with the Taliban. The people who we have now bombed out of existence, and this not many months ago. The book says that the negotiators said to the Taliban, you have a choice. You have a carpet of gold, meaning an oil deal, or a carpet of bombs. That's what the book alleges.

CNN followed the story with another on the same topic but interviewing the two authors, which are making precisely the same argument I have been making here in the United States since September of 2001. It is this kind of separate evidence derived from independent sources and research other than my original work that acts to corroborate the argument. In a court of law that it what separate evidence from different sources is called, "corroborating evidence."

Two Developments This Morning Raise Questions About What Bush Administration Was Willing to Do in Pursuit of Oil

Aired January 9, 2002 - 07:10

PAULA ZAHN, CNN ANCHOR: Two developments this morning raise some questions about what the Bush administration was willing to do, allegedly, in the pursuit of oil both domestically and internationally. Vice President Richard Cheney's office says administration officials met half a dozen times with the failed energy trading company Enron, including one meeting just days before Enron filed the biggest bankruptcy in U.S. history. And there are some disturbing new claims about America's relationship with the Taliban prior to 9-11.

The authors of a new book claim that the administration conducted secret oil negotiations with the Taliban and they claim those talks may have actually interfered with efforts to get at Osama bin Laden. The book is called "Bin Laden: The Forbidden Truth."

Joining us now from Paris are its authors, Guillaume Dasquie and Jean-Charles Brisard. Thank you both for being with us this morning.

GUILLAUME DASQUIE, CO-AUTHOR: Thank you.

ZAHN: Mr. Brisard, in your book, you claim before September 11 the U.S. administration cared more about its oil interests and the oil in the region than it did about getting Osama bin Laden. Let me put up on the screen a little bit of what is the, in the book along these lines. You say a source of stability in Central Asia that would enable the construction of an oil pipeline across Central Asia.

What evidence do you have that this is the case?

JEAN-CHARLES BRISARD, CO-AUTHOR: You know, there is some very important evidence and the first one maybe is the contract, deal signed in October 1995 between Enoch Carr (ph), an American, a famous American company, and Delta Oil, a Saudi Arabia company, and the Turkmenistan government so at the (UNINTELLIGIBLE) of Afghanistan. And according to this deal, the pipeline across, would cross the Afghanistan to take over Afghanistan some gas and oil which is inside now Central Asia.

So the deal and the negotiation with the Taliban and at the (UNINTELLIGIBLE) in Kabul was very hard and was very important because energy security for U.S. but also for all developed countries.

ZAHN: All right, but Mr. Brisard, or Mr. Dasquie, you go even further than that and you suggest that shortly after President Bush took office, his administration sent Christine Rocca (ph), who was an undersecretary of state for South Asian affairs, to Islamabad to sit down and talk with the Taliban. And you write, "Christine Rocca has met with Taliban officials only once, in August of 2001. She met with a Taliban representative in Islamabad. During that meeting, she once again pushed for the Taliban to turn over Osama bin Laden, as the international community had been demanding for more than two years. She also pressed the Taliban representative on humanitarian issues." Ms. Rocca never had any talks with the Taliban about oil and neither did any of her predecessors. And, in fact, what you write in the book is the exact opposite of that. What did you find?

BRISARD: Yes, that's right. Yes. You know, we find a lot of archives in Pakistan, Islamabad, about the meeting between Christina Rocca, who now works, of course, in the State Department. But before, during the '80s worked in the CIA and in the CIA she managed the relationship between the State Department and the Islamic group in Afghanistan.

So Christina Rocca is very important because she deals in her last meeting with the Taliban in Islamabad and for the Bush administration. And since the Bush administration arrived in last January with the first meeting with some Taliban officials in Washington like Mr. Ashimi (ph) in last March, she always says the same thing.

The thing is very clear. This is, you know, the control of Afghanistan for oil reasons. This is a strategy, a very important strategy aspect. And inside this fight, Osama bin Laden is, this is just a small criminal in terms for diplomatic issues.

So that's the reason why she discussed and there is a lot of evidence in the State Department archives that the reason why she discussed with the Taliban officer not to capture Osama bin Laden, but to deal with Taliban and to deal for oil reasons and energy security reasons.

Further light on secret contacts between the Bush administration and the Taliban regime was shed by this book which was released November 15th in France, and to repeat it's entitled *Bin Laden, The Forbidden Truth*, written by Jean-Charles Brisard and Guillaume Dasquie. Brisard is a former French secret service agent, author of a previous report on bin Laden's al Qaida network, and former director of strategy for the French corporation Vivendi, while Dasquie is an investigative journalist.

The two French authors write that the Bush administration was willing to accept the Taliban regime, despite the charges of sponsoring terrorism, if it cooperated with plans for the development of the oil resources of Central Asia. Former CIA director and ambassador to Pakistan, Richard Helms' niece was the individual called upon.

> After February 5, 2001 and the request from the Taliban for official recognition, it was....Laila Helms who received the assignment of orchestrating in Washington the new Afghan-American relations. Within weeks she made good use of her valuable diplomatic connections in order to arrange meetings between Bush administration officials and emissaries of Mullah Omar....In fact, from the beginning of 1999 until August 2001, there has existed in the United States a concerted and persistent desire to arrive at a solution to the Afghan question....On both sides the financial stakes are well understood. In the name of its energy policy, Washington will support a process of gradual international recognition for the Taliban. (*Bin Laden: The Forbidden Truth*, chapter: *Laila Helms-Profession: Lobbyist for the Taliban*, translation by David Jacobus, January, 29th, 2002)

Until August, 2001, the authors claim, the US government "perceived this regime [Taliban] as a providential movement. From 1994 to 1998, the United States expresses a relative benevolence toward the Taliban..." The Taliban, or "students of religion" as the name implies, were intertwined with oil and gas stakes in the region. "It explains why several States, along with the large oil companies, have targeted this group of 'soldier monks,' perceived as the only group capable of installing a strong government, a source of stability and security." (Ibid., Jacobus) And they were, as has been reported in the foreign press, and deceitfully denied relevance by the Bush administration.

> During the Taliban era, opium planting was forbidden, ... The rise of the Taliban was in some way a blessing in disguise for the Vienna-based U.N. body that has been fighting for a drug free world. In the last five years, opium production and drug traffic have been greatly reduced....But the fall of the Taliban has given opium farmers opportunities to replant the 'heavenly drug.'(By Seno Joko Suyono, *Tempo*, Jakarta, Indonesia, December 2, 2001)

Farmers who had been planting wheat for years rather than opium, under direct religious edict of the Taliban, have now begun to replant opium for cash, just as the violent Northern Alliance had been doing all along (not the Taliban) so as to provide funds to try to overthrow the Taliban regime; with American Special Forces and the CIA illegally aiding them well before

September 11, 2001. Mr. Bush and Mr. Blair have made the region safe for oil, not democracy, opium growers not wheat farmers, robbery and murder not peace and women's rights.

Today, January 31st, the region has returned to violent warlordism, crime and murder, robberies and the bags of donated wheat stolen and traded on the black market. "Their acts are so ferocious that they became intolerable. 'There were no robbers during the Taliban era,' starving Jalalabad inhabitant Abdullah Omari said." (Ibid., as reported in *World Press Review*, February, 2002, pg. 12; see also the *Christian Science Monitor* article, April 3, 2001, quoted elsewhere above in the present volume.) The only place which is safe for the people of Afghanistan is in the city of Kabul, where CNN and others film the new interim regime in its rather bland pomp and glory; a regime meant to secure the region for oil, not the people in democracy. Prior to August 2, 2001 the region was "up" for negotiation and meant to become a regime not unlike Kuwait and the Saudi regime as ally and the perceived puppets of the United States.

After August 2, 2001, this meant nothing less than in Central Asia the west will enable the construction of an oil pipeline across Central Asia, oil and gas exploration, by force now rather than negotiation. It was only when the Taliban refused to accept US conditions that "this rationale of energy security changed into a military one." (Ibid., Brisard and Disqiue)

By way of corroboration, one should note the no longer curious fact that neither the Clinton administration nor the Bush administration ever placed Afghanistan on the official State Department list of states charged with sponsoring terrorism, despite the acknowledged presence of Osama bin Laden as a guest of the Taliban regime. Such a designation, as with Iran and Iraq, would have made it impossible for an American oil or construction company to sign a deal with Kabul for a pipeline to the Central Asian oil and gas fields. Dick Cheney wasted no time, as Bush's head of the administration's energy policy, these talks between the Bush administration and the Taliban began in February 2001, shortly after Bush's inauguration. A Taliban emissary arrived in Washington in March with presents for the new chief executive, including an expensive Afghan carpet. But the talks themselves were less than cordial. Brisard said, "At one moment during the negotiations, the US representatives told the Taliban, 'either you accept our offer of a carpet of gold, or we bury you under a carpet of bombs'." This statement has been attributed to the book *Bin Laden* itself, which is incorrect; my personal translator of the text, Mr. David Jacobus, tells me these remarks were mentioned in interviews with the authors (where another party present told them what was said) and not an assertion of their own in the text. Nevertheless, it remains a twice corroborated statement below.

As long as the possibility of a pipeline deal remained, the White House stalled any further investigation into the activities of Osama bin Laden. What really became an important point, for at least CNN, the authors argue that John O'Neill, Deputy director of the FBI, resigned in July 2001, in protest over this obstruction. O'Neill told them in an interview, "the main obstacles to investigate Islamic terrorism were US oil corporate interests and the role played by Saudi Arabia in it." It is somewhat a bizarre coincidence, that Mr. O'Neill accepted a position as security chief of the World Trade Center after leaving the FBI, and was killed on September 11.

Confirming Naiz Naik's account of the secret Berlin meeting noted above, the two French authors add that there was open discussion of the need for the Taliban to facilitate a pipeline from Kazakhstan in order to insure US and international recognition. The increasingly unfriendly environment of the United States and Taliban talks ended August 2nd, after a final meeting between US envoy Christina Rocca and a Taliban representative in Islamabad.

This one book alone clearly does not supply the definitive evidence for a court of law, as the evidence against bin Laden; "all roads lead to...," admittedly did not provide any legal evidence as well, as was placed at the outset of the compilation of charges Mr. Bush and Mr. Blair passed around immediately following the 9/11 air attacks. But having reviewed the book by having it translated myself by one of my clients (the above mentioned Mr. David Jacobus) and having done independent research regarding the Caspian region, the reason for the present volume that is, I must state somewhat hesitantly, yet categorically, there is indeed sufficient evidence to make precisely the charges that 1)"one of" the political objectives, certainly not the only one, but "one of" the objectives is without doubt to remove the ruling Taliban from power to open the way for the long-sought-after pipeline route through Afghanistan, into Pakistan with its ultimate destination, India. And 2) The Bush administration did in fact recognize the Taliban as the government of and the sovereign state of Afghanistan, making the aggression against the state of Afghanistan and the removal of the ruling Taliban a *delict* in international law. It becomes then, my somewhat saddened duty, as an American, to inform the reader that my country is in violation of international law, violation of all international norms, relations, and in violation of human rights.

That this is not a conspiracy is abundantly clear; that this is what the corporate-state would do, will always do, has always done, is clear as well. The evolution to corporate Empire, with *Corporatism* as ideology, cannot really be fundamentally argued against by the well-read and reasonable people; that Mr. Bush Junior has picked-up, predictably, where Mr. Bush Senior left-off, is no longer in dispute either. But for it to succeed, for the American-led Empire to see fruition, it must work in both silence and without United States Constitutional domestic intervention; without U.N. international intervention. Afghanistan is but the beginning, not the end-all to this coming regime.

The only reason to silence critics over this is to provide a safe harbor for such activities now and in the future. There is no such thing as a perfectly just and fair, equal or non-corrupt society. There is always and everywhere the grasping hands of those who want more power, more wealth, no matter how they can get it, no matter what laws stand in the way. It is not just that power corrupts and absolute power corrupts absolutely, that is abundantly obvious to all with any small historical knowledge, but that it is so predictable in its results.

Persons in power also have the all-too-human tendency to believe in good faith that the "right" answers to moral and political issues just happen to be the ones that consolidate and
enhance their own power. Moreover, because these individuals
have power, they possess a disproportionate ability to convert
their answers into society's answers. (Steven H. Shiffrin, *Dissent, Injustice, and the Meanings of America,* Princeton University
Press, pg.92)

A brilliant and experienced (life experience) philosopher once wrote,
"Those who are fearful cannot be tolerant. Politicians who are weak and vulnerable cannot endure opposition, any criticism, any dissent, because they
are always insecure. Intolerance rescues those who are afraid of the danger
of defeat in open competition." (Mieczyslaw Maneli, *Freedom and Tolerance,*
Octagon Books, 1987, pg. 178) Regarding the White House's efforts to silence
any and all criticism of Mr. Bush, and a media fully prepared to aid in that
effort, this same author made this important point which applies today more
than ever: "Corruption is inseparable from any form of government. It is the
nature of every government to impose secrecy so as to silence its critics."
(Ibid., pg. 292)

This has been understood for ages, yet today, January 31, 2002, it is lost
on the media and the rest of the country. The tendency to authoritarianism
has always been present in government, but it has, as well, been ever-present
in the monopoly corporate world; there is no dissent in this private sphere
either. Like government, totalitarian tendencies in a leader, or "Totalitarianism, as trait or totality, escapes social scientists because of their innocence...
The first rule of totalitarianism is silence, and the isolation it implies....From
the outside one cannot recognize totalitarianism until it reaches the bizarre
stage of expansion by force, repression by overt terror, unmitigated madness."
(Earl Shorris, *The Oppressed Middle, Politics of Middle Management, Scenes from
Corporate Life,* Garden City, New York: Anchor Press, 1981, pp. 3-10) It was
the view of Mr. Maneli that "Mass propaganda in a mass society, the 'selling'
of ideas, of presidents....tends to channel thoughts into a one-track, one-way
flow of alleged obviousness. It is a pseudo 'common sense' which, together
with blatant irrationalism, has become one of the most dangerous enemies of
reason in modern, industrial democracies." (Maneli, Ibid., pg. 333)

CHAPTER FOURTEEN
Afghanistan: The Planning Stages

In every age...
the ultimate sources of war are the
beliefs of those in power:
their idea about what is of most
fundamental importance and may
therefore ultimately be worth a war.
—EVAN LUARD

Aggressive warfare was to be the key
mechanism by which [the totalitarian temper]
fulfilled their destinies. Thus, imperial agriculture's
hunger for territory would find an equivalent in the
supposed necessity to physically control the
natural resources necessary to feed an
industrial economy.
—ROBERT L. O'CONNELL

If I knew something that was useful to me, but
it would hurt my family, I would evict it from my thoughts.
If I knew something useful to my family,
but not to my nation, I would try to forget it.
If I knew something useful to my country, but harmful
...to the human species,
I would consider it a crime.
—MONTESQUIEU

WAR PLANNING

THIS WAS DESTINED TO BE THE MOST DIFFICULT chapter written for this volume. It is much too interpretive, compared to the others, too subjective and therefore controversial. I've gone ahead with it because I have a sense of it, a feel that it may bear fruit, be true, that is to say, and maybe the facts borne out by a full investigation by the United States Senate or a joint House and Senate. But this is so unlikely that it was the main reason not to include it at all. I will, therefore, have to let it stand as pure speculation. Speculation based on my personal research work in several related fields and some circumstantial evidence. This is all to say only this: I think what is argued here may just be valid. Nobody is expected to agree.

There were what are often referred to as insider accounts published in the British, French and Indian media that may have revealed that United States government officials had threatened war against the Taliban ruling Afghanistan, during 2001, but well-before 9/11/01. It was reported at least once that this included the prediction, made in July, that "if the military action went ahead, it would take place before the snows started falling in Afghanistan, by the middle of October at the latest." Everyone knows that Mr. Bush Junior's administration began bombing this poverty-stricken country October 7th, and ground attacks by US Special Forces began October 19th, 2001. As of this writing (January 25th) these raids have yet to end. Since bin Laden's presumed escape to who-knows-where, there is more talk than ever to go after Iraq, Syria and Somalia; Sudan and Yemen have each been named as possible targets.

I have spoken to my client base for some time to focus their reading in the foreign press, and only read the American press for anecdotal evidence of what Mr. Bush is saying, not doing. According to more left-leaning journals and websites "The American media has conducted a systematic cover-up of the real economic and strategic interests that underlie the war against Afghanistan, in order to sustain the pretense that the war emerged overnight, full-blown, in response to the terrorist attacks of September 11." (wsws.org) "The pundits for the American television networks and major daily newspapers celebrate the rapid military defeat of the Taliban regime as an unexpected stroke of good fortune. They distract public attention from the conclusion that any serious observer would be compelled to draw from the events of the past two weeks: that the speedy victory of the US-backed forces reveals careful planning and preparation by the American military, which must have begun well before the attacks on the World Trade Center and the Pentagon." (Ibid.) In case the reader was not aware, the speedy victory has already found its glitches: During the middle of January, over 5,000 Taliban soldiers with their commanders not only escaped altogether with 450 tanks, armored personnel carriers and assorted anti-tank weaponry, but have now begun their guerrilla war against the American convoys and Northern Alliance troops. They are hiding amongst the villagers who are protecting them and supplying them. The beginning is here, it is hardly over in Afghanistan. This is ignored by the American press.

While I do not always agree with the far-Left in America, socialists operating in foreign lands very often get their facts very straight indeed. They have to, they are on the margins like never before. I believe in dissent wherever it originates from. Let us hear it all; then let us sort it out. I look to verify that which I do not agree with, not discount it outright because I do not care for the ideological slant or the purported agenda. There is some smoke here from the international left, and so to this assertion above.

The myth-making in America might be said to have begun with one of America's leading advocates, for some five years running, of the policy proposal to remove the Taliban from power in Afghanistan, so as to bring about a change in leadership "more acceptable to the international community, the oil companies and their financial supporters." (House Hearing on The Silk Road Strategy, chapter five above): American myth number one is that "everything changed" on the day four airliners were hijacked and nearly 4,000 people killed. I have already argued, the illegal US military intervention in Afghanistan, according the below account, was improvised in less than thirty days. Deputy Defense Secretary Paul Wolfowitz, actually claimed that only "three weeks went into planning" the military onslaught. (CNN, November 18, 2001)

Afghanistan and oil pipelines

It can be argued from the circumstantial evidence that the United States had been "contemplating" war in Central Asia for at least a decade. During 1991, following the defeat of Iraq in the Persian Gulf War, *Newsweek* magazine published an article headlined "Operation Steppe Shield?" It reported that the US military was preparing an operation in Kazakhstan modeled on the Operation Desert Shield deployment in Saudi Arabia, Kuwait and Iraq. The only reason for a war on Kazakhstan would be in the interests of oil. It has the single largest deposits in the Caspian region, and is, now well-known, to be virtually land-locked. The way Mobil Oil, Exxon and BP and other large oil firms could get their oil out of the region was through "oil swaps." Oil swaps are the more dangerous means to see one's oil delivered as there is the risk of being caught in international bribery schemes. The oil one holds in a landlocked region is swapped with (paper agreements) oil holding between the one or several parties, in return for their oil (often already in a tanker somewhere) and an added fee. Other than this process, which has several American companies being investigated under the 1997 international legal agreements against bribery, there is but one way. Pipelines are the only viable answer for transit of the oil. But why would America think a war in Kazakhstan was important? One writer speculates well on just this point.

American oil companies have acquired rights to as much as 75 percent of the output of these new fields, and US government officials have hailed the Caspian and Central Asia as a potential alternative to dependence on oil from the unstable Persian Gulf region. American troops have followed in the wake of these contracts. US Special Forces began joint operations with Kazakhstan in 1997 and with Uzbekistan a year later, training for intervention especially in the mountainous southern region that includes Kyrgyzstan, Tajikistan and northern Afghanistan. (Patrick Martin, November 20, 2001)

I have not been able to verify that the US Special Forces were training for an intervention in Afghanistan, per se, but that they were there in the regions noted is a fact. As pointed out in the above chapters the route chosen for a pipeline was through Afghanistan and not just for cost consideration, though that is true also, but the firm policy formulation of isolating Iran and Iraq from oil markets by circumventing an Iranian route; this was of major strategic energy policy concern. Russia had in the past been the main player in most every negotiation (I argue in chapter nine and again here, they will remain so) and this was a concern in American governmental and non-governmental circles over the past six years. This will remain a concern also. Mr. Bush believes Russia will play ball with him while he *goes his own way* on everything else, including the Missile Defense Shield. Vladimir Putin goes his own way as well, Mr. Bush, and the recent filing below demonstrates this:

Caspian News Agency:

17:22 25.01.2002/ Russia/parliament/North-South/ratification

Russian State Duma to ratify agreement on North-South international transport corridor.

Moscow, January 25, 2002. (CNA). Russian State Duma will ratify agreement on North-South international transport corridor, press service of Russian Transport Ministry informed CNA. On Thursday the international relations committee recommended the parliamentary lower chamber to ratify the agreement signed between *Russia, India, Iran and Sultanate Oman* on September 12, 2000 in ST. Petersburg. It's noteworthy the Indian parliament has already ratified this document. According to expert's data, annual income from corridor exploitation is estimated at USD 5-6 billion. (my italics)

The Russians today intend to pursue a pipeline transit route through Iran. Over these last six years and presently, the Afghanistan pipeline transit route was pressed forward by Unocal, and six or eight major national political figures like Dick Cheney and Richard Armitage, which "intensely lobbied the region" and others which negotiated with the Taliban regime. As pointed out, these talks in 1998, soured because of the bombing of United States embassies in Kenya and Tanzania. Osama bin Laden was held responsible by our CIA. To summarize briefly, in August of 1998, Mr. Clinton ordered the launch of some eighty cruise missiles on alleged bin Laden training camps in eastern Afghanistan. The Clinton administration demanded that the Taliban hand over bin Laden, economic sanctions followed. Bin Laden sold some of the missiles that did not explode to China.

Now this is where speculation from ascertainable facts can get an analyst in trouble. But there is growing evidence daily now that these events are correctly interpreted. Only history will bear out the veracity of the following. Throughout 1999 the US pressure on Afghanistan increased.

On February 3rd of that year, Assistant Secretary of State Karl E. Inderfurth and State Department counter-terrorism chief Michael Sheehan traveled to Islamabad, Pakistan, to meet the Taliban's deputy foreign minister, Abdul Jalil. They warned him that the US would hold the government of Afghanistan responsible for any further terrorist acts by bin Laden. According to a report in the *Washington Post* (October 3, 2001), the Clinton administration and Nawaz Sharif, then prime minister of Pakistan, agreed on a joint covert operation to kill Osama bin Laden in 1999. The US would supply satellite intelligence, air support and financing, while Pakistan supplied the Pushtun-speaking operatives who would penetrate southern Afghanistan and carry out the actual killing. (Ibid. Martin)

The Pakistani commando team was up and running and ready to strike by October 1999, the *Washington Post* reported. One former official told the newspaper, "It was an enterprise. It was proceeding." Clinton aides were arguably excited at the prospect of a successful assassination, with one declaring, "It was like Christmas." Then the attack was aborted on October 12, 1999, when Sharif was overthrown in a military coup by General Pervez Musharraf, who halted the proposed covert operation. The Clinton administration had to settle for a UN Security Council resolution that demanded the Taliban turn over bin Laden to "appropriate authorities," but did not require he be handed over to the United States. (Martin, Ibid.) An important last point to remember.

Now comes Mr. Bush Junior, a man who claims he has special proof that "all roads lead to bin Laden," but he cannot show the proof, not even in a duly constituted court of law. No, instead he illegally sets up a military tribunal system to hold secret trials with secret evidence with a death penalty which can be imposed by the "military judges"... "by a two thirds majority..." but with this additional proviso... "of those present." Two thirds of those present? The propaganda, the demonization (or specie-ization as noted elsewhere), against al-Qaida and the Taliban, and Osama bin Laden in particular, and each perhaps does deserve to be repudiated and some even arrested and tried as others have been, has gone uncontested. It is deliberate and ongoing, still, as late as January 31st, 2002. This war on a Muslim nation-state cannot be ignored forever. I have long stated that the Arab people, the Muslims throughout the world, have been relegated to the "new Jews," in Hollywood, the mainstream media and the governments of many of the richer countries. The racism inherent in a majority of white Americans endorsing this war has been obvious to all. There are, according to Mr. Bush and Mr. Blair, of course the "good Arabs" and the "bad Arabs." Here is what one commentator wrote not too long ago during April 1991 regarding our good versus bad Arabs, during Bush Senior's *jolly little war*.

> No one appears to have taken note of the fact that Jews are forbidden to set foot in Saudi Arabia under the threat of death.... Has anyone culled the ranks to make sure that no Jews slipped through, and since thousands of Protestants have been circumcised, what if some poor kid is grabbed as he urinates? How does he prove he's not Jewish? If he just happens to have a crucifix hidden away, he can be whipped and stoned for being a Christian. It's somewhat better than being put to death for being Jewish—a practice we once deplored bitterly but which is now entirely acceptable in our new ally—but still it makes one wonder about the 'good Arabs' we are ready to die for in a struggle against the 'bad Arabs.'" (Howard Fast, *War and Peace, Observations in Our Times*, 1993, M.E. Sharpe, Pg. 256)

According to an account published November 2nd 2001, in the *Wall Street Journal*, written by Robert McFarlane, former national security adviser in the Reagan administration, McFarlane was hired by two wealthy Chicago commodity speculators, Joseph and James Ritchie, to assist them in recruiting and organizing anti-Taliban guerrillas among Afghan refugees in Pakistan. Their principal Afghan contact was Abdul Haq, the former mujahedin leader who was executed by the Taliban after an unsuccessful attempt to spark a revolt in his home province. (Ibid., Martin and *The Wall Street Journal*)

McFarlane held meetings with Abdul Haq and other former mujahedin in the course of the fall and winter of 2000. These meetings are with private citizens while Mr. Clinton (his hands full) did nothing to discourage these meetings. Then, according to journalist Patrick Martin, "After the Bush administration took office, McFarlane parlayed his Republican connections into a series of meetings with the US State Department, Pentagon and even White House officials. All encouraged the preparation of an anti-Taliban military campaign." During the summer, long before the United States launched air-strikes on the Taliban, James Ritchie traveled to Tajikistan with Abdul Haq and Peter Tomsen, who had been the US special envoy to the Afghan opposition during the first Bush administration. There they met with Ahmed Shah Massoud, the leader of the Northern Alliance, with the goal of coordinating their Pakistan-based attacks with the only military force still offering resistance to the

Taliban." This activity reported by Martin, if accurate, violates the Geneva Conventions and the United Nations Charter as I have noted thoroughly in Chapter One. If it was known to the government of the United States, and one cannot see any believable reason why the government would not be aware, then the government was in clear violation of the above accords.

Finally, according to McFarlane, Abdul Haq "decided in mid-August to go ahead and launch operations in Afghanistan. He returned to Peshawar, Pakistan, to make final preparations." In other words, this phase of the anti-Taliban war was under way well before September 11." (Ibid.) This had to have been acknowledged within the belt-way even if there was never any written authorization. Laila Helms was intimately involved during the two administrations.

The *Washington Post,* on November 18th, 2001, Bob Woodward stated the "CIA has been mounting paramilitary operations in southern Afghanistan since 1997."

Woodward provides details about the CIA's role in the current military conflict, which includes the deployment of a secret paramilitary unit, the Special Activities Division. This force began combat on September 27, using both operatives on the ground and Predator surveillance drones equipped with missiles that could be launched by remote control. The Special Activities Division, Woodward reports, "consists of teams of about half a dozen men who do not wear military uniforms. The division has about 150 fighters, pilots and specialists, and is made up mostly of hardened veterans who have retired from the US military."

Here, again is the important and mostly overlooked point: according to Woodward, "For the last 18 months, the CIA has been working with tribes and warlords in southern Afghanistan, and the division's units have helped create a significant new network in the region of the Taliban's greatest strength." This means that the CIA was engaged in some level of overt attacks against the Afghan regime as early as 1999, some time after our US House of Representatives were deliberating the Silk Road Strategy with Unocal and until the spring of 2000, well over a year before the suicide hijackings that destroyed the World Trade Center and damaged the Pentagon.

The British-based *Jane's International Security* reported March 15, 2001, that the new American administration was working with India, Iran and Russia "in a concerted front against Afghanistan's Taliban regime." It is now well-known from many sources that India as well as the Russians were supplying the Northern Alliance with military equipment, advisers and helicopter technicians, and the magazine at the time noted this as well, adding "both India and Russia were using bases in Tajikistan and Uzbekistan for their operations....Several recent meetings between the newly instituted Indo-US and Indo-Russian joint working groups on terrorism led to this effort to tactically and logistically counter the Taliban." According to this report "Intelligence sources in Delhi said that while India, Russia and Iran were leading the anti-Taliban campaign on the ground, Washington was giving the Northern

Alliance information and logistic support."

On June 26, 2001, the magazine *IndiaReacts* reported more details of the ongoing efforts of the US, India, Russia and Iran against the Taliban regime. "India and Iran will 'facilitate' US and Russian plans for 'limited military action' against the Taliban if the contemplated tough new economic sanctions don't bend Afghanistan's fundamentalist regime." This is, again, a clear violation of intervention into the cultural elements of the regime as well as its nation-state sovereignty. At this stage of military planning, the US and Russia were to supply direct military assistance to the Northern Alliance, working through Uzbekistan and Tajikistan, in order to roll back the Taliban lines toward the city of Mazar-e-Sharif "A scenario strikingly similar to what actually took place over the past two weeks" of December 2001, as Patrick Martin correctly pointed out. According to Martin, "An unnamed third country supplied the Northern Alliance with anti-tank rockets that had already been put to use against the Taliban in early June. Diplomats say that the anti-Taliban move followed a meeting between US Secretary of State Colin Powell and Russian Foreign Minister Igor Ivanov and later between Powell and Indian Foreign Minister Jaswant Singh in Washington." This covert military pressure on the Taliban was taking place while there were ongoing trade and economic negotiations from other US diplomatic personnel on the economic front; did the US think the Taliban would fail to "link" the two areas of concern?

The BBC's George Arney reported September 18, 2001, that American officials had told former Pakistani Foreign Secretary Niaz Naik in mid-July of plans for military action against the Taliban regime: "Mr. Naik said US officials told him of the plan at a UN-sponsored international contact group on Afghanistan which took place in Berlin. "Mr. Naik told the BBC that at the meeting the US representatives told him that unless Osama bin Laden was handed over swiftly, America would take military action to kill or capture both bin Laden and the Taliban leader, Mullah Omar. "The wider objective, according to Mr. Naik, would be to topple the Taliban regime and install a transitional government of moderate Afghans in its place—possibly under the leadership of the former Afghan King Zahir Shah. Mr. Naik was told that Washington would launch its operation from bases in Tajikistan, where American advisers were already in place. He was told that Uzbekistan would also participate in the operation and that 17,000 Russian troops were on standby.

Mr. Naik was told that if the military action went ahead it would take place before the snows started falling in Afghanistan, by the middle of October at the latest."

Four days later, on September 22, the *Guardian* newspaper confirmed this account. The warnings to Afghanistan came out of a four-day meeting of senior US, Russian, Iranian and Pakistani officials at a hotel in Berlin in mid-July, the third in a series of back-channel conferences dubbed "brainstorming on Afghanistan." These are the meetings where the two French authors of *Bin laden: The Forbidden Truth* independently reported on this also. So one is getting corroboration from several sources, independent of each other to the effect that Mr. Bush and his collection of past private Caspian regional lobby-ists, now turned Administration officials, have been planning all along this *jolly little war.* (Ibid., Martin)

The participants in the meetings included Naik, together with three Paki-stani generals; former Iranian Ambassador to the United Nations, Saeed Rajai Khorassani; Abdullah Abdullah, foreign minister of the Northern Alliance; Nikolai Kozyrev, former Russian special envoy to Afghanistan, and several other Russian officials; and three Americans: Tom Simons, a former US am-bassador to Pakistan; Karl Inderfurth, a former assistant secretary of state for south Asian affairs; and Lee Coldren, who headed the office of Pakistan, Af-ghan and Bangladesh affairs in the State Department until 1997.

The meeting was convened by Francesc Vendrell, then and now the depu-ty chief UN representative for Afghanistan. While the nominal purpose of the conference was to discuss the possible outline of a political settlement in Af-ghanistan, the Taliban refused to attend. The Americans discussed the shift in policy toward Afghanistan from Clinton to Bush, and by August 2, 2001 and earlier, they had strongly suggested that military action was an option. Recall, again, the Taliban had been ridding the region of opium growing.

While all three American former officials denied making any specific threats, Lee Coldren told the *Guardian*, "there was some discussion of the fact that the United States was so disgusted with the Taliban that they might be considering some military action." Naik, however, cited one American declar-ing that action against bin Laden was imminent: "This time they were very sure. They had all the intelligence and would not miss him this time. It would be aerial action, maybe helicopter gunships, and not only overt, but from very close proximity to Afghanistan."

The *Guardian* summarized: "The threats of war unless the Taliban sur-rendered Osama bin Laden were passed to the regime in Afghanistan by the Pakistani government," As the entire world now knows, the Taliban refused to comply.

Did the US government plan the war well in advance, using the shock of September 11, which made it politically feasible, by gathering-up ignorant public opinion at home and giving Washington leverage on allies, so-called, abroad? This conclusion will be very hard to prove although there is much evidence to argue it. I also might add, would anyone even care now? Both the American public and dozens of foreign governments were stampeded into supporting military action against Afghanistan, in the name of the fight against terrorism. The Bush administration targeted Kabul without present-ing any evidence that the Taliban regime was responsible for the World Trade Center or anything other than what amounts to "their own business" domes-tically. The overt political objective, somewhat achieved now, of removal of the Taliban can only be for the reasons argued in this book: oil and pipelines. (The entire article titled *US planned war in Afghanistan long before September 11*, by Patrick Martin, 20 November 2001 can be viewed on the wsws.org web-site.)

276 The Hydra of Carnage

This targeting of Afghanistan's Muslim population as somehow culpable, along with al Qaida and Osama bin Laden amounts to something more than just simple demonizing of these people. Given that it certainly has been made clear by Mr. Bush, he does not intend to stop with Afghanistan; he intends to "root out the evil doers" wherever he finds them.

It is my belief, no, my conviction, that Mr. Bush Junior along with his gaggle of senior advisors, most of which came from the old Bush Senior regime, have planned this war for some time. The plan to remove the Taliban is well-known and had been offered as a solution to the "pipeline" issue since 1997. It would be very hard to believe that Mr. Bush did not have a military plan, some operational plan, in place well before September 11, 2001. Mr. Patrick Martin should be commended for his efforts at raising this specter from beneath the rubble of this devastated country. This excerpt below was written during 1984 but it applies today more than ever.

> The first stage of a new Holocaust has started. The victim has been singled out and clearly marked. The world knows the nation and the state by name. Its geographical location is defined. The bill of indictment has already been made known to the victim, to the future executioners, and to the more or less indifferent onlookers and bystanders. The remaining task is simple. The propagandists will day after day repeat the charges in order to assure that at the decisive moment no one will doubt that the death of the victim is a necessity or represents eternal justice and that it will bring relief and benefit to all. (Maneli, Ibid., pg. 259)

Black Tuesday

One question remains. If the war was planned well in advance of September 11, 2001, and that the events of that day simply triggered a greater aggression against Afghanistan which was already in the works, how many people may have actually known about the air attacks themselves prior to them being deployed? It must be obvious that some few within the hijacker's network knew; if Osama bin Laden, which has been constantly alleged, had something to do with the planning, or just knew of its plan, then how many others as well? Were there others still, completely outside of any terrorist network or this growing international guerrilla movement, who may have been privy to its planning stages?

These questions will probably never be answered definitively but they will haunt the conspiracy circles, not to mention criminal investigators, for decades to come. The problem with conspiracy theorists is they always go too far. If it could be proven that "someone" gained financially from the air attacks, but never proven "who" the crackpots on both the left and right, theorize, huddled in some dingy room conspiratorially themselves, that the conspirators, therefore, *ipso facto* (they like words like that) must be George

Bush Junior, or certainly the Senior. They may be dismissed out of hand but that does nothing to diminish the facts. Should there be sufficient empirical evidence, facts, to demonstrate "someone" did gain financially, and demonstrated that they therefore knew of the attacks, then this still must be reported and investigated exhaustively. And it was and it is being investigated, just not here in America too much nor publicly anywhere else. The source? The United States Stock Exchange.

According to one author with considerable background, "Investigators will be looking at transactions starting with those that can be most easily identified as suspicious. Already enough has emerged to indicate that some trades were almost certainly made based upon advance knowledge of the Black Tuesday attacks" Trades in American Airlines and United Airlines stocks were traded in amounts and at times which caused the Security Exchange Commission's investigators to look into it. According to the author, here is what was found in the beginning stages of their investigations:

· Between September 6th and 7th, the Chicago Board Options Exchange saw purchases of 4,744 *put options* on United Airlines, but only 396 *call options*. Although there was no news at that time to justify so much "left-handed" trading, United Airlines stock fell 42 percent, from $30.82 per share to $17.50, when the market reopened after the attacks. Assuming that 4,000 of the options were bought by people with advance knowledge of the imminent attacks, these "insiders" would have profited by almost $5 million.
· On September 10, 4,516 *put options* on American Airlines were bought on the Chicago exchange, compared to only 748 *calls*. Again, there was no news at that point to justify this imbalance; but American Airlines stock fell 39 percent, from $29.70 to $18.00 per share, when the market reopened. Again, assuming that 4,000 of these options trades represent "insiders," they would represent a gain of about $4 million.
· No similar trading in other airlines occurred on the Chicago exchange in the days immediately preceding Black Tuesday.
· Morgan Stanley Dean Witter & Co., which occupied 22 floors of the World Trade Center, saw 2,157 of its October $45.00 *put options* bought in the three trading days before Black Tuesday; this compares to an average of 27 contracts per day before September 6. Morgan Stanley's share price fell from $48.90 to $42.50 in the aftermath of the attacks. Assuming that 2,000 of these options contracts were bought based upon knowledge of the approaching attacks, their purchasers could have profited by at least $1.2 million.
· Merrill Lynch & Co., with headquarters near the Twin Towers, saw 12,215 October $45.00 put options bought in the four trading days before the attacks; the previous average volume in these options had been 252 contracts per day. When trading resumed, Merrill's shares fell from $46.88 to $41.50; assuming that 11,000 option contracts were bought by "insiders," their profit would have been about $5.5 million.

· European regulators are examining trades in Germany's Munich Re, Switzerland's Swiss Re, and AXA of France, all major reinsurers with exposure to the Black Tuesday disaster. (Swiss Re estimates that its exposure will be $730 million; Munich Re expects to pay out as much as $903 million.) It is not clear if any trades in these stocks ring alarm bells; and some negative earnings news announced shortly before the attacks means that a certain amount of unusual selling may have been a normal market reaction and not anything more sinister.
· Amsterdam traders have noted that there was unusual trading activity in KLM Royal Dutch Airlines put options before the attacks.

   This author is no alarmist. But these investigations should be followed closely. His own disclaimer is here repeated: "This is very much a developing story, and we can be sure that more — and more accurate — numbers will emerge soon. Investigators will be examining transactions starting with the few days immediately before the attack, and then working backwards; and similarly, they will be looking first at trades in the most obviously affected securities." (Don Radlauer, ICT Consultant; *Black Tuesday: The World's Largest Insider Trading Scam?* The author is an expert in electronic banking and cash management, and qualified as a floor trader for the New York Futures Exchange.)
   There is no evidence of any wrongdoing by anyone at this point and this is only important if the investigators are assuming, or are convinced, that some of the trades were made "based upon advance knowledge of the attacks." If that were the conclusions "they will obviously try to trace these trades back to determine who initiated them." There is a law on the books in the United States called "Misprison of Felon," although not all nations have such a law. What it amounts to is this: If someone had prior knowledge that a felony was about to be committed and failed to notify authorities, they can face up to a five year felony prison sentence for just having had that knowledge. This law was used often during the violent militia activity here in the United States; it was the one tool which, in the end, ended much of the criminal and conspiratorial activity of these group's members.
   Therefore, here in America at least, anyone who had detailed knowledge of the attacks before they happened was, at the very least, an accessory after the fact, if not being charged with being an accessory to the planning itself which would be much more difficult to prove. Don Raudlaur then argues that the "overwhelming probability is that the trades could have been made only by the same people who masterminded the attacks themselves." Only here does Radlaur err, in my opinion. That may not be the case at all. Those who masterminded the air attacks would likely have kept it within a small circle of friends, but that is not to say some "other" player, maybe not involved in the planning at length, might not have gone their own way and saw an opportunity to make a bit of money without the mastermind ever knowing. In fact, it is doubtful those which masterminded such an attack would have cared

one whit about making any money off the operation. Nobody could possibly think Osama bin Laden, a legitimate millionaire if not billionaire, would have even considered it. Nor, if my theory holds, would any international guerrilla soldiers seen this as worthy of their efforts and the high-level of personal honor (no matter what else one thinks of them) necessary to be such a guerrilla.

It is prudent to understand one's enemies, which includes not giving them greater or worse attributes than they have; this will only confound you (or investigators) and make them seem more evil (larger than life) than they are in reality. Something Mr. Bush has single-handedly managed to accomplish with bin Laden. That was likely the intent on Bush's part of course, to demonize the scapegoat is a primary objective in war-making.

The difficulty will be in tracing the transactions to their real source. The trading is likely to have been done under false names, and as Radlaur points out, "behind shell corporations, and in general to have been thoroughly obfuscated." I part with the author only in that he hypothesizes that bin Laden could have done this, because of his already well-known skills at hiding assets and moving funds wherever he wished to finance terrorism in the past. This hypothesis rests on the assumption that Osama bin Laden was the mastermind, something not even the virulence of Tony Blair has succeeded in proving to anyone not already disposed to believe it. It is highly unlikely these transactions were made under orders from Osama bin Laden, even though we are "dealing with an expert in masking ownership of corporations and making covert deals." (Ibid.)

That someone may have had prior knowledge of the attacks is not something without historical precedence and anyone inside the loop of any of the industrialized nations or lesser developed nation's intelligence communities, could have acted in such a manner. But the conspiracy buffs will undoubtedly see Mr. George Bush (both of them), or Dick Cheney having set up the shell corporations, for intrigue runs deep in their shallow minds. This is as unlikely as bin Laden having done so. One cannot make our own Mr. Bush, or Britain's Mr. Blair, any more unlikable than they might be. Millionaires, and certainly billionaires, do not leave paper trails and do not violate such mundane laws of any land. I am opposed to Mr. Bush's imperial war-making, and Mr. Blair's unseemly support of the same, for precisely the reasons this volume outlines; no more, no less.

CHAPTER FIFTEEN

USA Freedom Corp.
Domestic Surveillance

*September 11 was a tragic day in our Nation's history
and the history of the world.
No American, and no civilized person, would wish the
evil of that day on anyone. So much grief and sorrow
were inflicted on so many of our fellow citizens,
and people around the world.
Yet we also know that out of tragedy,
strength and hope and even good can come.
One of the best ways to counter
evil is through the gathering momentum
of millions of acts of service and decency and kindness.*
—PRESIDENT GEORGE BUSH JR.

*To be locked into one's ethnicity is to be blind
to the claims of others; to go beyond ethnicity is to
expand one's consciousness of the world.*
—EUGENS GOOGHEART
The Reign of Ideology

USA FREEDOM CORP
CITIZEN BLOCK COMMANDERS

PRESIDENT GEORGE BUSH JR. HAS INTRODUCED what to many will seem a rather new concept. He calls it his citizens *USA Freedom Corp.*, his executive order (see appendix four) brings this into existence. But the concept is not new at all. Hitler's Germany used it, Italy's Mussolini used it, Stalin's Russia perfected it. It is the turning of citizen against citizen, a war of all against all, with a twist. It has as one of its intended effects to mobilize seniors, college students, truck drivers and mail carriers into an activity they have no qualifications nor skill sets to perform; and no amount of "volunteer" training through this program will give them these skills. Here is how it is intended to begin. Everything below is taken directly from the presidential initiative. I have purposely left out the significant areas where one may find little argument, these being that of asking for volunteer help and training for medical, disaster, and emergency services help; these everyone concerned can find no problem with. But what I outline below is what will be spoken of less and the text of the initiative has this as the key fundamental change in how America behaves domestically. This president is serious and the level of funding and the federal agencies involved spell this out. "**The President is requesting more than $560 million in new funds in Fiscal Year 2003** to support this new citizen service initiative." The new initiative forms, among other things the following key to the initiative:

A newly created Citizen Corps to engage citizens in homeland security:

The new Citizen Corps will consist of Citizen Corps Councils. It will engage Americans in specific homeland security efforts in communities throughout the country. These initiatives include a Medical Reserve Corps, a *Volunteers in Police Service Program, a doubling of Neighborhood Watch, a new Terrorist Information and Prevention System,* and a tripling of Community Emergency Response Team members.

Establish Citizen Corps Councils

Citizen Corps Councils (Councils) will be created at the local level throughout the country. *Councils will have flexibility to determine the jurisdictions they cover,* and FEMA will coordinate with the Governors and their state Emergency Management Offices and, where applicable, state homeland security offices, to ensure councils represent citizens throughout the state. (italics are mine)

These "Councils" are to determine the "jurisdictions they cover," is an important reference point. I have lived in seven US states and two foreign countries. I have, for over twenty years, after leaving the military and corporate world behind, been active in public affairs and political activity of one sort or another. I say this by way of explaining only this: I understand my countrymen better than most; I know how we have changed and seen the paradigm shift to the far-right, displacing any sense of popular pluralistic discourse and even thinking. Talk-hate originated on the street and spilled over into talk-radio, it is now apparent on every network talk show inclusive of CNN; there is to be no dissent; this has been addressed already. The paradigm shift to intolerance began in earnest almost to the day Bill Clinton became president; there is only some correlation here, as the shift was predictable well before that day and not substantive enough to place blame on Mr. Clinton and his aggressive spouse. Even a paradigm shift is evolutionary. This increasing level of intolerance applies to both the militia-right and multicultural-left. What has developed is an *intolerance for difference* which cannot be ignored. With Bush's *Councils* here is why the intolerance can no longer be ignored:

> Other members of the Councils would include leaders from law enforcement, state, and local fire and emergency offices, businesses (especially security firms), school officials, faith-based groups, public health organizations, mental health and educational groups, veterans groups, and neighborhood watch organizations. Other participants may include representatives from non-profit organizations, community foundations, and other institutions with local presence and the ability to build capacity. The Citizen Corps Councils are intended to reach all segments of American society and should represent the diversity of each local community.

It is the areas of "non-profit organizations" and "other institutions" which is clearly problematic. The assumption that diversity will, or would be allowed to be represented is more than problematic, it is highly suspect. From both the right and left, we have organizations which already practice racism and bigotry of every sort; it is the sad depleted heritage of America's original pluralism gone ugly. On the right we have anti-Semitic militia groups which often cross-membership with the aging and rather silly racist KKK and too many "faith-based" groups veiled behind racism and intolerance. Those which remain in rhetoric only should be ignored, their political views, no matter how repugnant, are protected free speech and assembly; the federal authorities did then, and still do leave them be. (Ignored for now at least, which is the problem with this initiative as you will see below.) Those which were violence prone, armed illegally and operating in secrecy based upon what they called "red cells" are different. Therefore in the latter case, and only where there was substantial evidence, I periodically consulted with two federal law enforcement agency's intelligence divisions. These individuals were acting in a criminal capacity and that is where surveillance should remain. It is not too well-known outside of federal law enforcement intelligence agents' circles, but where Mr. Timothy McVeigh, our first official domestic terrorist of any repute, was concerned, he was "in fact" a member of a militia cell and often acted as a body guard to at least two national militia leaders, so-called. That these same leaders will state McVeigh was "never" a "signed-up" member of any militia has a two-fold reasoning: 1) there are others like McVeigh out there which must be protected by these groups and 2) the militia leaders, so-called, inherent cowardice and terribly obvious to all, membership money-raising goals for personal power. Mr. John Trochman of the Militia of Montana wanted nothing so much as a seat at the table of federal law enforcement right along with Morris Dees of the Southern Poverty Law Center. (More on SPLC below)

The factional local Republican parties have, as well, often brokered a kind of bigotry which borders on Christian inquisitional reactionary fervor. The bombings of abortion clinics, the beatings of homosexuals, the attacks periodically on Asians in the past, and now (thanks in part to Mr. Bush's heightened rhetoric) Arabs, Persians, Muslims and non-Muslims alike have increased tenfold. It is no longer entirely safe to have skin of brown, it will begin to get a lot more un-safe with this paranoid initiative adopted.

Mr. Bush's efforts to expand citizen surveillance of other citizens will be abused, that is assured. Let us mention the average, less-informed, paranoid American women, mostly older white women. From personal experience I can tell you there is a rampant paranoia running through the (mainly) white suburban middle-class women and a same paranoia in the rural lower middle-class white women, where, for one instance, men with the perfectly legal right to carry a side-arm with a CWL, a proper "concealed weapon's license," is concerned is suspect. I have seen the feigned look of "terror" on the face of more than one woman when they accidentally "notice" a man armed. Now if it is a white fellow that resembles a husband or father in dress and appearance, that is often overlooked; call this the "good-ole-boy-that's-okay" syndrome. But if not, whether white or brown or god-forbid, black, these women are on the phone in a heart-beat to 911. After what you read below, what Mr. Bush imagines his new surveillance of all against all will achieve, will be its opposite. (I could be wrong in how I am arguing this as the paranoia and turning all against all may be the general principle desired by the administration's elite)

It is not the right-wing alone which practices a level of paranoia which resembles clinical pathology more than anything else. America's progressive-left (represented by, in part, the Anti-Defamation League [ADL] and Southern Poverty Law Center [SPLC]) has long been active in "spying on" and targeting other citizens whose political and cultural views are not shared with the afore mentioned. These local "non-profit organizations" often travel veiled, no differently that the white racist groups often do, calling themselves "human rights groups." It is well-known in law enforcement circles that these groups on the left are not entirely honest in their advertisement of purpose. (They are, as often as not, homosexual "rights" groups with an agenda to match their needs.) One of the best studies regarding these organizations of, often illegal activity (they have faced prosecution on more than one occasion), is researcher and analyst Laird Wilcox and his research titled *The Watchdogs: A Close Look at Anti-racist Watchdog Groups*, which he finds violate every tenet of fair play and often break the law, in an effort purportedly to identify dangerous white males (that would only include heterosexual, Christian, and gun-owners which are white) with latent or outright racist views. It is clear that many of the antiracist organizers, self-proclaimed spokesmen and many of their members and financial contributors are racist themselves, only racist against white heterosexual males (Christian or not), and are practicing what Wlilcox identifies as "ritual defamation" as one of their more effective and abusive actions.

> In Canada,... which has more strict libel laws than the United States, false charges of anti-Semitism brought B'nai B'rith Canada and its League for Human Rights, the approximate equivalent of the ADL in the United States, a libel action that cost the organization $400,000. The case, brought by Winnipeg teacher and former Progressive Conservative candidate Luba Fedorkiw in 1987, was the largest defamation award in Canadian history. (Mary Jane MacLennan, *The Winnipeg Sun*, 26, November 1987, and *Watchdogs*)

This Bush initiative will further give these kinds of reckless and dishonest groups and leaders, often with a very personal ideological agenda of their own (racism being but one) even more power to reek havoc amongst the fellow citizens they do not like. "The entire history of the ADL's relationship with government agencies has yet to be written. However, in working through a large stack of FBI documents obtained under the Freedom Of Information Act (FOIA) request, it becomes clear that the organization has labored long and hard to ingratiate itself with federal law enforcement authorities, ostensibly as "experts" on their own enemies." (Wilcox, *Watchdogs*, p.39) The Bush initiative will in fact give them some level of unwarranted and dangerous "authority" in their ruthless behavior as "Federal representatives from key agencies with local and regional offices, especially FEMA, DOJ, HHS, VA, Environmental Protection Agency (EPA), U.S. Department of Transportation (DOT), U.S. Department of Agriculture (USDA), Corporation for National and Community Service (CNCS), and the U.S. Postal Service will also be involved as appropriate and work with their state and local counterparts to help support the work of the Councils." The effect of giving many of these groups and individuals a semblance of legitimacy by allowing them to participate in the "Councils" as they are now to be called, will, actually in effect, create an environment of hate and the pursuit of every kind of injustice against anyone someone does not like or holds a grudge with.

In the case of the Right-leaning Volk, anyone some post office employee, takes a dislike to, will start to slowly imagine all sorts of things about this "other's" behavior, "wasn't that an odd package he received" and "does he have a gun in that car rack behind his seat," or "there have been several letters from Cairo lately..." To be brown, have an accent, be new to the area will be sufficient cause for these new "terrorist experts" to make the TIPS call.

In the case of the Left-leaning, anybody some local "human rights watch" group or self-proclaimed "expert" on racist hate-group's membership (and they all claim this "expert" status regarding right-wing groups) sees who travels through the region, stays over at someone's home, downs a beer at the local Karaoke bar, will be the target of "the TIPS call." Mr. Bush is wise in setting up a separate "hot-line" for all this, as it is going to be very busy indeed. If you feel I may be exaggerating my argument read on.

"The Councils will be responsible for developing a community action plan, including a local assessment of infrastructure vulnerabilities and possible threats, available local resources, and how to best organize and expand local efforts. The community action plan will coordinate the community-based prevention and preparedness efforts, such as Volunteers in Police Service, Neighborhood Watch Programs (NWP) *(with a new terrorism prevention focus)*, Medical Reserve Corps, and Community Emergency Response Teams." (My italics)

It is the "with a new terrorism prevention focus" that is absurd. It is, very often, the paranoid Neighborhood Watch crowd that should set off the brain bells in every rational noggin. To see just how absurd read the following definitional paragraph set out in the initiative:

Develop a Volunteers In Police Service Program (VIPS)
Since September 11, the demands on state and local law enforcement have immeasurably increased. Resources are being stretched further than ever at a time when the country needs every available officer out on the beat. Some local police departments are turning to civilian volunteers to supplement their forces. These programs draw on the time and considerable talents of civilian volunteers and allow law enforcement professionals to better perform their front-line duties.

....To ensure that existing NWPs are incorporated into these new efforts, Neighborhood Watch Program Coordinators or their designees will organize the efforts of the local NWPs and would be appointed to sit on the Citizen Corps Councils.

This is going to be something to see. Those of you (maybe in Great Britain for example) that just cannot imagine how paranoid Americans were before September 11, will be shocked to see what they are like now, and what they will become when this creature of centralized executive power evolves. And it is an *executive* function with offices in the White House. How does the federal government get the average paranoid to enlist in the active pursuit of the same? Incentives, incentives...money and prizes, designations and awards ceremonies, a soft title (NWP officer Bob, Ma'am.) and little window decals and bumper stickers is all it takes in the USA. Think how nice they will look with their little American flags flapping off their car antennae.

Create Community Designation Program

Although no community can protect against all threats, we can provide incentives for local communities to take comprehensive steps and to maintain those efforts over time. The "USA Freedom Communities" program will be a voluntary initiative that will give a special designation to communities meeting certain criteria related to preventing and responding to terrorist threats. The criteria can include, among other things, the following measures: creation of a Citizen Corps Council; operation of VIPS, Neighborhood Watch, Medical Reserve Corps, and CERT training; **strengthening all-hazard community planning;** improving public awareness and education; and persuading citizens to support local first responders. Governors, working in cooperation with Mayors, other local officials, and FEMA, will determine whether or not a community has met the criteria for designation.

I want to live in a *special designated* **USA Freedom Community**...like a hole in the head. Does anyone even know what the *all-hazard* community *planning* is? I do. I reported on it years ago when writing about FEMA's newest grant of powers. It has, no longer, since about 1995, have anything to do with natural "hazards" like hurricanes and floods. The new definition in law is regarding public disturbances like the Seattle WTO protests, the Los Angeles Riots, and the presumed ability of FEMA to prevent these kinds of events by the deployment of pentagon assets. The military that is.

Double Neighborhood Watch Programs and Add a Terrorism Prevention Component: The Department of Justice will work with the Neighborhood Watch Program (NWP) to incorporate terrorism prevention into its mission. The goal would be to double the number of NWPs over the next two years. DOJ will make grant funding available to Neighborhood Watch for additional training and increased capacity through the National Sheriffs' Association.

Create Operation TIPS: Terrorist Information and Prevention System

As part of the Citizen Corps, Operation TIPS — the Terrorist Information and Prevention System — will be a nationwide mechanism for reporting suspicious terrorist activity — enlisting millions of American transportation workers, truckers, letter carriers, train conductors, ship captains and utility employees. Operation TIPS, a project of the U.S. Department of Justice, will start first as a pilot program in ten cities in America, affecting more than 1 million workers. Applications from cities will be accepted in Fall 2002 for inclusion as one of the pilot programs.

The very suggestion that "utility workers" and "truck drivers" and "train conductors," are to be trained to "identify potential terrorist threats" is an outrage. One can imagine the rush from cities on the brink of bankruptcy to get the direct funds and future "matching funds" the President has offered-up as what some will see, quite appropriately I should add, as outright bribes. The criteria for the choice of these routine and mundane, often bored to death workers, is that "Operation TIPS will establish a national reporting system that would allow these workers, who have routines and are well positioned to recognize unusual events, to report suspicious activity to the appropriate authorities. Every participant in this new program will be given a Citizen Corps: Operation TIPS information sticker that could be affixed to the cab of the vehicle or placed in some other public location so that the toll free reporting number would be readily available to report any suspicious activity." A TIPS sticker *Readily available to report suspicious activity?* "Well positioned to recognize unusual events"? Not satisfied with garnering the subtle active law enforcement role of truck drivers and utility workers, Mr. Bush goes even further; now we are getting into Monty Python territory: He enlists the senior citizens and lowers the age for participation from 60-65 to 55 years of age.

> **Public safety.** Seniors will volunteer part-time with and for police departments and nonprofit organizations supporting public safety. They will carry out vital tasks including organizing neighborhood watch groups, community policing, victim assistance, fingerprinting and other tasks that free officers and other professionals to do front line work.

> *The Citizen Service Act of 2002*
> In support of the challenge to every American to serve, the Administration will submit proposed legislation, the Citizen Service Act of 2002, with the following objectives:
> · To support and encourage the greater engagement of citizens in volunteering;
>
> · To provide greater assistance to secular and faith-based community organizations, including those that address the homeland security needs of the nation;....

One wonders if the seniors in question might not include some of those feeling inadequate, stogy retired generals on CNN mentioned elsewhere, and retired for good reason. And what is the incentive for the aged and low-income elderly, often low-income for entirely obvious reasons, to enter into this volunteer program? Money of course, which makes it somewhat less voluntary than at first blush. To wit:

Enhance uses of current postservice benefits to allow a volunteer to have not only education awards but also options to use the funds for a downpayment on a home, job training, or health care costs....In both the Foster Grandparent and Senior Companion programs, members are low-income, serve 20 hours per week, and receive a modest stipend of $2.65 per hour... The FY 2003 budget will call for providing senior service opportunities for more than 100,000 volunteers. These individuals will support the following efforts:

Expanding training. The Administration will support additional training for projects and senior volunteers in areas such as homeland security.

Some of us have not been terribly impressed with the American youth these past several years. Not only do they come to college illiterate they leave illiterate. The campuses have become a battleground of intolerance. The right-wing CAUSA crowd (Rev. Moon's) Republican ultra-conservatism battling left-wing gay and lesbian factions, human rights groups and post-modern critiques of everything form literature to law. Multiculturalism is fightin' words and pluralism is selling out your ethnicity for assimilation. On the one hand, if you are not ethnic (wearing uniquely colored cloths) you have no standing, on the other, if you are not white (and going-for-it) you are not too bright (the MBA crowd). Never has American academic life been so unruly and un-academic in its thinking. So what does Mr. Bush want to do with this divided and disheveled lot?

Providing Greater Service Opportunities for College Students
The Administration will submit legislation to amend the Higher Education Act to require every college and university to devote 50 percent of its Federal Work Study funds to community service, commonly known as Serve Study. In any given year, at least five percent of the students will be expected to work in the homeland security fields of public safety, public health, and emergency preparedness.

And with that I shall close this chapter and the book as well. A short *postscript* follows which I had intended to call my *conclusions*, only to realize I have not come to any.

POSTSCRIPT

...corporate decision making is the most powerful
single force in socializing and politicizing the American public.
Leading corporations own the leading news media
and advertisers subsidize most of the rest.
They decide what news and entertainment will be made
available to the country;
they have direct influence on the
country's laws by making the majority of the
massive campaign contributions that go to
favored politicians; their lobbyists are
permanent fixtures in legislatures.
—BEN H. BAGDIKIAN

Sometimes, in exceptional and reflective natures,
the distraction and the triviality of life, even of healthy life,
become oppressive, and a sympathy with the necessarily
excluded goods pursued by contrary moralities
renders one's own morality pathetic and almost remorseful.
Then mystical aspiration, renouncing everything
for the love of everything, may overflow the mind.
Victory or prosperity for one's own people or
one's own civilization will no longer seem an ultimate
or unqualified good.
—GEORGE SANTAYANA

War, what other thing is it than a common
manslaughter of many men together,
and a robbery, the which, the farther it sprawleth abroad,
the more mischievous it is?
—ERASMUS

POSTSCRIPT:

DO WE LIVE IN AN GLOBAL EMPIRE IN THE MAKING, an American-led, corporate empire? Is *Corporatism* is its ideology and its source of power? Is globalization the necessary means to achieve its full fruition? technology its sword and shield? These questions, or remarks, will never be believed by most, never read nor heard by most, certainly not Americans. This too may be why this "global regime of economic interdependence," as it is now properly called, the perceived empire of international governing institutions and its perceived American-led Roman legions, will likely achieve its main goals over the next few decades. War is always seen as a necessary means to many of the ends desired by the elite; always have been, and nothing has changed human nature for the better; nothing has brought about a "kinder, gentler nation" here at home in America; nothing suggests other national leaders will decide to not join the ranks of Empire rather than be left out altogether (Mr. Tony Blair a fine example). To quote at length one of America's most respected international relations experts:

> Specific economic concerns and contentions will then merely transmit the conditioning-to-causal impact of the attendant frictions to either more fundamental or operationally more influential factors, and may transmute combative predispositions into politically significant acts liable to precipitate military conflict. In either case, whether the concern is primarily domestic (internal stability assured by security of ruling-class tenure, itself based on viable employment and consumption levels for the lower classes) or external ("national" security based on assured material capability), it will be viewed as reflecting basic needs. (George Liska, *The Ways of Power*, 1990, Basil Blackwell, pg.322)

These two specific sources of the decision to go to war as opposed to risking a United Nations peace settlement, which I have argued was the lawful thing Mr. Bush should have pursued all along, was not pursed because it may have garnered true and fair elections in Afghanistan. (The western states still could have gone after Osama bin Laden as we did Panama's Manuel Noriega, Serbia's Slobodan Milosevic and the terrorist known as "the Jackal," using other means.) But true and fair elections in Afghanistan, which may have not removed the Taliban from power at all, but instead assured them a majority vote from their people, was something Mr. Bush and Mr. Blair could not tolerate. The Taliban are never going to be allowed a seat at the UN table of the new interim governing body. Which will go some to prolong a guerrilla war in Afghanistan alone for years to come. Also, lawful elections under the aegis of the United Nations with the Taliban winning would not achieve the "other" objectives of securing the pipeline through Afghanistan and isolating to a greater degree Russia and Iran from the world's oil markets. (This is now and has been, the declared "strategic energy policy" position of both the Clinton and Bush administrations all along) Liska's next remarks on war bear quoting again in addition to the above:

> The needs can, and often will, bear on access to foreign trade (markets) and primary strategic commodities (raw materials), not least when revenues from foreign markets outstrip the efficacy of domestic fiscal and monetary mechanisms in averting economic depression—and so long as the "strategic" raw materials ranging from timber for naval stores in the seventeenth and eighteenth through coal and iron in the nineteenth to petroleum and a range of rare metals in the twentieth century are essential for the naval or military and the industrial trade posture of a power. (Ibid.)

Here is the argument in the clearest of terms. There can be no contestation if one has any grasp of the economic downturn in America (lower class unemployment and consumption) coupled with Alan Greenspans's Federal Reserve's improbable task of using "domestic fiscal and monetary mechanisms in averting economic depression." Interest rates are already hovering around the enigmatic zero and the economy is collapsing rapidly, job losses are going to run in the several millions by the end of 2002—unless, so the argument goes, Mr. Bush does something—which is what he is doing. (He will fail in this latter regard.) Add to this, the summer, 2001 California energy crisis tied to America's placing United States "energy security" as its number one "long term" strategic policy goal and the picture could not be more in focus. These "linkages," as they are referred to in IR language, are fundamental to any understanding, although the common man almost always simply believes whatever "his leader" tells him. There is no excuse though for anyone posing as a journalist or reporter to be quite as common.

> Such linkages suggest that, across their range, the interplay between the requirements of "power" and "plenty"—of "defense" and "opulence" — within the determinants of crisis-type upheavals is as constant as it is circular. (Ibid.)

Liska then defines this perception of this American-led Global *Corporatism* in a way he probably may not have noticed at the time: "The comparative primacy of the 'political' and the 'economic' goals and stakes is not to be decisively clarified by the fact that sea powers tend to be more overtly concerned with plenty and continental states with power, and the mercantilist doctrines stress state power while liberal-capitalist dogma emphasizes societal plenty." (Ibid., pg. 323). The American-led empire with its ideological foundation of *Corporatism* is both a sea power and a continental power, it is both "overtly concerned with plenty" and with "power," is now both "mercantilist" [state power] and "liberal-[monopoly] capitalist," which "emphasizes societal plenty."

Power and plenty. The world is never really all that different in the end, century after century, and Americans are just some, in a long line of individuals, which shall find they have thrown away liberty for security, opulence for a short-lived selfishness, though with a despicable grandiosity, an arrogance, about who they really are on the true scale of things. The American people will be the big losers, second only to the Afghans, in the long run, as this newest form of Empire, being global as all empires strive to be, is multinational corporate-led; and these corporations are no more American than a British, French, German or Japanese; no less internationalist than a Russian firm or Chinese.

Bush's State of the Union

It was argued in the British *Guardian* newspaper on January 31st, 2002, immediately after President Bush's State of the Union address, that "Mr. Bush, in his black-and-white way, has clearly convinced himself that in what he calls the 'decisive decade in the history of liberty,' his duty, mission and calling is to direct the triumph of good over evil at home and abroad. 'America will lead by defending liberty and justice because they are right and true and unchanging for all people everywhere,' he declared."

When an editorial this clear admits of one's own country's leaders as delusional and very dangerous, and that country is an ally rather than enemy, one must give pause. Is the *Guardian* going too far, or is Bush? On the premise that Mr. Bush was to lead, presumably everyone in the world now, Imperially?, by defending liberty and justice "everywhere" the *Guardian* added this:

> This is a premise fortified by falsehoods and underpinned by a delusion. The principal falsehood is that the policies Mr. Bush now advocates are dictated by an ongoing terrorist menace. They are not. Primarily they are the products of conservative Republicanism, set dangerously loose in September 11's aftermath.

It is fairly irrelevant that Mr. Bush spoke so much on the American economy in this address, as I have written too often to date, the US president has no such power over the domestic economy. This is smoke and mirrors, and jobs will continue to be lost, bankruptcies will escalate and the economy will face its recession, if not worse. It is a *business recession*, not something the mall-fodder (consumers) can buy their way out of. For lack of a greater analysis here I suggest the reader seek-out my Strategic and Economic Analysis *Special Report, 2001* on my website for what this entails. But it is what Mr. Bush said regarding his, war on all fronts rhetoric, that is important. The *Guardian* states it well:

September 11 undoubtedly bound the American nation. But it did not blind it. Sooner or later, Mr. Bush, self-styled universal soldier for truth, will have to stop pretending that tragedy gave him a free hand to remake America and the world to fit his simplistic, narrow vision - or risk having voters and US allies end the pretence for him. For this is the delusion under which he labors. And a very dangerous delusion it is too. (*George Bush's delusion: Tragedy does not give America a free hand*, Leader, Thursday January 31, 2002, "http://www.guardian.co.uk")

Indeed, it is a very dangerous delusion Mr. Bush labors under. It is my hope, in a small way, that this volume goes some to "end the pretence for him." As an American, but as Nietzsche might have added, really "a good European," so as to distance myself, as he did from the German people, from my countrymen's virulent xenophobia and ultra-nationalism, which has yet to die a proper death in the hinterlands, I must, therefore, consider the possibility we may be approaching an age where Empire is what these Volk want to see evolve. That this is no simple perception of "others" out there, but becoming too verifiable and empirical, is then, the real problem. There is only one way this latest evolution to empire can gain ground. There has to be, delusional maybe, external enemies, seen as large enough, frightening enough to the mass of men, that in its name Mr. Bush can reign. These frightening "evil doers" as Mr. Bush likes to call them, certainly are present, in much smaller numbers though, throughout the world. It is American *Corporatism* and our global reach which has, in some greater or lesser degree, helped to create them; it is our very own American-led western corporate structure, perceived by billions of people the world over, as being that Empire. It certainly is not envy on these people's part; this argument betrays the very arrogance and alienated narrow point of view which so many throughout the world detest in American tourists.

No, for Empire to succeed, for *Corporatism* as ideology, and it is an ideology, to win the future, there must be enemies, great enemies. They must be perceived as present in numbers sufficient enough to count, evil enough to instill fear and loathing in the common herd. History has shown us a most effective way to bind the mass, control the people, herd the herd.

Scapegoats: The Pomp and Ceremony

The Empire, as with all governing states, since the dawn of time, has always needed the "scapegoat" to keep its communities in order, obedient and fearful. OJ Simpson played the part well, although unwillingly like most; there will be many others. All this is great theatre to some, the cynical and indifferent. Osama bin Laden, and only less so, Mullah Omar of the Taliban, are today the most important, fabricated out of whole cloth, scapegoats for the United States' citizenry facing recession, job losses and a fear generated by a president setting out to generate precisely this level of fear. Scapegoating has been the rule not the exception throughout history. Often the aging king or careless prince would be scapegoated, targeted for execution, and not unusually with some level of pomp and ceremony, for whatever ills the community had suffered over the past years, leaving the idea that all would be different now that the failed king was replaced. In America, long having to endure the fact that we have no King or Queen, therefore a lack of true national *pomp and ceremony*, the masses seek its satisfying delusion elsewhere. America must have its periodic scapegoat.

Some thought those days were long gone. Has the practice been entirely eliminated in our more civilized cultures? One respected author thought not: "For when a nation becomes civilized, if it does not drop human sacrifices altogether, it at least selects as victims only such wretches as would be put to death at any rate. Thus the killing of a god may sometimes come to be confounded with the execution of a criminal." (Sir James G. Frazer, *The Golden Bough*, New York, Macmillan, 1958, pg. 667)

> ...[t]here is an intimate relationship of complicity between a community and its scapegoats. The community's continued existence requires scapegoats; while the scapegoat, whether consciously or not, continues to provoke the community through semiotic excess. Leaving aside the moral problem, the scapegoats most brilliant moment is at the time when this provocative nature culminates in execution by the community. (Masao Yamaguchi, *Towards the Poetics of the Scapegoat*, in *Violence and Truth: On the Work of Rene Girard*, Stanford University Press, 1988, pg. 188)

The scapegoat has not left us. The need to instill an unwarranted amount of fear in the citizenry is also not without precedent. One way to keep the scapegoats alive is with a constant influx of new ones over a longer period of time. Should Osama bin Laden not provide the scapegoat's execution, die a simple death of illness or disease (i.e. without Mr. Bush's desired pomp and ceremony, theatre that is), it will not only be the excitable Mr. Bush and the ever trenchant Mr. Blair who is disappointed. Americans wanted a public execution of the man whether he actually had anything to do with September 11th or not. Should he die a quiet death without American's need, lust for blood, another shall be named, and named again, and again, damned equally as well.

One certainly does not want to see this war go on and on, nor what Mr. Bush personally wants to see happen, but as I have stated in this volume throughout, you will not defeat a guerrilla army, especially a global one, without their specific grievances being addressed. By not recognizing any grievances from any quarter, Mr. Bush and Mr. Blair guarantees this protracted war against Empire. The guerrilla needs his war to be protracted. For one instance: If Osama bin Laden was involved with 9/11/01 and his alleged al Qaida network, Mr. Bush still ignores the primary grievance of bin Laden and his network, as well as now, the Saudi regime and its people. By not getting American soldiers out of the two Holy Lands. Mr. Bush feels he cannot budge to any request, not even one from a beleaguered ally. Right before this book went to press I found I had to include this below from that indomitable spirit of Great Britain, Robert Fisk:

> [The] Washington Post, no less, has reported that the Saudis want the Americans to quit and the commentators are silent. Not so US Secretary of State Colin Powell. For him, the American presence in Saudi Arabia may last until the world turns into "the kind of place we dreamed of." American troops in Saudi are not only a deterrent to Saddam, he said at the weekend, they are a "symbol" of American influence. Could al-Qa'ida have a more potent reason for continued resistance? The "occupation" of Saudi Arabia remains the cornerstone of Osama bin Laden's battle against the United States, the original raison d'être of his merciless struggle against America. And here is Mr. Powell proving, in effect, that Washington had ulterior motives for sending him into the Gulf. When he added that "we shouldn't impose ourselves on the Government beyond the absolute minimum requirement that we have," the phrase "beyond the absolute minimum" tells it all. The United States will decide how long it stays in Saudi Arabia? not the Saudis; which is exactly what Mr. bin Laden has been saying all along.
>
> (Robert Fisk: **Congratulations, America. You have made bin Laden a happy man** *'We are turning ourselves into the kind of deceitful, ruthless people whom bin Laden imagines us to be.'* The Independent, UK, 22 January 2002)

The kind of place we dreamed of? Whose dream Mr. Powell? Whose "symbol" symbolizing what?

There is only way to assume greater power centralized into fewer and fewer hands; centralizing the federal government in the United States has been in process for over fifty years and everybody knows. The greater centralization of federal power into the hands of the White House is being furthered each month with each new set of executive orders emanating from the mansion in D.C.; fear is the only way it can be achieved. The scapegoating does the job well. Mr. Bush has passed some twenty new orders, decrees, imperial edicts is more proper (many of them on December 28th, 2001, a very busy day), redefining the "Succession of the Heads of the Department of State, Defense, Labor, Treasury, etc.," to assure only his own appointed personnel remain with power should resignation or death take his anointed. Mr. Bush is well-known for his almost pathological need for "loyalty." The American continuity of government paradigm has been set out for years in emergency decrees and other past executive orders, but Mr. Bush must be sure of *who* it is that retains "official" bureaucratic power if Empire is to thrive; therefore, that it is his own hand-picked people and not some "other's." To make war on the world without asking the United States Congress for its opinion (let alone the United States Constitutional mandate of [only] Congress to declare war itself) and to turn his presidential face against the War Powers Act of 1973, Mr. Bush passes yet another Executive Order:

> Sec. 2. Section 7 of Executive Order 13223 is deleted and revised to read as follows: "Based upon my determination under 10 U.S.C. 2201(c) that it is necessary to increase (subject to limits imposed by law) the number of members of the armed forces on active duty for the Department of Defense beyond the number for which funds are provided in the appropriation Act for the Department of Defense, which, by virtue of 14 U.S.C. 652, applies to the Department of Transportation with respect to the Coast Guard, the Secretary of Defense and the Secretary of Transportation may provide for the cost of such additional members under their respective jurisdictions as an excepted expense under section 11(a) of title 41, United States Code." GEORGE W. BUSH, THE WHITE HOUSE, January 16, 2002.

The only power the United States Congress had retained under the War Powers Act of 1973, was the power of the purse. If the President did not remove troops out of hostilities in contravention of Congressional oversight, the Congress simply would deny funds to the Pentagon to proceed, and whatever other Departments might be affected. Mr. Bush has, once again, shown his princely worthiness of Machiavellian skills.

The empire is coming to fruition, its outlines becoming clearer, the flesh beginning to show on the skeletal beginnings of five decades of effort on the part of so many global elite, tireless in their quest. Only a fool would call this a *theory* at this point in history, let alone a conspiracy. And I do not call it such a thing nor have I ever believed such nonsense. What I see is what has always been, always will be, always a part of human nature; greedy men clutching for power, grasping for plenty. I see just what is. "To say of what is that it is, or say of what is not that it is not, is true." (Aristotle, *Metaphysics*, translation, Christopher Kirwan, Oxford, OUP, 7.27., 1993)

There are too many, very many indeed, who see in Mr. Bush's further centralization of power in the executive branch as a good sign. Mr. Cheney on CNN during January, claimed that for thirty years the power of the presidency had been diluted to almost nothing, claiming in a huff of staggering arrogance that those days were over, and Mr. Bush and he, were "now the White House" and "they were going to return the power to that office." Of course this is a complete falsification of the truth as anyone who has followed the executive orders and process of centralization of power during those same thirty years; the White House has centralized more power to itself than at any time in the country's history. That is to say, Mr. Cheney lied. Mr. Bush easily abrogates international treaties (since 1963) on anti-ballistic missiles, something which has never happened before, still under the pretext of a threat based wholly upon September 11. The *Guardian's* Matthew Engel in Washington, Friday, December 14, 2001, notes this with this hopeful caveat: "Perhaps Europe will get the message from this: the administration did not change fundamentally on September 11. Karl Rove, the president's political strategist, said it out loud this week: 'He is the same president now as he was before. What you see is what you get.'" What is this school-yard bully's language?

Yet there are those who see in this as being a process they can live with, and almost always it is Republican partymen which feel this way, because Mr. Bush does not represent their personal enemies, and almost always it is Democratic partymen like Bill Clinton who are those perceived enemies. Those who see, no feel, this way, are utterly mistaken. This power centralized will not remain in Mr. Bush's hands alone; it will not be returned to the people after some six year time limit (it never does); the power will grow exponentially instead, year after year. Only to one day be placed in the hands of someone much more power-mad than even Mr. Bush seems to be. To those that fit the above Republican mold, this someone which may assume the mantle of President some years from now, may be your enemy in the end. But in the end, all power centralized and usurped, under any pretense, will always fall into the hands of the enemies of freedom and liberty, the enemy of all people, Republican conservatives and liberal Democrats alike. On things that matter, there is little difference between the two factions.

Those of us who fail to fit so easily and simply (as in simpleton-like) in these two categories, always find both factions our enemies as they are factions; club opinion is always and everywhere the enemy of liberty. Though to mention this one shall certainly be labeled the all-inclusive invective, the anathema hurled by the dutiful followers of privilege, the epithet hosed at those who would speak of such potentialities: One shall be, in a stroke of a pen, the blast from the mouth of the "recognized" talking-heads, the charge (like a felony indictment) leveled..."conspiracy theorist."

Indeed, I would argue that those who would charge the likes of us out here who see the world clearly, as seeing a conspiracy and therefore way off base (which we would then be), are the very "types" (archetypically) which truly wish to join the ranks of the elite; they are the ones who desire nothing less than more power personally; the ones who want a seat at the table of the elite we all know full well exist openly, visibly and with little need these days to ever conspire. These mainstream media critics of independent social critics are the ones who lust more than most for opulence and plenty; these critics of critics know what they are doing when they charge the able, honest and well-read with being conspiracy theorists; charged as being anti-American; charge the clear-eyed with being naive and misinformed; charge the wide-awake with being wrong-headed, or worse. "The person who claims to know the truth and is certain that others with an opposing view are the captives of illusion is a potential despot." (Eugene Goodheart, *the Reign of Ideology*,

Columbia University Press, 1993, p.19) They are the dissemblers, it is they who are the artful prevaricators, they are the incite-full against the insightful. It may be that it is "they" who charge the "other" with being a conspiracy theorist because it is they who would like nothing better than be offered the bribe; nothing more than the gross advantage from birth; nothing less than the raw power from selling out; the grant of unearned privilege. I may be as uncertain as ever about what I have proposed here in this volume. I only ask that it be given a hearing, maybe asking too much that it be a *fair* one.

I take my lead from Nietzsche as I here speak out. "One may speak with the greatest appropriateness, and yet so that everybody cries out to the contrary,— that is to say, when one does not speak to everyone." (Human, All-Too-Human, aphorism 295) I take my lead from Nietzsche and place a question mark after my firmest convictions, throw them out, kick them off the cliff, when facts bear witness to their obsolescence. I understand convictions are often the nemesis to reasoned thought and discourse, inclusive of my own. *I take my lead from Nietzsche, and therefore place a question mark after my own name as well.* Dissidence is the meaning of America if anything is. I fear I must dissent.

Now, it is a curious assumption of religious moralists that their precepts
would never be adopted unless people were persuaded
by external evidence that God had positively established them.
Were it not for divine injunction and threats everyone
would like nothing better than to kill and to steal and to bear false witness. Un-
doubtedly, there is little integration or integrity
in most men's characters;
there is only habit and a plodding limitation in life and mind;
and if social pressure were not added to lack of opportunity
disorderly lives would be more common than they are.
But decency, at least verbal decency or conventionality,
establishes itself automatically in human society;
a relative decency of course, according to the age
and breeding of the circle concerned,
but a decency very sharply enforced,
since nothing is more intolerant than club opinion.
These spontaneous and local codes coerce the individual,
but they claim no divine authority.
On the contrary, one of the most powerful means
of exercising moral pressure is to impose a very special code,
avowedly that of only one class or country or profession.
The contrast to legal and public standards is often a chief part
of this private allegiance;
the excitement and danger of being lawless
are merged in a sense of superior privilege and enlightenment.
Pride, vanity, esprit de corps, secret oaths,
backed by the intense vigilance and quick vengeance
proper to secret societies,
can work up the special conscience and zeal of party men
almost to madness;
and the isolation of the conspirator
from the rest of society binds him the closer to his gang.

—BY GEORGE SANTAYANA
DOMINATIONS AND POWERS: REFLECTIONS
ON LIBERTY, SOCIETY, AND GOVERNMENT

APPENDIX ONE

The Folklore of Corporatism
The Coronation of George

Typically nowadays a prince, while young
is rapidly corrupted by vicious counselors who instill
in him their own lust for power, regardless
of the hideous damage and suffering
inevitably inflicted upon the common people
when their schemes are executed.
—ROBERT P. ADAMS ON SIR THOMAS MORE

But you will say, that the rights of sovereigns must be maintained.
it is not for me to speak unadvisedly about the acts of princes.
I only know this, that summum jus,—*extreme right, is often*
summa injuria,—*extreme wrong;*
there are princes who first decide what they want, and then
look out for a title with which to cloak their proceedings.
—ERASMUS

THE CORONATION OF GEORGE

AS SOCIETY BEGINS THE SLOW AND INEVITABLE PROCESS of replacing its older religions with a new faith, regardless of its makeup, a period ensues whereby the existing terminology no longer explains properly the old nor the new. Old terms remain in use even while they are no longer descriptive of reality. Yet during the transition period, when the new faith begins to displace, for many people, the older beliefs and ceremonies, there is no word , no turn of a phrase, that explains precisely what is taking place: although many new words are being coined each year, they are words about the details, about this or that aspect, but remain without a foundational usage overall. A new language is needed.

It is here that is troubling for the analyst, whether using a descriptive or analytical approach. The analytical philosopher too cannot help but use old terms redefined or metaphors in place of clearer prose. Nevertheless, to see the clear outlines of the new regime, whether political, economic, or religious, each is in a sense a new faith. Most political factions and parties are nothing more than surrogate religious beliefs overlaying issues that replace lost hopes and failed faiths in other areas of society. Even atheism for many of its adherents is but a replacement for the mystical yearning for personal satisfaction, spiritual renewal, or as rejection of some religious bases of cultural aspects the individual has need of without the old tradition.

Thus the analyst finds that to describe the present coming regime, called many things (Global Regime, global regime of economic interdependence, The New World Order, etc.), must simultaneously depict the economic aspect of what it is, the political power that brings it to fruition, and the glue that holds it together. It is the glue that has the religious trappings and terminology describing the other two. That it can be described as a new religion is the same reason all "isms" can: fascism, communism, racism, feminism, all partymen are of a religious faith; Republicans and Democrats as much as Mensheviks and Bolsheviks. The new global religion which has taken hold of the American psyche is *Corporatism*. The clearest manifestation of its pure faith is materialism. As with most religions the thing it is called and thing it acts upon are synonymous and interchangeable. Corporatism is the name we give to the regime of materialism that people have replaced their old faiths with. But other than this simple deduction, the analyst is left with little descriptive terminology to further describe the how, the who and the what it will encompass, what it will mean when in full bloom. The term Globalization or Globalism has been addressed by this author elsewhere and for many years.

Faithful Terminology

I have utilized the religious terms of Christianity and Catholicism, Priests and a Pope, Jesuits and missionaries because of two overriding reasons: first, it is Christianity that is being replaced, even in Christian churches, with materialism and Catholicism is the only true Global Christian church whose metaphorical symbolism fits the Corporatism replacing it; secondly, Corporatism is replacing Buddhism, Judaism and virtually every faith in America, first, but ultimately the world over.

One hopes the Catholic reader will understand there is no disparagement directed at Catholicism nor any religion. Any insult in the use of these metaphors should be placed squarely upon the heads of government and corporations that are taking on the aspect of preaching a gospel of greed and power as the *one best way*: a phrase utilized in engineering and technology similar to Taoism's *The Way*, or the path; a similarity not so coincidental as one might think at first. It is this faith in progress, proselytized by technology's prophets, designed by mystical engineers that make religious metaphors the only ones useful. It also helps a great deal that this new religion, Corporatism, is believed upon religiously by its adherents. One need only sit in on a Microsoft seminar and see the swooning Mass, Pope Gates opening and the message of salvation *preached*. Materialism took hold of the Mass well before Gates was chosen by the internal mechanism, very like the Bishops' vote, declaring him Pope. That the general population follow materialism as faith and greed as need can hardly be contested. LOTTO, and Stock Market speculation by the poorest segments of society has taken on the aura of tithing; tithing their way into the present heaven on earth of worldly goods and goodies.

My small consulting firm often receives more phone calls in a day (not clients) from missionaries of Corporatism, MCI, AT&T, and a host of others; you begin treating them the way one snarls at Jehovah Witnesses when they invade your privacy on a random Sunday. The last two that showed up while I was chopping wood for winter, not my favorite chore, I smiled and told them I was a Nietzschean and I killed God. Of course Nietzshe never said any such explicit thing, it was his character *The Madman* in *Zarathustra*. What he implied and later made specific (through characters in his works) was that it was Christians that had killed God by their hypocrisy and vice.

To understand a future, a possible cultural problematic, one must use deductive reasoning, know something about men (knowing about women will not help, they're finding the *male* in themselves) and have had some significant life experience, diversified enough to draw upon many ideas and hopefully some remnant of wisdom. Even then, it remains just your one best guess. In taking this essay seriously I am trying as much to create a picture in one's mind. Paint a picture. A metaphorical parody. One must understand first what the regime is before you can begin to understand what may happen. Within this context is what I do think that little sprout of a Bush will attempt to achieve once crowned emperor (small "e") and take the world and America where the big Bush had intended, before being unseated single-handedly by that little up-start Lord Perot; (this will not change if Bush's ox is Gore'd). Maybe the reader will gain some insight into at least one possible future based upon one analyst's insight.

The Folklore of Corporatism

Every new religion must displace the old traditions. It has been pointed out often just how tenaciously the obsolete Gods thrash about in an effort to survive. The old never passes over to the new without a fight. The fight is already over and Corporatism has won the day; it has not as yet won the minds of the old believers and old priests and so confusion reigns. In part, the old believers cannot understand the new folklore of Corporatism because they attempt to understand it using the old words, the old language and the old definitions.

To understand the new Priesthood requires understanding how they have redefined the terms of the debate. President George Bush Jr. will have as his main responsibility pressing forward the new language and semantics, guided by the best scribes the state can summon to service, to explain to a bewildered herd that what is new is not new but the same old they have always known. His primary focus will be to adapt old institutions and ancient rituals to the new; diffuse further state power over to international governance and its international bodies; no differently than when the Pope, of ancient times, over-laying pagan religious practices with Catholicism's new rites, while the old was still in practice by the converted. Bush II, the little sprout, as father and emperor must use old words, old names, old dogmas to convince the stupefied faithful that the new paradigm is but the old dressed-up in less worn-out robes.

The people remain believers in free enterprise while free enterprise has been utterly decimated by regulatory agencies, confiscatory taxation and the managed centralizing economy now called our *mixed* economy. "Mixed" sounds better than "managed" so mixed is utilized to make comforting the transition to a non-free enterprise system. This does not imply anything like a socialist economy, the means of production remain in the hands of private for profit individuals; it is, though, at the same time not free to all, but only free for those with the right connections, fraternal and corporate, and thus not free at all.

Mergers and acquisitions, ongoing since the Reagan and Bush Sr. and Clinton era, continue apace with no end in sight. It shall be never-ending. Media scribes in corporate employ betray their ignorance each time they "see the end in sight," with mergers a thing of the recent past. There shall never be an end to the centralization of power and corporate combinations. In fact, the process of downsizing and consolidation has not even begun compared to what is yet to come.

It is this shift, a very real paradigm shift, that has been growing clearer since 1979 that the little sprout, President George Bush Jr. must put back on track, keep on track, and make up for lost time regarding it. Globalization is a process of altering the way the world does business. Altering the way people perceive it is as important to achieving it. If the masses think there is to be great and sudden change, they shall surely panic. Although the change is as rapid as any in the past, accelerating with a different feel, but accelerating without question, the message must smooth and sooth every fear, every discontent. Bush Jr. couldn't be more perfect for the job. Nobody will hear the deceptions, the deceits, the falsehoods. They cannot hear over their own chatter, their own epic poems, their own voices singing praise unto themselves.

What will the agenda be during the next eight years Bush and Company (literally speaking, "Inc.") reign over the transition to Global Corporatism, that will surely succeed? There is little question that the agenda will be that same plan, structure, drive, pressed forward that Bush Sr., the mighty Oak, outlined and successfully guided world-wide for twelve years. The direction has never changed: Clinton signed off on each significant Bush (Reagan) policy and proposal once finalized. The process under Clinton was slowed to a crawl, but NAFTA and GATT with the finalized World Trade Organization (WTO) were Bush's corporate dreams. There shall be a new Multilateral Agreement on Investments, whether through the OECD (which failed by a slim margin due to France's and Germany's rejection of two fundamental areas, rapid transit and cultural) or the World Bank, or the International Monetary Fund. Corporate Governance may bring it about with little legislative effort involved. But pass it will, within three years of Bush Jr. seizing the reigns of power. Fast-track legislation must pass immediately (Clinton lost that only because Republicans voted against their own wishes to foil a Democrat in office); both aisles shall line up when the new call comes from on high.

Also the two latter agencies along with the Export-Import Bank will be strengthened and expanded. China will be granted Most Favored Nation Status (a Bush deal going back to the days when Bush was Ambassadorial Liaison to China and Ambassador to the U.N.). China's application and accession into the WTO will be accepted within that three year period. These are must-do's for the new regime and the little sprout will press them vigorously. The timing less important than the deed.

What we are also going to see is a loosening of the Justice Department's criteria under anti-trust laws allowing an even further monopolization of key industries. Especially the technology field will become more centralized, monopolies more acceptable and little deference paid to smaller start-up firm's ability to compete. Competition is out. The redefined canonical term *competition* shall still be used religiously, as pointed out above, so the confused masses can still mouth the phrase *"but we're free,"* as competition shall exist less as a reality than as something managed from above between the giant monopolies. This was always implied in *managed competition* for both the general economy (national governance) and industrial sectors of importance globally (corporate governance). Thus we shall see the Nietzschean Eternal Return of a *National Industrial Policy* chaired by Corporatism's best and brightest lights.

It is here that serfs, peasants and most experts miss entirely. The government within government, as represented by the corporate structure is no different than the government of the public sector. The private sector, the you and I as subject and labor, taxpayer and subsidy recipient, have no government representing our interests. The people no longer have an *America* that represents them versus the old view of democratic governance, nor an aristocracy nor monarchy. The nation in *nation*-state no longer exists. Nation has always meant that body of people that formed the State to represent them and protect their interests and unalienable rights. For thirty years that entity has not existed except in language; it exists in the flock's mind as faith and the sacred; it has not existed in the guarantees outlined in the United States Constitution since the seventies. The nation (people) no longer have representation but obligations; they have areas to obey and conform; they have the police power ever watchful over their continued obedience; they have duties to the State, but no liberties, no rights whatsoever. What remains of Rights is the light heartedness of fashion and dress, T.V. and the Internet, personal proclivities that do not matter like sexual preferences and abortion rights. But in all things that matter they have no rights, only obligations.

So whose rights and liberties does the State, then, represent? For whom do the rulers (Bush, et al) govern? Whose rights and privileges, freedom and whose free-*enterprise* is protected and promoted? We have all heard the term, but think it means something from our past catechism, our past faith and ceremonies. In the *corporate*-state, the *corporate* has replaced the *people* in a *nation*-state configuration that has no relationship to the past terminology still in use today. The new religion of Corporatism shall use the terms "Nation," "free enterprise" and "free-market" as long as the *people* (the nation) remain believers in the old faith. The old taboos will hold. The old sermons retold. The old priests from the left and right shall supply the dialectic. But they shall supply apologia for dead gods and dead faiths.

Apologia Corporatus

Here is the argument, still, from the *progressive left* opposing the further power of the corporations now cleverly called *transnational corporations*: We, the people (meaning the progressive vanguard only) must oppose the ever growing belief in the hidden hand of Adam Smith; everywhere we see the growth of free enterprise and laissez faire globalizing the planet, leaving ever more poor with the entrepreneurial rich the only winners.

Per Contra

From the conservative right opposing the socialist domination of government policies, we hear this: We, the country (meaning the elite think-tank experts only), must continue aiding the developing countries in adopting our standards of free markets and free enterprise as the only remaining ideology that works; it has proven itself with the collapse of socialism as evidence that our American system of *laissez faire* is the only viable alternative to centralized collective economies. Socialism is dead, free enterprise has won.

Laissez faire is either the global threat and socialism remains untried; or socialism is evil versus *laissez faire* salvation. Democracy is but a footnote to both.

Preaching the Faith

The false arguments emanating from both sides are false because they are the old religions which are dead; their gods are dead but the tribal priests don't know it yet. As catechism and myth, the one side hurls anathemas at the other while their congregations faithfully pray for a favorable outcome. That neither faith can see is no surprise to the new religious leaders of Corporatism and the corporate-state. It is the new corporate religious leaders that guide these false arguments so the new faith can have the time necessary to convert its own flock, and that of the others as well.

The priests of the new religion (corporate CEOs) and their Jesuits (politicians) send their missionaries (economists and business diplomats) forth to convert new lands and new peoples to the new faith with sacred texts authored by scribes (lawyers). There is but one God — Efficiency; there is but one true manna from heaven — Money; there is but one enemy representing Evil — Competition; one Satan — Adam Smith is that dead Satan. Isis burial rites must wait though, as he has proven useful to the new faith and priests of Corporatism, as summoning up his name is akin to drawing a circle and summoning a spirit. Corporatism does not care that the one belief sees Adam as the way, the glory and the light, while the other faith, Aleister Crowley-like, believe they summon Adam the evil and the darkness. Corporatism's priests know he is long dead and has no effect on the outcome as both religions have been replaced already.

The new religion has as ideology and faith all the above, but the practical side is important. The ideology has as purpose nothing short of replacing both socialism and free-enterprise through usurpation of all that is useful in both; creating a synthesis between the competitive and the centralized; between the too-free of the one, and the un-free of the other. *Corporazione*, is *Neither Left nor Right* as argued by Zeev Sternhell (Hebrew University of Jerusalem). The actual and important means of production remain in the hands of only the Chosen that understand the synthesis between the one and the other. Other industries, unimportant in both need and significance globally and heavily burdened by taxation, regulation and lack of credit, fall away like so many maple leaves burdened by a winter out of season; tinder, under the managed competition by the Church of Monopoly, it is Corporatism's *Inquisition*.

Vatican II - Propaganda Two

Corporatism's Canon needs the progressive left to incessantly argue, anathematize the free-marketer, argue competition and *laissez faire* is the root of all evil. *Corporatism* needs the conservative right to incessantly argue in favor of it, anathematize the socialists, argue socialism is the root of all evil. All the while Corporatism goes its way destroying both socialism and free enterprise wherever it plants its faith. It conquers foreign lands and converts the heathen; converting pagan chiefs and witch-doctors is as easy as ever: bring bells and whistles, bobbles and trinkets, guns to help them kill off each other's best warriors, blankets to keep them warm and whiskey to keep them soft.

Managed competition eliminates real competition for a virtual competition that is managed by the corporate Priests working closely with each other's scribes and theologians (boards of directors) and the Jesuit priesthood of State governance. That any one individual often has worn both robes makes the progress that much easier. That they are never interfered with by the older religious factions makes the going smooth. Those of the older dead faiths are not part of any planning, prospectus, nor even heard from within the hallowed ground of the corporate sanctum sanctorum. They occasionally receive invitations to Corporatism's elaborate ceremonies to be entertained and allowed to entertain the hope that they still matter. They may clink a goblet with a new priest; give a sermon to the proper faithful who are humorously tickled to see these remnants still vigorous with renewed zealotry; write new books proclaiming to the new priesthood their message of hope; tongue tied to find their enemies in the congregation along with their own flock. None the wiser.

The easiest way to manipulate the Left-over older faithful is to invite them to such ceremonial functions and give them a place at the table. Flush with themselves and intoxicated with the wine of self-importance, they are slowly absorbed into the new faith piecemeal. Soon their sacred institutions begin to crumble. The progressive left's listener sponsored radio stations first merge programming with National Public Radio (NPR: Government Corporate Radio), then see no reason not to take Corporatism's charity, since their congregation drifted away to look for their failing faiths elsewhere. Soon the cathedrals and churches of the old faith crumble and are sold off like so much real estate to the corporate barons of the new religion. None the wiser.

The other older Right-eous are even more easily converted to the new faith. Also invited to attend Priestly religious ceremonies and allowed to drink from the same goblets, they too are asked to give a little recital for their betters; they too believe they are there to enlighten this flock. But many of these older faithful actually believe more stubbornly because unlike their lazier smarmy left-over counterparts they have owned their own business or worked in the real world, looking down their conservative noses at the motley tribal preachers from the left. They can be as easily converted to the new faith though, which shall crush their own, by simply placing them on the board of directors, without portfolio, of one of the great industrial empires which symbolize the monopolist's mythos. With their new found revelation and a substantial flow of manna, seemingly from nowhere, yet believing they *earned it* just as before through their entrepreneurial skills, they slowly soften their vitriolic vituperate, admonishing less, conforming more. In any case, as a past believer in *laissez faire*, it was always implied as business maxim and creed: *compromise is good business.* This symbolic ceremony to monopoly mythos, eliminating *laissez faire*, is very good business indeed.

The New Emperor

The overview above, defining the new religion and noting the passing of the older faiths, was necessary to understanding what emperor little sprout will adhere to as principle and law. What will he allow to pass unnoticed and what willful lie need he pontificate upon to the Mass so as to maintain their illusions and delusions? In short what can we likely expect from this Sun of Bush? Clearly nobody believes him to be his own man. He has never owned a real business, successful and failures alike, that were his — made by him — his own initiative. This is no self-made man; a Bush made Bush. The little sprout and friends of Bush made the sprouting shrublet into the millionaire we see strutting Princely across the stage of history. Every time the little sprout got into trouble one of Bush's close allies baled him out; not unlike allies baled Bush out of the Persian Gulf maneuvers financially, as though the entire effort had more to do with Bush & Co.'s corporate hegemony over the Middle East than nation-state arguments. In fact, the little sprout and Bush's rolodex are but one and the same.

Throughout the past it's been the same,
In this, all's in accord;
Emperor' sons, they stake their claim;
Country Boss and tyrant Lord.

And life goes on, with Emperor's Own,
Ruling all that's known.
Emperor's Own, on Father's throne.
His shadow not his Own.
(Human All-Too-Human, Hulet, 1999)

The First Blow to History

The Middle East may have been the first blow delivered by the new religion, the corporate faith, as the country seemed ever ready to persecute the foreign heathen with no better understanding than the crusaders of the past. It marked the beginning of the fall. An Inquisition. The fall, as in Adam (without the rib removed); America's fall from faith, marked at the time by just how little the peasants cared that Bush Sr. prosecuted a crusade against an

Islamic Persian horde while his little sprout, having received loans and investments from the nursery's friends, was on the board of directors of Harken Oil, with drilling rights off the coast of Bahrain, an ally that tithed substantially for both efforts. That the deal off-shore made little sense (to the sprout's firm) since it had no capability to drill off-shore, this received no notice; that Daddy's firm Zapata Oil did, which no thinking agnostic could miss the point here, mattered less and the little sprout slipped away. Even after he sold Harken stock for a substantial gain shortly before Harken went belly-up, which did cause the Securities Exchange Commission to review the insider deal; nobody thought that the Bush Sr. appointed SEC Head would gather much steam against the little sprout, who once again slipped away. The point here is becoming clearer, the little sprout is the perfect corporatist man. No entrepreneur, no free enterpriser, no *laissez faire* past at work here, but the very opposite: no risk, guaranteed success even when failure is assured due to residual competition and his own incompetence. Corporatism intervenes to protect its own, everyone else is left to fail; one of the only times one hears Corporatism's Priests return to *laissez faire* reasoning is when other than Corporatism's elite fail, then bail-outs violate the faith's catechism that to fail is also the market at work, the hidden hand visible in other than our failures but always very hidden indeed when taxpayer's and some Priest's rolodex bail out yet another chosen's venture.

His baseball stadium deal is a study in corrupt financing of a private deal by taxpayers and crooked loans. Even the matching funds the "owners" were supposed to put "up-front" against the taxpayer's much larger stake, was never really put up at all, but paid out over precisely the years necessary to fulfill it with ticket sales (a one dollar private tax by Bush & Co. per seat!). No risk, no competition: use the peasant's (taxpayers) coin and loans from money changers you sit on the board of directors with. This is the heart of Corporatism, not *laissez faire* entrepreneurial competitiveness; there is no free market at work here. The only hand hidden is the one doing the taking.

> *monopoly raises prices (taxes)*
> *on consumers (subjects)*
> *while lowering costs (theirs)*
> *by eliminating competition.*

This understanding of the little sprout as Sun of Corporatism is needed so as to see with unclouded vision how he will handle his years in service to the Crown. Whose interest will he serve? We find his global corporate interests of interest.

We shall now call him just Bush as the little sprout has begun to flower.

Some Scenarios

Everybody knows that the present economic boom is the worst bubble in world history. Alan Greenspan, the current Fed Chairman, is the real author of the false boom and the absurd valuations of the largest corporation's stock

(Microsoft the most obvious over-valuation) by manipulating interest rates downward and keeping wages in check by threatening a rate increase; this, Priest Greenspan calls wage inflation. The Fed no longer fights inflation as indicated by the increase in the money supply (inflation) by monitoring M1 and M2 indicators (a thing of past dogma) but by wage inflation (oxymoronic term) as indicator. Whenever wages trend upward, indicating labor is beginning to reap the benefits of the up-turn in the economy, the Fed raises interest rates to throw just enough workers out of work so as to keep wages down. In whose interest? Corporatism of course. Unemployment figures can serve the same precedent. Too many people working, full employment? This is a bad thing and a correction is needed, more unemployed that is, so workers do not begin demanding higher wages nor being offered them as well because of a shortage of workers (they are all laboring to pay the annual levies in taxes and prices which are the corporate tax).

Simultaneously, the Fed, under Lord Greenspan has orchestrated the largest increase in the money supply (inflation) in the nation's history. This, in part, coupled with foreign investors and institutional investment, is the vapor of the bubble; the stock market could climb to 10,000 before the year 2001. The threatened and predictable crash that could come from such excessive speculation is well understood on Wall Street and any thinking agnostic feels some little jitters about the whole thing. But knowing there is no hidden hand, no market driven forces at work here can both alleviate the fear and go some distance towards understanding what may happen under Bush the Second's rule. First, let us assume the threat, the bubble, is real and Bush & Co. know this well. What might we expect from Bush 2001.

Again we must reiterate the fact that the current boom is manipulated by the Federal Reserve Open Market Committee under the visible hand of Lord Greenspan; there is no hidden hand. The priestly progressive left-overs do not know what they are talking about as usual. But Lord Greenspan cannot orchestrate a slow burn-off, a down-turn manipulated and controlled, a controlled burn as one might do to a nasty vine patch. His Lordship has orchestrated the boom and intends to be inscribed into history as the man that did so. Bush & Co. on the other visible hand, already has the best theologians in the State advising him about precisely this topic. Bush & Co. may not intend to await a calamity from outside — hurricane, floods, earthquakes and wars all can send the market downward as has already been the case: increased volatility with Asian financial crises the most obvious. Even the even-handed Greenspan knows this. Bush & Co. may replace Greenspan within the first year of his Administration. He will, if my assumptions hold about whose interests Bush really serves (& Co.), replace him with another Paul Adolph Volker. Unless Lord Greenspan is willing. His job will be to manipulate the stock market and economy back to some rationale: and do it by any means necessary. A slower down-turn, a controlled burn-off.

This may be a harsh outcome for many, as there will be more losers than winners where individuals are concerned. The largest corporations that make up the top forty industrials and the top seven high technology firms will suffer but little over the long term. They are so overvalued in many cases, the correction will gain for them in stability what the paper wealth loses. The individual investor, not anticipating the outcome, having no scribes on the inside, will be wiped out. Especially in the bloated tech industry, where the youthful ignorant peasants are pregnant with the lust for more. Should this scenario be played out Bush & Co. will have served Corporatism faithfully and well. The largest monopoly corporations operate world-wide under a global reach that has no end in sight. They will be less affected at home, this place you and I call home, that is, by what happens under such a controlled, contrived burn-off, than by the continued effort by Bush & regime to expand globally.

Another way Bush will serve the global corporate interests here at home is by increased defense spending, increased budgets for the CIA, NSA and all branches of government where taxpayer's subsidize these same corporations from the so-called private sector. This constant ongoing subsidization in behalf of the elite corporate monopolies insulates these Lords and Barons from the effects of policies that put to ruin the unimportant subjects of the realm. Remember, there is no private sector in the new religion, only the peasant sector. There is the temporal government of business, building roads, airplanes and communications networks (which keeps it all together) and there is the spiritual government that preaches the faith to the flock, and enforces the temporal government's dictates. But they are the same government: not two sides of the same coin: the same coin; that when you render unto Caesar you render through the one unto the other. There is no hidden hand, but two highly synchronized hands, one the right hand the other the left hand: the two visible hands of secular Gods. In whose interest do you tithe the greatest share of your levy but to Corporatism?

Bush & Co. shall therefore increase regulation of all businesses which the largest concerns can easily pay while they also lobby for greater regulations over themselves (this shows their alleged benign side by caring for the environment for instance, knowing smaller competitors cannot afford to take on the added expense). More wealth shifts to the largest corporate monopolists not through the hidden hand of *laissez faire* but through the managed competition and manipulated market of the mixed economy. A win-win for elite Corporatism. Bush & Co. will have to be seen to be in capitulation with environmentalists and progressive agendas masking real outcomes. In whose interest does he serve? Corporatism, not business interests; the latter would mean serving the general population's interest which includes the smaller independent large corporations. Bush & Co. serves the *corporate*-state, the *nation*-state is gone. That bible rewritten.

Bush & Co. shall increase taxation across the board to help the peasants thrown out of work by the down-turn. Increased funding for social security and welfare: this is the compassionate conservative at his best. Again, the largest corporate monopolies do not suffer lordly levies. They are often the recipient of manna's *receipts*. The tax laws drawn up at the same time rules of incorporation were redefined, at the same time the IRS was formed, at the same time of the founding of the Federal Reserve System (1913-1915), is seen by conspiracy theorists (often incipient excommunicated scribes) as significant for their wrong—headed beliefs. A not understood fact: that the taxes you and I and independent smaller large corporations pay, are not the same taxes, subsidies, grants, tax breaks and relief that the largest monopolies pay, or don't pay, but receive; that we are taxed entirely differently, and everybody ought to know this, is not well known at all. I could only wish I had been burdened, as the Lords of Oil were, with the 1979 Windfall Profit's Tax — a faux-tax — paid by the consumer (like the one dollar private tax per seat levied at Ranger Stadium by the little sprout) levied at the well-head and only increased revenue by reducing tax obligations, for the Barony.

There is but one way to solve the magisterial problematic the new scribes will outline for Bush & Co. regarding the Social Security pyramid scheme. How to get the youthful serfs to seek employment within Corporatism's new paradise? How doth one get the sons and daughters of working peasants to work well and pay their fair levy towards the retirement of each others' idle grandpeasants? The coin from the youth must be collected as booty and passed through as Treasure(y) to support the changing demographics of the future vacationers. To support the down-turn Bush & Co. one day shall re-institute the draft; selective service, though never selecting the priestly caste's chosen seed, shall give idle hands, always the devil's workshop, busy work; Corporatism's ventures in far-off lands shall need many simple minds and simple tasks done by somebody. And the tasks needing done? rebuild the State's infrastructure, clean-up toxic dump sights, feed the victims of hurricanes and flood, shelter disaster victims, plant trees, and build roads in lands where Corporatism's coach traffic finds less than desirable conditions. Indeed, there is much to be done that Corporatism certainly must not be *privately* burdened with. Recall the most massive undertaking in the Old Tradition's past? who paid for Lord Henry's Fords to have fine bridges of steel and roads of concrete and tar? A subsidy fit for a King.

What of those serfs, the untouchables, which refuse the service selected for them to serve their *country*? Homeless souls that reject the new religion's catechism and dogma: hard work, get ahead, efficiency, busy hands are happy hands, go along to get along, compromise, conform, keep up with the Mall-fodder, you can't fight city hall, there is only one best way...etc., ad nauseam? Yes, we know how troublesome these wandering lost souls can be to those trying to tread the life fantastic. Round them up, house them on abandoned military bases. Legal within the already written into law under the previous Bush Sr. & Co. watch: *Base Closures and Realignment Commission*. One applauds the prospect if one is weary of stepping around the outstretched palms a-begging, over the outstretched limbs a-sleeping, in our every village and hamlet.

But it would be wise indeed to recall your history as well: the rights granted the State to round-up the homeless grants the same right to the State to levy additionally upon your fortune. Could one possibly suggest that Corporatism's church feed the hungry, house the homeless, heal the sick, aid the needy? Not even the old traditions did it, by what right do any of us have to burden the new religion with virtues we failed to acquire, obligations we failed to fulfill? After all, Corporatism's great theologian Dwayne Andreas spoke to this very issue as Priest of Archer Daniels Midland Corporation: To the question, "Isn't there enough food to feed the starving in the world"? Father Andreas's rebuttal was memorable and now part of the Book of Everlasting Wisdom, "It isn't that there is not enough bread but that they have no money."

If they followed the true faith, prayed for efficiency and the strength to see Corporatism as The Way, they too would suffer a less unfavorable fate. One would do well to remember such sage advice from the future faithful filling the ranks of priest and scribe, theologian and elder, director and higher ranking lords, as indeed they believe as Father Andreas. The future is clear to those with eyes to see.

> No one would have dreamed in the Middle Ages that the despised creed of the trader and the money lender - a creed of selfishness and worship of the then lowest material values - should rise to be a compendium of everything most respectable in temporal affairs .

...So sayeth scribe Thurman W. Arnold, circa 1937, as he struggled against the old traditions, towards social reform, bringing the mantra of managed competition to the then bewildered herd of one religion ...the *laissez faire* faithful, into restless synthesis with the other religion...democratic socialism. The priests of each faction then did not see the light of pure enlightenment, "efficiency," the Aura of "Organization," the catechism of "Control": Corporatism, unknown to the New World called America. America the naive, they thought they needed a Constitution. Foolishly, they thought they needed free enterprise. Slavishly, they thought bigger might mean Monopoly when it all just meant a better way to distribute the goods produced by workers more "efficiently." Anti-trust laws were the, then, religion of an archaic individualism, an individualism that saw government's intervention into the *market* as an evil. Scribe Arnold, promoted to Jesuit, or Assistant Attorney General, Anti-trust Division of the Justice Department, emerged as the government's leading advocate of Corporatism; with Jesuit-like wisdom, that word, *Corporatism*, was never spoken.

Arnold, while scribe, pressed for managed competition and government/corporation co-operation, found himself using the old religion's sermons to, "...illustrate a common belief that social remedies could be found in the formulation of principles rather than in control and organization. In this respect radicals and conservatives were exactly alike." Lord Arnold became a *fellow* with Corporatism's finest think tank, the *Institute for Policy Studies;*

the bewildered progressives still think, even today, that this is a bastion of liberal left religious dogma; Lord Arnold knew that to achieve the synthesis that would redeem the world to Corporatism he would have to control and organize the left, while others controlled and organized the right. His success is today evident everywhere. His prospect of building "practical organization (s)" to achieve such things as "distribution of goods to the poor," has been almost entirely accomplished. Indeed, every area of life today is organized and controlled by one side of Caesar's coin or the other: corporate governance or public governance; the temporal government or the spiritual government: Corporatism rules as the only *one best way*. Subjects taxed through prices by the one, and levies by the other.

If one of the serfs or peasants or, if these terms betray your sensitivity of it too much, one of the subjects of the realm, want to understand the coming global corporate-state, the global regime of economic interdependence, the Global Regime writ large, one must listen to what they mean by what they say. Ignore what you think they mean. Understand the turn of a phrase, the slippery semantics of corporate Jesuitism. Lord Arnold again informs us: but only by seeing the ingenuity of his arguments against the old American beliefs, ones he no longer could abide, can one hear what lie he is saying. The Master speaks:

> (Yet) the thinkers about government had no objective grasp of the place which the corporate myth was playing in society. Even the social doctors believed in the fantasies of the great organization for which they prescribed, or else adopted the point of view of missionaries to the heathen and prescribed an alien set of fantasies without regard to the fact that they were planting them in uncongenial intellectual soil. And thus, since all cures based on this unreal conception of the social structure seemed worse than the disease, the notion of *laissez faire* was sure to be adopted sooner or later by all those who actually remained in power. However, the laissez faire of the theoretical economists was far different from the *laissez faire* of the business government. To the prince of business, *laissez faire* meant only that his principality should not be interfered with by an attempt to put the dreams which supported the spiritual government into actual practice. Therefore, the *laissez faire* economists constantly advocated free trade, while *laissez faire* businessmen insisted on letting protective tariffs alone.

Can the subject of the realm see the deceit in the terminology applied to one thing when describing an entirely different thing? The *laissez faire* businessman differs entirely from the corporate monopoly businessman. The monopoly capitalist has no tolerance for the free enterprising entrepreneur. The free market remains free only if the corporate monopolist, who cannot achieve his monopoly status without government decree, is forced to act according to the rules of free enterprise. Corporatism's first tenet must be to merge government power and corporate power as one. Co-operation shall come with a National Industrial Policy appointed by Bush & Co., return of Capital Gains tax reform shall be their first objective. Fast-Track legislation must happen in Bush's first term. The utter excommunication of the Federal Trade Commission: Anti-Trust Division, emasculated and to play the part of eunuchs to Corporatism's monopoly harem.

Domestic Discontent

Some authors still believe in the old-time religion and argue that it is *government* that is the barbarian at the gates of liberty. That government is the real enemy. That the largest corporations need protection from this enemy of free enterprise. What these tribal priests fail to grasp is that the government is, or was, the only power that could stem the tide of complete domination by barbarians of the new Corporatism and her monopolies in all goods that matter. The anti-trust laws were originally drawn up to fight the formation of monopolies in all industries. Scribe Arnold has it inscribed that these efforts failed because in the end, these giant organizations were needed to supply the goods people wanted and their size was a necessary component. He doth protesteth too much. Monopoly is not only about size, it is about absolute control of the organization of power that eliminates competition: the only way to stop the *price leadership* (price-fixing) every monopolist practices, was enforcement of anti-trust laws. Lord Arnold's deceptions allowed the very formation of monopolies while feigning opposition to corporate corruption. By arguing against *laissez faire* dogma as doctrinaire archaism, he helped (along with the living scribes at the Institute for Policy Studies) eliminate the solution to Corporatism and corporate monopolies: *laissez faire*.

We see these same scribes of Corporatism (on the left-hand) arguing against the de-regulation of business in America as selling out to *laissez faire* dogma, as caving in to the hidden hand of free enterprise: they lie; beginning in the Reagan era, de-regulation has been the battle cry of Corporatism's corporate crusaders and raiders. *Laissez faire* was protected by the spiritual government, by regulations, by anti-trust laws; by protecting competitiveness; by fighting monopoly practices and price-fixing. De-regulation aids the corporate Lords to Take-Over anything they desire worth having. Conservatives (on the right-hand) applaud stupidly the de-regulation that will utterly end any hope that *laissez faire* and free enterprise might survive; confusing any business with big-business. Instead, now, we have the *corporate*-state: a government within a government. An empire within empire. *Imperium in Imperio.*

The Barbarians Return

The Pagan Future

The new religion, materialism, is an incredibly powerful and pagan enterprise. Like it or not Christianity was a great civilizer, even taking into account the atrocities and crusades. The new regime of Corporatism reflects nothing so much as a return to a barbarian past, pagan and primitive. Corporatism will be inquisitional in defense of its own. It will act as barbaric as any pagan horde hoarding its booty and pillaged wealth, as materialism is its only creed. It is in this fashion that even devout Christians and Jews will deface their own temples with greed supplanting every creed; children do not need parents, they need greed; mothers do not need children, they need status; man does not need woman, they need more credit. Nothing of the old will survive, nothing of virtue, honor nor courage can survive. Only awaiting the call to arms for manna, arms outstretched to the sky, the new faithful pray, not for their child, their spouse, their life. They pray for Federal Reserve notes.

America will be abandoned at some point in time. It has begun the process already in corporate desertions to off-shore anywhere. When the future Multilateral Agreement on Investment finally has its day under Bush & Co. the smaller corporations and subsidiaries, along with subcontractors of significant size will follow. America as America will only remain in the myths the old faithful pour out in tears of lost hopes. Gone forever will be the middle-class of anything. The streets will fill with the worst sorts of degenerates and criminality will take over each inner city. Crime will be the only out for many to survive.

DRUG WARS REVISITED

To maintain the illusion through this slow burn-off, that America is still a God-fearing Christian nation, the State will continue waging its holy war upon those that lost the first rounds. Drugs will be entirely tolerated while we selectively make war on them. The occasional televised trial of a drug kingpin will mark the day for the old faithful to still believe in their faith; "virtue and goodness comes with a fight," they will piously mutter, shaking their head at the criminal's pagan behavior, who argue "it's not about drugs but about dead Presidents," Federal Reserve notes. The faithful will never see the real drug addiction of those trying the little thieves — the addiction to money, greed and material gain as the way to salvation and survival — exactly like the Bloods and Crips. Exactly like Microsoft. Exactly who do you think the drugs are sold to? inner city poor? Which is why drugs are tolerated while the *high* priests perform magnificent rituals to *zero tolerance* mythos. First the poorest disenfranchised go pagan out of necessity, then the creed is adopted out of greed by those not disenfranchised, then the greed is adopted by the middle-class out of need. The need for the creed of materialism is why they are so easily converted from followers of older faiths that ask too much and give too little materially.

All the old taboos are gone, many with good riddance, but ousted too were virtue and nurture; honor and fathers; courage and dignity; modesty and honesty. The last, honesty, is so well gone, one cannot find even one rare individual, not living in a cabin in the woods, that could even give you a definition of what that word is supposed to mean. One of the sacred teachings of Corporatism, already adopted by the priests of the left-hand, is that there is no truth, no right, no wrong, everything is relative to what you want and how you personally feel about it, whatever the topic. This cultural defect, sometimes coyly coined as relativism or post-modernity, always was the scripture of monopoly capitalism. That the monopoly capitalist system's enemies of the left-hand began with relativism as first gospel of Marx, helps some to explain why they have adopted Corporatism's creed, while desperately trying to maintain their (false) opposition as faith. As hypocrite, Christians first adopted Corporatism's creed of materialism, which implies relativism, which helps to explain why they desperately try to maintain their (false) opposition as faith.

While all of this is human, all-too-human, no hand-wringing implied, it does little good to think in terms of political reform measures, stopping the decay, correctives and salves. Waste your time praying to God to end the heresy if you like. But your prayers are lost under the incense and priestly smoke of hosannas for manna to yet another god. huyhnhnm to Yahoos might attain more but look as foolish. Truly we are upon the twilight of these idols.

APPENDIX TWO

To amend the FREEDOM Support Act to authorize the President to waive the restriction of assistance for Azerbaijan if the President determines that it is in the national security interest... (Introduced in the Senate)

S 1521 IS

107th CONGRESS

1st Session

S. 1521

To amend the FREEDOM Support Act to authorize the President to waive the restriction of assistance for Azerbaijan if the President determines that it is in the national security interest of the United States to do so.

IN THE SENATE OF THE UNITED STATES

October 9, 2001

Mr. BROWNBACK introduced the following bill; which was read twice and referred to the Committee on Foreign Relations

A BILL

To amend the FREEDOM Support Act to authorize the President to waive the restriction of assistance for Azerbaijan if the President determines that it is in the national security interest of the United States to do so.

Be it enacted by the Senate and House of Representatives of the United States of America in Congress assembled,

SECTION 1. WAIVER OF RESTRICTION ON ASSISTANCE TO AZER-BAIJAN.

Section 907 of the FREEDOM Support Act (Public Law 102-511; 22 U.S.C. 5812 note) is amended—

    (1) by striking 'United States' and inserting '(a) RESTRICTION- United States'; and

    (2) by adding at the end the following:

'(b) WAIVER- The President is authorized to waive the restriction in subsection (a) if the President determines that it is in the national security interest of the United States to do so.'

APPENDIX THREE
51 Largest Corporations

RANK MARKET VALUE
2000 1999   Billions of U.S. dollars

1	2	GENERAL ELECTRIC	U.S.
$520.25			
2	8	INTEL	U.S.
416.71			
3	9	CISCO SYSTEMS	U.S.
395.01			
4	1	MICROSOFT	U.S.
322.82			
5	4	EXXON MOBIL	U.S.
289.92			
6	70	VODAFONE AIRTOUCH	Britain
277.95			
7	6	WAL-MART STORES	U.S.
256.66			
8	27	NTT DOCOMO	Japan
247.24			
9	38	NOKIA	Finland
242.19			
10	5	ROYAL DUTCHISHELL	Neth/Britain
213.54			
11	15	CITIGROUP	U.S.
209.86			
12	10	BP AMOCO	Britain
207.51			
13	122	ORACLE	U.S.
204.01			
14	3	IBM	U.S.
192.49			
15	13	NIPPON TELEGRAPH & TELEPHONE	Japan
189.16			
16	23	DEUTSCHE TELEKOM	Germany
187.25			
17	16	LUCENT TECHNOLOGIES	U.S.
183.34			

18	17	AMERICAN INTERNATIONAL GROUP	U.S.
173.50			
19	12	MERCK	U.S.
172.87			
20	18	PFIZER	U.S.
171.52			
21	32	TOYOTA MOTOR	Japan
170.52			
22	77	LM ERICSSON	Sweden
158.05			
23	84	NORTEI NETWORKS	Canada
152.39			
24	31	SBC COMMUNICATIONS	U.S.
149.03			
25	43	FRANCE TELECOM	France
148.71			
26	11	COCA-COLA	U.S.
131.97			
27	82	EMC	U.S.
126.19			
28	21	JOHNSON & JOHNSON	U.S.
124.55			
29	20	AMERICA ONLINE	U.S.
121.76			
30	33	HEWLETT-PACKARD	U.S.
120.14			
31	91	SUN MICROSYSTEMS	U.S.
119.62			
32	96	TEXAS INSTRUMENTS	U.S.
118.23			
33	141	TOTALFINAELF	France
116.32			
34	41	HOME DEPOT	U.S.
112.38			
35	37	DELL COMPUTER	U.S.
111.55			
36	7	AT&T	U.S.
109.10			
31	19	BRISTOL-MYERS SQUIBB	U.S.
108.80			
38	14	WORLDCOM	U.S.
107,57			
39	29	NOVARTIS	Switzerland
105.96			
40	76	WARNER-LAMBERT	U.S. 105.92

41	42	TIME WARNER	U.S.
103.65			
42	30	6LAX0 WELLCOME	Britain
102.12			
43	24	BANK OF AMERICA	U.S.
94.86			
44	171	VIACOM	U.S.
94.41			
45	26	BRITISH TELECOMMUNICATIONS	Britain
93.70			
46	34	HSBC HOLDINGS	Britain
93.30			
47	28	ROCHE HOLDING	Switzerland
92.38			
48	25	BERKSHIRE HATHAWAY	U.S.
89.13			
49	36	BELLSOUTH	U.S.
87.88			
50	69	WALT DISNEY	U.S.
87.66			
51	22	PROCTER & GAMBLE	U.S.
87.49			

www.craigbhulet.com

APPENDIX FOUR

EXECUTIVE ORDER
ESTABLISHING THE USA FREEDOM CORPS

By the authority vested in me as President by the Constitution and the laws of the United States of America, it is hereby ordered as follows:

Section 1. Policy. Building on our Nation's rich tradition of citizen service, this Administration's policy is to foster a culture of responsibility, service, and citizenship by promoting, expanding, and enhancing public service opportunities for all Americans and by making these opportunities readily available to citizens from all geographic areas, professions, and walks of life. More specifically, this Administration encourages all Americans to serve their country for the equivalent of at least 2 years (4,000 hours) over their lifetimes. Toward those ends, the executive departments, agencies, and offices constituting the USA Freedom Corps shall coordinate and strengthen Federal and other service opportunities, including opportunities for participation in homeland security preparedness and response, other areas of public and social service, and international service. The executive branch departments, agencies, and offices also will work with State and local governments and private entities to foster and encourage participation in public and social service programs, as appropriate.

Sec. 2. USA Freedom Corps. The USA Freedom Corps shall be an interagency initiative, bringing together executive branch departments, agencies, and offices with public service programs and components, including but not limited to programs and components with the following functions:

recruiting, mobilizing, and encouraging all Americans to engage in public service;

providing concrete opportunities to engage in public service;

providing the public with access to information about public service opportunities through Federal programs and elsewhere; and

providing recognition and awards to volunteers and other participants in public service programs.

Sec. 3. USA Freedom Corps Council. (a) Establishment and Mission. There shall be a USA Freedom Corps Council (Council) chaired by the President and composed of heads of executive branch departments, agencies, and offices, which shall have the following functions:

serving as a forum for Federal officials responsible for public service programs to coordinate and improve public service programs and activities administered by the executive branch;

working to encourage all Americans to engage in public service, whether through Federal programs or otherwise;

advising the President and heads of executive branch departments, agencies, and offices concerning the optimization of current Federal programs to enhance public service opportunities;

coordinating public outreach and publicity of citizen service opportunities provided by Federal programs;

encouraging schools, universities, private public service organizations, and other non-Federal entities to foster and reward public service;

studying the availability of public service opportunities provided by the Federal Government and elsewhere; and

tracking progress in participation in public service programs.

(b) <u>Membership</u>. In addition to the Chair, the members of the Council shall be the heads of the executive branch departments, agencies, and offices listed below, or their designees, and such other officers of the executive branch as the President may from time to time designate. Every member of the Council or designee shall be a full-time or permanent part-time officer or employee of the Federal Government. Members shall not be compensated for their service on the Council in addition to the salaries they receive as employees or officers of the Federal Government.

Vice President;

Attorney General;

Secretary of State;

Secretary of Health and Human Services;

Secretary of Commerce;

Secretary of Education;

Secretary of Veterans Affairs;

Director of the Federal Emergency Management Agency;

Chief Executive Officer of the Corporation for National and Community Service;

Director of the Peace Corps;

Administrator of the United States Agency for International Development;

Director of the USA Freedom Corps Office;

Director of the Office of Faith-Based and Community Initiatives.

(c) <u>Chair</u>. The President shall be the Chair of the USA Freedom Corps Council, and in his absence, the Vice President shall serve as Chair. The Director of the USA Freedom Corps Office may, at the President's direction, preside over meetings of the Council in the President's and Vice President's absence.

(d) <u>Honorary Co-Chair</u>. The President may, from time to time, designate an Honorary Co-Chair or Co-Chairs, who shall serve in an advisory role to the Council and to the President on matters considered by the Council. Any Honorary Co-Chair shall be a full-time or permanent part-time employee or officer of the Federal Government.

(e) <u>Meetings</u>. The Council shall meet at the President's direction. The Director of the USA Freedom Corps Office shall be responsible, at the President's direction, for determining the agenda, ensuring that necessary papers are prepared, and recording Council actions and Presidential decisions.

(f) <u>Responsibilities of Executive Branch Departments, Agencies, and Offices</u>.

Members of the Council shall remain responsible for overseeing the programs administered by their respective departments, agencies, and offices. Each such department, agency, and office will retain its authority and responsibility to administer those programs according to law;

Each executive branch department, agency, or office with responsibility for programs relating to the functions and missions of the USA Freedom Corps as described in section 2 of this order shall be responsible for identifying those public service opportunities and coordinating with the USA Freedom Corps Council to ensure that such programs are, if appropriate, publicized and encouraged by the Council; and

Upon the request of the Chair, and to the extent permitted by law, the heads of executive branch departments and agencies shall provide the Council with relevant information.

<u>Sec</u>. <u>4</u>. <u>USA Freedom Corps Office</u>. (a) <u>General</u>. The USA Freedom Corps also shall be supported by a USA Freedom Corps Office (Office), which shall be a component of the White House Office. The USA Freedom Corps Office shall have a Director who shall be appointed by the President. The Director shall be assisted by an appropriate staff within the White House Office.

(b) <u>Presidential Recognition to Participants in USA Freedom Corps Programs</u>. In addition to supporting and facilitating the functions of the Council listed in section 3 of this order, the Office shall support the President in providing recognition to volunteers and other participants in programs and activities relating to the functions and missions of the USA Freedom Corps as described in section 2 of this order.

<u>Sec</u>. <u>5</u>. <u>General Provisions</u>. (a) The White House Office shall provide the Council and Office with such funding and administrative support, to the extent permitted by law and subject to the availability of appropriations, as directed by the Chief of Staff to the President to carry out the provisions of this order.

(b) This order does not alter the existing authorities or roles of executive branch departments, agencies, or offices. Nothing in this order shall supersede any requirement made by or under law.

(c) This order does not create any right or benefit, substantive or procedural, enforceable at law or equity, against the United States, its departments, agencies, or other entities, its officers or employees, or any other person.

Congress of the United States
House of Representatives
Washington, DC 20515—4702

January 31, 2000

To Whom It May Concern:

Craig Hulet has been an invaluable advisor. Whether the issue is MAI, GATT, NAFTA, or the more general question of the growing power of trans-national corporations over our institutions and everyday lives, Mr. Hulet provides a heavily researched, coldly logical analysis where others too often delve with emotion, biases, and disinformation. His work should be widely disseminated. His conclusions should be very carefully considered.

Sincerely,
Jack Metcalf